THE ENGLISH CLERGY
The Emergence and Consolidation
of a Profession, 1558–1642

THE ENGLISH CLERGY

The Emergence and Consolidation
of a Profession
1558–1642

Rosemary O'Day

1979
Leicester University Press

First published in 1979 by Leicester University Press
Distributed in North America by
Humanities Press Inc., New Jersey

Copyright © Leicester University Press 1979

Designed by Douglas Martin
Phototypeset in V.I.P. Bembo by Western Printing Services Ltd, Bristol
Printed in Great Britain by Unwin Brothers Ltd,
The Gresham Press, Woking
Bound by Redwood Burn Ltd,
London and Esher

British Library Cataloguing in Publication Data
O'Day, Rosemary
The English clergy
1. Church of England – Clergy
I. Title
262'.14   BX5175

ISBN 0 7185 1167 0

The publication of this book has been assisted by a grant from the
Twenty-Seven Foundation

To My Father and Mother
(Reverend and Mrs T. H. Brookes)

Contents

Tables

Abbreviations

A.H.R.	*American Historical Review*
B.I.H.R.	*Bulletin of the Institute of Historical Research*
B.L.	British Library
Borthwick I.H.R.	Borthwick Institute of Historical Research, York
B.R.L.	Birmingham Reference Library
C.C.	Church Commissioners
C.C.R.O.	Cheshire County Record Office
C.H.R.O.	County of Hereford Record Office
C.S.	Camden Society
C.S.P.D.	*Calendar of State Papers Domestic*
C.U.L.	Cambridge University Library
D.N.B.	*Dictionary of National Biography*
D.W.L.	Doctor Williams' Library
E.D.R.	Ely Diocesan Records (Cambridge University Library)
E.H.R.	*English Historical Review*
G.C.L.	Gloucester City Library
G.D.R.	Gloucester Diocesan Records (in G.C.L.)
G.L.MS.	Guildhall Library MSS
H.R.O.	Hertfordshire Record Office
H.J.	*Historical Journal*
H.M.C. Rep.	*Historical Manuscripts Commission Report*
I.T.L.	Inner Temple Library, London
J.E.H.	*Journal of Ecclesiastical History*
J.H.I.	*Journal of the History of Ideas*
L.C.R.O.	Leicestershire Record Office
L.C.C.R.O.	London County Council Record Office
L.J.R.O.	Lichfield Joint Record Office
L.P.L.	Lambeth Palace Library

L.R.O.	Lincoln Record Office
N.L.W.	National Library of Wales
N.R.O.	Northampton Record Office
P.C.C.	Prerogative Court of Canterbury
P.R.O.	Public Record Office
P. and P.	*Past and Present*
Q.S.R.	Quarter Sessions Rolls
R.H.S. Camden Ser.	Royal Historical Society Publications: Camden Series
S.P.	State Papers
S.R.	*Statutes of the Realm*
T.B.G.A.S.	*Transactions of the Bristol and Gloucester Archaeological Society*
T.R.H.S.	*Transactions of the Royal Historical Society*
U.B.H.J.	*University of Birmingham Historical Journal*
V.E.	*Valor Ecclesiasticus*
W.R.O.	Worcester Record Office
W.S.L.	William Salt Library, Stafford
W.P.	Will proved

Glossary

caveat	A claim to the right to present to a benefice and a warning to the ordinary not to admit the candidate of any other claimant to the living in question. Entered in the diocesan registry. It had no force of law.
collation	Direct admission of cleric to living by the ordinary.
commender	Person nominating cleric to patron.
composition	Agreement by which tithe payment of parishioner is fixed at a given amount for a given length of time. It could involve commutation but not necessarily
de iure patronage	Patronage by right. Legal ownership of advowson.
duplex querela	The form of action open to a cleric whom the ordinary refuses to institute to a living to which the cleric has been presented. The action is heard in an ecclesiastical court.
hac vice patronage	This patronage is not held by right but by grant from the *de iure* patron for either one or more presentations. Nevertheless, such a patron *pro hac vice* has a legal right to present under the terms of the grant and should not be confused with a commender.
induction	Admission of a cleric to the temporalities of a church living.
institution	Admission of a cleric to the spiritualities of a living.
modus decimandi	An agreement of a general nature by which the tithing custom of a parish is established and the amount to be paid for specific tithes is fixed. It does not necessarily imply commutation to a money payment and could be written or unwritten.
nominator	On occasion a *de iure* patron might grant to a

suitor not the right of *hac vice* presentation to a living but the right to nominate a client to the *de iure* patron. This protected the nominator against other suits; it also ensured the *de iure* patron's right to veto and left him as the formal presenter of the cleric to the ordinary.

patron   Owner of advowson.

presenter   He who presents the cleric to the ordinary for admission to a particular living. There may be a distinction between the presenter and the nominator.

procurations   Payments due to the ordinary on visitation.

Puritans   I have adopted the loosest possible definition of
and   'puritan' and 'puritanism'. The puritan is
Puritanism   essentially still a revivalist Protestant, who resists the institutionalization of Protestantism within the English state which conservative Protestants have succumbed to. He differs not in doctrine from the men who support the settlement but in attitude. His spirit is essentially critical, revivalist and outspoken. Thus there may be degrees of puritanism and elements of puritanism even in the most conservative defenders of the Elizabethan and Jacobean Church settlements. This loose definition appears to me to accommodate certain apparent contradictions: in individual careers where a man may at one point be identifiably puritan and at another conservative (a progression which may often be noted when the man becomes part of the institutional hierarchy himself); in the similarities of view held by Protestant bishops and so-called puritan activists on a number of matters; in fact puritans themselves were not unified in their constructive suggestions concerning Church organization (for example, there were those who shared a very clericalist approach – the presbyterians – and those who thought in terms of the relationship between pastor and congregation). The puritan is one who, from a Protestant standpoint, is not content with the Church settlement, says so and intends to act. He places other Protestants in a defensive position.

As contemporaries used the term loosely, so, I think, must we.

quare impedit Legal action brought in civil court by patron against the bishop on his refusal to institute patron's presentee to a living.

synodals Payments due to the ordinary on visitation.

Preface

This book grew out of work connected with my University of London Ph.D. thesis (1972) which prompted me to a closer examination of the English parochial clergy as a professional group during the period between the Reformation and the civil wars. I am greatly indebted both to Professor Patrick Collinson and to the late Professor James Cargill Thompson, my erstwhile supervisors at King's College, London for their constant support, encouragement and inspiration. I owe much also to the encouragement given me by Professor F. J. Fisher, who co-supervised my thesis during the year 1970–1, and by Professor Kenneth Charlton. I owe an especial debt to Dr Molly Barratt of the Department of Western Manuscripts at the Bodleian Library and to the staff of the Staffordshire County Record Office and the Lichfield Joint Record Office (especially Dr David Robinson and Miss Jane Isaac) who have been very generous with their time. I extend my thanks also to the staffs of the following libraries and record offices: Gloucester, Hereford, Lincoln, Norfolk, Northamptonshire and Worcester Record Offices; Borthwick Institute of Historical Research (York); Dr Williams' Library; Guildhall Library, London; Institute of Historical Research; Inner Temple Library; Lambeth Palace Library; National Library of Wales and, of course, the British Library, the Cambridge University Library (Mrs Dorothy Owen) and the Public Record Office. The examiners of my Ph.D. thesis, Professor Joel Hurstfield and Dr Claire Cross, have offered much constructive criticism of my general thesis, as has Professor C. W. Dugmore. As this is also a general monograph, one of my greatest debts is to scholars in the field of ecclesiastical and social history, whose labours have permitted me to generalize. I have sought to acknowledge my indebtedness to such scholars throughout the work. Discussions in the Tudor Seminar and the Seventeenth Century Seminar at the Institute of Historical Research have helped me to crystallize my own ideas concerning aspects of the subject. I would like to thank Gerald Aylmer for his constant and quiet support of my work, both in encouraging me to initiate the research and also in inspiring me to continue.

A number of institutions and foundations have offered me financial support in undertaking the research for this book. I should like to acknowledge my considerable debt to the Trustees of the Eileen Power Memorial Studentship for awarding me the Studentship in

1970–1; to Imperial College, London for an I.B.M. Fellowship in computerized analysis; to the University of Birmingham School of Education for a Research Fellowship, 1971–5; to the S.S.R.C./ D.F.G. Exchange Scheme for an academic visit to Universität Tübingen in the Summer of 1977 and to the British Academy/ Folger Library in the Summer of 1976.

I would like to thank the following for permission to publish in whole or in part work previously published by me.

The Journal of Ecclesiastical History for parts of chapters 2, 5, and 14.

Transactions of the Royal Historical Society for chapter 8, here greatly abbreviated.

Leicester University Press, for chapter 9.

I extend my thanks to the Secretary to the Press, Mr Peter Boulton, who has spent much time and effort on the book and whose criticism of it has been most valuable.

My husband, Alan, has been a source of constant encouragement (not to say, prodding!) and practical help in the preparation of the book. Andrew's assistance has helped me to keep the task in perspective, for which I thank him.

Rosemary O'Day, The Open University, April 1978

1
The career structure of the clergy

The development of the professions in early modern England is of profound importance to the social and economic historian. The emergence of large professional groups having a common academic, institutionalized training; an accepted internal hierarchy, rules, regulations and codes of conduct; and similar interests, ambitions and life-style, made a great impact upon society. Although it is true that none of the professional groupings (clergy, lawyers, doctors, and the newly emerging teaching and civil service groups) formed separate economic classes, it is equally true that they formed vocational and social groupings, often self-perpetuating, which to some extent stood outside any rigid class system. Although they were, themselves, increasingly monopolistic, the professions offered such opportunities as there were for social mobility via education in Tudor and Stuart England. Each profession was conscious of offering a service to the community – an essential service – and felt itself to possess the monopoly in this respect. The mid-seventeenth century saw the professions defending their monopolies against all-comers. Dr Hill has drawn our attention to the anti-professionalism of the interregnum period.[1] The development of such monopolistic groups is of interest for more mundane reasons: if, for example, the clergy were separated from the laity in life-style to a great extent, is the historian justified in using sources such as clerical diaries, memoirs, wills and inventories for a study of lay society?

The treatment of the professions by historians has been patchy and has been confined in the main to describing the type of training which members underwent and the nature of professional organization. Professor Kenneth Charlton wrote a stimulating article in 1969 which attempted to provide a working definition of a 'profession' and to discover whether there was a separate teaching profession in the later sixteenth century.[2] Significantly enough, he made little mention of the parochial clergy in this study. Patrick Orpen, a student of Kenneth Charlton, has more recently recognized the professional status of the clergy and argued that teaching was primarily 'a form of outdoor relief for the underpaid or aspiring cleric'. Most attention, however, has been accorded to the medical and legal professions.[3] Carr-Saunders and Wilson in *The Professions* explicitly exclude a consideration of the clergy as a profession because its functions are spiritual. Others accept that the clerical hierarchy constituted a professional group but neglect the parish clergy.

Down until the Reformation the secular clergy could be seen to comprise two groups: the educated, non-resident, beneficed clergy who had a definite career structure which led ultimately to high office in Church or State; and the unlearned, resident parochial clergy – vicars and assistant curates – who had no training to speak of, no career structure, and little or no group solidarity. Historians appear, unaccountably, to have missed the immense transformation which the secular clergy went through in the post-Reformation period. By the end of the sixteenth century a new situation had arisen: now the resident cleric, however humble, was much better educated than the majority of his medieval counterparts and it was not only the higher clergy and dignitaries or absentee rectors who possessed university degrees. Moreover, there was now an awareness on the part of the hierarchy of the need to control clerical recruitment at parish level and to educate the lower clergy. Such awareness was a necessary prerequisite for the professionalization of the clergy and it is in line with the attempts to control entry into all the other ancient professions at this time. Although many parish clergy had not attended university at the end of Elizabeth's reign, the improvement in the educational level at this end of the scale had an enormous impact both upon the emergence of the profession itself and on its future relations with the laity.

To some extent the improvement in the educational standards of the parish clergy was the natural outcome of the educational revolution but it was also, in part, a direct response to the changed *raison d'être* of the clergy and to the improved career prospects of graduates in the late sixteenth century. There were, for example, deliberate attempts by Crown, hierarchy and laity to consolidate the clerical profession. The universities functioned as seminaries; puritan colleges were founded to produce fit, preaching ministers; the bishops (or rather some of the conscientious) dedicated themselves to programmes of in-service training; the canons of the Church and the statutes of the realm all worked to restrict the cleric's participation in non-clerical or non-intellectual pursuits; and more and more emphasis was placed upon the cleric's pastoral duties, in accordance with the beliefs and practices of the Reformed churches.

Several doctoral theses have dealt with the parochial clergy of the period, but they have been chiefly concerned with issues other than the consolidation of the clerical profession. They have provided us with the basic information necessary to assess whether the parochial clergy truly formed a profession and if so, why, but they have not seen the study of the parish clergy in this context. Similarly, Professor Collinson's *The Elizabethan Puritan Movement* supplies abundant evidence of the positive contribution of puritanism to clerical professional awareness and consolidation in general, without defining the issue. If these works permit us to conclude that the clergy were conscious of their professional position by the early seventeenth century, they do little to provide answers for some of the more important questions about this profession. Was the clerical group a social as well as a vocational one? Was it monopolistic, divisive, restrictive, exclusive? Was its claimed status as a profession recognized by the laity? Are we to agree with Dr Tyler that the status of the clergy was low and declining in the reign of James I? Did the career structure of the clergy accommodate or frustrate the ambitions and expectations of its members?[4]

To answer these questions we must explore several areas – the many influences at play on the personnel and organization of the clerical community; the life-style of that community; and the relationship between the clerical community and the laity – and, to begin with, describe and analyse the career structure of the clergy over the period as a whole.

Almost the only direct contributions to our knowledge of clerical career structure after the Reformation have been the works of Mark Curtis and Paul Seaver. Professor Curtis suggested that a huge surplus of graduates kept out of permanent benefices in the Church of England produced in the 1620s and 1630s a disgruntled group of alienated intellectuals, filled with burning resentment against the establishment in Church and State. Professor Seaver discussed the careers of puritan lecturers as part of the 'educated élite within the Church of England'. The parish clergy, as such, have been neglected, yet during the period 1540–1640 the personnel of the English Church underwent apparently radical changes which must have had important consequences for the Church and for society as a whole. This was particularly true of the parochial clergy, both beneficed and unbeneficed. Few of the clergy involved wholly at the parochial level (that is, those who did not also hold a prebendal stall or diocesan office, and who formed the majority) were graduate in the 1540s and 1550s. At Lincoln approximately one-fifth of the Henrician, Marian and Elizabethan ordinands still in the diocese in 1569 were graduates. Edwardian ordinands were noticeably better qualified but far fewer in number, as only small numbers of men had been ordained during Edward's reign. Michael Zell has shown that in Canterbury diocese the proportion of graduates in the 1550s was actually lower than that during Warham's episcopate (1503–32). (The case of London was exceptional – of 87 incumbents in 1553, 63 were university educated, or 72.4 per cent.) If we turn from this generally dismal state of affairs to the situation in the 1620s, we find that by then recruitment into the Church at parish level was overwhelmingly graduate. What was the impact of this transformation upon the career prospects and patterns of the parochial clergy?[5]

It may be that this transformation of the clergy from a grammar-school educated into a university educated group had less radical effects upon career patterns in the long term than might be expected. Although at first graduates may have been preferred to livings at the expense of non-graduates, once every ordinand possessed a degree the qualification no longer provided a positive advantage to the cleric seeking his first living or subsequent preferment. The absence of a degree may have proved a disadvantage to earlier recruits in their quest for further preferment, but it is probable that the operation of patronage, both at primary and subsidiary levels, was still dictated primarily by considerations of local origin, kinship and connection, with education acting as the deciding factor in only a minority of cases.[6]

There was, however, some wider geographical mobility which seems to have occurred via the universities or the metropolis. The ordination lists of the diocese of London give us some indication of what was happening. For example, 42 deacons ordained between 1598 and 1628 were of Yorkshire origin. Not one returned home to Yorkshire or the north: 13 remained in the universities (mainly as Fellows), nine found work in Essex, four held positions in the City of London, three lived in Middlesex, Surrey and Kent claimed two apiece and, finally, seven found employment in other counties in the south-east and London. Thirty-two men from Scotland were ordained and all remained in the south. The same pattern was re-peated in the case of ordinands from other northern and midland counties. This behaviour is sharply differentiated from the pattern revealed in provincial dioceses. For instance, of 282 ordinands at Chester during the first decade of Elizabeth's reign only 53 (18.7 per cent) stated that they came from outside the diocese. The majority of these originated from nearby dioceses such as Lichfield, St Asaph and Hereford, although one man came from Worcester and another from Chichester. Some of them may already have been employed in Chester diocese when they took orders, although non-graduates who had only resided in the diocese briefly when they took orders would still have had to return to their home diocese for ordination. This occurred with three men who gave Chester as their place of abode when ordained deacon but were living in Hereford a year later when they returned to Chester for ordination as priest. At an ordina-tion in Lincoln, in May 1569, 68 out of 93 men ordained deacon (73.1 per cent) claimed Lincoln as their place of origin, and of 73 admitted to the priesthood, 52 (71.2 per cent) came from the diocese. Of non-graduates ordained at Ely in the 1560s, almost all came from the diocese, with a few coming from Norwich or Lincoln. Most graduates at the time chose to be ordained either at London, Ely or Oxford; non-graduates were forced to stay in their home dioceses. Graduates had the opportunity to make new connections at the university and this led to somewhat greater geographical mobility – although one must balance this·with a consideration of the geographical complexion of the various college communities at the universities, which were often very restricted. The pull of the south-east was certainly felt by graduates. A breakdown of London ordinands of London origins draws attention to the fact that most stayed in London or the universities, that mobility was restricted to the Home Counties, and that very few went as far as the Midlands. There was graduate mobility into London but not, to any significant extent, out of it. The evidence points to the conclusion that while comparatively few men were entering dioceses such as Chester, Lincoln or Lichfield at parish level without local connections, far more were flooding out of northern and midland dioceses into the more populous and economically prosperous areas of the south and south-east.[7]

A university education was probably the decisive factor in allowing this mobility: it broadened the horizons and heightened the ambitions of the clergy, and gave many the opportunity to receive orders in a diocese of their choice without evidence of origin, residence or title. During the first decade of Elizabeth's reign many of the graduate clergy were immediately absorbed into university employment or into appointments in cathedral chapters. Because patronage was still distributed largely through local connection, many graduates not wishing to return home and not succeeding in their quest for a benefice elsewhere looked instead to the capital where there were more opportunities for employment. Many of the graduates ordained at Ely in the early 1560s were destined for immediate preferment outside the realm of parochial responsibility. Thomas Steward, M.A., of Cambridge, was ordained both deacon and priest in 1560 specifically to take up a prebend at Ely at the age of 34. Matthew Hutton was also ordained deacon to take up a prebend in Ely. John Whitgift, M.A., was ordained both deacon and priest to become chaplain to the Bishop of Ely. Gilbert Holland remained in his Fellowship at St John's College, Cambridge, after taking deacon's orders. Robert Beaumont, in exile under Mary, now Lady Margaret Professor of Divinity, was ordained to become Archdeacon of Huntingdon. Nicholas Wendon, M.A., had been Archdeacon of Suffolk since 1559 but only took deacon's orders in 1560. He also held two livings in plurality. In 1570 he was deprived of both livings for not being in priest's orders. Thomas Fennye, M.A., was another who apparently never undertook any parochial responsibilities, first serving as prebendary of St Paul's and then as a university preacher.[8]

One can scarcely argue then that the number of graduates ordained in the 1560s had a dramatic effect upon the parochial situation: only in London were there surplus graduates in unremunerative posts and London, even in the 1550s, had attracted graduates. Otherwise the situation in the first decade of Elizabeth's reign was remarkably similar to that of the pre-Reformation Church. The non-resident clergy were university educated, and socially, geographically and economically quite mobile: the parochial clergy were of local origin, modest education, and had little prospect of further preferment. This seems true even when one bears in mind recent research on the new role of cathedral prebendaries in pastoral work, and the increased emphasis upon their residence.[9]

Yet the post-Reformation Church was committed to the task of reforming its clergy and of finding well-educated and vocationally suitable men to fill its parishes, even down to the poorest rectories and vicarages, many of which were currently standing vacant. The attempts of the hierarchy to change the situation will be considered later in the book and here we shall do no more than note that the number of graduates being produced by the universities increased dramatically during the later sixteenth and early seventeenth centuries, to the Church's advantage. For various reasons more and more intending clerics attended the universities and the impact of this educational revolution was being felt in some dioceses as early as the 1570s. The impact was slower in backward dioceses such as Chester and Gloucester, but it was felt. By the 1620s new recruitment into the Church was almost entirely via the universities. As there were still non-graduate clergy ensconced in freehold benefices throughout the country, it would take some time before the parochial clergy themselves were wholly graduate, but this was, nonetheless, an important improvement and had considerable repercussions as far as the career structure of the clergy was concerned.[10]

There can be little doubt that most of the new ordinands had been motivated to attend university not only for ideological reasons (many were convinced that a good pastor had to be a well-educated man) but because they felt that their promotion prospects would be thereby considerably improved. This may have been true in the first instance – perhaps as late as the 1590s and early 1600s in the south-east, and rather later in the north and parts of the Midlands – but there came a time when a degree was so commonplace that it offered no guarantee of a first benefice, let alone further preferment, and the old considerations of local connection, kinship, money and so on exercised as powerful an influence as ever. Patronage, although sometimes operating via university-made connections, still worked primarily within a local framework. For example, Francis Leeke, baronet, later Earl of Scarsdale, had been a pupil at Southwell School and had attended Caius College in the 1590s. After three years there, he went to the Middle Temple. Succeeding to the estate in Sutton, Derbyshire, he had the *de iure* right to present to five Derbyshire livings. Educational connections figured in two of the presentations which he made. In 1627 he presented John Baies, graduate of Caius and Master of Southwell School, to Pleasley. William Smithson, educated at Oxford but a student of the Middle Temple and the son of one of Leeke's contemporaries there, was presented at Ault Hucknall. Leeke presented Godfrey Platts, a Cambridge man, to Sutton but the other two men whom he favoured had strong Derbyshire connections. Francis Tallents, a non-graduate, was of a Derbyshire family. Elisha Bourne, assistant of Mickleover, was the brother of an eminent Derbyshire preacher of Northamptonshire birth – Immanuel Bourne.[11]

By the seventeenth century the clergy were probably not significantly more geographically mobile than their predecessors. This is not to say that there was no geographical movement. The chain of connection or kinship which secured a man preferment might stretch over several counties. Moreover, as we have seen, university connection did present some opportunities for patronage for those seeking to escape their county of origin. London and the university towns still attracted young recruits like magnets. The puritan connection also seems to have acted as a vehicle for geographical mobility in some cases. Yet an examination of the careers of clergymen in the 1620s and 1630s does not suggest a decline in the number of clergy finding preferment in their native area. The operation of patronage within a local framework seems to have been reinforced by the growth of clerical dynasties after the Reformation and by the system of grants of next presentation, whereby significant numbers of the clerical, legal and medical professions, and of the lesser gentry, yeoman and husbandman classes acquired patronage which they used in favour of kinsmen and acquaintances.[12]

Some general conclusions concerning the career pattern and prospects of graduate and non-graduate clergy in the late sixteenth and seventeenth centuries may be reached through a study of patronage itself, but it is extremely difficult to chart the pattern of geographical and economic mobility in the career of the average cleric. What was the nature of an ordinand's first appointment? If he failed to obtain a permanent living immediately, was he forever shut out of the ranks of the beneficed? How many times did a cleric move during the course of his career? How far did he move when he moved? The career of each man was necessarily stamped with individual characteristics and the historian should not force all into one mould for his own convenience. Moreover, the type of information available limits the extent to which one can answer these queries. It is rarely possible to obtain detailed and equivalent information about the careers of a substantial group of clergy during the period. As a beginning it has been possible to perform a reasonably detailed analysis of patterns of mobility within the archdeaconry of Coventry for the period 1540–1632. It is *not* claimed that the evidence from this small population is definitive, nor that it can be applied unquestioningly to the national clergy of the day.[13]

According to the 1563 return, the archdeaconry contained 109 churches, including free chapels and donatives. The institution records of the diocese cover 98 benefices to which presentations were made via the bishop. Some of the cures presented to were technically churches without institution, but were apparently under the bishop's cognisance nonetheless.

During the 90 years from 1540 to 1630, 438 institutions were made. Thus, on average, each living might have been expected to change hands some four times during this time (4.4 times). In fact the distribution of vacancies was rather more irregular than this might suggest. The period 1540–80 saw 242 of these institutions (55.25 per cent) and that between 1620 and 1630, 66 (15.0 per cent). The rate of turnover during these periods was almost twice that of the years 1580–1620 when 130 institutions took place (29.6 per cent). Within the 20-year period 1540–60, an exceptional period for many reasons, every living had the expectation of being left vacant at least once; from 1580–1600 only two-thirds of the benefices were likely to fall vacant at all.

The relative instability of the years 1540–80 can be explained both by the insecure political–religious situation and by the high death rate which prevailed, especially during the years 1557–9. The influenza epidemic of these years probably did more to aid the Elizabethan hierarchy in their attempt to instal Protestant clerics in benefices than did the policy of deprivation of the obstinate. Of 33 vacancies in the years 1557–9, 29 were caused by death (87.8 per cent). The clergy as a group were presumably particularly vulnerable to disease. The average number of institutions for these three years stood at 11 (suggesting an overall death-rate among the parochial clergy of 9.85 per cent if we take the average number of deaths per annum as 9.66 per cent for these three years) as against the average for the remaining years of this period of just over five per annum, itself high. The early years of Mary's reign had seen a number of deprivations but it was the period 1560–80 which saw the highest number – some 13. This period also saw a rising number of vacancies occasioned by voluntary resignation and cession: at least 31 out of a total of 124. The proportion of deaths was still high – 61 out of 124 vacancies were occasioned by death. This suggests a death rate of 3 per cent among the beneficed clergy of the archdeaconry.[14]

Table 1

Vacancies in the archdeaconry of Coventry: 1560–80

Cause	Number	Percentage
Deprivation	13	10.5
Resignation or cession	31	25.0
Death	61	49.2
Unknown	19	15.3
Total	124	100

It is the figures for 1620–29/30 which may cause most surprise. After a period of 40 years when stability was the rule and when a man might well expect to remain in one living for above 20 years, the number of vacancies in a ten-year period suddenly doubled the average for previous years (6.6 as against 3.2). This phenomenon does not appear to have owed much to increased mobility but rather to an increased number of deaths. Forty of the 66 vacancies (60.6 per cent) occurring in these years were occasioned by death. Unfortunately the information regarding the reasons for vacancies during the preceding 40 years is disappointingly fragmentary, but from total figures for the period it seems reasonable to suppose that the number of vacancies caused by death was lower between 1580 and 1620 and that, therefore, the overall death rate was below that of 1560–80. The death rate for beneficed clergymen during the period 1620–30 was quite high, approaching the levels of the early and mid-1550s but still half that of the late 1550s (4.08 per cent).

Too much weight should not be attached to these bald statistics. Some of the institutions were quashed within a month or so and such instances very slightly inflate the resignations column and the impression of mobility. Moreover, one cannot be sure how many deaths resulted simply from old age, although one might assume a normal death rate of 2 per cent among the clergy, rising perhaps to 5 per cent in time of plague, epidemic or dearth. The 'high' death rate of 1620–30 may have been the result of long-term immobility following a large number of new institutions in the period shortly before 1580 and a subsequent period of low death rate. The figures suggest the impact of bad harvest, epidemic or plague during the 1620s.

The clergy of the archdeaconry were rather immobile – they averaged a 20-year stay in their respective benefices. It seems probable that this pattern was strengthened rather than weakened during the period when new recruits were becoming better qualified and apparently more numerous. Was this a reaction? Were those ensconced in benefices either unable or unwilling to move in the face of the onslaught of new men? This might in its turn have meant that the older clergy were finding it increasingly difficult to obtain patronage, although the number of resignations recorded during the period of stability does not appear to have been lower than usual and 27 per cent of vacancies in the 1620s were occasioned by resignation. Probably it should be concluded that it had always been difficult to obtain fresh patronage once beneficed. When Sir John Coke begged John Jemmat to become minister of Melbourne, Derbyshire, Jemmat commented, 'Neither is your honour ignorant that when a man is once settled in a pastoral charge his best friends cease to make enquirie after any better preferment for him, yea though he live in a most uncomfortable meanness.' Undoubtedly, this stability made the situation more economically difficult for new recruits seeking benefices. It would seem from the Coventry data that it was the reign of James I which offered the poorest employment prospects because of the low number of deaths. If the improved situation of the decade 1620–30 was felt nationally, the succeeding period was one of slight relief on the employment scene, yet an increased number of vacancies may not have been sufficient to compensate for a growth in the overall number of recruits.[15]

This data suggests that the historian's picture of the employment prospects of the clergy over this long period hinges on the changing death rate. The number of clergy moving from one benefice to another or resigning a benefice in favour of a relative remained fairly constant. The periods 1540–80 and 1620–30 are aberrations from the norm, not because there was high mobility but because there was a high death rate. Infiltration of graduates into the parishes of this archdeaconry was gradual, despite high graduate recruitment into the ministry and expansion of educational opportunities within the diocese, because there were only a few vacancies per annum.

This type of analysis, useful as far as it goes, presents a 'type' and is in danger of distorting the interpretation of clerical career structure unless it is tempered by a sound knowledge of individual case histories. Whereas each living within the archdeaconry averaged four vacancies during the period, some livings changed hands more often and some rather less often.

There is some information regarding the group of clergy in Coventry archdeaconry in 1584 which may throw light of a more personal kind on this matter. Every year 5 per cent of the livings changed hands, sometimes passing to new recruits, sometimes to 'foreigners' from outside the archdeaconry, and sometimes to clergy already established in the archdeaconry. This very gradual change of personnel preserved continuity in the Church. In the 98 benefices already noted were an interesting cross-section of old and new recruits to the ministry.[16]

Table 2

Institutions of clergy in Coventry archdeaconry

Institutions	Date	Percentage of total
6	pre–1558	7 over 26 years
7	1558–63	8 over 21 years
33	1564–74	39 over 10 years
39	1575–84	46 over 1 year
Total 85[1]		Total 100

1.Including pluralists, this covers 91 benefices; information is not available for the institution dates of six beneficed clergy.

The group who had held their livings prior to 1575 were obviously sufficiently conformist to have satisfied the Church authorities. Few of the entire group had held other livings before institution to the living which they held in 1584. Although the mean length of incumbency for the group was 28.77 years, there was a sharp deviation from the mean (15.23). A more accurate statement would be that there was a substantial number who resided in a single living for between 25 and 50 years, and a small group who held their livings for 12 years or less.

The men instituted in or since 1575 are of especial interest as they form the group among which, presumably, death took least toll. On the whole their careers were long and, although there is some evidence of geographical mobility, many retained the same benefice throughout their working life. Not all of those who resigned their livings did so to move elsewhere – for example, William Porter resigned the vicarage of Kinsbury after 31 years service; Richard Harbert vacated Wolfancote voluntarily after 37 years; and when Richard Hill resigned Radway vicarage in 1620 after 40 years occupancy it was to make way for a relative. The total number of resignations was small, the chief reason for vacancies being death. Those who did move elsewhere included Gedion Hancocks, a Marian exile as a youth, and Vicar of Willoughby for 24 years. He succeeded his father Thomas to the living in 1578 and left it in 1602 for the rectory of Fitz in Shropshire. He died in this second living, to which he had apparently been presented by a *hac vice* patron, in 1616. Pluralism within the archdeaconry was rare and normally involved neighbouring parishes. Luke Smith, Rector of Birmingham since 1578, obtained the parsonage of Solihull in 1590 and held both until after 1639. Roger Ellyot already held two livings in 1584. John Barwell held Stockington rectory in 1584 and three years later acquired Newton Regis. Roger Barker had held two livings in plurality until 1572 when he resigned Ashow. It was only three years, however, before he obtained Newbold vicarage; this he held in plurality with his old living of Cubbington until 1581. In that year he resigned Cubbington, retaining Newbold until his death in 1604. Of the five pluralists who held both livings in the diocese only one was a non-graduate. Several men held benefices outside the diocese before 1584 (14 or 35.8 per cent of this small group) and two of these were pluralists who continued to hold an extra-diocesan living with that in Coventry archdeaconry.

At least 21 of the group instituted in or since 1575 had held no previous benefice, although they may have acted as curates for very short periods (53.8 per cent). Five others had held another benefice in the diocese previously (12.8 per cent: one of these is included in the above total of 14 and two were pluralists within the diocese in 1584 or later).

A very few men involved in the total 1584 list were later preferred elsewhere in the archdeaconry. Thomas Rotton, curate of Ansty chapel in 1584, moved to Meriden in May 1589 and remained there until 1618. Richard Seale, having served as curate of Bobbenhull for four years, was presented to Marton vicarage in 1587; he vacated it on his death in 1623. John Fox, assistant curate of Newton Regis, entered Kinsbury vicarage in 1586 and Baxterley rectory in 1591. He held the two livings in plurality until his death in 1627. The only one in this group who actually held a cure with freehold before further preferment was Henry Williams, LL.B. – he made a sensible move from the small living of Meriden to the much larger and more comfortable Aston. The other moves represented a step up the ladder for curates of free chapels and donatives or assistant curates. John Fox had exceptional good fortune – perhaps because he was the only curate who had had a university education and possessed a preaching licence. He was the only assistant curate to receive preferment out of the group. This seems to bear out Michael Zell's suggestion that during the 1550s few assistant curates ever moved into the ranks of the beneficed clergy and to indicate that there was little change in this pattern. Even in the late sixteenth century the clergy were divided at parochial level into two distinct, rarely overlapping, groups, the beneficed and the unbeneficed clergy. From the Coventry data it appears that it was the perpetual curacy or the free chapel rather than the assistant curacy which represented the road to a benefice for those who failed to secure one at ordination.

The existence of a class of permanent curates during the reign of Elizabeth and after is suggested also by the careers of a number of Chester ordinands. William Duxbury of Chester diocese was ordained priest there in 1564/5: during his career he held four separate curacies in the diocese and is last heard of in 1605. In 1576 James Martindale was ordained deacon at Chester; it was not until 1583 that he was admitted priest after several years as curate of Ormskirk. In 1590 he became curate of a chapelry, Padiham; by 1595 he was preacher at Holcombe/Tottington chapel. Sometimes these curates were immobile: Alexander Horrocks was curate of Deane Parish Church from 1614–50; James Kershaw served Newchurch in Rossendale through the years 1578–1623. Clearly, however, most occupied more than one such position during their careers and sometimes these were of short duration. Gilbert Astley, who held at least three Chester curacies, was more typical, serving as curate of Todmorden, Rochdale, from 1590–1611 and of Turton chapel, Bolton, from 1596–1622. Technically, many of the curates were not clergy at all but readers. Thomas Wainwright had been styled 'curate' of West Derby chapel for six years before he took either deacon's or priest's orders: on admission to Liverpool chapel in 1598 he was ordained both deacon and priest on the same day and he remained there until 1622. Such a position could act as an apprenticeship for the ministry – Otes Bradley was five years unordained reader of Denton chapel, Manchester Collegiate church, before ordination as deacon and priest in 1595.

In examining the careers of 42 curates ordained at Chester one is aware that the sample is small and also that the records conceal the fact that 'curate' was a word used to cover a multitude of occupations – reader, assistant curate, deputy, curate of a free chapel, perpetual curate. Those who were readers had served 'apprenticeships' of about five or six years before taking holy orders. Those who were curates of chapelries often held more than one position as curate during their careers but their positions would be of fairly lengthy duration. It is more difficult to distinguish between assistant curates and deputies in the lists. There is no evidence of any movement between chapelries and freehold benefices and many of those serving as curates of chapels or parish churches were evidently men of mature years.

If a group of men in the Coventry archdeaconry in 1620 is examined, the basic similarity to the cohort of 1584 is startling. Of course, there is considerable overlap in personnel between the two groups. Careers are again lengthy, although perhaps a little less confined to one benefice. There is one evident dissimilarity between the two groups: whereas in 1584 out of a total group of 123, 41 laid claim (often dubious) to a university education (33 per cent), in 1620, of the total group of 113, 73 had a verified university training (64 per cent). Thus, by the 1620s, university expansion had had a marked effect at parish level, whereas in 1584, although university expansion itself was under way, recruitment of graduates into the parishes was as yet slow.[17]

Eleven men had moved from curacies of one kind or another within the diocese to the benefice which they held in 1620 (12.7 per cent of the group of 86 beneficed clergy) and some allowance should be made for curates moving in from elsewhere. A further three had held livings in the diocese apart from that held in 1620. Added to this number are eight men who had served a cure of souls in another diocese (9.3 per cent of the beneficed). There is evidence of very little pluralism – what there is consists of an extra-diocesan living being held with that in the archdeaconry.

Whereas more of this group apparently started their careers within the archdeaconry than was the case with the earlier cohort, there seems to have been more mobility from one benefice to another at the later date. Twelve clergymen beneficed in the archdeaconry in 1620 acquired further livings after this date, some of them held in plurality (13 per cent had further preferment). Thirteen of the curates in the 1620 group obtained preferment to a benefice (48 per cent of the curates listed) either inside the archdeaconry or elsewhere in another diocese. This is in marked contrast to 1584 when only five curates apparently secured freehold benefices subsequently. Perhaps one of the more noticeable developments in the 1620 listing is the number of men who actually served as curates in the livings to which they were later presented. This indicates that 'being on the spot' to agitate for patronage mattered as much if not more than local origin – it was connection which counted. Thus John Prior, a student at Oxford, was admitted curate of Allestrey in May 1620. Three years later the vicar, Robert Bostocke, an Oxford M.A., resigned and Prior was admitted in his stead. This might represent an arrangement between the two men at the outset: Bostocke was a pluralist and in a position to bargain. On the other hand, there may have been pressure from the Bishop, Morton. Samuel Buggs had served as curate of St Michael's, Coventry, for five years before institution as vicar and there is little doubt that his favour with the corporation of Coventry acted to his advantage. Robert Chadborne was instituted Vicar of Stoke in 1627 but had been curate there for at least seven years past. Richard Abell had long been curate of Mancetter before institution there in 1622. This development was common to the rest of the diocese of Lichfield. Being in the area gave a man some advantage over clergy from elsewhere seeking employment, except where the patron concerned had his eye on someone specific from outside or had arranged to sell the right to present.

Julian Winsper held three cures without institution and one vicarage in the archdeaconry during his career. Some with apparent advantages, however, did not gain immediate preferment. John Ennewes, son of the Rector of Bilton, did not find placement upon ordination but, after serving as curate of Brownsover chapel for some years, stepped into his father's place at his death in 1621. Whether he knew that his future was secure is uncertain. Henry Smitheman must have found it somewhat more difficult to find patronage. Although he had a Cambridge B.A. degree, he held an assistant curacy and a cure without institution for 19 years before eventually obtaining preferment to Lillington vicarage. Perhaps significantly, the same two curacies had been held by his predecessor at Lillington, Ralph Wilding, who also found a benefice after a long wait of 28 years. Having spent 12 years in a chapelry, Thomas Sibley was presented to Marton vicarage, the first of two livings which he served prior to the civil war.

These examples point to further conclusions. It was still from free chapels and perpetual curacies that preferment was easiest, and these seem on occasion to have formed an intermediate step between an assistant curacy and a regular benefice. The personnel of churches with cure of souls but without institution was fairly stable, although there was more tendency to move from them than from freehold benefices. The cures were normally small and impoverished but they offered a degree of independence and prosperity not to be found in the assistant curacies, with which they are so often confused. However they did not offer security: the curate possessed no freehold and his position was subject to the patron's pleasure. By this date, however, more assistant curates *were* finding preferment and there is a suggestion that the position was becoming part of the career ladder for the clergy as it had not been in the 1580s.

The two groups of parochial clergy in 1584 and 1620 present a picture of lengthy clerical careers, continuing the tradition of the pre-Reformation and Reformation periods which had been interrupted during the chaos of the 1540s and 1550s. The evidence indicates a changing pattern, however. In the earlier period most clergy obtained a benefice early if they were ever to achieve preferment. Once obtained, this benefice was likely to prove the cleric's one source of livelihood for a goodly number of years – until retirement or death. There were a very few pluralists but actual movement from one living to another was comparatively rare. There also seems to have been a significant class of permanent curates, who never attained the status of curate of a chapel let alone of vicar or rector. Some men in churches without institution were able to move into freehold benefices. By 1620 more men were serving two or more benefices during their careers, several coming in from other dioceses to take up preferment or later moving on into another jurisdiction. Pluralism was more rare. The pattern of movement from a cure of souls without institution to a benefice is more definitely visible, and the importance of local connection and presence is evident. However, a graduate ordinand – even one with strong local connections – did not at this stage automatically obtain a benefice at ordination: he might be forced to serve in a curacy or even to act as an assistant curate, reader or schoolmaster for some years. On occasion, the road to better preferment and security was a long one for both graduate and non-graduate. For a very few graduates success never came but most, if they lived, secured a niche in the establishment eventually. By 1620 several assistant curates were obtaining freehold benefices. There is thus not the same sharp distinction in the seventeenth-century Church between non-beneficed and beneficed clergy – it was becoming more usual for an ordinand to serve a waiting period of this kind before obtaining a benefice.

It is, of course, dangerous to assume that all clerics were seeking to make further moves. A chapelry may have been the height of ambition for some clergy, given their qualifications and their assessment of the situation. For the uneducated or the lazy any one of the lower rungs of the clerical ladder could provide a stipend equal to what they could have expected in other walks of life; various perquisites such as fees for writing wills or teaching children to read and write; and work which was slightly less arduous and of improved status. Moreover, obtaining a living in the first place was a relatively expensive business and it probably took many clergy several years of economic husbandry before they could contemplate further moves. The subjection of the beneficed to taxation and subsidy payments and our lack of precise information concerning the payment of curates makes a straight economic comparison between assistant curacies and curacies and freehold benefices difficult. No doubt the difficulty of obtaining patronage did reflect the shortage of vacancies during this period and the wait must have been frustrating for many, but one must at least entertain the possibility that some of the beneficed and unbeneficed were not ambitious, and that some of those temporarily shut out of freehold benefices found in their positions a degree of independence and status which was not uncongenial.

The ordination lists of the different dioceses lend substance to the claim that recruitment into the ranks of the clergy was steadily increasing during the period in question and placing additional pressure on available vacancies. Exact comparisons are difficult to achieve as ordinations in each diocese varied from year to year – a fall-off in numbers at Peterborough might be compensated for at Oxford – and as ordination lists do not exist for all dioceses. Total numbers do seem to have increased but by how much we simply cannot be certain. It is the eventual coupling of the improved quality of the ordinands (first felt in the 1580s) with the general increase in numbers which is most significant and which had most effect upon career structure. Some questions remain unanswered: did improved recruitment mean that it was now easy to fill those very poor livings rated at below £5 in the *Valor*? Was it now more difficult to obtain dispensations to hold livings in plurality?

The lower average age of late Elizabethan and early Stuart

ordinands presumably had an initial effect upon the prospective number of vacancies. Although the situation may have eased somewhat in the 1620s there was a backlog of men waiting in curacies and teaching posts who filtered into newly vacant livings, as well as ever-increasing pressure from new and technically well-qualified recruits. In combination these factors probably wiped out any possible advantages brought about by a slightly increased death rate. The increase in the number of ordinands did not have to be large to create a difficult situation, because margins were always small.

Yet at Peterborough recruitment into the ministry during the five-year period 1620–5 was over five times as great as that of the equivalent period 1585–90, and almost twice as great as that of the period 1611–15/16, and it was now almost entirely graduate. The number of ordinands at Oxford was either as high or higher than that of Peterborough. Neither set of figures show real decline until the late 1630s. Only if it could be proved that these centres were growing entirely at the expense of provincial dioceses could the effect of this expansion be minimized, but there is every indication that other dioceses, while not expanding as ordination centres in the same way, were holding their own. These facts may prompt us to question the assumption that the status of the clerical profession was low at this time but, as the following argument demonstrates, it is probable that the impact of increased clerical recruitment was moderated by certain factors.[18]

Professor Curtis postulated that in the seventeeth century the universities were directing more graduates and students into the Church than the Church could accommodate in sufficiently lucrative, secure and prestigious positions. He suggested that the average cleric of the period might expect a career of 30 years or slightly more after ordination as deacon at 23. This conclusion was based on two samples. Neither group was exclusively clerical and it might be said that the inclusion of a sample of men included in the Dictionary of National Biography biassed his conclusions in favour of the long-lived.

Possible objections to Mark Curtis's method prompted an analysis of a purely clerical group – 125 ordinands at London between 1600 and 1618 for whom information was available. The results supported Mark Curtis's general view of the longevity of the clergy, but with a significant modification. He estimated that the average life span of a cleric was between 60 and 63 years; with no correction, the London information gives an average life span of 57 years. The average career of matriculands of Caius who later became ordained was 29 years 8 months: Professor Curtis suggested, without further explanation, that this be corrected to 27 years 6 months. He admitted that the average represented careers in a range from

Table 3

Pattern of ordinations: Oxford and Peterborough dioceses: 1570–1642

OXFORD

Date	Total no. ordinands	Deacons	Priests	Deacons and priests	Total no. ceremonies
1570–5					
1585–90					
1591–5					
1605–10	545	298	228	19	30
1611–15	786	458	324	4	21
1616–20*	537	281	244	12	19
1621–2/3 (Mar.)	290	181	109		8
1628–9	197				8
1630–5	698	400	293	4(+1?)	29
1636–40	346	178	167	1	25

* But no ordinations recorded between March 1617/18 and May 1619, when three ceremonies would have been normal.

Although equivalent information is not available for all years in these two dioceses, the table does make plain the fact that the pattern of recruitment varied in both and that the rate of recruitment at certain times might differ quite sharply from one diocese to the next. At Oxford, for example, recruitment reached a peak in the early years of the seventeenth century, while figures at Peterborough did not really rise noticeably until the years 1611–15. If the somewhat inadequate figures for Oxford in the 1620s tell us anything at all, Oxford suffered during this decade, picking up again in the early 1630s. Peterborough had boomed in the 1620s but numbers showed a marked decline in the 1630s; by the last half of the decade figures at Oxford were also dropping. The two dioceses were, apparently, the major ordination

PETERBOROUGH

Date	Total no. ordinands	Deacons	Priests	Deacons and priests	Total no. ceremonies
1570–5	285	128	100	57	136
1585–90	209	58	57	94	
1591–5	101	11	20	70	
1605–10	234	116	115	3	29
1611–15	609	304	281	24	142
1616–20	921	468	450	3	189
1621–5	1199	620	567	12	
1626–30	964	464	500		
1631–40	649	377	272		
1641–2	175	100	75		

centres in the country. In using the table care should be taken to realize that the total number of ordinands represents the total over the time span specified and not the total of separate individuals ordained. The figure for deacons is normally taken as a guide to the number of recruits, but, once again, allowance should be made for professional casualties of one type or another. The number of men ordained deacon and priests on the same day (by licence) dropped dramatically after 1604 – there was no slackening off in the attempt to restrict the practice in later years, rather the reverse. The number of ceremonies at Oxford was kept low, with only a few ceremonies by special faculty; at Peterborough far more small ceremonies occurred.

4–50 years but ignored the significance of this distribution within the range, which was so scattered as to make his use of a corrective meaningless. The mean length of career of London ordinands was 32.1 years but there was a marked deviation from the mean: the standard deviation being 14.74. There seem to have been very few professional casualties among these deacons: only two out of 125 ordinands had careers of less than six years in length. It is certainly significant that while 33.6 per cent of the clergy had careers of between 15 and 30 years, a further 40.8 per cent had longer careers of between 31 and 50 years' duration. Thus a substantial percentage were exceeding by some years the length of career suggested by Professor Curtis on the strength of the mean alone.[19]

Using the above figures for length of career with Professor Curtis's method of estimating the total number of vacancies in the kingdom per annum may suggest that he was underestimating the extent to which the Church was over-supplying its needs, as there would have been about 281 vacancies as opposed to 327. However, there is every reason to suppose that his estimate of 427 graduates and students entering the Church from the universities per annum is a gross overestimate, as he omits to take into account the large number of ordinands remaining in the universities for at least a part of their careers. At London, between a third and a half of all ordinands returned to the universities. Moreover, it may be that there was some easing of the situation in terms of vacancies at the very time when this increase in recruitment was at its most startling. Extreme reliance on the *average* conceals the fact that the placement situation within the Church was subject to continual change, not only because of fluctuations in the numbers of recruits to the Church but also because of a fluctuating death rate.

Is it indeed possible to estimate by what margin the Church was over-producing new clergy? In the decade 1616–25 the diocese of Peterborough alone was apparently fulfilling a third or more of the Church's personnel requirements. Between 1616 and 1620, 471 men were ordained deacon – almost all graduates; between 1621 and 1625, 632 men were admitted. There were professional casualties amongst this group but, if the London analysis may be relied upon, they were few. By this date Oxford and Peterborough were the ordination centres *par excellence*, but if between them they were catering for two-thirds or more of the Church's need for beneficed clergy, it seems possible that the Church was over-supplying its needs over the country as a whole, but this takes no account of ordinands not following parochial careers (that is, those taking college fellowships or pursuing other professional careers). In the absence of complete ordination lists from Lincoln, Chester, Durham, Ely or Hereford it is, moreover, impossible to say whether ordination numbers elsewhere were *more* than supplying the deficiency in total numbers at Oxford and Peterborough. The distortion of the ordination rules (and thereby the geographical pattern of ordinations) as a result of escalating university numbers cannot be exaggerated.

Mark Curtis's argument in his *The Alienated Intellectuals* hinges on his contention that over-recruitment was keeping many well-qualified men out of secure posts in the Church. There is no doubt that the quality of curates had changed by the 1620s. In 1584 no curates in Coventry archdeaconry were graduates and only one had attended university. A licensing book for the period 1601–4 in Coventry and Lichfield diocese reveals that most readers and curates admitted were not in orders and that only one was a graduate. By the 1620s and 1630s the situation was changed. Many graduates were assuming temporary posts of very little status or income. Some were not even styled curate but 'reader': George Fyrchild, B.A., was appointed reader at Bloxwich chapel, Walsall, and Philip Perry, M.A., was licensed reader of Maxstock, Warwickshire, in 1637. Most graduate curates and readers combined their post with one of teacher or schoolmaster. Some of them later found preferment but it is difficult to trace their later careers because the civil war has robbed us of the necessary information. Moreover, some of those who acted as 'preacher' while serving a curacy or teaching in a school were undoubtedly equivalent to lecturers, and their positions may have been reasonably remunerative and challenging.[20]

It is also true that recruits in the seventeenth century tended to be younger than entrants during the 1560s and 1570s. The average age at ordination had now fallen to approximately a year above the canonical minimum, the average now being 24 for a deacon and 25 for a priest. Between 1614 and 1632, 39 men were ordained at Lichfield below the canonical age. At London also the rules regarding age minima were waived occasionally. Sometimes the age cited in the London lists does not tally exactly with that given at the university, but what is important here is that the authorities did not turn away candidates when they claimed a lower age than was technically required: whether the relatively low age of these ordinands made them less resentful of serving an 'apprenticeship' before attaining a permanent living is a moot point.[21]

Out of a group of 337 clergymen subscribing on institutions to a benefice at Lichfield between 1614 and 1632, at least two-thirds were entering their first benefice. The age at admission of 41.3 per cent is known: 50 men were between the ages of 26 and 30 at institution (35.9 per cent of the group for whom age is known) and 28 men (20.14 per cent) were aged between 31 and 35. Such figures suggest that preferment, if it came, came quite early in a man's career. 'Apprenticeship', where it was served by graduate recruits, was normally under six years' duration and rarely over nine years. The average age for appointment as a London lecturer was 30, and we should remember that this represented a high point in the career of a well-qualified cleric.[22]

If one concludes that there was increasing recruitment into the Church in the seventeenth century and that this was of a predominantly graduate nature, then the main issues are why was there this overproduction and was it absorbed into the career structure of the Church and its allied professions (university and school teaching; lectureships) satisfactorily or not? Letters such as the one below from Edward Golty in 1617 suggest not.

> Right Worshipful Sir after pardon craved for my bold presumption in writing unto your worship. These are in all humbleness to desire you to be a means unto Mr Ralph Symonds my father in law that he would not be unmindful of me concerning the obtaining of a church living for me that I may make some better use and employment of my time than I have done hitherto for I have been now in orders almost this twelvemonth. And he that hath once set his hand to the plough and looks back he is not fit for the kingdom of God. They that are God's ministers they must be workers and labourers both in life and doctrine. And it grieves me not a little that the small talent of knowledge which God hath lent me should be all this time hidden in the ground of an unfruitful heart like unto a candle put under a bushell which although it hath light in itself yet it ought rather to be set upon a candlestick that it may show light unto all these that are in the house. Grief oppressed me and sickness of body hath hitherto prevented me from doing my self that good which otherwise I should have done; so that I may not unfitly compare myself to the disabled man in the Gospel which had lain xxxviii years at the pool of Bethesda; and while he was coming to wash himself in the troubled water, another steppeth down before him; many of my juniors and acquaintances hath outstripped and stepped before me because I have had no friends to stand at the pool's mouth to help me in when the water is troubled (that is) when there are many suiters and all strive to be made whole and to obtain their wished desires. I received at Michaelmas last a 100[li] in part of my wife's portion: let him bestow the best part of it for a gratuity upon them that will help him to a living. Let an Angel move the water. (And if he want means) let him make friends of the unrighteous mammon that he may but purchase for us an earthy habitation whilst we remain in this miserable world. Thus desiring your worship's aid and furtherance, I most humbly take my leave with my hearty prayers to God for the continuance of your health and prosperity and rest at
>   Your worship's command
>   Edward Golty
> Aylsham, 6 January 1617.[23]

However, one must be cautious in one's use of a single example. Golty's letter does suggest the existence of fierce competition for benefices in the second decade of the century and the need to buy oneself into a living at this date and as such it is interesting. It provides some support for Mark Curtis's viewpoint, but it is a single example and, moreover, it comes from the year 1617. If the figures pertaining to Coventry and Lichfield are reliable, then this was still within the period when vacant livings were most scarce, although this would soon be replaced by an easier period when competition was not so fierce.

In the course of the book we shall be seeking the answer to the question, why was the Church a popular profession in the early seventeenth century? As to whether overproduction was of such a magnitude that it could not be dealt with, resulting in large numbers of disgruntled and ambitious clergy jockeying for position and expressing disgust and frustration, one can say that the extent of overproduction itself has probably been exaggerated and that no account has been taken of compensating factors. It may also be that the dramatic situation in the capital, where non-beneficed clergy were certainly numerous, has distorted the national picture.

A study of the parish clergy from the 1540s until the civil war demonstrates that the career pattern of the clergy underwent certain real changes during the post-Reformation period. Indeed, one might say that the lower clergy now possessed a career pattern whereas prior to the Reformation they did not. There is more evidence in the seventeenth century of clerical mobility from assistant curacies and lectureship to livings and from one living to another than there is in the sixteenth century. The Church has become a career even for its most humble recruits and the clergy, as a consequence, are subjected to the pressures of a career structure. This book will attempt to show that these changes had multifarious roots in ecclesiastical policy, lay opinion, the patronage system, demographic change, the educational revolution and so on. It will also be seeking to establish the extent to which the clergy had become a profession as a result of these changes. It is but a first step to draw up a tentative picture of this changing career structure at parochial level, quite another to explain it.

2

The context

Until recently contemporary historians had given little attention to the late medieval parochial clergy. In his book, *English Parish Clergy on the Eve of the Reformation*, however, Peter Heath dispelled many of our preconceptions and misconceptions about the clergy of the period. Since then the work of other historians, notably Christopher Haigh, has made us aware that wide regional differences in clerical standards prevailed but, nevertheless, Peter Heath's generalizations provide a useful working hypothesis as to the state of the pre-Reformation clergy.

> Far from perfection though most of the clergy undoubtedly were, their ignorance, negligence, indiscipline and avarice have been crudely magnified by commentators; to a large degree the Church seemed to be keeping the distance which separated the clergy from the ideal as narrow as society and history would permit.

In other words, until a more rigorous education was both available to, and within the pockets of, the clergy, a higher standard of learning in ordinands was unlikely to obtain. In any event, ordinaries could not ensure that the better-educated ordinands went into parochial service. Moroever, although bishops were firm in their rejection of the unfit from benefices, they were helpless when the presentee possessed a papal dispensation. Certain types of pluralism and consequent non-residence also were regarded as a social and economic necessity, although they had been stripped of their most scandalous features.[1]

Mr Heath portrays the situation as a necessary compromise with reality: 'the Church had to content itself with the art of the possible'. Certain revolutions – political, social, intellectual – were necessary before the situation could itself be revolutionized. For instance, an upsurge in the education of the laity might serve to push educated clerics out of the choice administrative and political positions and into pastoral work. Similarly, clerical discipline would have been improved by the abolition of the minor orders. An emphasis upon the pastoral as opposed to the priestly function of the clergy would also have affected attitudes to standards. Of course, the bishops might have changed the situation somewhat by example and by the exercise of imaginative schemes of reform.[2]

Peter Heath assumes that the bishops did not often set the needed example or set in motion reform programmes because they did not feel that the situation was desperate, but recent work, especially that of Margaret Bowker and Stephen Lander, has tended to show that some of the bishops of the early sixteenth century were reforming bishops of this type. It was through visitations and sessions of the diocesan ecclesiastical courts that bishops were able to maintain the standards of the dioceses. The courts seem to have been undergoing reform in the 1520s but to have been permanently weakened by attacks during the 1530s. As Stephen Lander concludes,

> The Chichester courts may present an especially clear picture of reorgan-
> isation and reform in the 1520s and of decline in business and efficiency
> over the early Reformation, but it was a picture . . . that is apparently
> applicable in varying measures to other dioceses.

The shocks administered to the system during the period seem to have crippled the Church courts as agents of social and moral control among the laity although there is some evidence that their disciplinary role with regard to the clergy was still important down to the civil war.[3]

During the period of the Henrician and Edwardian Reformation itself both Crown and bishops were more concerned with the problems raised by opposition to the new measures than with standards of clerical learning or moral uprightness or residency. The response of the parochial clergy to the Henrician and Edwardian measures over the country as a whole remains to be charted although historians working on certain counties or dioceses have provided us with several valuable indicators of the general response. Professor A. G. Dickens suggested that on the whole the parochial clergy offered little resistance to the new measures. For the most part the clergy were content to follow the example of their bishops and archbishops and to implement government policy in the parishes even when they privately disagreed with it. Few seem to have objected to the severance of the link with Rome and it was ceremonial and sacramental change which bothered them most – leading some to participate in the Pilgrimage of Grace or the Western Rising of 1549. In Kent, Dr Michael Zell concludes, opposition to the new practices and doctrines in the Henrician period was 'common but not constant, . . . usually disorganised but occasionally found support in more powerful quarters; . . . that it involved a scattered collection of parochial clergy and some zealots among the religious'. Because the clergy voiced their discontent and the laity reported their ministers, the Archbishop of Canterbury was able to control but not to halt this clerical opposition. In fact, the government (in the persons of Cranmer and Cromwell) seems to have been amazingly tolerant of clerical opposition: only those who actively sought martyrdom were persecuted and there were no large-scale deprivations of recalcitrant clergy. In Lancashire Dr Christopher Haigh describes a different situation. Geographically large parishes made ecclesiastical control difficult, information was hard to obtain and reforms almost impossible to implement. Rich but socially unattractive benefices repelled educated and reform-minded clergy and therefore limited the spread of new ideas in the county. Hence, here in the north-west, clerical and lay opposition to the Henrician measures were as one and were fed by the late enthusiasm for traditional Catholicism in the north. Detection of the seditious was more problematic when laymen supported their clergy and organization of opposition became a reality.[4]

Although, on the whole, one is tempted to agree with Professor Dickens that clerical opposition was scattered (whether easily controllable as in Kent or less easily so in the north-west), one must recognize that even unstated opposition provided an environment conducive to conservative rather than reformed religious life within the parishes. Acceptance of the official Reformation did not mean enthusiasm – and enthusiasm on the part of the clergy was necessary if Protestantism were to thrive. In saying this, one has to remember that the Henrician Reformation was not Protestant although some of its supporters were. It was thus natural that there should be no purge of conservative priests during the early Reformation. Continuity of personnel was one of the hallmarks of the period, even down to the 1570s and 1580s. The Marian purge of 1554 was the most rigorous – involving perhaps 2,000 deprivations – but of the men deprived of their livings then many were instituted to others reasonably quickly. Elizabeth I found it necessary only to deprive a few hundreds of the clergy serving her 9,000 parishes. All this seems natural when it is recalled that the Reformation had not proceeded all that far among the Edwardian clergy and that Elizabeth later did not want a Protestant clergy but a loyal one.

Clerical enthusiasm for the Edwardian régime may have varied from region to region. Whilst warning us against geographical determinism, Dr David Palliser reminds us that between 1549 and 1553 a far higher proportion of parochial clergy in London, Essex, Suffolk, Norfolk and Cambridgeshire chose to marry than was the case in Yorkshire, Lincolnshire or Lancashire. (Of course, the enthusiasm of the bishops in persecuting married clergy has some influence on these figures. Moreover, marriage did not necessarily imply acceptance of Protestantism although it does seem to indicate a rejection of conservatism.) Although isolated examples of clerical enthusiasm for the new ideas can certainly be found and although individual bishops were trying hard to Protestantize the clergy during Edward's reign, the span of the reign was too brief to have achieved significant results at parochial level. What the Edwardian period did ensure was that some men of stature, clerics, gentry and merchants, cared sufficiently for the new beliefs and objected so strongly to the reintroduction of Catholicism that they were willing to go into exile for their cause. Enthusiastic Protestantism among the clergy at parochial level had to await the return of the Marian exiles from the Continent, with their strengthened resolve and the missionary example of the Swiss Reformed churches ever in their minds.[5]

As chapter 9 will suggest, the theology of the Reformation itself put the status of the clergy in doubt. The *raison d'être* of the regular clergy was removed and with it the regular clerical orders. The justification for a secular clergy was not abolished but was radically changed. Here was not a mediating priesthood but a pastoral ministry. Martin Bucer's *De Regno Christi* of 1551 contained an interesting appeal to King Edward VI to 'take in hand immediately your universities and the colleges which are part of them' to provide sufficient ministers of the new variety. Bucer saw the universities as vocational training schools with colleges assigned to the various professions – law, medicine, Church. Some of the colleges would become seminaries, concentrating on a study of Scripture. The universities should be totally under the control of Reformed academics.[6]

Bucer's four-fold division of the Reformed ministry into preachers, doctors, pastors and deacons found favour with English Reformers such as Cartwright. Many had had close acquaintance with the ideas while in exile: however, although there were parallels in the English ministry of the later sixteenth and early seventeenth centuries, the division was never clearcut and was never adopted in its pure form in the post-1558 period. One man commonly combined the several functions except where additional support was needed. Whatever the precise function of the minister, his role was not priestly and his knowledge of Scripture and his personal example became all important.

The clergy of the Reformation were being judged by new standards and one of the more interesting phenomena of the period is the appearance of the clerical survey which attempted to assess the state of the clergy according to these new criteria of excellence. The most famous early example of this is Bishop Hooper's visitation of Gloucester in 1551; 311 clergy were examined as to their knowledge of the ten commandments, the Apostles' Creed and the Lord's Prayer in English: 171 could not repeat the ten commandments and 33 of these could not say where they occurred in Scripture. Ten did not know the Lord's Prayer and 27 did not know its author. This emphasis upon the knowledge of the vernacular Scriptures is new and is intimately related to the role of the clergy as teachers as well as to the place of the Scriptures as an authority in the Reformed Church.

Such examinations of the clergy are a common occurrence in the period down to 1604 and beyond, but what they tell us as historians about the state of the clergy as opposed to the attitudes of the examiners is debatable. As F. D. Price notes, the test was whether the clerics could recite the passages by rote, not whether they were familiar with their content and import – 138 of the 171 who failed to recite the ten commandments perfectly could locate them in the Bible. There was scarcely a long tradition of familiarity with the Scriptures in English and various translations of the biblical passages current during the early Reformation may well have confused the clergy. Moreover, the test does not indicate that the clergy were in other ways unlearned, ignorant, illiterate or vocationally unsuited. The survey's chief value lies in that it highlights the concern of the bishops or of puritan clergy to improve the biblical knowledge of the clergy – thus laying secure foundations for scripturally based preaching and better teaching – and that it shows the rate at which this change was taking place.[7]

The clergy of the 1540s and 1550s clearly did not meet the new standards of learning required of them although, as Dr Barratt and Mr Heath agree, it is improbable that there were many who could not read or write by 1558.

How precisely the clergy were to be educated was an issue which taxed the Church's leaders throughout our period. The reigns of Edward and Mary saw some important developments which were later acted upon. Bucer not only advocated college 'seminaries' but also local schools which would offer compulsory scriptural and catechistical education and a broader humanistic curriculum. Such schools would be directed to seek out potential candidates for the ministry and send them to the seminaries. During Mary's reign the English congregation at Frankfurt set up a university with an academic purpose. Experience of the Reformed churches made English Reformers aware of the importance of the teaching function. The teaching of teachers (i.e. clergymen) might take place at godly universities (as at Frankfurt) or, failing this, at parochial level through prophesyings, exercises and the like. The Reformers rarely saw the local grammar schools as fulfilling this further training role although, in practice, the common combination of schoolmastership with pastoral function or lectureship meant that the schools did fulfil this specific function of educating future ministers. A significant number of ministers are praised for encouraging and teaching candidates for the ministry. The formal separation of functions is more difficult to pinpoint. Whereas historians used to see the lectureship as a purely doctoral office, recent research suggests that many incumbents and curates also held lectureships, thus combining pastoral, doctoral and preaching functions. Whoever was thought to be responsible for the training of ministers (universities, the most learned ministers or specifically appointed lecturers), there was agreement that clergymen should be trained to serve cures.[8]

Along with these more fundamental changes in the whole approach to clergy, there occurred several changes in the outward face of the clergy. The most notable of these was, of course, the appearance of clerical marriage. As the problem of sexual incontinence among the clergy in the pre-Reformation period seems to have been serious, clerical marriage was probably more important than has usually been thought. Certainly it seems that clergy of the less conservative variety attached some importance to their right to marry. Hilda Grieve, for example, suggested that marriage rather than political or religious recusancy was the real issue for which clergy were willing to sacrifice their livelihood in the Marian period. Of 93 deprivations in Essex between 1553 and 1558, 88 were for marriage. Incontinent priests were meted out far less severe penalties, indicating that the authorities did associate the act of marriage with religious and political intransigence. The reformers of the early Elizabethan period certainly believed that married clergy were Protestant: marriage was an expression of rebellion against the Catholic faith; failure to marry laid the Protestant credentials of a clergyman open to doubt. Although many of the deprived Marian clergy were given other livings after renouncing their wives, many appear to have turned to secular occupations until the return of Protestantism under Elizabeth. The desire to marry may have been one of the more important factors in dissuading youths from pursuing a clerical career down to the 1580s. Although Elizabeth tolerated a married clergy, the status of a clerical wife was still uncertain, the obstacles put in the way of marriage considerable, and the livelihood offered too meagre to tempt many.[9]

The period 1536–80 saw a distinct turning away from the Church as a career. The number of ordinations fell during Henry's reign because young laymen anticipated that the benefices which were vacant would go to ex-monks from the dissolved religious houses. The competitive nature of the search for a benefice before 1536 helped to further convince laymen that entry into the ministry was not wise. There is evidence that the fall in recruitment, while it benefited both secular clergy and ex-religious, acted to the advantage of those secular priests who had been unbeneficed prior to 1536. There seem also to have been few ordinands during Edward VI's reign. This was perhaps partly due to the fact that Edwardian bishops expected higher standards of their clergy than the laity were able, given the state of educational provision, to attain, but the uncertainty surrounding the religious settlements must have played a large part in discouraging recruitment among the young in the 1540s and 1550s. Not only was the complexion of the régime always changing but also the exact status of the Protestant clergy was in doubt. Historians have tended to assume, therefore, that the continued lag in recruitment between 1550 and 1580 coincided with the low point in ministerial status, but this is not entirely true. Despite the anticlerical sentiment of many of the laity in the 1540s and 1550s, the Reformation acted to raise the status of the lower clergy. One has to remember that the Reformation itself (rather than Henrician policy) had not really made a big impact upon the people of England before the reign of Edward at the earliest and most probably not until the reign of Elizabeth. From about 1560 onwards the advanced Protestants in England and Wales were working hard to instil in the minds of the people the importance of the pastoral and preaching functions. Individual clergymen or lay patrons fostered the education of promising youth. This activity came to fruition with the generation who were eligible for ordination in the late 1570s and 1580s. In other words, the Church was already seeming a more attractive prospect for the fathers of sons born in the 1560s and 1570s but these sons had to be *educated*. It was a movement which coincided with the multiplication of grammar schools and the eventual expansion of university undergraduate education. As on the continent, the ministry became more popular as a career when its status rose and standards of admission became more rigorous, not when it became more lucrative. Looked at in this way, it seems reasonable to suppose that the shortage of clergy in the 1560s and 1570s was the result of doubts cast upon the status of the ministry much earlier during the English Reformation when Protestantism had as yet little hold upon the minds of the people. The Protestant insistence upon an educated clergy meant that the lost ground of the 1540s and 1550s could not be made up instantaneously. Thus it is not until the 1580s that the parishes of the kingdom were properly served.[10]

The acute shortage of clergy in the Reformation period can be documented, and it seriously undermined the prospects of pastoral care and spiritual education of the laity which both the lay and the clerical leaders of Protestantism envisaged as the ideal. Non-residence and pluralism were common (although perhaps not so common as might have been expected, given the shortage of ministers), particularly in areas of the north where parishes were already too large and remote from episcopal control. For the first time, laymen were admitted, indeed invited, to an active role in the ministry as a temporary expedient. The situation presents a curious anomaly. Just as more emphasis was being placed on the importance of pastoral care, it was being withdrawn from many congregations.

This may have had several effects – it perhaps gave a certain impetus to lay religious independence; it perhaps made more people aware of the need for pastoral care and spurred some into the ministry because the chance of placement was now self-evidently good; it certainly did nothing to improve the level of lay religious education and meant that new ideas did little to penetrate some vast areas of the north.

While it is true that, over the country as a whole, as many as 10 per cent of livings were vacant in 1561, the seriousness of the situation varied from county to county, diocese to diocese, and town to town. It was, for example, more serious in the populous areas of Canterbury and London than in Oxford or Gloucester diocese. Lincoln appears to have found it difficult to fill her benefices until the 1580s. Of course, Lincoln was a large diocese but in 1576 there were 77 vacancies in the archdeaconry of Stow and Lincoln alone: all but five of these livings had been filled by 1585.

The records for dispensations for pluralism can tell us something about the incidence of non-residence throughout the country. A living might technically be filled and yet not have a resident incumbent for more than a small part of the year. Between 1560 and 1565 the Archbishop's Court of Faculties issued 735 dispensations for pluralism. In 641 cases the diocese was noted. Dispensations were fewest on the ground in Wales, the north, the north-west and the midland dioceses. The proportion of dispensations was high in London, Exeter, Peterborough and Salisbury. The incidence of pluralism and, in consequence, non-residence, remained low in Coventry and Lichfield. However, many of the dioceses with little pluralism (Chester, York, Coventry and Lichfield, for example) had large parishes with many chapelries dependent upon a mother church. Whether the incumbent of such parishes could serve such a large area adequately was always open to question and many of the inhabitants of outlying chapelries may not have been much better off than those of parishes which had no resident incumbent. To approach the issue of pluralism or non-residence from a strictly statistical vantage point would therefore be unwise.[11]

Whatever the exact situation, the occurrence of non-residence and the shortage of ministers to fill cures combined made for a serious pastoral deficiency in the early 1560s.

This was the state of affairs which greeted the returned Marian exiles at the beginning of Elizabeth's reign. Professor Collinson has noted that for every returned clerical exile who refused a place in Elizabeth's Church, there were five who were offered and accepted preferment therein. Bishoprics, archdeaconries, deaneries, prebends and benefices went to the exiles at the beginning of the reign and to their protégés during the first 16 years of the reign. The radical churchmen came into office, again quoting Professor Collinson, with 'the most progressive intentions'. Although they were very involved in Church politics – in attempting to influence the general religious settlement – the returned exiles demonstrated a close interest in the plight of English and Welsh congregations. Attitudes to the function of the ministry nourished on the continent showed themselves in diocesan administration. The concern of the bishops for pastoral care and preaching in the parishes was often frustrated by legal, economic, social and political obstacles but it was, nevertheless, a constant concern. There were many who shared the interest in adequate pastoral care who had not been in exile. But the community of the returned exiles continued when they took office in the Elizabethan Church, and they provided a hard core of concern which influenced their fellows. They provided the early and enthusiastic leadership for Elizabethan Protestantism. Their enthusiasm was important because it had been fed by successful example – that of the continental Reformed churches – and because it was contagious. In the course of this work it has not been possible to deal in great detail with the efforts of *all* the exile bishops to reform the ministry, but the case study of Bishop Bentham of Coventry and Lichfield helps to underline the point and to show just how difficult it was to make any headway in the context of the early Elizabethan settlement.[12]

3

The Reformed episcopate and its problems: a case study

After Elizabeth's accession the Church in England was in a confused condition. The queen envisaged a politique settlement which, although Protestant, was not Reformed, thereby enabling her to avoid both international conflict and open internal rebellion. This meant that the established Church must not follow too closely the radical changes in ceremony, doctrine and administration associated with the continental Reformed churches, yet Elizabeth was compelled to recruit the necessary new bishops and chief ecclesiastical officers from amongst the returned exiles and other convinced Protestants who were committed to just such changes.

Many of these men were unwilling to participate in the new settlement. For example, Alexander Nowell may have been offered and rejected the diocese of Coventry and Lichfield and Thomas Sampson those of Norwich and Hereford. Those who eventually agreed to accept office often did so after a period of real indecision. In general this reluctance to accept preferment to bishoprics was due not to a dogmatic objection to episcopacy as such nor even only to the strong associations of the office with the papal past but rather to unfavourable land exchanges which Elizabeth was making a condition of appointment. Those who agreed finally did so because they preferred not to allow control of the Church to pass to others. They hoped to mould the settlement from within and to make the Church in England a Reformed Church on the continental model. Until the mid-1570s it appeared that they were to some extent succeeding in their aim but Grindal's confrontation with the Queen concerning the employment of 'prophesyings' seems to mark a definite turning point in the direction of the Church of England's development.[1]

In 1559, however, the hopes of the radical Protestants in England were pinned upon the figures of such as Thomas Bentham, who at 46 succeeded Ralph Bayne to the see of Coventry and Lichfield. Bentham had been turned out of his fellowship at Magdalen College, Oxford, during Mary's reign and had in 1554 escaped to exile in Zurich.[2] Later he had become preacher to the English congregation in Basle and, by 1557, having refused office in the Church of Frankfurt, was a resident of Geneva. Very late in Mary's reign, however, he accepted an invitation from the Protestant congregation in London to become their pastor, and a letter survives from him to Thomas Lever recounting some of his experiences in this capacity.[3] While abroad Bentham married one Mawde Fawcon of Suffolk. Primarily a scholar, he was also a man of conviction: having braved the fires of Marian London, he was expected by the returned exiles to stand as steadfast in the comparative calm which now prevailed.

The bishop, however, was beset by several immediate and urgent problems, those of finance, politics, and personnel being foremost. On his entry to the diocese it became evident that it would be by no means easy to devote his whole attention to reforming the administration and ministering to the people of the diocese. The see was large and parts of it troublesome. The four archdeaconries of Coventry, Derby, Shrewsbury and Stafford were reputed to contain numerous Catholics ready to cause trouble at any moment and Coventry archdeaconry already boasted a radical Protestant congregation of some size in its capital city. The diocese contained over 500 cures, including peculiar jurisdictions, perpetual curacies and chapelries, and had a population of approximately 125,144 according to the return of 1563.[4] This population was distributed unevenly: the archdeaconry of Coventry contained the largest urban centres of the diocese although it was not the most populous. Coventry, inhabited by perhaps 2,200 persons, was acknowledged by Bentham who described it as 'the cheyfe citye of all thes parties of your majesties Realme' and the vicarage of St Michael's within it as 'beyng the greatest cure of any one benefyce within my whole diocese'.[5] This archdeaconry contained also the centres of Birmingham, Nuneaton, Solihull, Aston, Hampton and Sutton Coldfield. Coventry itself was not as prosperous as it had once been. Bentham attributed the declining revenue of St Michael's, Coventry, to 'the decay and impoveryshement of thinhabitants of the said citye'. Technically the archdeaconries of Derby and Stafford were more populous than Coventry but they covered a much wider area (only half of Warwickshire was situated in this diocese, whereas the entire counties of Staffordshire and Derbyshire were within its bounds) and they contained fewer towns. Perhaps most significant from the administrative point of view was the fact that several of the reasonably large towns were exempt from episcopal jurisdiction: these included the City of Lichfield with 400 households; Wolverhampton with 323 households; and the parish of Bakewell with its seven chapelries which represented an enclave of population within Derbyshire equivalent in size to that of Coventry. These peculiar jurisdictions were to prove a thorn in the bishop's side during the years to come.[6]

Bentham's perilous economic position soon made itself felt. He entered the see at a considerable disadvantage: as he complained to the Queen, he had incurred necessary personal debts while waiting to enter the see but had no personal fortune with which to pay them off and no connections in the provinces to provide him with loans to do so. He was greeted with a claim for first fruits and subsidy payments and he had inherited certain debts from his predecessor. Even in normal circumstances it would have been difficult to muster together enough money from the surplus estate revenue to pay such extraordinary sums immediately and live adequately, and Bentham had no personal resources upon which to draw. However, his position was even more difficult – the normal yield from the episcopal estates was not available to him and would not be for some time. He was unable to collect the rents from his various properties, including those of Lichfield, Hanbury and Gnosall, and Mr Harcourt refused to yield the total rents from the castle and manor at Eccleshall in Staffordshire for a period including the vacancy of the see and ending at Michaelmas 1560, because of expenses incurred during that time.[7] The bishop was even unable to take possession of the parsonage house at Hanbury because of the pretended title of Christopher Bayne and Christopher Grene.[8]

Bentham regarded these financial difficulties as strictly temporary. There is no indication that he thought himself incapable of meeting regular demands on income once he had rights to Eccleshall and Hanbury restored to him and collected due monies. Yet Bentham's approach to these *temporary* difficulties had a profound long-term effect upon episcopal finances.[9] He succeeded in reclaiming Hanbury through a suit in Chancery but at considerable cost. Quite apart from high legal costs, Hanbury was laid waste and the bishop still had difficulty in collecting back rents and profits. Moreover, Bentham was forced by financial necessity to let out the rectory for a period of 21 years in 1566.[10] Long leases of other properties were made to the Crown as his episcopate progressed.[11] Like other of his contemporary bishops, Bentham had trouble with his predecessor's debts. The collector of subsidies, Thomas Boult, proved difficult to manage.[12] The see had escaped Elizabeth's policy of compulsory exchanges relatively unscathed however, and Bentham appealed to the Crown for release from some of his debts, apparently successfully.[13] For the rest, he appears to have entered into some personal indebtedness to cover immediate expenses and to have lived frugally. One of his most positive contributions to the financial management of the see was a survey of episcopal revenues.[14]

Like so many of his contemporaries on the episcopal bench, Bentham lacked any administrative experience and, not surprisingly, he found the task of administering the diocese and satisfactorily conserving its resources beyond his abilities. He saw his main avenue of escape in further borrowing and more careful management of existing revenues – the Crown was initially sympathetic but was evidently unwilling to offer any long-term solution to episcopal poverty. As time passed it became increasingly difficult for Bentham to raise loans within the diocese because he could offer little by way of surety: his lack of local connections apparently acted against him in this as in other respects. Cumulatively, he was worsening rather than improving the see's financial position.[15]

For the first year of his episcopate at least, a high proportion of Bentham's time was consumed by his financial predicament and resulting legal suits. He was considerably frustrated by this and in April 1561 he appealed to Sir Clement Throckmorton for help in legal matters so 'that I may the rather folowe my vocation, whitche is my cheyfe desyre as knowethe God'.[16] Yet, despite the apparently disproportionate concern of his correspondence with money matters, the impression gathered is that Bentham took his pastoral duties seriously and was fighting against all odds to perform them well. His efforts evidently did not satisfy his radical Protestant colleagues who had not been made bishops. Both Thomas Sampson and Thomas Lever upbraided him for not exercising his pastoral charge as well as he might by administering a true, fatherly discipline.[17] Typically, Bentham accepted their right to criticize but strove to impress upon them the realities of the situation. As he said to Ralph Egerton,

> I heare say that I am moche slaundred of negligence, coldnes and weaknes, whitch maney other grevous faults. Whereunto I say nothyng, but wyshe theym that slaunder me yf they wold do more and better in my place. What they be I knowe not but I beleve they never felt suche a burden as I am compelled to beare dayle. Beyng so many wayes vexed as I am and havying so littell helpe and comforth as I fynd, no marvayle yf I satisfy not all mens expectation, for indede I do not content myselffe . . .[18]

In the main he concerned himself with the situation in Shropshire and in Staffordshire where he had his normal residence. His chief concern was that in large areas of the diocese, and especially in Staffordshire and Shropshire, the Reformation seemed scarcely to have done more than skim the surface. Many of the leading notables were found to be either openly recusant or hostile to the new settlement. In addition, a significant proportion of the incumbents, including the Archdeacon of Derby, had remained at their posts regardless of religious change.[19] In Staffordshire, during Edward's reign, only three men are known to have resigned, none for religious reasons.[20] About 85 chantry priests were dispossessed but most were re-employed within the area.[21] Under Mary there seems to have been little nonconformity amongst the Staffordshire clergy, although 42 married clerics were deprived in the diocese.[22] A truly apathetic attitude to the establishment of the day seems to have prevailed amongst the laity as well as the clergy. Whereas the removal of long established shrines, as well as new, met with little or no resistance and whereas Bishop Lee had confidently reported a lack of support for papal claims or the cause of the Pilgrimage of Grace, in 1558 Bishop Bayne's visitation revealed no pockets of Protestantism within this archdeaconry.[23]

However, as there was no outward opposition to the introduction of Protestant forms and even a willingness to accept the benefits of the new system, so there is also evidence that the people and the clergy in 1559 were loath to relinquish the old ways. Bentham was aware of a hard core of Catholicism among the clergy of the diocese: this must have come to his notice when he acted in the Royal Visitation of 1559 for the diocese and received the subscriptions of its clergy. He needed to remove the obstinate and apathetic and replace them with suitable Protestant recruits, preferably well-educated, but in the light of national recruitment problems and his own lack of patronage this was impossible, and Bentham's approach to improving clerical personnel in the diocese had to follow a more oblique course. Firstly, he tried to suppress Catholic practices. In 1560 Bentham told Mr George Lee that he would not prosecute the case of Henry Techoo further, 'who serveth not his cure as he ought to do' and 'hayth hyd iiii of theyr Images with theyr cases or tabernacles', making it clear meanwhile that he could 'not suffer those that beare ii faces in one hood, to marry & love Images etc'.[24] Henry Techoo, Vicar of Monford, Shropshire, had been one of these deprived for marriage under Mary and had apparently re-entered the living at the accession of Elizabeth.

The situation may have been to some extent the product of confusion. After Elizabeth's accession none knew which path she would opt for apart from the necessary renunciation of papal authority. Clergy and laity in the more remote corners of kingdom were even less aware of the queen's intentions than were the returned exiles. Moreover, it probably took some time for the news of the actual settlement to filter down into the parish units, particularly when the officials in command were often Catholic, if not papist. Many must have been under the delusion that the return was to the Henrician situation, with a Church not acknowledging the Pope but in other respects Catholic, rather than to one more akin to the Edwardian. In addition, there may have been a feeling, strengthened by Elizabeth's equivocation, that this change was to be short-lived like the others. On 12 October 1560, the bishop wrote to George Torperlaye of Salop on this very point, instructing him to visit the churches of that archdeaconry and remove the images which were still retained, noting the names of those who refused, that they might be presented to the bishop to answer for their resistance:

> For as moche as I do planly understand by experience of my selfe in many places made, that the most part of churches within this part of my diocese haithe not onely yet theyr altars standyng but also theyr images reserved and conveyd away contrarye to the Quens maiesties Iniunctions, hopyng and lookyng for a newe day as may be thereby coniectured . . .[25]

These considerations do not explain away the fact that there was reputed to be a strong recusant population in Staffordshire and Shropshire throughout the period under discussion. Allegiance to the old faith was not easily eradicated amongst the clergy either: when William Barrett, Rector of Longford, Shropshire, made his will in 1571 he bequeathed his soul 'unto almightie god my maker and redemer to be assocyate to the companye of our blessed Ladie Sanct Marie the virgin and all the holye saints of heaven'.[26]

In any event, the problem of enforcing conformity to the settlement was an immediate one. Bentham realized that the root of the problem lay with the clergy: during the year which the Letter Book covers, several clergymen were called before the bishop to explain their nonconformity. In 1559 only 29 Derbyshire incumbents had subscribed to the settlement.[27] The situation in Stafford archdeaconry was known to be bad. Thus at the beginning of 1561 Bentham instructed Richard Walker, at this time Archdeacon of both Stafford and Derby, to search out popery in his jurisdiction by means of visitation. Walker was to concentrate in particular upon the manner in which the bounds of the parish were beaten at Rogationtide:

> they must syng or say the ii psalmes begynyng *benefyc anima mea domino* in Englyshe with the letanye and suffragyes thereto with some sermon or homelye of thanks gevenge to god and movyng to temperancye in theyr drynkynge yf they have anye. Here you must charge theym to avoyd superstition and suche vayne gaysynge as the used the last yere and in no case that they use either crosse, taper, nor beades, nor wemen to go abowte but man . . .[28]

Yet conducting visitations at second hand and summoning recalcitrant priests into his presence were not solutions and Bentham knew this. The main objection to this form of pastoral care was akin to that levelled at the bishop himself – that of remoteness. Moreover, the higher court of the diocese, the bishop's consistory, seemed to the critic to belong not to the bishop but to the civil lawyers. Efficiency and not quality of pastoral care was the goal of these courts, and even the achievement of this end was dependent upon the officials in control.[29] Much of the business conducted in this court was equivalent to civil litigation – tithe, testamentary, defamation and marital. Many of the office cases brought by the official principal, acting in lieu of bishop and chancellor, were concerned with the administration of the diocese in conformity to the law and the mass of ancillary injunctions and canons, rather than with the correction of the flock through a fatherly discipline. The Reformers saw it as ineffective in barring the scandalous from communion, the mark of a true discipline. The judge of this court was possessed of great discretionary power: the administration of the *ex officio* oath, which impelled men to self-incrimination, could in no way be considered brotherly in intent. From awareness of this situation arose a demand for the introduction of the Reformed discipline, of fatherly correction of the faults of the flock by its pastor, who sought to restore them to the fold whilst, meanwhile, protecting the sacrament from defilement.[30]

Two main solutions to this problem were possible: the removal of the existing hierarchy and its replacement by a reformed system of one type or another, or the revolutionizing of Church government from within through its hierarchy. Those who accepted sees, although they did not regard the intial settlement as permanent, were by their office usually committed to the latter route as the practicable one. They might hope that eventually the number of dioceses might be multiplied and likewise the number of bishops and that, until that time, they would be allowed to use the learned and preaching members of their clergy to assist in the administration but, generally, the system of imparity was accepted – of one minister supervising a group of those less able or learned, instructing them and offering counsel and correction.[31]

There is much evidence that Bentham involved himself intimately in the administration of ecclesiastical justice within the diocese – hearing many lay and clerical cases in person on a regular basis and seeking to expedite justice in the consistory. He involved himself in both correction and instance cases. Conscientious as he strove to be in these matters of discipline, it was clear that a successful job could not be done by one man, especially one who was increasingly preoccupied with financial worries and personal litigation. Allowing for this and for the unwieldy nature of the diocese, some division of responsibility was evidently necessary. As the clergy were in grave need of reformation themselves, and as the Queen and others were opposed to delegating disciplinary powers to the parochial clergy in the Reformed manner, the bishop had to look to his officials and a few educated clergy for help. It was unlikely that Elizabeth would ever countenance the proliferation of bishops or 'superintendents' which some Protestants sought, although the hopelessness of the plan was not entirely appreciated. On the other hand, it was feasible that a bishop should associate with himself in the business of government and pastoral work a number of the leading clergy of his diocese. Bentham appears to have projected an extension of this delegation of responsibility, initially on a very informal basis.

Notice should be taken here of the extent to which the bishop relied upon Thomas Lever, his Archdeacon of Coventry. Bentham's correspondence contains several letters to Lever, mostly offering advice on the technicalities of his office. Generally the tone is one of deference and Bentham reacted without rancour to Lever's criticisms of his administration of the diocese. To what extent was Lever following detailed episcopal instructions in the government of Coventry archdeaconry and to what extent was he a power in his own right?

There is no evidence that Bentham himself initiated prophesyings, as had Bishop Curteys in Sussex, and it was to Lever that the exercise at Coventry owed its origin early in the reign. Lever always acted as moderator when in Coventry and another moderator was the radical John Oxenbridge. Clearly the group was concerned largely with the improvement of clerical knowledge of the Scriptures. Bentham approved of this aspect of the meetings, only expressing concern when he found that the moderators and speakers tended to obstinacy regarding the use of clerical apparel and the Book of Common Prayer.[32]

Eventually the method of associating the clergy under a moderator for these purposes spread within the archdeaconry. Professor Collinson has noted that when Oxenbridge established a similar prophesying at his home living of Southam, Bentham remained in ignorance of the act.[33] The initiative here clearly came from someone other than the bishop. Bentham's part in the government of Coventry is put further into perspective by evidence contained in a letter from Bentham to the Privy Council in November 1564. The bishops had been instructed to make returns concerning the Justices of the Peace within their respective jurisdictions, commenting upon their religion and recommending suitable men for appointment. Bentham duly reported his views concerning the Bench in Staffordshire, Shropshire and Derbyshire, with special reference to Staffordshire where he lived and with due acknowledgement of the help which he had received from diocesan officials. When it came to Warwickshire, however, the bishop declined to make any personal comment:

Forasmuche as myn abyding is far of from that parte of my Dioces, and partely through good Justices of Peace, & partly by the diligence of myn Archdeacon, Mr. Leaver, & other Rurall Deanes, I have bien litle trobled with any matters, by meanes whereof I have not travilled so miche that way to get any understanding by myn own experience. I do here confes to your honores that I iudge this former certificate made good and sufficient for that shye . . .[34]

On this occasion he appears to have rubber-stamped Lever's certificate of the state of Coventry archdeaconry.

This letter and the reliance which Bentham was evidently placing upon Lever during the first year of his episcopate further suggest that for five years at least the archdeacon had some considerable freedom in the running of Coventry. The archdeaconry was in fact far more accessible to Bentham than were parts of Derbyshire or Shropshire. Lever may have been allowed some degree of independence because of his position as *archidiaconus major*.[35] The situation is probably largely attributable to Lever's seniority among the exiles and the consequent respect for him which was felt by Bentham, however: Lever was barred from preferment because of his own obstinacy and for no other reason. This does not mean that Lever and the bishop were working in conflict with one another; indeed the contrary is true. It was simply because their ideas were in accord that Bentham was able to allow Lever a free hand. Bentham was not in close contact with the prophesyings in Coventry and Southam and the fact that he was unaware of the Southam prophesyings may have been due not to an unwillingness and fear on Lever's and Oxenbridge's part that he should know of its existence, but to the fact that Bentham had chosen to delegate the responsibility for this part of his diocese to Lever, preferring not to be troubled by such matters, especially when they were so in harmony with his general policy.[36] Bentham's only caution was that the enthusiastic Protestant congregation of Coventry should not burn itself out by enthusiasm but remain steadfast in its faith.[37] There is little doubt that Bentham gave Lever power in the diocese because he held him in esteem. He seems to have entrusted Lever with the selection of suitable ordinands at the beginning of the reign, whereas similar instructions were not sent to the other archdeacons.[38] Perhaps one is influenced by earlier views of Bentham's character in assuming that the bishop was only too relieved to pass some of the tedious and tortuous work of administration onto someone else's shoulders. In any case it is Lever rather than Bentham who emerges as the dominant figure in the diocese with regard to blue-prints for administrative reform and the organization of the clergy.[39]

Bentham's recognition of Lever's 'quasi-episcopal' standing in Coventry is not, however, a unique instance of the bishop relying on fellow clerics to fulfil important pastoral and administrative functions although it is the most startling. In the first year of his active episcopate he appears to have leaned quite heavily upon Robert Aston or Ashton, Rector of Mucklestone and Vicar of Sandon in Staffordshire. Aston was a Cambridge graduate who was deprived of these livings because of his marriage during the Marian period. Apparently he was restored to both benefices at Elizabeth's accession. Bentham had few graduate clergy at his disposal and it was probably because of this as much as because of Aston's religious persuasion that he delegated responsibility to the latter. He acted in the capacity of surveyor of the bishop's lands. That he was considered to be one of the bishop's right-hand men is borne witness to by a number of letters written to him during 1560 and 1561 and seems proven by the fact that in 1564 Bentham recommended him for appointment as a Justice.[40]

Within Shrewsbury archdeaconry the bishop entrusted certain duties to one Thomas Ashton, a preacher and first schoolmaster of Shrewsbury School. To Ashton was given the task of hearing cases within the area and reporting his findings to the bishop. In 1561 Ashton was preferred to a living in Lincoln diocese and Bentham wrote anxiously to the Archbishop of Canterbury, begging that Ashton be allowed to hold the Lincoln benefice *in absentia* whilst remaining resident at Shrewsbury:

> Further wheras one Mr. Aston a godlye preacher within thes parties of my dioces ys preferred to a benefyce within the dioces of Lincolne, whereupon he shold by order of lawe be resident, my reqest and desyre to your grace ys that yt wold please the same to shewe so moche favor as your grace may lawfullye do unto the said Mr. Aston, for that he haith nowe begonne a good work to the furtherance of a Schole in Shrewsbery whiche yf he shold presently departe were lyk either not to proceed or els moche therebye to be hyndred. In consideration whereof . . . you shall not onely do a greate pleasure to the towne of Salop but allso to me in thes parties of my dioces whiche have here no other preacher but hym.

In 1576 Bentham was called upon by Grindal to report on the prophesyings in the diocese. Bentham noted that the exercise at Shrewsbury was held fortnightly on Thursday, commenting that he 'did long stay the exercise at the beginning, because' he 'would have had Mr. Thomas Aston to be moderatour thereof' but then Aston had left the county and been replaced by other preachers.[41]

There were others also upon whom Bentham relied for help in his pastoral and judicial work: Thomas Bickley, B.D., and Fellow of Bentham's old college; Peter Morweyn, his personal chaplain; the Registrar; the Chancellor of the Diocese; and, to a certain extent, the archdeacons of the remaining jurisdictions.[42] His relations with Richard Walker, Archdeacon of both Stafford and Derby, do not appear to have been on the same level as those with Lever. Clearly these were informal arrangements but there are signs that Bentham wished to associate the group of leading ministers in the administration on a more regular basis.

Bentham's projected revival of the office and function of rural dean has often been noted. Evidently he wished to restore the role of the dean as administrator of discipline by reviving the dean's correction court, which had by this time been swallowed up into that of the archdeacon. Such a project would have complied with the radical desire to see that a pastor in close contact with the people should correct them for their faults rather than an impersonal court at the seat of administration – such men would fulfil the role of *chorepiscopi*. Generally, however, it has been agreed that this proposal was never acted upon, although the similarity between the function of the rural dean and that of the moderator of prophesying has been pointed out. Yet it now seems possible that Bentham did act upon these instructions and had, indeed, already acted upon them. In his letter to the Privy Council in 1564 he mentioned 'the diligence of myn Archdeacon, Mr. Leaver and other Rurall Deanes,' evidently referring to his right-hand men in the diocese and to Augustine Bernhear, Rector of Southam.[43] It is not possible to say whether these men were ever officially appointed rural deans, for no administrative records appear to be extant for the period 1560–5. Indeed it does not really matter whether these men were officially thus styled, rather it is important that Bentham treated them as such and expected them to fulfil the duties of a dean. Probably it was customary for the rural dean to occupy a particular living – the radical rectors of Southam appear to have been associated in the work of the archdeaconry during Overton's episcopate also – but this was natural because the better educated ministers and preachers were generally presented to the wealthier livings in the diocese.

Evidence from elsewhere, moreover, suggests that the role of rural dean was by no means as formal and insignificant as some have assumed. Rural deans were automatically appointed at the yearly synods in Ely diocese. At Bury St Edmunds the rural deans were instructed to certify inductions. In York the deans possessed probate jurisdiction. These are, admittedly, rather formal functions. In Worcester diocese, however, as late as 1603, the bishop sent the following order to 'Mr. Feryman deane of the deanrie of Blockley' concerning

a collection for Geneva . . . and the suppressing of such ministers in this diocese as will not observe the forms of common prayer and administration of Sacraments appointed . . . for the better execution of both which your paine is requisite to call together to some fitt place the Clergie of your deanrie, and to acquaint them therwith, takinge order with every incumbent that he with the church-wardens or sidesmen of his parish see this collection made . . . and you to bring it unto me . . . For the other point that you truely adevertise me under your hand what Ministers in your deanrie, either Incumbents or Curats do not observe the forme of the booke of Common prayer.

In Gloucester there survives on the cover of a document the heading,

'A note of the Deanes of all the Deanryes within the Diocesse of Oxon, 1596', although the listing itself is missing.[44]

One is surely tempted to conclude that Bentham, who had openly professed a wish to give the rural deans a meaningful role within the diocese, did in fact appoint deans and use them. Because the men chosen in this capacity were often those of radical Protestant persuasions there was always the danger that they would end up in opposition to, rather than co-operation with, the episcopal régime. The case of John Oxenbridge is a prime example of such a situation. Both Bentham and his successor, Overton, sought to use Oxenbridge's talents to good effect. Opposition from the Privy Council forced the bishops to reject the help of the puritan preachers because of their nonconformist tendencies. In Overton's return of 1593 Oxenbridge is described as 'eruditus sed sismaticus'. In 1596 he was brought before the Consistory Court at Lichfield and confessed that:

> he the sayd Oxenbridge did publiquelie ordayne and appoynte a publique and solemne faste at a certen sett and appoynted daye which was solemized and celebrated in the churche of Sowtham by sondrie preachers Whereunto did repayre and come a great multitude and many hundreds besydes his owne parishioners And that there was the same daye three severall sermons preached by three severall persons . . .

For this offence Oxenbridge was suspended and the fruits of his living sequestered. The flirtation between the bishops and the puritan clergy within the diocese was for the time at least well and truly ended, more as the result of political pressure than because the bishops of Lichfield were unwilling to employ these activities to their own advantage.[45]

Bentham, and later William Overton, sought to use the leading clergy of the diocese, whether rural deans by title or not, to supervise groups of clergy and to educate them. At a time when few ministers with good academic qualifications were being ordained, it would have been folly even to contemplate removing all those clergy who did not meet the high specifications of the Protestant ideal at Elizabeth's accession. The institution lists at Coventry and Lichfield for the period May 1560–70 illustrate that only a very few clergy were deprived, despite the small number of clergy who subscribed.[46] It may be that those who were deprived were the more prominent supporters of the Marian régime in the diocese after the initial deprivations of the 1559 period. This was certainly the case with the pluralist Anthony Draycott who had been Archdeacon of Stow in the diocese of Lincoln and Chancellor of both Lincoln and Coventry and Lichfield dioceses during Mary's reign, being noted as a great persecutor of the Protestants.[47] He was deprived of all his preferments in 1560 and imprisoned in the Fleet. Additionally, the removal of these men may have been motivated by a more mundane concern. There was a crying need to implant at least a core of well-qualified Protestant clergy in the diocese, to serve as the leaven in the lump. At this date such men could only be attracted by reasonably lucrative prospects and many of the men deprived were in just such livings. Moreover, the new bishop was accompanied by an army of new officials and chaplains for whom the old régime had to make way.[48]

Certainly there seems to have been a concerted effort on Bentham's part to encourage the substitution of learned men for those who were deprived, and to promote the presentation of like men to other livings as they fell vacant. On occasion this led to a further abuse, that of pluralism. For instance, Peter Morweyn, Bentham's chaplain, was presented to Norbury rectory after the deprivation of Henry Comberford, lately Archdeacon of Stafford. Morweyn was also presented to the living of Longford, Derbyshire, on the removal of John Ramridge.[49] The small amount of patronage at the bishop's disposal made it difficult for him to find preferment for others but he tried to use his influence. On 25 August 1560 he wrote to Dr Weston, his chancellor, in the 'behalfe of William Mansfield for the parsonag of Boylston voyd by lapse', to which the chancellor instituted him three days later. Bentham was unable, however, to secure the presentation of the staunchly Protestant Richard Stonnynaught to Wirksworth vicarage, as he had promised Sir Ambrose Cave to attempt. The grant of next presentation belonged to Richard Taylor by concession from the Dean of Lincoln: Taylor presented John Hyron to the living, again vacant by deprivation. Similarly, an instruction to Dr Weston to institute Richard Foxe to the living of Curdworth in Warwickshire met with no success and Foxe had to wait four years before obtaining the living of Baxterley.[50]

That Bentham found it difficult to place men of his own choice in vacant livings is understandable: out of 147 separate presentations during the period 1560–70 the bishop was responsible for five only, and of these three had fallen to him through lapse. Of the remainder, the great majority were made by laymen. Evidently this situation was alleviated somewhat by petitioning the Crown to present episcopal protégés to livings in the gift of the lord keeper. In this way Bentham successfully nominated 13 clerics to livings within the diocese during his episcopate. It seems that he was constantly searching for opportunities to exercise patronage although he was willing enough to adopt as his own the protégés of Protestant notables such as Cave. Archdeacon Thomas Lever was also influential: he petitioned the lord keeper successfully on behalf of seven clerics, all presented to livings within his archdeaconry. At least two of these seven clerics were noted for their puritan leanings.[51]

Questions of preferment aside, Bentham was anxious not to lose such good ministers as he had. This has been shown by his anxiety to retain Ashton's services at Shrewsbury. The case of Hugo Symons, Vicar of St Michael's, Coventry, illustrates a different aspect of the bishop's predicament: the more able ministers were unwilling to remain in poor livings which had been further improverished during Mary's reign. Bentham desired Cecil's

> ever redy helpyng hande in the sute of. . . Mr Simons . . . who as he is greatlye charged with the arrerages of his vicaredge (whitche as I can learne hitherto dyd onelye growe in the tyme of the late intrusor) so sence his restitution made in the Quens Majesties visitation he haithe sought good occasions diversleye boethe to me and otherwyse to leave and gyve upp the saide vicaredge agayne, for that he is not able to paye the arrerages demaunded.

If Cecil acceded to his request it would,

> not onelye ease hym of a greate burden, but allso do a greate pleasure to the cytye of Coventree, and a singuler benefytt unto me, whiche have greate nede of suche ministers in my hoole dioces for he ys learned, godly and sobre in his doyngs.

Bentham felt so strongly in this regard that he also petitioned the Queen on Symons' behalf.[52]

Meanwhile, Bentham was anxious not to have to reject such learned or godly men as were brought to his notice. On 16 November 1560 he thanked the bishop of Worcester for granting a lay reader's licence to one Cole, urging the bishop to ordain Cole for a ministry within Coventry and Lichfield diocese, 'for I lack many good ministers'.[53] He attributed the lack of learned ministers to the fact that livings in the diocese were notoriously inadequate, and to the fact that he himself had no personal patronage to distribute. He attempted some remedy in his own impropriate rectories by augmenting the incomes of the vicars.[54]

At the heart of the problem, however, was the small number of well-qualified ordinands and the small number of learned and godly men already incumbent on benefices. Bentham's main solution to the problem of inferior personnel lay with schemes for the instruction of the clergy who were already ensconced in livings. In 1561 he instructed his archdeacon at Stafford to appoint New Testament texts to 'be lerned withowt the book' by all curates: at the next visitation they were to be examined. His injunctions of 1565 again attempted to enforce private study among the diocesan clergy.[55] Moreover, he took an interest in preaching, seeking to organize the preaching activities of the clergy under his own leadership. Roger Morrice, the bishop's seventeenth-century biographer, noted:

His industrious promotion of the truth, by his frequency in the Minis-
teriall worke hee was a preaching Presbyter (& I will hope) a preaching
Bishop, that as in many other Bishops, soe in him Queen Elizabeth's
proverb (as it is said) may bee falsified, that when shee had made a
Bishop shee had mar'd a preacher.

The bishop's correspondence suggests the truth of this appraisal. In
August 1560 Bentham instructed the Dean of Lichfield, Laurence
Nowell, to go and preach at Seckington, Warwickshire; in the same
month he asked Thomas Lever to go and preach at Shrewsbury. In
November he preached himself at Swinnerton, Staffordshire. He
was concerned to retain the services of preachers such as Thomas
Ashton and Hugo Symons. At this time, when the population of the
diocese outside a few urban centres was, if not Catholic, certainly not
ardently Protestant either, the bishop and his leading ministers were
possessed of a considerable missionary zeal. For the same reasons he
thought the prophesyings

> not only profitable both for the ministers & the people, but also very
> necessary . . . For it seemeth to me here in the Countrey that to be the
> only way both to increase learning in the simple & ignorant, & to
> continue the same clear in the Learned without rust or disuse of the
> same, for what they learn godly in the exercise they may fruitfully teach
> their Parishioners at home.

Such gatherings were clerical gatherings first and foremost, with a
dominant teaching function. The object was to educate the parochial
clergy in the Protestant faith: the ministers so taught would relay the
message to their individual congregations. Such a system attempted
to make good undeniable deficiencies in the system of clerical
recruitment and to provide some remedy for the grave shortage of
preachers at a time when missionary expertise was most crucial to
the realization of Protestant hopes.[56]

It is evident, therefore, that Bentham could not tackle his personnel problems in a straightforward manner. The clergy already within
the diocese were in grave need of reformation, either with respect to
education, morality or religious sympathy; the bishop, however,
could not remove the obstinate or unsuitable and replace them with
learned ministers or even with enthusiastically Protestant ministers.
More than limited use of deprivation was prevented by the law and,
in any case, where was a bishop to obtain enough suitable men to fill
such vacancies if he created them? Most bishops were forced to
ordain, if not indiscriminately then according to minimal standards,
in order to fill such vacancies as occurred naturally. As will be shown
later, there was an acute national shortage of educated clerical
recruits: even had the bishops possessed the necessary patronage and
even had they been untrammelled by the law, they could not have
filled the benefices with graduate clergy. As the following chapters

seek to demonstrate, the bishops did try to surmount the legal and practical difficulties involved in pursuing an ordination policy but in practice the Elizabethan episcopate, at least, had to employ the same sort of measures that Bentham used. He tried to 'educate' the clergy who were already in the diocese but, meanwhile, initiated a policy whereby the services of such good men as he had were widely used. The plan involving the use of rural deans, for instance, insured that the less able and perhaps obstinate parochial clergy be controlled and influenced by trusted henchmen who were responsible to the archdeacons and to the bishop. This side of the plan was perhaps as important as the administrative which is normally stressed. Certainly it was hoped that the system would make the execution of the Church's discipline more personal and just, but it was also a way of providing a means to lessen the influence of unsuitable clergy upon their parishes and of bringing the laity into contact with the more able diocesan clergy. The attempt to bring sermons to outlying districts can be viewed in the same way: at a time when it was impossible to license many preachers without lowering standards beyond belief, it was nevertheless necessary to educate the laity into Protestantism and a few chosen clergy were employed for this purpose. The exercises provided a similar occasion for the education of both laity and clergy in knowledge of the Scriptures.

Having said this, it is not claimed that the bishops made full use of their opportunities to influence clerical standards within the dioceses. In all probability attempts were inconsistent. Bentham, as had been shown, was prevented from giving his full attention to the problem of personnel by overriding problems of finance and politics. Even so, it is clear that some of the attempts to improve clerical education, although connived at by the bishop, were not initiated by him. Not a free agent, because in the last resort shackled to the queen's wishes, it was perhaps inevitable that the bishop should delicately pursue a policy of *ad hoc* attempts to improve clerical standards, withdrawing hastily into his shell when more definite and ambitious plans, with political consequences, met with resistance from queen, Privy Council and archbishop – the extent to which the bishop was willing to brave this wrath from above obviously varied with the individual concerned. However, the *ad hoc* character of episcopal attempts to improve personnel was not altogether the result of political timorousness but rather of poor communications within the diocese – often the bishops failed to fill livings which fell into their gift by lapse, thus missing an opportunity to exercise independent patronage, but more often than not this meant that they were unaware of the vacancy, or, of course, that no suitable candidate was available.

4

Recruitment

As we have seen, the bishops shared an *ad hoc* approach to the solution of the problem of recruiting well-qualified Protestant ministers.[1] Some, however, attempted to achieve greater control over clerical recruitment, using conventional and unconventional means at their disposal. While the case of Bentham at Lichfield demonstrates that the bishops could attempt to influence in a direct way the choices made by lay patrons, on the whole this was an unreliable and unsatisfactory method. For the most part the hierarchy had to rely upon a more subtle and indirect type of pressure – that of restricting the catchment area from which the prospective patrons could select their men.

Theoretically, at least, this could be achieved through the medium of the ordination examination, by the rejection of unsuitable candidates for the ministry. Traditionally the right of examining ordinands belongs to the archdeacon, although when this proved inconvenient the bishop had the right to appoint some other fit person to fulfil the function. The rules had been drawn up at a time when ordinands were few and the archdeacon well able to conduct a rigorous examination in person of all candidates. In the sixteenth and seventeenth centuries the archdeacon still commonly examined ordinands. In London, Archdeacon John Mullins acted as examiner in the 1560s; in Coventry and Lichfield Archdeacon Thomas Lever conducted the examinations. It seems though that the archdeacon often acted in association with other diocesan officials and prominent clerics; in Ely diocese this is clearly illustrated. In 1574 Dr Thomas Ithel, LL.D., sat with the archdeacon as examiner: he acted thus at many examinations over a 20-year period. On occasion the Archdeacon of Ely delegated his function to others. For instance, on 14 and 15 March 1577 candidates were examined by Dr Randall and Mr Bancroft.[2]

What form did these examinations take? Documentation is scarce on this point and it is possible to describe fully only the method employed at Ely in the late sixteenth century. This was a period of extensive experimentation regarding the form of examination, however, and the situation at Ely during this period should not be viewed as typical of all dioceses.

In accordance with medieval rules and practice, the Archdeacon of

Ely or another examiner called together prospective candidates a day or a few days before the ordination was scheduled to take place. Thus for an ordination taking place on 17 April 1580, the examination was held on the 14th and 15th of the same month. The articles of examination were based on the requirements of the canons, which were themselves modified during the Elizabethan and early Stuart period. At Ely in 1561 11 interrogatories were administered to ordinands which were designed to establish name, age, place of habitation, possession of a good reputation, literacy (both reading and writing), religious zeal, serious vocation, and knowledge of Latin. These rules, which conformed to Edwardian specifications, were modified in 1571. The canons of that year stipulated that the candidate should make an account of his faith in Latin in accordance with the 39 Articles of 1562. In addition these canons envisaged a situation where as many as possible would be university educated. In 1575 regulations concerning entry into deacon's orders were formulated: henceforth a deacon should be 23 years of age and should remain a deacon for one year before becoming a priest. Moreover, the rules of 1571, regarding the presentation of letters dimissory from the diocese of origin or long dwelling when a candidate sought to be ordained elsewhere, were reiterated; it was further ordered that none shall be admitted to orders unless he possessed benefice or title. In 1585 Whitgift reinforced these rules, further regulating the use of letters dimissory and appointing 24 years as the minimum age for ordination as priest. Again the ideal was set forth of a wholly graduate clergy or at least of one well learned in the Scriptures and giving a good account of its faith in the Latin tongue. The articles for Canterbury province of 1585 and 1597 and the canons of 1604 finally confirmed these requirements.[3]

The nature of recorded replies to examinations at Ely in the 1570s and 1580s suggests conformity to these modified regulations, at least as far as the form of questions went. In 1574, for example, Owen Lewyes, B.A., seeking ordination as priest,

> readethe well & understandethe the latten tonge well, And the good zeal he bearethe to gods word movethe him to take uppon him this function, he answerethe to An Article or question well, well studied in the scriptures, And writethe as followethe.[4]

Just how rigorous were these examinations? Peter Heath, discussing the situation in pre-Reformation England, maintains that little documentary evidence contradicts the view of Colet and More that archdeacons were possessed of a great reluctance to turn away candidates. However, a record of examinations was kept at Ely in the sixteenth century and entries were meticulously and faithfully made for all examinees whether they passed the test or not. The Ely examples indicate that in this diocese, at least, standards were fairly high. On 21 March 1561 32 candidates presented themselves to the archdeacon for examination: of these five were rejected outright and one was bound over for a year. By the later 1560s the rejection rate appears to have been even higher. Thus in December 1568, 30 men were examined, seven not admitted, and five admitted conditionally. In April of the same year out of 41 candidates, 12 were denied orders and two respited. In April 1580 eight men were rejected out of 35 examined. Clearly approval in this diocese was no mere formality.[5]

It is possible to establish in a general way the qualities which the Ely examiners regarded as essential in ordinands. Most of the men denied admission at Ely appear to have been rejected because of insufficient knowledge of the Scriptures. Six of the seven denied in December 1568 were turned away on these grounds. Against inadequacy in this respect good qualifications or testimonials seem to have held little sway. In April 1568 Nicholas Wallys, seeking admission as a deacon, discovered that neither his B.A. nor the fact that he was 'comendyd in good behavior from Mr Dean and others' over-ruled the decision of his examiners that he was 'in the scriptures ignorant' and therefore not to be ordained.

Certainly, in no case does it appear that either possession of a degree or residence in a university protected a candidate, the letters testimonal of the said college being ignored when the personal examination afforded contrary evidence. In December 1568 two of those rejected were students of St John's, Cambridge; one a graduate of Gonville and Caius, Cambridge; one a student of Christ's College, Cambridge; and another of Pembroke Hall, Cambridge. The same pattern was repeated in the mid-1570s.

There were, of course, other reasons for refusing a candidate ordination but frequently it is impossible to determine on what grounds the candidate was turned away. An ordinand's religious opinions may sometimes have stood in his way, although no direct evidence of this is contained in the Ely lists. Often the reasons for rejection are completely concealed: of Anthony Iveston, B.A., of St John's, Cambridge, in 1580, we are merely informed that he 'was not thoughte mete to procede & therefore was not admitted'. Occasionally candidates were dismissed because of some deficiency in their letters testimonial, although in June 1561 John Dawsbury, Fellow and B.A. of Magdalene College, Cambridge, was admitted despite the fact that he was unable to present letters testimonial until the Master of his college returned to Cambridge. Several other persons received acceptance conditional upon the production of such testimonials. Natives of Ely, dismissed on such grounds, normally possessed some other disqualifications. For example, John Clarcke, rejected in 1561 having failed to produce testimonials, had no degree and was too young, aged only 21.[6]

The attitude to those from outside the diocese who failed to produce the requisite letters dimissory appears to have been somewhat more severe. In April 1568 William Oxenshawe of Huntingdonshire, Deacon, failed to present the said letters and also showed himself ignorant in the Scriptures: he was immediately rejected. When William Ashton of London diocese presented no letter a decision regarding his admission was deferred until the bishop could examine the case.[7]

At an early date the Ely examiners demonstrated some hesitation about admitting men to orders who were comparatively advanced in years, responding to Archbishop Parker's directive of August 1560. The ordination of June 1561 was the first following the announcement of Parker's ordination policy. Twenty-four men were examined, 14 of whom were non-graduate. The ages of 10 of the group are known; six were over 35. Only one of these was denied admission outright – John Hemyngton of Brandon in Norfolk, aged 57 – but Richard Toll of Wychford Bridge, 38, and Richard Skynner, 66, of Cambridge, were referred to the bishop for a decision. Both men were eventually admitted to the diaconate. This hesitancy on the part of the examiners is in contrast with their behaviour in July 1560 when five none-graduates were admitted to orders despite the fact that at least four were over 30.[8]

It may be, however, that Parker's directive concerning the background of clerics was having considerably more effect than his warning concerning age alone. It was important to the Church that new recruits had been 'traded and brought up in learning'. The possibility that an ordinand of fairly advanced years and no education had not been thus set apart for the ministry from his youth was much stronger than that in the case of a young man or a graduate. It is true that, on the whole, the age of graduate candidates for orders at Ely was considerably lower than that of non-graduates.

The presumption would be that a non-graduate seeking entry into the ministry, particularly into the diaconate, after the age of 30 was of 'base occupation'. The examiners would examine the candidate's life and credentials with especial care to establish vocational suitability. Thomas Whitehead, a candidate in 1561, had been a servant at King's College, Cambridge, for 20 years and was admitted readily. Two men who exceeded the age of 39 were admitted in March 1561/2 despite poor scriptural knowledge because they were already in deacons' orders. The examiners felt no similar responsibility towards Henry Funston, lector of Norwich diocese, who was aged 60 and possessed of poor Latin and scriptural ability, simply because he was not a member of the profession.[9]

The examinations at Ely were conducted by the archdeacon and other senior diocesan personnel but discretionary power lay with the bishop. Problem cases were referred to him for a final decision. The examiners themselves freely admitted those candidates who fulfilled the letter of the law. More surprisingly they felt it within their power to admit several who had insufficient knowledge of the Scriptures – always, however, making the candidate in question enter into a bond to improve his learning in this respect. In March 1561 20 men were bound by obligation to this end and all but one of them were admitted upon this condition. When Thomas Michel of Brokesbye, Leicestershire, was questioned he was said to understand the 'latten tonge well' and to be 'reasonablye well exercised in the scriptures' but was 'bound alsoe for his further diligence to learne withowte booke the Epistle to the Romans & Render an accompte thereof brieflye within one halfe yere nexte after the date hereof to Mr Bancrofte'. But beyond exercising this type of discretion the officials were not willing to go. When William Reynolds, aged 49, claimed personal knowledge of the bishop as a qualification for ordination, the examiners, not wishing to offend one of the bishop's protégés and, moreover, unwilling to let anyone evade the test by spurious claims, did not examine him further, reserving the case to the bishop's discretion, probably because of the candidate's advanced age.[10]

If a man who had initially been denied orders presented himself again at a later date his acceptance was by no means automatic. John Dun, aged 30, 'Curate of Westwrattinge' for 12 months past, sought deacon's orders at Ely in December 1574; he was not admitted. In April of 1575 he presented himself once more for examination but 'he being examined was fownd unfit and unhable to enter into the ministrye And therefore was not admitted'. Likewise, Lancelott Ellys, B.A., of Clare Hall, and Henry Mason of Trinity College, Cambridge, were denied orders twice. Ellys was already a deacon. Thomas Everard, B.A., student of Clare Hall, was finally admitted deacon in April 1576 after two previous rejections.[11]

At the same time, the examiners invited objections from the laity to the candidates being examined. Statutory publication of the administration of orders appears to have been observed. At Worcester it was asked in 1560 that if 'any man knowe any fawlte or impedymente in any of the parsons whose names ben here undre wrytten why they shuld not be made decons or ministres let him appere in his lordeshippes cathedrall churche of worcestre upon sondaye'. Whether any objections were levelled at candidates in this way or whether they were heeded, it is impossible to tell.[12]

The Ely evidence seems to suggest that ordination examinations were rigorous in that they demanded conformity to the regulations and in that both graduates and non-graduates alike were expected to measure up to certain standards. Was the situation at Ely typical of the rest of the country, however? It may seem strange that so many men were rejected at Ely at a time when the shortage of adequately trained clergy is said to have been serious. In addition an unusually large proportion of Ely ordinands were graduate at an early date. Could it be that both phenomena were peculiar to Ely? The Bishop of Ely was the visitor of the University of Cambridge. In fact several of the ordination examinations took place in the chapels of various of the colleges of the universities.[13] The diocesan officials here, as at Oxford, were living in a fool's paradise. Elsewhere the shortage of educated clergy was grave and was acknowledged to be so, despite Parker's view that the situation in 1561 was improved.

Does this mean, however, that officers elsewhere were less willing to reject blatantly unsuitable candidates for the ministry? Dr Owen argues from silence in the records of London diocese that only one person was denied orders during the year 1559–60 despite the fact that one in seven of the incumbents were of 'base occupation'. This is a dangerous argument. In order to estimate fully the number of persons refused orders, a record of actual examination such as that extant for Ely is required. At Ely the names of candidates who failed the initial examination did not appear in the subsequent records of subscription and ordination; on occasion someone who passed the examiners would not be admitted on failure to subscribe, or upon rejection at the actual ceremony. Whatever the explanation for stray evidences of rejection in subscription books and ordination lists, it remains true that only a report of the actual examination is a reliable guide to the rate of rejections.[14]

It does seem reasonable to suppose, however, that the standards of various diocesan examiners varied in accordance with the quality and number of candidates presenting themselves. It is also true that there was an understandable reluctance on the part of officials to reject candidates. This was due to the unwillingness of the bishops to encroach upon the rights of patrons. The business of ordination was intimately, indeed inextricably, connected to that of presentation to benefices. The rejection of a candidate with influential backing at ordination was a serious encroachment upon the sole initiative of the patron: the references presented by a man seeking ordination, institution or licensing were more than testimonials to his good conversation; they were a challenge to the authorities to refuse that person preferment, backed by such weighty means as he could muster. Yet while the bishops might fear alienating the local gentry in some cases, more often than not they were faced by patrons of relatively humble status. Officials would doubtless weigh such considerations before coming to a final decision. It is more likely, however, that indiscriminate admission into the Church occurred because of awareness of a grave shortage of personnel to exercise pastoral functions.[15]

In certain dioceses, as has been indicated, the situation was not as critical as in others. At Oxford as well as at Ely examiners were in a position to reject even unsuitable graduates. This may be explained by the geographical position of these dioceses. Moreover, there was perhaps a backlog of Protestant graduate ordinands who had not entered the Church during Mary's reign, but in the case of a diocese such as Chester, for example, it was impossible to insist upon a graduate ministry even during the 1580s because few graduates were presenting themselves. Equally in a diocese so affected by vacancies in its parishes as Canterbury or London in the early days of Elizabeth, over-rigorous examination of candidates was undesirable.

Yet, as will be shown, by the early seventeenth century, and particularly by the 1620s, the conditions which had prevailed at Ely during the 1560s and 1570s were almost universal in English dioceses. Because of the influx of graduates into the Church as a whole, examinations could be exacting even in dioceses normally forced to accept whatever persons offered themselves, whether qualified or no. It is tantalizing that the historian is faced with a lack of direct documentation just when a comparison with sixteenth-century procedure would be most instructive, and is forced back upon examples taken from literary sources and inferences drawn from extant ordination lists and subscription books.[16]

Rejecting tradition, the canons of 1604 assumed that the responsibility for examining ordinands lay with the bishop. If he was unable to preside personally, he should delegate his powers to cathedral dignitaries or leading preachers of the diocese. The Chancellor of Hereford diocese was accustomed to conduct examinations there. By the 1620s Thomas Morton, Bishop of Lichfield, was insisting upon examining candidates himself. His secretary noted that Morton 'trusted not his own chaplains in this sacred business, though otherwise very able and learned divines'. There is, of course, the possibility that some sort of preliminary selection took place before the bishop examined ordinands, but this is unlikely. The bishop was now fulfilling the role of examiner as well as that of court of appeal in difficult cases. The Crown no doubt supported such a step as a block to the ever encroaching influence of the puritan preachers in such matters. It was probably a simple matter to transfer responsibility to the bishops owing to the experimentation in the form of ordination examinations during the later Elizabethan period.[17]

The increasingly graduate composition of ordination lists everywhere during the second decade of the century is apparent. This was certainly the case at Lichfield, yet Bishop Morton appears to have used this as an opportunity to make the questioning of candidates more and not less searching. Several references to the form of his examinations exist. His secretary, Richard Baddiley, recorded that Morton was diligent in his attempts to secure a university-trained clergy:

> He never ordained any for priests and deacons . . . but such as were graduates of the university (or otherwise well qualified in learning:) And for a tryall of their parts, he always appointed a set time to examine them in university learning, but chiefly in points of divinity; and in this he was very exact, by making them answer syllogistically, according to their own abilities.[18]

John Shaw, of Christ's College, Cambridge, acted as lecturer at Brampton near Chesterfield for a few years and then applied to Morton for a licence to preach within the diocese: 'he finding him young and newly come from Cambridge, was strict in his examination. He enquir'd, what questions he gave in the schools when he was senior batchelor, and disputed very scholastically with him upon them.'[19] In this way Morton was able to keep his finger upon the pulse of the diocese. By subjecting all his clergy to a searching test in points of religion he was able to bar from the ministry all who did not measure up to his required standards. Jonathan Jephcott reported that Morton 'was counted very severe in examining candidates' and that he 'rejected several' who presented themselves for orders.[20]

Of the severity of Morton's examinations we have little direct evidence; the subscription books contain the names only of those admitted to ordination. They do, however, show that Morton admitted some men to orders on conditional terms. In 1623, Peter French, B.A. and curate of Rugeley, Staffordshire, was ordained deacon but made to promise that he would not seek ordination as priest without the bishop's prior approval. At least four other candidates were admitted to the diaconate on similar conditions during the next eight years.[21]

It is interesting that Morton did not assume that one who possessed a degree was automatically suited for the ministry. He took care to examine each candidate according to his own abilities; realistically, he could not expect a grammar-school man to answer questions fitted to those of graduate status, whereas he could expect the former to have equivalent religious education. Implicit in this was an assumption that lack of a university education, however undesirable, did not make a man unsuited to the priesthood: lack of scriptural learning did.

It seems probable that Morton, at least, did not search too deeply into the question of the conformity of the ordinands before him. Apparently on occasion he permitted learned men to subscribe with mental reservations. When Bishop of Chester he had ordained Richard Mather, who subscribed but with no conviction and little intention of conformity. He acted in a similar manner towards Shaw when licensing him as preacher. It is apparent that Morton believed that these men should conform but he sympathized with the puritans in matters of doctrine and respected those who were learned and good preachers. Because of this he was reluctant to lose their services and tolerated them within his diocese as far as he could, striving to bring them to conformity by persuasion. Unfortunately the nonconformist clergy appear to have been misled by Morton's sympathy, expecting him to tolerate more than he could or wished to as a bishop of the Church.[22]

The overwhelming impression obtained from the Lichfield evidence is that candidates were denied admission on grounds of insufficient scriptural knowledge rather than of nonconformity – as long as they made a token subscription – or of non-presentation of letters testimonial and dimissory. Now that the majority of ordinands were graduate, letters dimissory were rarely required. Of course, this meant that the bishop often had little check on the ordinand's origins and had to rely increasingly upon the evidence of personal examination.

There is considerable evidence that the bishops in the seventeenth century were taking advantage of improved recruitment and turning away unsuitable candidates for the ministry. Despite the existence of official requirements regulating entry to the profession, however, the decision about suitability was essentially a subjective one. In the 1630s the Bishop of Oxford was complaining to Laud that his own attempts to prevent the ordination of unsuitable men were to no avail because 'having refused to give orders to twenty or thirty at an ordination, most of them have addressed themselves to other bishops, and of them received orders, not only without letters dimissory but without such qualifications as the canon requires'. Yet this does not imply corruption on the part of other bishops, or even negligence. The standards set down by the Church were minimal standards and they gave the bishops ample room to exercise individual discretion in interpretation. At Gloucester, for example, Bishop Goodman maintained that he was forced to 'ordain some very mean ministers . . . to supply cures as mean'. Yet these men were graduates who technically fulfilled the canonical requirements but who were judged by Goodman to be vocationally unsuitable. The bishops had to be in a favourable position to discriminate between good and mediocre material; in some areas they were hard put even to reject the downright unworthy.[23]

It seems correct to conclude that in the late sixteenth century and increasingly in the seventeenth century bishops were in a position to raise the standards required for ordination. There was considerable regional variation, however. In those areas least affected by university expansion, men of inferior education were admitted. A bishop's attitude to the importance of various aspects of the office of priest would also affect his decisions. He might place preaching above all other necessary functions and admit a good preacher who was only dubiously conformable; his interpretation of the requisite level of learning might be very different from that of a colleague; he might place excessive value on testimonials. Despite these provisoes, the bishops did utilize ordination examinations to control recruitment and, allowing for certain restrictive factors, they succeeded in doing so.

Table 4

Summary analysis of the Ely ordination book: 1560–80

A

Date of ordination examination[1]	Place of ordination examination[2]	Examiners
5 July 1560	?	Archdeacon of Ely
(11 July 1560)	(Ely Cathedral)	(? Mr Wysdom)
7 June 1561	Lady Chapel of Ely Cathedral	Mr Wysdom, Archdeacon of Ely
(8 June 1561)	(Armitage Chapel, Ely)	
21 March 1561/2	Lady Chapel of Ely Cathedral	Mr Wysdom
(22 March 1561/2)	(Downham Chapel)	
15 April 1568	Ely Cathedral	Thomas Ithell, LL.D.,[3]
(16 April 1568)	(Ely Cathedral)	John Parker, clerk
18 December 1568	Jesus College Chapel, Cambridge	Thomas Ithell, Mr Barnwell, M.A.
(21 December 1568)	(Downham Chapel)	
19, 20 December 1569	Jesus College Chapel Cambridge	?
(21 December 1569)	(Erithe Chapel)	
18, 19, 20 Dec. 1574	Trinity Parish Church, Ely	John Parker, Archdeacon of Ely, Thomas Ithell, LL.D.
14, 15 April 1575	Jesus College Chapel, Cambridge	John Parker, Thomas Ithell,
(17 April 1575)	(Doddington, Isle of Ely)	John Randall, LL.D.

Date of ordination examination[1]	*Place of ordination examination*[2]	*Examiners*
27, 28 September 1575	Jesus College Chapel, Cambridge	John Parker, Thomas Ithell,
(29 September 1575)	(Ely Cathedral)	John Randall
15 April 1575	Downham Chapel	John Parker,
(15 April 1575)	(Downham Chapel)	——— Scott, M.A.
(19 April 1576)[4]	(Downham Chapel)	
29 April 1576	Downham Chapel.	John Parker, Thomas Scotte, M.A.
14, 15 November 1577	Jesus College Chapel, Cambridge	Dr Randall, Mr Bancrofte
(17 November 1577)	(Ely Cathedral)	
28, 29 March 1578	Jesus College Chapel, Cambridge	John Parker, Dr Randall,
(1 April 1578)	(Ely Cathedral)	Dr Ithell, Mr Bancrofte, & 'others'
18, 19 December 1578	Jesus College Chapel, Cambridge	John Parker, Richard Bancrofte,
(21 December 1578)	(Ely Cathedral)	Dr Randall, Dr Ithell, & 'others'
14, 15 April 1580	Jesus College Chapel, Cambridge	John Parker, Richard Brydgwater,
(17 April 1580)	(Downham Chapel)	LL.D., John Randall, Richard Bancrofte, M.A.
17, 19 December 1580	Round Church in Cambridge	John Parker, Richard Brydgwater, John Randall,
(21 December 1580)	(Downham Chapel)	Richard Bancrofte

1. Dates in brackets give dates of corresponding ordination ceremonies.
2. Places in brackets give corresponding ordination ceremony locations.
3. Dr Thomas Ithell was Master of Jesus College, Cambridge, which must explain the use of this chapel for ordination examinations.
4. It is probable that this is a mistake for 29 April 1576.
Reference to the above table shows that examination records do not survive for several Ely ordinations during this twenty-year period.

B

Date of ordination ceremony	Place of ordination	Examination record	MS references
11 July 1560	Ely Cathedral	Yes	fos. 52r and v, 67r–69v
24 November 1560	Ely Cathedral	No	fos. 52v and 53r
8 June 1561	Armitage Chapel, Ely	Yes	fos. 53r, 70r–74v
22 March 1561/2	Downham Chapel	Yes	fos. 53v, 75r–80
19 December 1563	Downham Chapel	No	f. 81r
25 November 1564	Ely Cathedral	No	f. 81v
29 July 1565	Parish Church (Fennydrayton)	No	f. 82r
26 May 1566	Erithe Chapel	No	f. 82v
24 August 1566	Parish Church (Conington)	No	f. 83r
15 September 1566	Parish Church (Fennydrayton)	No	f. 83v
23 March 1566/7	Parish Church (Conington)	No	fos. 83v–84r
21 September 1567	Erithe Chapel	No	fos. 84r and v
16 April 1568	Ely Cathedral	Yes	fos. 85r 55r–60r
21 December 1568	Downham Chapel	Yes	fos. 85v, 60v–63v
21 December 1569	Erithe Chapel	Yes	fos. 86r, 64r–66v
27 March 1569/70	Downham Chapel	No	f. 86v
22 March 1569/70	Ely Palace, Oratory	No	f. 86v
2 June 1570	Downham Chapel	No	f. 87r
21 September 1570	Parish Church (Fennydrayton)	No	f. 87v
21 December 1574	Ely Cathedral	Yes	fos. 40r, 2–4v
17 April 1575	Doddington, Isle of Ely	Yes	fos. 38v, 5v–8v
29 September 1575	Ely Cathedral	Yes	fos. 39r, 10r–11v
15 April 1576	Downham Chapel	Yes	fos. 40r, 12r–13r
19 April 1576[1]	Downham Chapel	Yes	fos. 38v, 12r–13r
12 August 1576	Parish church (Doddington)	No	f. 40v
21 December 1576	Ely Cathedral	No	f. 41v
17 November 1577	Ely Cathedral	Yes	fos. 42v, 15r–19r
12 January 1577/8	Downham Chapel	No	f. 44r
1 April 1578	Ely Cathedral	Yes	fos. 43v, 19v–21v
21 December 1578	Ely Cathedral	Yes	fos. 44v, 22r–25r
17 April 1579	Parish Church (Doddington)	No	f. 46r

Date of ordination ceremony	Place of ordination	Examination record	MS references
5 July 1579	Parish Church (Doddington)	No	f. 45v
30 March 1580	Downham Chapel	No	f. 49v
17 April 1580	Downham Chapel	Yes	fos. 49r, 25v–32r
21 December 1580	Downham Chapel	Yes	fos. 51r, 32v–37v

1. This may well be a mistake for 29 April as an examination was held on that day.

C

ref. referred
n.a. not admitted
a. admitted
ref. a. referred but finally admitted
c.a. conditional admission

Examination 5 July 1560
No. examined 14
No. accepted 14
No. of graduates examined 6
No. of students examined 3
No. of graduates rejected 0
No. of students rejected 0
Ages
Graduates 20, 24, 25, 36, ?, ?
Students 21, 25, ?
Non-graduates 50, 32, 37, ?, 46

Examination 21 March 1561/2
No. examined 32
No. accepted 27
No. of graduates examined 4
No. of students examined 3
No. of graduates rejected 1
No. of students rejected 1
Ages
Graduates 29, 24 (n.a.), 23+, 28
Students 26, 23, 24 (n.a.)
Non-graduates 55, 24, ?, 29, 41, 43, 26, 50, 40, ?, 40, 46, 28, 24, 24, 24, 50, 24, 47, 23+, 54, 44 (n.a.), 60 (n.a.), ?, ?,

Examination 7 June 1561
No. examined 24
No. accepted 22

2 were rejected but 4 were referred and the outcome was recorded for only 3 of these – therefore possible that only 21 were finally ordained.

No. of graduates examined 9
No. of students examined 1
No. of graduates rejected 0
No. of students rejected 0

Ages
Graduates 29, 30, 21, 24, 30, 34, –?, ?, 23
Students 24
Non-graduates 55, ?, 24 (ref.), 21 (n.a.), 57 (n.a.), 22, 25, 38 (ref.; a.), 50, 66 (ref.; a.), ? (ref.; a.) 40, ?, ?

Examination 15 April 1568
No. examined 42
No. accepted 28
No. of graduates examined 17
No. of students examined 6
No. of graduates rejected 2
No. of students rejected 2

Ages
Graduates ?, 24, 24, 23, ?, 24, 22, 24, 23, 24, 22, ? (n.a.), ?, 21, ? (n.a.)
Students 21, 23 (n.a.), 24, 24, 25 (n.a.), 22,
Non-graduates 24 (n.a.), 24, 23, 28, 24, 24 (n.a.), 25 (n.a.), 25, 26, 24 (n.a.), 49, 21 (n.a.), 20 (n.a.), 40 (n.a.), 46, 25, 24 (n.a.), 42 (n.a.)

Examination 18 December 1568
No. examined 30
No. accepted 23
No. of graduates examined 14
No. of students examined 8
No. of graduates rejected 1
No. of students rejected 4
Ages
Graduates ?, ? (c.a.), 23, 30, 24, 23, ?, 22, 22, 23 (n.a.), 23, ?, 25, 24
Students 21, 22, 23, 21, 25 (n.a.), 24 (n.a.), 26 (n.a.), 22 (n.a.)
Non-graduates (24), ?, 39 (n.a.), 40, 25, 25, 26, 30 (n.a.), 'of age sufficient' for priest

Examination 19, 20 December 1569
No. examined 32
No. accepted 20
No. of graduates examined 14
No. of students examined 10
No. of graduates rejected 1
No. of students rejected 5
Ages
Graduates 26, 26, 26, 34, 22, 24, 22, 26, 26, 25, 22, ? (n.a.), 23, 23
Students 22, 23 (n.a.), 25 (n.a.), 25, 25 (n.a.), 35 (n.a.), 22, 22, 23, 24 (n.a.)
Non-graduates 27, 26(n.a.), 40 (n.a.), 25 (n.a.), 25 (n.a.), 23 (n.a.), 23 (n.a.), 22

Examination 18, 19, 20 December 1574
No. examined 10
No. accepted 8
No. of graduates examined 5
No. of students examined 1
No. of graduates rejected 0
No. of students rejected 0
Ages
Graduates 40, 24, 25, 26, 29
Students 24
Non-graduates 30 (n.a.), 49, 23 (n.a.), 30

Examination 14, 15 April 1575
One man, Henry Mason, was not noted as having subscribed on 17 April. Neither was he admitted to orders on that day. He had received, however, a good examination report. In the list he is noted as a graduate but in September of the year was listed as a student only.

No. examined 21
No. accepted 13
No. of graduates examined 10
No. of students examined 4
No. of graduates rejected 1
No. of students rejected 3
Ages
Graduates 24, 24, 23, 23, 24 (n.a.), 24, 24, 24, 26, 25
Students 30 (n.a.), 24 (n.a.), 26 (n.a.), 24
Non-graduates 26, 24 (n.a.), 25, 30 (n.a.), 40 (n.a.), 26 (n.a.), 25

Examination 27, 28 September 1575
No. examined 11
No. accepted 7
No. of graduates examined 2
No. of students examined 5
No. of graduates rejected 0
No. of students rejected 2

Ages
Graduates 25, 30
Students 23, 24, 23, 24 (n.a.), 23
Non-graduates 23 (n.a.), 29 (n.a.),
   34, 46

Examination 15 April 1576
No. examined 8
No. accepted 8
No. of graduates examined 6
No. of students examined 1
No. of graduates rejected 0
No. of students rejected 0
Ages
Graduates 25, 25, 31, 26, 25, ?
Students 24
Non-graduates 24

Examination 29 April 1576
No. examined 6
No. accepted 6
No. of graduates examined 5
No. of students examined 1
No. of graduates rejected 0
No. of students rejected 0
Ages
Graduates 27, 24, 24, 24, 24
Students 30
Non-graduates 0

Examination 14, 15 November 1577
No. examined 21
No. accepted 18
No. of graduates examined 16,
No. of students examined 4
No. of graduates rejected 0
No. of students rejected 2
Ages
Graduates 24, 25, 24, 25, 24, 25, 23,
   28, 23, 23, 24, 25, 23, 25, ?, 25
Students 24, 26, 23 (n.a.), 23 (n.a.)
Non-graduates 24 (n.a.)

Examination 28, 29 March 1578
No. examined 11

No. accepted 11
No. of graduates examined 7
No. of students examined 1
No. of graduates rejected 0
No. of students rejected 0
Ages
Graduates 30, 28, 25, 24, 23, 24, 24
Students 24
Non-graduates 24, 25, 25

Examination 18, 19 December 1578
No. examined 20
No. accepted 17
No. of graduates examined 10
No. of students examined 5
No. of graduates rejected 0
No. of students rejected 1
Ages
Graduates 29, 24, 23, 24, 24, 24, 24,
   25, 24, 37
Students 24, 23, 25 (n.a.), 23, 24
Non-graduates 28 (n.a.), 28 (n.a.),
   24, 25, 23

Examination 14, 15 April 1580
No. examined 35
No. accepted 26
No. of graduates examined 27
No. of students examined 2
No. of graduates rejected 3
No. of students rejected 1
Ages
Graduates 24, 25, 24, 25, 26, 24, 25,
   26, 30, 24, 24, 27, 23 (n.a.), 24, 24,
   24, 24, 26, 28 (n.a.), 23, 24, 28, 24,
   24, 25, 26, 23 (n.a.)
Students 24, ?
Non-graduates 29 (n.a.), 24, 24 (n.a.),
   7 (n.a.), 27, 29 (n.a.)

Examination 18, 19 December 1580
No. examined 25
No. accepted 17
No. of graduates examined 19
No. of students examined 1

No. of graduates rejected 5   (n.a.), 25, 30, 24 (n.a.), 24, ?, 24
No. of students rejected 1   (n.a.), 27
Ages   Students 26 (n.a.)
Graduates 25, 24, 26, 30 (n.a.), 23   Non-graduates Non-graduates 24
(n.a.), 24, 25, 29, 23, 28, 24, 25   (n.a.), 23 (n.a.), 30, 28, ?

D
Comparison of examination record and ordination list

Examination 15 April 1568   Ordination 16 April 1568

16 deacons
Laurence Washington M.A.
Hugh Byllett, M.A.
William Hayes, B.A.
George Dikonson, B.A.
Reginald Grovener, B.A.
William Morgan, B.A.
Richard Hycks, B.A.
George Best (student)
Hugh Brandon (student)
Robert Wells (student)
Barnabas Beneson (student)
Laurence Bancka (student)
William Clarcke (student)
Richard Baker, Curate of Harston

(admission on condition of   Thomas Stracock, Curate of Hardwyck
learning Epistle to Romans)   Thomas Wright of Ely

12 priests
William Clarke, M.A.
Richard Smyth, M.A.
Matthew Hollands or Hollme, B.A.
Edmund Franklyn, B.A.
Edmund Pryse, B.A.
Robert Boothe, B.A.
William Pollerd, Curate of Wilberton
John Gotobed, Petty Canon of Ely
John Worsley, Rector of Thurnyng
George Mahewe, Curate of Rampton
John Butterfeald of Queen's College

Men examined but not ordained
1. James Whittacres, 23, student, St John's College and deacon by
   Bishop of Ely – not admitted as priest – poor understanding of Latin
   and Scriptures – f. 56v.
2. James Thornton, 24, of Hinton – not admitted as deacon – lack of
   Scriptural learning – f. 56v.

3. Miles Downham, 24, Vicar of Hinxton and deacon by Bishop of Ely – not admitted as priest – 'not exercysyd in the scripturs'.
4. William Oxenshaw, 24, Curate of Hallywell, Hunts. – already deacon – not admitted priest – no letters dimissory; poor understanding of Scriptures.
5. Richard Biggs, 25, of Wallsover – not admitted deacon.
6. Andrew Burnett, 24 – 'somewhat ignorant in the Latyn tong therfor examynd in full'.
7. William Reynollds, 49, of Tydd St Giles – 'he hath exhibityd letters of his comendacion from Mr Adam he redyth well & sayth he is otherways well known to my L. byshopp of Elye' – f.58v – admission delayed until approval of bishop obtained.
8. Richard Ryding, 25, of Christ's College.
9. Henry Pyck, of Christ's College, B.A., – letters testimonial from Master and Fellows.
10. Nicholas Wallys, 20, B.A. of Peterhouse, – letters testimonial from Mr Dean and others – good Latin but 'in the scripturs ignorant'.
11. John Fenton, 52, of Wallsover (?) – letters testimonial from Mr Styward and others – bad understanding of Latin and Scripture.
12. John Hall, 21, scholar in Ely grammar school, – Latin passable, 'small understanding in the scripturs'.
13. Edward Townson, 20, scholar in Ely grammar school – as above.
14. William Tuthill, 40, of Swaffham Priors, – 'symply' understanding Latin and Scriptures.

This comparison demonstrates that one cannot assume that a list of those actually ordained also includes a full list of those examined or, more specifically, the names of those who were rejected at the time of examination.

5

Experiment

If the medium of ordination examination offered the bishops the means to control personnel recruitment, many felt that the method was in need of refinement and improvement. The canonical requirements for ordination as a priest were that an ordinand must have a title to a benefice before admission; there was no stipulation that either hierarchy or congregation judge his suitability for acting as pastor to that particular flock. Many also felt that the formal examination was too hurried and superficial really to gauge a candidate's vocational suitability.

In the 1570s Archdeacon Thomas Lever drew up 'notes for some reformacon of the mynistrye and mynisters' to be observed in the Church until some official rules were promulgated. These notes constituted an integrated plan for the admission of men to the priesthood and to benefices and for the supervision of their ministry once they were ensconced in their livings. In addition they laid down detailed instructions regarding the administration of the sacraments and concerning the duties and behaviour of readers and other Church officers. Lever rightly saw the problem as one whole: an artificial distinction is imposed by dealing with the question of ordination examinations separately from the control of institutions and from attempts to educate and supervise the beneficed and unbeneficed clergy. Lever's project took into full account the stumbling block raised by the impropriation of livings by laymen. He saw that the situation where one man might present to a living a highly unsuitable clerk without effective hindrance and certainly without the assent of the congregation must be altered. Rules governing the admission of men to orders were a necessary but an insufficient remedy for the cancer of irresponsible lay patronage.[1]

The first clauses of the notes deal with the actual admission of men into orders and are worthy of detailed comment. Lever reiterated the rule that no man should be ordained without a title to a living or cure, but added that he would likewise be disqualified by inability to preach or administer the sacraments. His concern was not with the problem of maintaining newly ordained clerics physically but with the establishment of a truly pastoral ministry. The office of a priest implied responsibility for a congregation and not simply initiation into a mystery or even entry into a professional group – here were to be no barristers who did not practise, no teachers who never taught. All those ordained would simultaneously be admitted into cures of souls. Lever was striking boldly at the many men in orders who remained in the universities and who never ministered to a congregation.

Lever went further than this, for the examination which he envisaged was to be conducted on several levels. He demanded that the congregation join with the patron in assenting to the presentation of the man in question. The power of the parishioners to challenge a nomination in an indirect way had always existed in the system of letters testimonial and in the publication of ordinands' names before the ceremonies. But this new plan took as its starting point the positive assent of the parishioners themselves to the presentation of a particular man as their minister. The initiative still remained with the patron but the laity was given a strong negative voice, especially where the patron was non-resident.

The responsibility for seeing that the candidate was presented to the parishioners for inspection *before* ordination, Lever laid squarely upon the shoulders of the archdeacon or other examiners. When the parishioners had voiced their assent, the archdeacon should preach a sermon or exhortation regarding the mutual duties of minister and congregation. Lever extended these proposals to cover the admission to benefices of men already in orders.

The vigilance of the authorities should not end at institution. A cleric who did not perform his duties must be suspended and, if he failed to reform himself within a given period, 'utterlie deposed from the ministrie'. Lever's was no attempt to educate the clergy or test the extent of their learning but rather to reform the ministry and to reject all those who did not comply with standards rigorously enforced at pastoral level.

Lever's projected reforms were not original: in the continental Reformed churches it had long been the practice for the processes of selection and examination for the ministry to be dependent upon the availability of vacant charges – the ministerial office being regarded as a pastoral rather than as a priestly one. Such ideas were taken up by many. In England Udall discussed the question of ordaining to a particular charge only, rather than to the ministry in general; much later the Westminster Assembly entered into debate on the matter. There were, of course, occasional deviations from the pattern – for instance, the Swiss Reformed Church tended to ordain rather more ministers than were required, but most of the surplus were in fact given missionary charges. The Westminster Assembly later decreed that a candidate for a benefice must preach three sermons before the congregation of a vacant living; after this a deputation would go from the congregation to the presbytery to intimate approval or disapproval of the minister.[2]

Most of the other experiments in controlling recruitment of the lower clergy concentrated upon transforming the traditional patronage system into one more amenable to hierarchical control. In most, however, there was an underlying appreciation of the fact that those unworthy of a pastoral charge in the Reformed Church of England should never be allowed to enter orders in the first place. In 1584 *Certain Advertisements* were published in the diocese of Coventry and Lichfield by Bishop William Overton. Ordinands were to be subjected to a searching examination at quarterly sessions by the bishop, his chancellor or chancellor's deputy and four learned preachers. The motivation for this was boldly stated, 'for that to help the lamentable inconveniences frowing to the Church of God by the insufficient ministry, they are not only to be sifted which are already made ministers, but also a diligent care and foresight is to be used that only sufficient men be admitted to the function hereafter'. Yet the emphasis of the *Advertisements* was upon the examination of presentees to benefices. The examiners would, on the first day of the month in the consistory court, test the gifts and learning of the party concerned and after conference record their estimate of his performance in a book specially kept for the purpose. Because letters testimonal had been found unreliable guides as to vocational suitability in the past, the prospective incumbent would be submitted to a second searching test of a different type. He would enter his future charge and exercise his ministry there for a probationary month. If no complaints were heard against him after that period, he was entitled to appear before the ordinary, take an oath that he had not obtained the benefice by simony, and be admitted formally to the benefice.[3]

While it is true that these advertisements were in the main a 'local application of the Privy Council's articles', it is also apparent that they owed much to ideas already current in this diocese. The chancellor, Thomas Becon, had favoured similar ideas in his reform experiment in Norwich in the late 1570s; Overton himself was anxious to conciliate the puritan ministers of his diocese – in 1582 he had come under serious attack from William Axton, minister of Moreton Corbet, Salop, for his conduct of ordinations and institutions without the advice of the 'Eldership' and without testing the candidates' 'gifts'. Overton's was an isolated, radical attempt to enlist the help of the puritan preachers in selection of personnel, to give the congregations a voice in the choice of their ministers, and to guard against careless, corrupt or inefficient exercise of patronage by patrons. The implementation of this plan would have meant that bishops were able to follow institutional policies instead of reacting in an *ad hoc* fashion to the actions of individual patrons.[4]

Why the scheme aroused such hostility is an interesting story. The project was probably seen by the bishop and his chancellor as merely setting the seal of approval upon what was already widely practised. The association of the puritan preachers with the work of the diocese was in harmony with existing practice.[5] Throughout the country patrons of puritan persuasion were allowing congregations a veto in the choice of their ministers. Their concern was that the actual right to choose be untouched: if the initial choice of the patron found no favour with the congregation it was still he, not the laity, who chose the replacement. However, the scheme floundered because of the unpropitious moment at which it was launched and because of the particular circumstances in which it was brought to the attention of the Privy Council. At the time Whitgift was being criticized for alienating the local gentry.[6] Overton's plan, while essentially *confirming* a fairly common practice, did make the congregation's veto a right rather than a privilege freely granted by individual patrons. No longer would the patron overrule the objections of people and hierarchy if he so chose. In addition, the years 1584–5 saw numerous petitions to the Crown asking for some toleration of nonconformity in puritans.[7] The petitions were couched in moderate terms, having as their core complaints against the episcopate. Most of the Privy Council were impressed but the Archbishop remained unmoved. Schemes such as that at Lichfield offered the Church more control over patronage but at what cost? The cost of conceding the puritans' point and of allowing their chosen system of Church government to creep in with official connivance seemed a high one. Then Overton lost even the potential support of the Council. The scheme was put into operation with respect to all presentations to livings and in 1584 Overton had to explain to the Crown why he had refused to admit William Jennings, a Crown presentee, to Church Eaton rectory, Warwickshire. Tampering with the patronage rights of the Crown, and in open liaison with radicals such as John Oxenbridge, Overton had truly overstepped the mark.[8]

In these circumstances was it any wonder that the hierarchy turned away from innovatory policies which threatened to infringe existing patronage rights or to bring to the attention of the Crown too thoroughgoing an attempt to bring this Church 'but halfly reformed' into line with the continental churches? Yet experiment of a more moderate kind continued with a view to compromising with the existing recruitment situation. If the bishops were not to be allowed to enlist the participation of learned preachers and congregations in selecting ministers, they could still hope to educate the insufficient candidates once they had entered the profession. In a general sense such attempts met with approval both from the hierarchy and from the Crown, although the methods used to achieve re-education of the ministry were open to intense critical scrutiny.

In the reigns of both Edward and Elizabeth royal injunctions ordered that clergy with dubious academic qualifications should undertake supervised biblical study. Both Parker's *Advertisements* and the canons of 1571 delegated examining responsibility in this sphere to the archdeacons and their officials in the visitation procedure. Different officials interpreted these general orders in various ways. In London in the 1560s and 1570s Archdeacon John Mullins held biennial meetings of ministers; a prior assignment was given to non-preachers of four or five chapters of the New Testament 'to reade and studie . . . diligentlie till the halfe yeare come up'. On the day appointed all met in a given church and were queried 'of sutch places as seme to have anie hardnes. And thei answer according to ther skill.' The archdeacon explained any points which had raised problems. These meetings generally lasted for four or five days at a time and steady progress was made during the decade: between 1561 and 1576 the group had covered the New Testament and was about to study the Apocalypse. Unfortunately, of course, inadequate preachers escaped the system altogether. No changes were made in the method until the mid-1580s, although in 1581 the system was extended to the archdeaconry of St Albans also. Here both non-preachers and B.A.s were required to hand in monthly *written* evidence of their scriptural studies to the local preacher or minister with an M.A. The official examined these scripts quarterly in order to assess progress.[9]

The years 1584–7 witnessed the introduction of a number of orders to improve the quality of the inferior clergy. These coincided with the accession of Whitgift, and complaints from both queen and Parliament. As noted, the convocation of 1584 regulated entry to the ministry and insisted on quarterly rather than biennial examinations of unlearned clergy. The system was set up almost immediately by Bishop Aylmer in London. Letters were sent out to his archdeacons reciting the new orders and demanding quarterly returns of clerics 'notoriously negligent or wilfully disobedient to the orders concerning the exercises'. At St Albans the clergy were divided into three groups for purposes of study and allocated specific, quite searching 'exercises'. The Archdeacon of London treated miscreants rigorously but there is evidence that the London clergy exhibited indifference to this and other projects of self-improvement despite official deterrents. In November 1585 non-attenders at the Michaelmas exercise were cited. Several were ordered to report performance of their assignments on the next court day; others were inhibited from their ecclesiastical functions until they had done so. Many successfully claimed exemptions; some rather less successfully pleaded illness, official business, old age or infirmity.

In 1586 Aylmer anticipated new articles to be laid down by the convocation of that year. He included all non-preachers below M.A. amongst the clergy to be supervised; ordered daily study and notes on a biblical chapter and weekly reading of a sermon from *Bullinger's Decades*; set up quarterly examinations by six or seven local preachers who were to report annually to the bishop or archdeacon; and laid down that negligence was to be rewarded by extreme ecclesiastical censure. As at St Albans, within the City three groups were set up for purposes of examination, each examined by experienced beneficed clerics from the City of London. All but one of the examiners were graduate and the exception was a preacher. It is even more interesting that several of the 15 examiners here were chaplains of either Aylmer or Whitgift and that all were of unimpeachable religious orthodoxy. Noteworthy also was the omission in their ranks of preachers of equivalent intellectual status but suspect conformity, such as Robert Crowley and Arthur Bright.

The new rules were soon put into operation – three months after Aylmer's visitation. A full list of parochial clergy was issued to the respective deans. Commissioners were to record the standard of performance of all persons not exempt from the trial and to hand their record over to the consistory court at a later date. The vicar general addressed the commissioners concerning the problem of non-attendance and in a letter to the archdeacons asked them to guard against a system of organized cribbing which had been prevalent in earlier attempts to examine the clergy. There is, however, some indication that ministers in the diocese made attempts to evade the new system: the number of preaching licences issued by the vicar general rose steadily from 11 (1584), to 19 (1585), to 24 (1586). Aylmer's forthright threats of deprivation for the non-attenders (which were of dubious legality before Whitgift's orders received the authority of convocation and which were in any event difficult of application) 'hint at the bureaucrat's impatience with administrative inefficiency'. Whitgift himself showed continued interest in the effects of the orders: prior to Elizabeth's last four parliaments he requested certificates of the quality of beneficed clergy admitted since 1584 in the dioceses. There were more positive incentives for the clergy to participate enthusiastically in the scheme. They could, for example, obtain a preaching licence if they progressed well in the course: five ministers in St Albans' archdeaconry obtained licences to preach in their own parishes within two years of beginning the exercise.[10]

Clearly, the implementation of these orders for the examining of the clergy in scriptural learning within the diocese of London was harnessed very much to a conservative desire to see an educated, conformable preaching ministry within the area. This desire was echoed in similar schemes practised in other dioceses – at York, Durham, Chester and Lincoln, for example.

As Professor Collinson has noted, there had in the 1560s and 1570s been 'a tendency of these schemes of extra-mural education to assume the shape of conferences organised for prophesying, something far from the intention of Queen Elizabeth'. Several of these had direct official supervision and approbation. There were five centres of prophesying within Essex; at each between two and five preachers 'moderated' and the remainder of the clergy were examined before a public audience. Bishop Curteys's Sussex prophesyings, arranged on a deanery basis, modified these practices: here the unlearned were examined in private and only the learned spoke in the public conference. These conferences, although officially inspired, contained innovatory features: the proceedings were in English; the laity were admitted to the meeting or to part of it; puritan ministers were often dominant in the proceedings; and theological works known as *commonplaces* were studied as well as the Bible.[11]

Other prophesyings were completely divorced from episcopal or archidiaconal control. The independence of the proceedings did not necessarily mean that the authorities were out of sympathy, however: at Norwich, Coventry and Northampton, for instance, the prophesyings were independent but condoned by the bishops. There were others, such as the more radical exercise at Southam, which existed without episcopal knowledge. Professor Collinson believes that the bishops in the 1570s were becoming increasingly appreciative of the value of existing prophesyings within their jurisdictions and more and more concerned to encourage the same with episcopal approbation and licence: hence the surviving orders with episcopal approval date from the 1570s. The Grindalian bishops, Cooper of Lincoln, Bradbridge of Exeter, and Curteys of Chichester, encouraged the exercises. Cooper ordered his clergy to frequent the exercise of prophesying on pain of ecclesiastical censure. Grindal's appointment to York signalled the creation of several exercise centres in Nottinghamshire, where the archdeacon compelled offenders to perform their penances. Yet the exercise grew out of the initiative of puritan preachers and gentlemen rather than of the bishops who approved them. Moreover, the exercises were given the support of local magnates and officials. Justices of the Peace attended the exercise at Southam; members of the Council of the Marches of Wales attended the Shrewsbury exercise.[12]

Yet in 1576 the queen ordered that the exercises should be suppressed within the province of Canterbury. Why? The servants of the queen – bishops and puritan preachers alike – wanted an energetic ministry, dedicated to preaching the gospel and bringing in a godly discipline. The queen, however, wanted conformity above all in her clergy to ensure the stability of her Church and to prevent the entanglement of England in religious wars on the continent. Elizabeth's attitude towards the exercises had always been hostile, although it was Archbishop Grindal's spirited defence of their worth which brought this hostility to the fore. She had earlier caused the exercises within Norwich to be attacked and had ordered the exercises in Lincoln and Hereford to be terminated. The catalyst for the queen's outright opposition to the system was provided by the reports of the radicalism of the Southam exercise in Warwickshire. Bishop Bentham suppressed the exercise, the Privy Council attempted to dissuade the queen from treating the other exercises similarly, and Leicester intervened to protect Sir Richard Knightley and the exercise's other supporters, yet it appears that behind all this was a deliberate attempt to halt the progressive government of the Church promoted by Grindal since his elevation to Canterbury. The attempt was probably instigated by Christopher Hatton, rival of Leicester (who supported the exercises) and later supporter of Aylmer, Whitgift and Bancroft. In his effort Hatton was considerably aided by Grindal's determined and pointed response to the queen's attack. He offered to the queen reasons for rejecting her policy. These took the form of reports from the diocesans expressing qualified approval of the exercises, indicating that their abuses had been corrected, that they were conformable, that they improved the quality of the ministry and instructed the laity. He cited precedents for the practice. He laid down proposals for reformation of the system, suggesting closer control and supervision by the bishops and the barring of the laity from speaking at the conferences. In December 1576 he wrote to the queen defending the practice and questioning tactlessly the queen's authority to ban it. As a result Grindal was suspended from his office. The prophesyings were suppressed.[13]

As observed, however, the halt to the prophesyings did not divert the hierarchy from conservative attempts to re-educate the ministry and improve its quality although it did remove one very promising tool to this end. Neither did it deter the preachers from combining together. Many convinced themselves that the royal ban did not cover private conferences of clergy, followed by exercises. Such exercises normally consisted of a public sermon preached once, twice or more a month on a rotational basis by local prominent preachers, a conference, and a dinner.

During Elizabeth's reign the hierarchy were making determined efforts to reform the ministry of the Church. The progressive first generation of bishops were interested in co-operating with the puritan preachers to this end. They initiated their own experiments but also gave their approbation to schemes originating in other circles. In the mid-1570s the situation altered. The queen forbade the bishops to ally with the preachers; she ordered the suppression of the vehicles of that alliance – the prophesyings; the progressive bishops gave way by death to a new, conservative bench, and notable upon it were John Aylmer, Bishop of London from 1576 and John Whitgift, Bishop of Worcester from 1577.[14] The hierarchy were still interested in the quality of the ministry but they were interested in making it conformable and in negating the influence of the puritan movement upon it as much as possible. They employed conservative means to their end although, as has been noted at London, they often did so most vigorously and with as fine a contempt as their progressive predecessors for the niceties of the patronage system. Moreover, before we assume that the queen's measure in suppressing the officially approved prophesyings was totally disastrous for the learning of the ministry, it must be stressed that from the late 1570s onwards the educational qualifications of new recruits into the ministry were steadily improving. Yet, as will later be noted, such changes in initial recruitment standards were slow to show themselves at parochial level, and the queen's repressive policy hindered the bishops in trying to bridge the gap between old and new recruits and did force some ministers into more extreme positions concerning the programme for reform in the English Church.

6

Jus patronatus

The ancient system of ecclesiastical patronage, unchallenged by what one historian has described as England's 'half-baked reformation', should be seen as one of the main reasons why England's new clerical profession of the late sixteenth and seventeenth centuries could not match up to the Protestant ideal in the final analysis. Because of this it is essential that we understand the intricacies of the patronage system and its operation and that we examine the attempts of certain groups to influence this.

It will already have been apparent that in attempting to reform the ministry and improve the quality of recruitment into the Church the bishops were faced with the almost insuperable barrier of the patronage system. It was partly because of negligently or corruptly exercised patronage that the bishops turned to the ordination ceremony as their main tool of direct control, and to 'in service' training as their indirect method. Of course, there were other barriers as well: there was a very short supply of graduates or well-educated non-graduates for some years and, therefore, the raw material with which the bishops and patrons were forced to work was unsatisfactory no matter how patronage was exercised.

Many lay patrons (and ecclesiastical ones also) were extremely jealous of their rights to present to benefices (advowsons) which they regarded as valuable property. A patron might well be prepared to grant a right of presentation to another as a favour or on payment of a fee, but he was not prepared to see his rights usurped and denied by any bishop.

In the next chapters we shall be examining the exercise of patronage in the English Church, but before doing this it is necessary to understand something of the law of patronage with which the hierarchy was forced to work and by which they were in the end defeated.

Benefices within the jurisdiction of the diocesan fell broadly into three categories where patronage was concerned: advowsons collative; advowsons donative; and advowsons presentative. The first were advowsons held by the ordinary himself, to which he presented or, more properly, collated his own nominees. The patron of a donative might admit his own candidate to the living without applying to the bishop for approval and institution. The patron of a presentative living, however, had to present his nominee to the ordinary for examination and for formal admission to both the spiritualities (institution) and the temporalities (induction) of the benefice in question. The ordinary exercised control over the holders of donative cures only after their admission: application had to be made to the bishop for a licence to serve the cure and contravention of the canon law could result in deprivation or suspension. The bishop's control over the occupants of presentative benefices was more immediate. It was technically within his power to prevent institution and induction of the candidate if he was felt to be unsuitable according to the Church's laws.

When a presentative living fell vacant through deprivation or resignation this fact was recorded by the registrar of the diocese and it was incumbent upon him to notify the patron of the living in question of the voidance. Should the living fall vacant through death, however, no formal notification could be made to the patron because the registry had no official record of deaths. In such a case it might well be some time before the existence of a vacancy was brought to the patron's attention – either by the relatives of the deceased, the congregation, or a suitor for a living.[1]

Once aware of the vacancy, the patron would probably attempt to find a replacement for the incumbent. There were certain immediate restrictions on his choice. By two statutes of Henry VIII's reign he could not present himself to a living. Should he wish to favour the son of the last incumbent, he would do well to ensure that the candidate obtained a dispensation to succeed his father to the living. Failure to seek such a dispensation, if discovered, would result in *ipso facto* deprivation. For most of the period it was quite possible for a deacon or even a layman to be presented and instituted to a cure of souls. Such a man, however, had to take priest's orders within one year of institution. Lawrence Nowell, brother of Alexander Nowell, Dean of St Paul's, was deprived of a benefice in Coventry and Lichfield diocese in 1553 for failure to comply with this condition. It was difficult to see that such a rule was observed and by a statute of 1663 it was laid down that although a deacon or layman might be nominated and presented to the bishop, the candidate must receive priest's orders prior to institution. By a statute of 1572 a patron was forbidden to present any man without a B.D. degree, or a preaching licence from one of the universities, or a dispensation, to a living worth more than £30 per annum. Crown and hierarchy hoped to use such benefices to attract learned men into the ministry. In 1573 Bishop Parkhurst of Norwich refused to admit the Earl of Sussex's presentee to the living of Diss because the cleric, John Hilton, had no B.D., licence or dispensation.[2]

When he had chosen his candidate, it was permissible for the patron to present his nominee to the bishop either verbally or in writing. The more formal procedure was preferred by both parties. Having received the presentation, the bishop was required to examine the candidate for his sufficiency within two calendar months and, by the end of that time, either to approve or reject him. Thus 'the right of patronage is really but a limited trust: and the bishops are still in law the judges of the fitness of the persons to be employed in the several parts of their dioceses'. The presentee was tested for fitness according to the minimal requirements of the Church. By 1575 it was technically impossible for a candidate for institution to be younger than 23 years of age, unless he had secured a dispensation. For example, the clerk of the faculties confirmed by letters patent a dispensation granted to Edward Fleetwood 'beinge xviii yeres of age to reteyne one benefice' in 1572 at a fee of £5 6s. 8d. In the same year only six other such licences were granted. Henry Marten, however, was permitted to hold a benefice for three years before receiving orders, on payment of 30s., as was Richard Webb.[3]

The nominee was tested also for his conformity to the laws concerning pluralism. These rules were under constant revision during the sixteenth century; briefly speaking they were designed to ensure that only the more learned clergy held livings in plurality and that, when they did so, the benefices in question were situated sufficiently close together to make their pastoral care feasible. Canons of 1571 ruled that the livings concerned should not be more than 25 miles distant from one another, although subsequent rulings in 1583, 1597 and 1604 extended this distance to 30 miles. These later canons attempted to check possible abuses by stating that only M.A.s and licenced preachers might be granted dispensations to hold in plurality. The livings in question had to be of low value. Strictly speaking, unless a cleric obtained a dispensation to hold an additional living preparatory to institution, he would be deprived of his original living *ipso facto* (as if he had resigned it) notwithstanding subsequent dispensation. Although zealous bishops did proceed in this way, it is evident that, in practice, dispensations were often granted retrospectively by the Archbishop's Court of Faculties and duly confirmed, perhaps some three years after the initial fault. Such licences were quite costly when related to the incumbent's clear yearly income and, in particular, to the quite heavy costs of entering upon a living.[4]

Certainly the standard of learning demanded by law was far from high although the bishop himself decided whether the candidate reached an adequate level of understanding of the Scriptures and of the Latin tongue. Standards could be raised or lowered to meet the requirements of the moment. As the availability of learned men increased during Elizabeth's reign standards were likely to rise far above the minimal demands of the law. A statute of 1562 laid down that knowledge of Welsh was necessary in a clerk serving in Wales. The presentee, by a 1575 canon, had to be willing to subscribe to the 39 Articles and to be able to give an account of them in Latin. John Gosnolde, *hac vice* patron of Gosbeck, diocese of Norwich, tried in 1573 to oust the incumbent of the living on the grounds that he had neglected to read aloud the articles of religion to the parish and was therefore *ipso facto* deprived. On institution to a vicarage the cleric might be required to perform an oath that he had not obtained the presentation through a simoniacal pact. If the candidate for a living had been ordained in a diocese other than that in which he was to be beneficed, he had to produce his letters or orders and letters testimonial before he could be instituted.[5]

The candidate could be refused for a variety of specific causes: broadly speaking, those offences for which an incumbent might be deprived under the canon law. The bishop might reject him for perjury before a judge, forgery, outlawry, simony, excommunication for 40 days, irreligion, heresy or schism, bastardy, age, or manslaughter. Moreoever, the bishop's knowledge of such an offence was sufficient: it was not necessary for the clerk to have been convicted in a court of law.[6]

In theory then the bishop had considerable freedom in examination and judgment of the man presented to him. In practice matters were rather more complicated.

The system was one of checks and counter checks, designed to prevent patrons abusing their privileges and bishops taking advantage of their position as ultimate judges of the sufficiency of ministers. Central to this system was the question of lapse. Left to themselves patrons might fail to fill livings in their gift and leave parishes unserved for many years. To prevent this it was ruled that should the patron not have filled a void benefice within six months of the occurrence of vacancy, the right of presentation to that place was vested in the diocesan. If the diocesan himself failed to present within six months of this falling to his lapse the right of presentation fell to the metropolitan for a further six months. At the end of this time the right of presentation *pro hac vice* belonged to the Crown. This rule applied to all livings but there is some evidence that neither patron nor ordinary was in practice bound to fill very poor livings (below £5 per annum) and that the continued vacancy of such livings was accepted by the hierarchy.[7]

In theory the problem of long-term vacancies in the mass of livings was surmounted. Lapse itself, however, could be, and sometimes was, abused by the bishops. Patrons were well advised to present some time before the six-month term was fulfilled because a bishop who was anxious to prefer his own candidate might well pretend that there was insufficient time to examine the true patron's nominee and thus claim the right of presentation by lapse. Also, should the bishop reject the candidate for unsuitability, the patron would have no time to present anew before the presentation fell into lapse to the bishop. There was a good deal of suspicion that bishops purposely caused livings to fall into their own gift through lapse, and the law courts to which the patrons might appeal for remedy were stern in their treatment of such cases. Contemporaries were well aware of the possibilities inherent in the device. In 1575, for example, the Master of Balliol granted his share of the advowson of St Lawrence Jewry *pro hac vice* to the parishioners but, aware of the possible refusal of the co-patrons, the Fellows, to confirm the grant, he decided to allow the presentation to fall into lapse in that event, because he could persuade the bishop to favour the parishioners' client. The Fellows did object to the grant; the Master allowed the living to fall into lapse; and the bishop did collate the parishioners' nominee.[8]

Safeguards against abuse were formulated. If a bishop failed to notify the patron of a living of its voidance in case of deprivation or resignation, via the registry, he could not claim lapse at the end of six months. When a living was voided for either of these reasons, the six-month period was counted from the date of notification and not from that of vacancy. If the lay patron's candidate were rejected the bishop was supposed to notify the patron by personal letter within 22 days. If this were not done, the bishop could not claim benefit of lapse when the patron did not present afresh. The patron himself, however, was bound to present again within six months of the initial notification of voidance and not of the notification of rejection.

Patrons might seek remedy in questions of patronage in the common law courts – normally in the Court of Common Pleas although the Crown could plead in any court it chose. When a case of *quare impedit* was brought against a bishop for rejecting a candidate or disturbing the right of patronage, the bishop was compelled to give specific cause for his action. For example, if he claimed that the candidate was heretical, he would have to cite the particular heretical opinions of the accused and the metropolitan would be required to pronounce the truth of the accusation. The bishop might well, therefore, have to answer articles in the ecclesiastical courts of appeal, the Court of Arches or the Court of Delegates. On occasion it was the rejected clerk who brought a case against the bishop. In this case the suit was fought from start to finish in the ecclesiastical courts, normally involving proceedings in the Court of Arches.

In 1572 Bishop Parkhurst of Norwich refused admission to one John Norton of Morlay, claimed right of lapse and collated his own candidate, George Gardiner, D.D., to the living. The patron, Owen

Hubbard, brought a *quare impedit* against Parkhurst, whose legal position was complicated. Parkhurst claimed in a reply to articles simultaneously brought in the Court of Arches that Hubbard had presented only three weeks before the living was due to fall into lapse and that the bishop had rejected the candidate not for lack of learning but for being *in famis*. On this issue hung Parkhurst's whole case. The court was suspicious that he had purposely rejected Norton and had omitted to notify Hubbard because of his anxiety to present Gardiner. Parkhurst argued that Hubbard had no right to present a second time to the living. The claim to present anew after an initial rejection rested upon the theory that a lay patron had insufficient expertise to judge a client's learning and that, therefore, such a patron should have a second opportunity for choice. For this reason ecclesiastical patrons, who were expected to be competent judges of qualifications and ability, had no right to second choice. Parkhurst accepted this position but claimed that Norton had been rejected not for lack of learning but for notoriously immoral behaviour which any man should have been aware of and able to condemn. Hubbard, therefore, had no claim to vary his presentation and Parkhurst was not bound to notify the patron of the refusal of his candidate. Guarding himself on all sides, however, Parkhurst purported to have instructed Norton himself to notify his patron of the decision. Parkhurst then observed that Hubbard had presented no further candidate during the six-month period.[9]

If Parkhurst could prove that Norton was truly notorious it would seem that he had a good case. Ecclesiastical patrons were never allowed to vary their presentations whereas lay patrons were allowed to do so if their first candidates were rejected on grounds of inadequate learning. Parkhurst may well have provided a precedent for the view that the lay patron was not permitted variance if his candidate were rejected on other grounds.

One can understand why the lay courts were wary of the bishops' use of presentations during lapse, yet the bishops allowed a huge number of legitimate opportunities to benefit by lapse to pass them by. The Crown was able to present to a large number of livings which had lain vacant for 18 months or longer. This position is to some extent explicable in terms of poor communications, particularly regarding livings vacant through death (the large majority), and the Crown's superior intelligence system as far as its rights went. At times, also, there was a shortage of clients seeking patronage, especially for poor livings. The bishops themselves were probably more keen to present to reasonably endowed livings. The bishop did have ready access to information concerning vacancies caused by resignation and deprivation and, where the livings were desirable, he was anxious to present to them by benefit of lapse. On such occasions he might employ highly dubious methods to ensure that the true patron could not present within six months, whereas he might normally be uninterested in the rights of presentation to other livings long since vacant.[10]

Although technically the bishop could reject a candidate for lack of learning, often he would be hard pressed to justify such an action if it came to court. The requirements of both canon and statute law were, in general, minimal, although particular livings might be reserved for graduates and preachers. Individual bishops in effect set their own standards, dictated partly by their own personal rigour and partly by the contemporary recruitment picture. For instance, in 1574 Bishop Cooper of Lincoln ordained one Thomas Morley as priest 'upon necessitie, although in the holy scriptures unacquainted' and refused to issue letters of orders (permitting institution, in effect) until Morley showed improvement in scriptural learning. In 1576 Morley was presented to a benefice but Cooper denied him institution because further examination had revealed his continued ignorance. Cooper ordered him to study for six months but, as at the end of that period he still proved unsatisfactory, the rectory was given to another. Eventually Morley was instituted to a vicarage within the diocese.[11]

However, for every bishop who was moved to adopt a hard line by the evidence of ignorance and evil living produced in a single case, there must have been many more who heeded the warning of legal process, especially when an influential patron was involved. In 1601 the Bishop of Lincoln denied institution to Shelton vicarage and was rewarded by a *quare impedit* in the civil courts. Bishop Brownrigg of Exeter defended the attitude of the bishops to the problem of the admission on inadequate clerics thus:

> the law of the land hath set that lowness of sufficiency in men to be ordained and instituted, that if the bishop refuseth to give orders or institution to a man presented by the patron, he is punishable by the judges: As I have heard, Archbishop Abbot was fined an hundred pounds in case he did not admit a clerk so meanly qualified as the law requires.[12]

Often no case was pressed or a suit (*duplex querela*) was brought by the clerk concerned in the ecclesiastical courts alone, where the bishop was perhaps more likely to triumph. Even then the candidate had the advantage in that he was merely required to fulfil the letter of the law. It was presumably to the bishop's advantage to reject the cleric on grounds of simony or immorality. When Thomas Atkinson brought a case of *duplex querela* against Parkhurst for refusing him admission to a second benefice, Parkhurst provided good proof that Atkinson was an 'ignorant asse'. He felt it necessary also to suggest that Atkinson was a papist and chosen as such by a popish patron.[13]

How common were suits brought by the patrons on behalf of particular clients rather than to protect their own rights of advowson? Cases of *duplex querela* were probably common enough but how often were they backed by causes of *quare impedit* sued in the common law courts? A patron would perhaps desist from legal action unless his right of patronage itself was being contested or disturbed. On 15 June 1574 Edmund Willock, pretended Rector of Hawton near Newark, diocese of York, was cited to appear as a result of a suit of *quare impedit* filed at Westminster by the patron, Francis Mollineux, Esquire. On 21 June Willock was deprived following a writ of the Court of Common Pleas and Mollineux was ordered to present. The court made it clear that his original nominee had been found totally unsuitable by examination and that he must vary his presentation, presenting a fit person. On 12 August 1574 Mollineux's new presentee, the Archdeacon of Nottingham, was instituted. Clearly Mollineux had brought the case not in defence of his client but of his own advowson. A similar conclusion can be drawn from the Parkhurst/Hubbard case. The patron felt peculiarly sensitive because the right of advowson was so easily obscured. It seems reasonable to suppose that the majority of patrons suing *quare impedit* did so when their own *jus patronatus* was being contested, either by the bishop independently or by a pretended patron. The absence of anything but fragmentary records for the Courts of Arches or of Common Pleas make such hypotheses difficult to test, but they seem reasonable in the light of current knowledge about the operation of the patronage system.[14]

Disputes about the whereabouts of *jus patronatus* doubtless arose most frequently out of the system of grants of next presentation employed by the advowson holders themselves. Owners of advowsons who did not wish to use an opportunity to present might sell or simply grant the right to present to a particular living for one time or specified number of times only. Other conditions might be imposed upon the use of the grant. Normally the transaction was carefully documented and recorded in the diocesan registry, thus protecting the patron in his ultimate ownership of the advowson. Confusion could and did arise when the advowson concerned changed hands.

The period after the dissolution of the monasteries is particularly notable for the large number of cases of contested patronage. Sometimes it was unclear whether the advowsons possessed by a monastic house had been sold or granted simultaneously with the monastic lands. More often, it was a question of whether grants of next presentation made by the religious houses before the dissolution were still valid against the claims of the new owners of the advowsons. As Dr Molly Barratt has pointed out, the religious houses had led the field in granting away rights of first and next presentation, the period prior to 1539 witnessing the largest number of such grants. Examples from Coventry and Lichfield are indicative of some of the ensuing struggles over patronage. For instance, in October 1562 William Leighton and John Braine entered a *caveat* against anyone else presenting to the living of Nestrange, Salop, claiming a grant of next presentation to the living (now in the Crown's possession) from the Abbot of Shrewsbury some 36 years previously on 1 March 1526. In October 1562, however, Robert Poyner came forward and claimed a later grant from the abbot, dated November 1536, and successfully presented John Powell, *litteratus*, to the living. The Crown, true patron, first presented in 1586. Sometimes the *de iure* patron was able to defeat such claims: this was apparently true of the living of Moreton Corbet, Salop. In May 1562 Robert Allein claimed the next presentation by grant from the Abbot of Haughmond, but in April 1563 it was the Crown which made the presentation.[15]

Complications sometimes arose when a rectory was leased by a lay rector who was also *de iure* patron: George Clerkson, farmer of the rectory of Walsall, Staffordshire, claimed that he was patron of the living during the term of the lease; the lay Rector, Thomas Wylbarne, Esquire, contested this view with a *caveat* in the same year of 1567. Apparently the living fell in lapse to the bishop in 1568. This case was probably made the more difficult because it had once been appropriate to the abbey of Halesowen.[16]

When a patron heard of a vacancy in a living which he controlled he was well advised to enter a *caveat* in the diocesan registry. This constituted a claim to the right of presentation and a warning to the ordinary not to admit the candidate of any other claimant without search to discover the true whereabouts of patronage. A *caveat* had to be entered after voidance had occurred: it was invalid if entered during an incumbency. It had no force of law, in that the registration of the *caveat* itself did not nullify subsequent proceedings. But a bishop was very ill-advised to admit a candidate if he knew that some other person was also claiming the right to present a client to the living involved and had registered a *caveat*. At this point the bishop should sue a case of *jus patronatus* in the consistory court to discover where patronage lay. The cost would be borne by either or both of the claimants. The diocesan could try such a case himself but nor-mally issued a commission for the trial. A jury of at least six clerics and six laymen (with a quorum of this number) was set up to decide the case. The decision of this jury was accepted by the judge and was binding, so that the bishop proceeded to institute and induct the man favoured by their verdict. But the issue might be further complicated if a third party, not represented in this suit, had been instituted meanwhile to the living involved.

The proceedings of *jus patronatus* commissions have rarely survived. The commissioners sat outside the consistory courts and recorded their proceedings in loose papers. It is worthwhile therefore to quote in detail one such case. On 22 April 1575 there was a double presentation to Sutton Magna rectory, Essex. On the death of the incumbent, Stephen Cawston, both Lord Robert Ryches and Isaac Wyott had presented their clients to the rectory. On 17 June 1575 the Bishop of London, Sandys, inaugurated a process of inquiry by six clerical and six lay 'jurates' and a commissioner sitting in the church of Sutton Magna. Public notice of the commission was to be given. The court was to sit on 6 July 1575, to call witnesses by citation, and to certify its decisions to the consistory court. Seven articles were answered by the jury on the basis of the evidence supplied to the court. It was thus established in what manner the advowson of Sutton was owned and by whom, and whether the true patron had made grants of next presentation to the rectory which might affect the current situation. In this instance the advowson was owned by two people: Isaac Wyott (who owned two portions of the advowson and claimed the right to present on two consecutive occasions in every three); and Mr Coverte (owner of the third part). Apparently Coverte had made a grant of presentation to Lord Riches who was now claiming the right to present. Wyott, however, through lack of contrary evidence, won the case on the grounds that he had not yet presented for the second time. His client was duly instituted just under a month later.[17]

If a bishop did not initiate a case of *jus patronatus* before instituting a candidate whose patron's right was unclear, he put himself in danger of proceedings by *quare impedit*. This was especially true when *caveats* had been entered. In such cases the bishop might be proved to be a disturber or hinderer of the lapse should the common law courts find against his decision. In fact, the bishops attempted to safeguard themselves against unnecessary and cumbersome legal proceedings by frequent employment of bonds. It was Parkhurst's view that it was not incumbent upon the ordinary to search the whereabouts of patronage unless he had due cause for suspicion, occasioned by a *caveat* to the contrary or evidence of a simoniacal pact. Otherwise the client was asked to take out several bonds. One of these would bind him to resign the living immediately if *jus patronatus* was found to exist with someone other than his patron. Another would commit him to automatic resignation if simony were proved against either him or his patron. A bishop who was not satisfied by the calibre of the candidate but loath to risk legal suit by rejecting him might enforce a bond compelling the clerk to study and produce certificate of his improvement in learning or to be deprived *ipso facto*.[18]

Conditional measures of this kind were very necessary for both bishops and patrons alike. The patron who was aggrieved might bring either a *jus patronatus* or a *quare impedit* and might in either case secure acknowledgement of his superior right of patronage. A *quare impedit* could not be sued for six calendar months following the vacancy. If the church had been filled for a period of six months, the patron who won the case (unless it be the Crown) could not oust the *de facto* incumbent. The remedy had merely ensured that the true patron's title was not prejudiced in any way in the future. However, the existence of a bond might well make recovery of the presentation possible if the ordinary wished to enforce its terms. If the living involved was still vacant, of course, the successful patron might have a writ issued to the bishop to present his candidate.[19]

The operation of patronage in the sixteenth and seventeenth centuries was complicated by the uneasy relationship between spiritual and temporal authorities. To the patron, however religious, the right of advowson was a treasured property right. To the spiritual authorities it was often just one more obstacle to true control of Church personnel. Apathy of individual bishops and poverty of communication alone dampened this fervour on the part of the hierarchy to achieve control. Nevertheless, an intricate system of checks and balances was required to maintain the temporal rights of patrons and the spiritual claims of the hierarchy. To make matters yet more involved, the right of advowson was often disputed amongst patrons, and bishops found themselves in the position of arbiters of patronage rights. Even if bishops were not actively contesting in their own interests the claims of a patron, they had to tread warily and be careful to admit no-one to a living without proof of his patron's rights or the protection of a bond. There can be little doubt that the bishops were generally at a disadvantage when it came to contesting directly or by-passing the choices made by other patrons, but the law of patronage also gave them rights of which the more energetic and determined on the episcopal bench could and did take advantage.

If the Church were to be fully reformed by the bishops (rather than by laymen) then such a situation was clearly unsatisfactory. The bishops needed a free hand to reform the Church's personnel at all levels and remould the clerical profession according to the continental model. The patronage system as it stood forbade thoroughgoing reform of this type. A determined bishop could use his rights to deny the very unsuitable places in the Church but he could not control recruitment to benefices on his own initiative in the ordinary course of events.

7

The puritans and patronage

Almost all the work which has been done on the operation of the patronage system in the early modern English Church has been connected with research into English Protestantism and, more specifically, puritanism. Some have seen puritan laymen making a concerted effort to succeed where the bishops were doomed to fail in completing the English Reformation by reforming the clergy. Dr Cross said that her 'study of the patronage of one member of the group, the third earl of Huntingdon, illustrates how militant Protestantism could be injected into the Church'. But taken overall it now seems unlikely that more than a fraction of the patronage exercised was governed consciously by a desire to further a religious movement. There is little evidence of a highly organized and widespread movement on the part of puritan patrons to reform the clergy – whether by purchasing blocs of advowsons or numbers of grants of next presentation. The puritan lay desire to use the patronage system to 'inject protestantism' into the Church was blocked by the ramifications of the patronage system in much the same way as was the episcopate's attempt. Advowsons were regarded as property by even the most ardent Protestants. The right to present to a living was seen as part of the wider web of patronage (or clientage) in society as a whole. Relatives, friends, servants and protégés all had claims upon the lay patron's resources. Even so, it must be admitted that the fraction of ecclesiastical patronage in the hands of active puritans was an extremely important fraction. It is vital that we should assess the impact of this patronage upon the composition of the profession at the parochial level.[1]

Over the country as a whole it appears that puritan patrons were markedly active in certain areas only. The work of Dr Barratt on Oxfordshire, Worcestershire and Gloucestershire directly contradicts Roland Usher's earlier contention that puritan patrons were purposely buying up blocs of patronage in an organized attempt to place puritan ministers in the parishes of England. But no-one would contest Usher's claim that in some dioceses and archdeaconries puritan patrons were in a position to introduce puritan clerics into the churches which they already controlled and to support them against episcopal action. The Earl of Warwick controlled many livings in Warwickshire, Northamptonshire, Leicestershire, Suffolk and Essex. Within the archdeaconry of Sudbury, Essex, Sir Robert Jermyn, Drew Drury and Lady Kydson, all ardent puritans, had the *de iure* right to present to some 23 livings between them. In Northamptonshire Sir Richard Knightley, Sir Edward Mountague and Sir Francis Hastings were leading patrons.

The position could change within a diocese: in parts of Coventry and Lichfield there was little evidence of a lay puritan movement and no single lay or ecclesiastical patron dominated the scene. There were, nevertheless, puritan enclaves: although there were no really large blocs of lay patronage, several patrons possessed small groups of advowsons which could be used to advantage in the puritan cause. Sir Francis Leeke, Baron Deincourt, held five livings in Derby archdeaconry and employed his patronage to prefer puritan clergy. Other patrons with a similar level of influence in the diocese were Sir Philip Stanhope, Earl of Chesterfield; the puritan earls of Pembroke; the Earl of Devonshire; the Earl of Bridgewater; and the Leveson, Corbett and Screvin families. Yet, in general, patronage was much fragmented in this large diocese, with the Crown possessing the largest bloc. However, it was not necessarily the scale of ownership which mattered most – the number of opportunities for the actual exercise of patronage was of far more significance for the enthusiastic patron. William, Viscount Mansfield, later Earl of Newcastle, for example, owned one advowson only in the diocese but presented to it no less than four times in six years. The puritan Leighs of Ruchall, Staffordshire, possessed two advowsons and presented twice to one of them, Hampstall Ridware, in the same period. Thus the patronage of Newcastle was as important during the period 1626–32 as that of someone who seemed far more influential on paper: for example, Sir Francis Leeke or Richard Leveson of Salop. A patron who never had an opportunity to present to the living in his gift was of little use to any movement.[2]

If puritan patrons did not control the majority of benefices (or even in some cases a large minority of them) their patronage was still extremely significant because the men whom they sponsored were by their very nature controversial; they were, in the eyes of the hierarchy, troublemakers *par excellence* and, moreover, they formed part of a 'brotherhood', an organized movement for reform which made them a force to be reckoned with even when their total numbers were small. Even if the bishop sympathized with puritan aims, he was on occasion forced by official instructions to discipline puritan ministers and sometimes to go as far as to deprive them of their livings. Moreover, the puritan clergy were *effective* troublemakers because they had the support of socially significant men whom the Church could not discipline and who, contradictorily, were often favoured at court. In Elizabeth's reign, Leicester, Warwick, Bedford and Huntingdon formed a powerful quartet of patrons furthering the Reformed Church cause. Some of this patronage was indirect. John Aylmer, once tutor to Lady Jane Grey, addressed a letter to Leicester asking for his support in acquiring the deanery of Durham, in the Crown's gift 'since Mr. Horne is sped of his bishopric'. Later Leicester and Warwick used their combined influence to persuade the queen to grant the deanery of Durham to William Whittingham, an acknowledged Genevan. Bishops Grindal, Horne, Sandys, Pilkington and Scambler all felt obliged to Leicester and it was commonly felt that Thomas Young, Archbishop of York, owed his promotion to him. It can be argued that an episcopal bench drawn from among the Protestant exiles was, under the circumstances, inevitable unless Elizabeth really scraped the barrel, yet it was surely a significant achievement in the light of future developments to ensure a bench of bishops so sympathetic to early puritanism. In the early years of Elizabeth's reign the puritan earls and exiled bishops were commanding a good deal of the patronage in the Crown's own gift in an attempt to secure a worthy ministry and they were working in reasonable accord. Often this meant that the entire upper echelons of a diocesan administration were in the hands of ardent Protestants. Grindal managed to secure four out of five archeaconries in London diocese, the chancellorship and some minor offices for fellow-exiles. The Dean of St Paul's and several of the chapter were also drawn from this group. In Coventry and Lichfield, Thomas Bentham, himself an exile, governed his diocese with the help of Thomas Lever, Archdeacon of Coventry, and the advice of other exiled bishops. The defeat of Grindalian churchmanship in the mid-1570s, with all its many implications for lay/clerical co-operation in reforming the ministry, can be regarded as extremely important for the history of the clerical profession in England.[3]

The puritan earls favoured some who were more truly troublemakers. John Field, for instance, was shielded by Leicester. Anthony Gilby, Thomas Wyddowes and Arthur Hildersham – all ministers at Ashby-de-la-Zouch, Leicestershire – were under Huntingdon's patronage. Ashby, in Dr Cross's words, had become 'the headquarters for the reform of the Church within the county and beyond' under Gilby's influence. Within their own direct spheres of control (the counties in which their lands or offices were situated and the court) the direct patronage of puritanism by the earls is evident. The Earl of Warwick, for example, petitioned the lord keeper on behalf of several clients when he had no personal patronage that he could offer – but this was in areas where he already held sway. Outside such regions, however, the situation was quite different. Huntingdon exploited to the full his opportunities for direct patron-

age in Leicestershire and, while President of the Council of the
North, in Yorkshire. He was also interested in the religious situation
in the diocese of Chester – despite the fact that the two palatine
counties were outside his jurisdiction. He was, however, a member
of the High Commission of the North which had jurisdiction in
Chester. He viewed the situation in Lancashire as crucial to the future
of Protestantism in the north – how could the commission enforce
the Reformation in Yorkshire, Cheshire and Nottinghamshire if
Lancashire remained the haunt of recusancy? In 1575 Huntingdon
combined with Grindal to attack the Chester mystery plays and in
1582 he recommended to the Bishop of Chester that lectureships be
founded in the diocese, but apart from this he could do little except
proffer advice – solicited or unsolicited – because he had no patronage rights in the area.

The evidence suggests that whereas aristocratic patronage of puritanism was extremely important at the top (where, for instance,
promotion to sees, archdeaconries, deaneries, or chancellorships was
concerned), the aristocrats had a more regionally limited patronage
when it came to the rank and file of the clergy. The distribution of
patronage rights had been dictated by chance rather than by a grand
design. For this reason, it was normally a local magnate who exercised most direct *de iure* patronage within a county. If this patron
happened to be an enthusiast for one religious position or another,
then this cause would inevitably be furthered in that region without
significant intervention from the aristocratic leaders of the Reformed
party who had a more important role nationally. It was only because
the aristocracy often had geographically more widely diversified
landed interests and advowsons that they seemed to dominate several counties.[4]

Dr Richardson discovered that in Chester diocese aristocratic
influence on the personnel of the Church was relatively slight. The
earls of Derby, although not puritan, were anti-Catholic and furthered the careers of several preachers of puritan persuasion. The
fourth earl, for example, invited puritan preachers to preach sermons
before him regularly. There is no evidence, however, that the Stan-
leys, earls of Derby, were deeply involved in lay puritanism within
the diocese. Dr Richardson concluded that gentry and merchant
patronage of puritanism was far more significant within the area and
it may be so that this was true of many other regions of the country.
He pointed out, however, that the cause was furthered less by the
judicious use of rights of presentation, *de iure* or *pro hac vice*, than by
gifts of money. Professor Jordan calculated that the Lancashire gentry gave over a fifth of that county's charitable funds and that a tenth
of the gifts made by the lesser gentry were designed for religious
uses. Richard Blackburn, puritan landowner of Newton-le-

Willows, in 1615 bequeathed £400 to endow a preacher at Newton. Other gentlemen founded and endowed chapelries or renovated existing ones. John Bruen of Stapleford, Cheshire, rigorously supervised the worship of his church, providing preachers when the incumbent was old and decrepit, presenting puritan clergymen to the place, stripping the church building of relics of popery and setting up in his house 'a miniature religious community' and 'puritan seminary' with widespread influence.[5]

Merchant patronage also had its place in the diocese. Thomas Aldersey contrived to introduce puritanism to the Cheshire parish of Bunbury by purchasing the tithes of the parish in 1594 and using them to endow a preachership and curacy which were relatively immune to diocesan interference. The London Company of Haberdashers acted as trustees to administer the benefice of Bunbury on Aldersey's death. In almost every case the clergy appointed to both posts were puritans and all were educated to at least M.A. degree level, in compliance with Aldersey's will. In the early seventeenth century the London merchant community appears to have been devoting more and more attention to the religious situation in their native counties. Jordan estimated that London merchants donated £29,000 to Lancashire charities but noted that the donors were largely natives of the county. In 1641 George Walker directed his *Exhortation for Contributions to Maintain Preachers in Lancashire* to these very members of the London merchant community. Support for Lancashire puritanism also came from local merchants and tradesmen. At the same time there was considerable financial support for individual puritan preachers in Lancashire from women.[6] In Lancashire one can see that lay patrons were instrumental in emphasizing one aspect of the clerical function – that of preaching, above all the mark of the Protestant ministry and, increasingly, the mark of the new profession.

In other counties where gentry patronage of the puritan movement was predominant the use of advowsons to promote the cause was more important, however. Dr William Sheils has made this very clear in his study of the puritan gentry in Peterborough diocese. In early 1573 the chancellor of the diocese was diligently rooting out evidence of clerical puritanism in Peterborough and thereby alienating a considerable body of opinion. He succeeded in depriving five incumbents from the Northampton area. However, 'having removed the offending clerics from their livings, the courts still could not undermine the local influence of the puritans in the face of strong support from all sectors of society in the area'. The diocesan could not prevent the same patrons presenting puritan clerics yet again to the livings in question. And of the five deprived, four continued to work in the area. Similarly, in the seventeenth century diocesan officials made a concerted effort to enforce the canons of 1604 and 16 puritan clerics were deprived, but gentry support of the cause which the government was seeking to suppress defeated the diocesan plan. Although individual puritans suffered as a result of deprivation, in several cases the patron responded by supplying yet another puritan clergyman to the vacated living.

An older generation of puritan clerics was being supplanted by a newer, more radical group of men. The bishops of Peterborough were attacking the wrong section of the puritan movement – had they been able to defeat the gentry puritan patrons, then and only then would they have stood a chance of stamping out the cause. As it was, puritanism suffered only a very temporary setback at the time; individual clerical careers rather than the movement were affected. Why was this allowed to happen? During the sixteenth century the bishops of Peterborough were unable to prosecute the puritan gentry in the ecclesiastical courts, for fear of social consequences. Thus in 1591 Bishop Howland stood by, helpless, while Margaret Fosbrooke presented William Kitchin, an outright nonconformist and non-subscriber, to the living of Cranbrook St Andrew. The situation in Peterborough diocese indicates that where patrons *en masse* were dedicated to a particular cause, even if they had not directly purchased large numbers of advowsons to advance it, and were uncontrolled by the ecclesiastical authorities, they could give effective support to a puritan clergy even against the determined action of the ecclesiastical courts. A cleric might be deprived for non-conformity but the courts could not deprive the patron of his right to present – this was the root of the bishop's problem, and it also had a marked effect upon the character of the profession.[7]

Once again this points to the conclusion that the chance distribution of patronage rights within an area was of crucial importance to the religious complexion of its clergy. In 1579, 42 of the 81 advowsons in the archdeaconry of Chichester were still remaining in the hands of the Crown or hierarchy. This in itself may have been a factor contributing to the relative freedom of West Sussex from puritanism. In contrast, by 1603, 63 of the 79 patrons in Lewes archdeaconry were laymen and here puritanism had a numerically stronger hold. However, the chance distribution of *de iure* patronage rights could be mitigated significantly by the system of granting away presentations to petitioners. This would seem to contradict Dr Seaver's contention that where advowsons were not owned by puritan laymen 'the established Church provided no mechanism by which Puritans could satisfy their demands, even if the influential laity of the parish were Puritan'. It would certainly be unwise to leap to the conclusion that few lay advowsons meant little or no clerical puritanism in an area. Moreover, many clergy of broadly puritan persuasion were probably preferred by patrons who had little or no interest in their cause. This meant that puritanism within some areas was essentially clerical in character (without the close ties with the gentry puritans exhibited in Lancashire, Northamptonshire, or East Anglia) and therefore much less secure against hierarchical threats, and more dependent upon the ability of the individual clerics to avoid episcopal censure.[8]

The puritan goal lay in true reformation of the Church on the continental model and the provision of a worthy, preaching ministry. When, after the consecration of John Whitgift as Archbishop of Canterbury in 1583, the official policy of the hierarchy was to deny the need for further reformation and to content itself with supplying a well-educated and conforming clergy, it became clear to lay puritans that their goal would not be achieved through institutional channels. This was true despite the sympathy of many of the bishops and other Church officials towards their views. Moreover, the distribution of patronage was such that control over the quality of the ministry was only truly possible on a regular basis in some areas. Until sufficient provision was made for the education of puritan ministers and until adequate income was offered to those following a clerical career, even command of patronage would not ensure such a ministry.

The outstanding example of puritan appreciation of this dilemma and of the link between patronage and adequately remunerated pastoral care is that evinced by the activities of the Feoffees for Impropriations. At the first recorded meeting of the 13 feoffees on 15 April 1626 they drew up articles to direct their work. The first of these provided that 'if any monys lands or tenements be hereafter given to them, the same shalbe imployed for and towards the purchasing of Impropriations for the meynteynance of the preaching of the word of God'. Impropriations had been acquired and returned to the livings concerned before this but the feoffees made no attempt to follow this example: they would use the revenue of the properties that fell into their hands to maintain a godly, preaching ministry but they determined to 'select and control the recipients of their benevolence'.

Similar projects had been suggested for the buying up of impropriations both by puritans and hierarchy: for example, in 1610 Bancroft had outlined such a scheme, and in 1620 a project had been mooted for using taxes and subsidies to buy in impropriations at between eight and ten years' purchase. In the hands of the hierarchy such projects would be turned to increasing the independence of the clergy *vis à vis* the laity – something far from the minds of the feoffees. The feoffees were tackling the problem piecemeal, using such monies as fell into their hands to buy impropriations and advowsons. London preachers strove to persuade the rich and pious of the city to donate sums of money to the cause. Between 1625 and 1633 some £6,361 6s. 1d. was contributed to the fund to increase the stipends of the St Antholin lecturers; real estate was bought by or bequeathed to the feoffees in fourteen counties; and in 1633 the group held 31 church properties and patronage in some 18 counties. Approximately 10 per cent of the income was devoted to augmentation of livings or establishment of lectureships. The feoffees were charged with supporting financially ejected ministers and their families. The authorities claimed that they also preferred to appoint curates or lecturers to their livings rather than vicars who would have been subject to episcopal approval and control. It was clear that far from seeking to make the clergy concerned more independent of lay influence the feoffees were determined to increase the control of the laity over the clerical profession and its activities.[9]

The members of the original group included four merchants, four lawyers and four ministers. Of the 16 members eventually involved in its work, 7 had been adventurers in the Massachusetts Bay Company, one (John Davenport) had been intimately involved with their affairs, and two had been members of the Providence Island Company. Three of the clergymen who were feoffees, Richard Sibbes, John Davenport and William Gouge, were also actively engaged in enlisting financial support for persecuted Protestants in the Rhine palatinate. Three of the lawyers were politically active and ardently puritan. In such a company one would not expect to find much support for an independent clergy of the type desired by Archbishop Laud.

The activities of the feoffees in the diocese of Coventry and Lichfield are of some interest, for here was an area where puritan patronage was not noticeably effective outside a few urban centres. In 1628, for instance, the advowson of St Alkmund's, Shrewsbury, was given to the feoffees by one of their number, Rowland Heylin. By the terms of a gift of Sir William Whitmore, the feoffees controlled the nomination of a preacher or curate at Bridgnorth and Claverley in 1629. In the same year the group bought the right of next presentation to St Martin's, Birmingham, for £100. The advowson to the vicarage of Neen Savage, Shropshire, was purchased for £80 in 1630; in addition the feoffees secured the right to nominate and maintain a curate and a schoolmaster at Kinver, Staffordshire. In 1631 the feoffees added to their list of advowsons those of Mayfield and Mainstone, Staffordshire, the latter at a cost of some £500. The feoffees, of course, had no power to deprive the ministers already serving these cures, however much they may have disapproved of them, although they could control the personnel of lectureships, curacies and schools. Certainly, they had no opportunity to present to St Alkmund's, where Thomas Lloyd was ensconced from 1607 until the end of our period. On 7 March the feoffees, represented by Rowland Heylin (who had previously been co-patron of the living), were able to present the puritan hymn writer, William Barton, to the living of Mayfield. The feoffees supported a preacher at Bridgnorth and a curate at Claverley. The former appears to have been one Thomas Wymall, who was later silenced by Bishop Robert Wright, and who seems to have preached until 1639, drawing parishioners from nearby parishes. John Cross, their preacher at Kinver, also attracted hearers from neighbouring parishes. Perhaps the most notable puritan receiving their patronage was Julius Herring, or Hearing, lecturer at Shrewsbury, who was eventually forced to leave England for Amsterdam after continual conflict with the Church courts.

It is true that in several cases the feoffees acquired patronage which was already held by men of puritan convictions; however, the feoffees as a group had several great advantages. They were able to mobilize puritan finance to further the cause in areas where there were no puritan patrons or where livings were too poor to support adequate ministers; they were, therefore, able to by-pass the benefice and concentrate upon the foundation and support of lectureships, when they were unable to buy advowsons. No matter where their impropriations lay, be it Buckinghamshire or Devonshire, they were at liberty to finance lectureships in entirely different areas if that was where the most need lay. Finally, as a group, and a London-based one at that, they had contacts with the cream of the puritan clergy and preachers and had a better idea of who was worthy of preferment than the local patron perhaps had. The efforts of the feoffees were doomed to failure, however, once the attention of the Laudian hierarchy was drawn to them. Yet for us their activities have an importance which is quite out of proportion to their actual impact upon the profession, because they show that puritan laymen were interested not only in improving the quality of the profession in Protestant terms but also in retaining continuing control over the clergy.

Organizations reaching the level of sophistication of the Feoffees for Impropriations were far from common. For the most part puritan patrons attempted to tackle the problem posed by the 'but halfly reformed' Church of England in a piecemeal fashion. One of the most perceptive studies of puritanism at the local level has been that of Dr Sheils who attempts to demonstrate the workings of puritan patronage in the diocese of Peterborough. Within the diocese the laity owned half of the direct patronage rights; the universities and ecclesiastical officials controlled only 8.4 per cent; the Crown and the lord keeper excercised the remaining patronage. The patronage in the hands of laymen 'generally followed the landowner pattern . . .

so that there was no great overlord of church livings in Peterborough diocese'. Within Rutland the two supreme patrons were the Cecils and the Harringtons, who each controlled seven advowsons. Both families used this patronage to support a puritan ministry of a moderate variety in the county. In Northamptonshire no one man controlled this much patronage. In the mid-county a group of Catholic gentry controlled several livings but their influence was balanced by that of the Mildmays and Mountagues, who owned eight advowsons between them. In the west of the county Sir Richard Knightley owned four advowsons, and used them to provide the radical focus for puritanism in the area. Most of the remaining patronage in the region was fragmented: the lord owned the advowson to his local church. In the east of the county patronage was similarly widely distributed. There was again some recusant strength. Informal co-operation between the families of Mildmay, Zouche, Lynne and Fitzwilliam provided a small nucleus of puritan clergy. As Dr Sheils stresses, this co-operation did not 'imply an organised attempt to implant puritan clerics but rather the natural friendship among like-minded neighbours'. On occasion puritans would make it their business to commend a puritan cleric to a neighbouring non-puritan patron who had a vacant living available. Thus in 1596 the puritan Henry Bourne (Browne) was presented to East Haddon by the *de iure* patron, Sir William Hatton, a man of no puritan views. Bourne made it clear that he had won the appointment through the efforts of Sir Richard Knightley, Mr Tate and Mr Tanfield. The importance of this web of local connection in the patronage system is most apparent, yet the web itself is invisible to the naked eye. Such utilization of social bonds could outweigh the surface disadvantages of little direct patronage. Dr Sheils demonstrates convincingly the manner in which active puritan patrons established a puritan nucleus among the clergy, the leaven in the lump, who proceeded to recruit other members of the clerical body to their cause.[10]

Individual patronage case studies tend to emphasize the degree of real control which the puritan patron sought to exercise over his protégé as a matter of course. There were all over the country patrons who went to considerable lengths to find worthy ministers for the benefices which they controlled. For example, Sir John Coke maintained a country residence at Melbourne, Derbyshire and he controlled the living even though he did not hold the advowson in his own right. He was particularly careful when filling the living, perhaps because he expected the incumbent to serve as household chaplain to the Coke family also. The cure fell vacant in 1639 upon the death of Richard Jones. The advowson belonged not to Coke but to the Bishop of Carlisle – Melbourne had ancient connections with that see, having acted as a convenient base to which the bishops could retire south of the Trent during troublesome times on the northern border – a connection borne witness to by Melbourne's fine Norman church, a veritable cathedral. In late 1639 Coke wrote to Thomas Morton, once his diocesan and now Bishop of Durham, asking for the nomination of a suitable successor to Richard Jones. Both Coke and Morton had been Calvinist spokesmen at the York House Conference. Morton obliged, giving the name of Richard Lowe, then serving a cure in Durham diocese. Coke accepted the nomination and presented Lowe. Hearing of Coke's action, the Bishop of Carlisle immediately wrote asserting his ownership of the advowson. He did not, however, object to Coke nominating a pastor for Melbourne, as Coke later explained to his son John. But Coke, wary of the volatile policies of many bishops and other patrons regarding their patronage rights, and appreciating the importance of a legal presentation in this context, told his son, 'I think, for Mr Loe's security, it will also be fit to have presentation from the bishop, which I will procure with speed'.[11]

At this time, Lowe had already been living in Coke's household for over a month and evidently proved a great comfort to the family. He was well loved by Coke's son and daughter-in-law, Elizabeth, who resided at Melbourne during Coke the elder's absences at court and for whose education in religion Coke had selected Lowe. Coke bestowed gifts of money and clothing on Lowe. He was anxious, however, that the attention of the ecclesiastical authorities in the diocese (now ruled by the Laudian Robert Wright) be not attracted to his new puritan protégé and he instructed his son accordingly: 'Yet let mee advise you not to cry him up too loud, that they eys of our churchmen bee not cast upon him, who can not indure anie confluence to those that go not in their idel way.' He had good reason to be wary: early in 1636 an office case had been brought in the consistory court against Richard Jones, the last incumbent, for nonconformity in respect of ceremonial. Jones had confessed that he had offended in the same way for the past ten years or so but promised to reform his ways.[12]

Coke's supervision of Lowe's ministry during the early days at Melbourne was quite intensive. Letters between the elder Coke and his son during December and January 1639/40 were often concerned with Lowe. The new minister himself was anxious to declare his intention of pursuing an active pastoral ministry. Coke became very worried by Lowe's extreme dedication to study, fearing for the cleric's health, but he encouraged his interests and those of his son by promising to provide 'any special books' which they might need for their studies.[13]

From the correspondence we gain an impression of a patron who sincerely wished to appoint a learned and diligent pastor to his home living and who was willing to foster his ministry in practical ways. The letters conjure up a picture of a vicar, living in a vicarage but a stone's throw away from the hall; provided with all the necessities of life and learning by his patron; and executing a ministry in the parish which found ardent support and direction from amongst the occupants of the hall, who strove to prevent the diocesan officials from discovering and curbing his activities. Meanwhile young master and chaplain together studied the Scriptures night after night, working with books provided by the patron.

Lowe's ministry at Melbourne, however, was of but short duration for he died within a year of his appointment – sometime in the summer of 1640. In August 1640 Coke wrote to Bishop Wright of Coventry and Lichfield, apparently greatly agitated by the news that Carlisle had presented a cleric named Goodwin to the living:

> Mr Lowe, our worthy vicar of Melbourne being dead I hear that one Goodwin, a man unworthy to succeed him, boasteth that he hath gotten a presentation from the Lord Bishop of Carlisle. I have therefore written both to his Lordship and to the Lord Bishop of Durham, my old friend, upon whose recommendation I nominated Mr Lowe, and expect every day to receive answer from them both. My request to your Lordship is that if Goodwin bring any such presentation to your Lordship you will be pleased to make stay of his institution and induction till I hear from the Lord Bishops; who I know when they are truly informed will not put upon us such a man as is here known to be incapable of the charge of so many souls, and besides without my help and assistance cannot find this poor vicarage for his turn.

Whereas Coke could not legally bar an unwelcome candidate from entering Melbourne, should the patron persist in his action he could and would withdraw all financial assistance and make life nigh on impossible for the presentee. It is not known how many livings were dependent upon local worthies for financial solvency but this type of arrangement may have been prevalent and could account for the apparent control which some non-advowson holders exercised over presentations.[14] Coke was determined that the next vicar of the parish should be someone with whose doctrinal and ceremonial position he was in sympathy – someone fit to be Coke's personal chaplain.

Evidently Coke's scarcely veiled threat brought success, for he offered the living to John Jemmat, a rising Essex preacher, in late August or early September 1640. He had offered Jemmat the same terms as Lowe had commanded, including financial assistance. Jemmat, however, asserted that there was 'just reason' for him not accepting the living.

First I am told by many that the roade is very dangerous, especially for ministers. Secondly I understand the living is of a very low value, not above 30li per annum, the double whereof would never yet keepe my house. And although I doubt not but that your Honour, your sonn and daughters would be helpfull, yet I conceive it wilbe noe wisdeom for me to remove from the sight of my kinred & ancient acquaintance to setle amongst them that are strangers unto me, where the meanes of mayntenance are in themselves incompetent and the accessions only arbitrary, so that when my charge is certaine my meanes shalbe uncertaine . . .

Jemmat desired independence and familiar surroundings so much that he accepted a lectureship in Essex shortly after hearing from Coke. (It is interesting that he chose this course in preference to that of a benefice, especially in the light of Professor Curtis's comments about the feelings of insecurity and resentment among lecturers.)

I accepted employment under another at Epping in Essex, where I am much desyred to continew both by the vicar and parishioners, who promise me 60li a yeare certaine besydes other things that will accrue. And they pleade that yf I come from them they have no hope to get one into the place that wilbe faithfull but a patron of a benefice hath his free choyer all the kingdom over . . . it's time to settle my familie somewhere after my long distractions, and I must confess I am somewhat affrayd to come so farr North with my wife and children at such a tyme of common danger, in winterly weather and where we have our acquaintance yet for to make.[15]

Here Coke was again supporting the advance of puritanism in Melbourne while being equally concerned to provide himself with a chaplain. Jemmat had been preacher at Berwick for three years when he was accused of sedition and removed from the lectureship in late 1639. His ministry had been exceedingly zealous. Secretary Windebanke had ordered Bishop Morton to dimiss Jemmat in the king's name. At this point Coke heard of the case; it is tempting to conclude that here Morton's influence was again at play. In view of Jemmat's removal from the extreme north to Essex it was small wonder that he proved unwilling to uproot his family and travel north again. Moreover, Jemmat knew that his success or failure at Melbourne depended upon a personal relationship with the Coke family. Their support and financial assistance could be withdrawn from him immediately if their views did not coincide. Understandably enough, Jemmat was unwilling to take the risk of entering into such a relationship without prior personal knowledge of his patron.[16]

By the 1630s the Coke family, represented by Sir Francis Coke of Trusley and Sir John Coke, his younger brother, of Melbourne, was one of the most influential in Derbyshire political and religious life.

Francis Coke allied with Henry Curzon to purchase a grant of next presentation to prefer the outspoken puritan Arthur Richards to Hartishorne. Both men were active in furthering the puritan cause and both sought to direct it in a positive fashion. Recipients of their patronage had to accept this relationship of semi-dependence. This was one aspect of the patronage relationship which was to have a marked effect upon the clerical profession as it developed throughout the century. There were those, like Laud, who dreamed of an independent clergy; there were those who saw the clergy as dependent upon the laity.[17]

One other aspect of puritan religious patronage has received a certain amount of attention recently – that exercised by town corporations. Christopher Hill has, on the basis of the examples of Boston, Ipswich, Lincoln, Northampton, Coventry, Warwick, Bedford, St Albans, Leeds, Gloucester, Newcastle, Norwich, King's Lynn, Yarmouth, Shrewsbury and Plymouth, concluded that most corporations tended to be puritan or, at least, anti-Laudian. However, it is wise to add here that corporations were in favour of a preaching ministry but that there is not all that much evidence that they supported the wholesale adoption of a presbyterian discipline such as that proposed by some puritan clergy. (Lay patrons as a body were more likely to sympathize with religious Independency than with Presbyterianism.)[18]

It was this overwhelming sense of the need for a worthy, preaching ministry felt by both puritan clergy and their lay sympathizers which led to one of the most, if not *the* most, remarkable attempts by the puritan movement to innovate. The office of parish lecturer, whose function was that of the doctor or teacher in the Reformed ministry of the continental churches, became a permanent feature of the late sixteenth and seventeenth century Church in an attempt to provide regular preaching in parishes where there were only the statutory monthly and quarterly sermons. The lectureship was not, of course, an exclusively puritan institution, but the impetus behind the movement for its establishment was undoubtedly primarily puritan and the clergy who staffed the lectureships were predominantly puritan. There was a dichotomy between those who wished to see in England a profession of the clergy containing the four distinct offices of the continental Reformed churches and those who were more than content with a clergy which allowed one man, the incumbent of a benefice, to perform all these distinct functions. 'Anglicans' who agreed that a preaching ministry was essential in the Church disagreed with the system of lectureships: they believed that preaching should not be divorced from the administration of the sacraments and that the real answer to the Church's present dilemma was better economic provision for incumbents to encourage the increasing number of university graduates to enter the ministry. Significantly enough, they saw the lectureships as aggravating the situation – they were merely creating further competition for limited financial resources. But for the puritans, both patrons and clergy, the institution of the lectureship permitted them to by-pass the benefice (where often they had no effective patronage and where always they were faced with potential hierarchical opposition and disciplinary measures) and ensure a preaching ministry for the Church. Those who paid the lecturers controlled their use of the pulpit and the tenure of the occupants in a way which had been denied to the parishioner who paid tithe to his rector or vicar or the patron who presented a client to the benefice. The patron of the lectureship (be it local magnate, corporation or group of parishioners) was now the agent of discipline. For the clergy the institution had real advantages. The command of the pulpit gave the zealous puritan preacher the opportunity to make his name known. He was able to avoid almost all participation in the 'compromising ministerial functions of the but halfly reformed church' (if he was not also an incumbent) and to evade discipline from the Church courts. It also had distinct disadvantages: many clergy were ambiguous in their attitude to lay intervention; more still resented the insecurity of their tenure and their relative lack of prestige within the profession. Some lectureships, such as those in London, were highly prestigious, however.[19]

We are talking here of the parish lectureships which were often, but not always, held by unbeneficed clergymen. Combination lectures, which have been studied in detail by Professor Collinson, made extensive use of the services of beneficed ministers and were an integral part of Church life, especially under James I and Charles I. These in no sense involved an attempt to by-pass the benefice system but were rather an attempt to make the best possible use of the preaching resources available in the established Church. 'Puritan' clergy were deeply involved in these combination lectures – just as were clergy who could in no way be described as puritan – but the combination lectures, to prevent confusion, cannot be talked of in the same breath as parish lectureships designed to present an alternative to the services offered by the established Church. They were not institutionalized and did not represent a separate rung on the professional ladder.[20]

The parish lectureship was more important to the puritans in certain areas than in others. In the City of London, for example, the puritan laity had singularly little opportunity to exercise patronage via the conventional channels. Seventy per cent of the parochial benefices were in the gift of the Crown and the Church (compared to a national average of five out of every six advowsons in the hands of the laity). In the 1580s 43 per cent of 129 London parishes had initiated lectureships; the percentage rose to 49 per cent by the 1590s and in 1630 about 90 per cent of livings had supported lecturers during the period of 1580–1630. During this period many of the lectureships were discontinued for a variety of reasons: the lecturer might be suspended; the expense of maintenance might prove too great. Despite this fact, it remains true that after 1580 one in four London parishes had an active lecturer, and that from 1610 until the Restoration the average never dropped below one-third.[21]

Lecturers were chosen by a plethora of methods. On occasion the parson himself was appointed to read the lecture (as at St Margaret Lothbury) or his curate was commissioned (as at St Dunstan in the East). Some vestries put up several candidates and put it to the vote: nominations seem to have come from puritan preachers, members of the universities, or the incumbent, but it appears that parochial influences were just as strong. On occasion outside pressure was brought to bear. At St Lawrence Poultney three local preachers gave sermons before the election. In the 1630s 13 London livings were themselves in the gift of the vestries concerned; here both the parson and the lecturer were commonly chosen by relatively free elections.

In almost all cases the duties of the lecturer were carefully defined. Commonly there were to be one or two sermons a week, but sometimes as many as four. Almost 72 per cent of London lectures in 1629 were delivered on Sunday afternoons, before or after evening prayer. Sermons were also often required on fast days or thanksgiving days. Lecture sermons averaged an hour in length and may have formed series of expositions on related texts. Often the willingness of the parishioners to support a said lecturer financially was closely related to the extent of his co-operation in fulfilling these defined functions. In 1649 the vestry of St Mary Colechurch offered their minister an annual stipend of £100 if he preached twice on Sundays or £52 if he preached only once on Sundays.

Town corporations throughout England also commonly employed preachers or lecturers. Dr Seaver has noted that,

> As urban élites found the Established Church unresponsive to their need for a preaching ministry or unable to meet it because of the poverty of urban livings, they gradually began to modify and adapt the complex ecclesiastical structure inherited from the middle ages to their own ends. Sometimes without even a nod toward the ecclesiastical authorities, almost always as a result of lay initiative, the town preacher emerged as the dominant clerical figure in the urban scene. The town, not the parish, was his province, and he was answerable less directly to the archdeacon and bishop than to the town magistracy.

In a sense, therefore, the town lectureship stood further outside the traditional ecclesiastical organization than did its London counterpart which was still closely connected to and responsible to the parish. However, this may be too simplified a picture as in some towns there were lectureships established in each of the parishes – as, for example, at Newcastle upon Tyne. Nothing really prevented town corporations subsidizing the incomes of town incumbents and encouraging a preaching ministry in that way but most still preferred to pay a sufficient salary to a preacher whom they could hire and fire at will, having laid down precise conditions of employment. Occasionally a strong puritan motivation was apparent in these conditions. At Ipswich in April 1585 the council ordered its lecturer to leave because of his non-residency, despite his orthodoxy. In 1600 the puritans gained control of the Lincoln council and as swiftly of its patronage policy: in May they ruled that the lecturer should not be an incumbent and should be resident; this disqualified the present lecturer, the incumbent, and permitted the election of John Smith, the future Baptist leader, as lecturer. But although puritanism was evidently dominant in some corporations (for example, at Ipswich where there was a tradition of appointing radical Protestant preachers) this was not always the case. At Oxford a much more varied selection of lecturers was appointed – some ecclesiastical careerists; some non-puritans; the occasional Laudian; and some declared puritans.[22]

Town preaching was not always supported entirely by the corporation. In 1608 money was left by a Barbary merchant to support a preacher at Ashbourne, Derbyshire; in 1631 £400 was subscribed by parishioners and handed over to the original trustees to support the divinity lecture. By 1636 the lecturer was John Hyron, who had been licensed to preach by the Laudian bishop, Robert Wright. A much more indirect patronage was exercised by those groups who merely chose to augment the stipends of preachers. The Mercers' Company of Coventry exercised no control over the selection of ministers for city livings (both of which belonged to the Crown) or the established lectureships, but they administered funds bequeathed by Mr Wheat to found three sermons per annum. Normally the man chosen to give these sermons was vicar of one of the city livings. From 1618 to 1633 Samuel Buggs appeared as lecturer – although in 1618 Staresmore, Vicar of St Michael's, gave one of the sermons and Buggs the remaining two. In 1634 Buggs' moderate Laudian successor, William Panting, assumed the duty and delivered the sermons annually until 1642. The company also sought to augment the income of the curates of both St Michael's and Holy Trinity by sums ranging from £1 to £5 per annum.[23]

This brief survey of lay puritan patronage enables us to reach certain tentative conclusions about its impact or potential impact upon the clerical profession. Statistically the importance of the puritan 'movement' has perhaps been exaggerated by historians. In many areas of England there were lay patrons of puritan conviction who possessed sufficient ecclesiastical patronage to ensure the existence of an energetic but often small nucleus of puritan clergy in those parts. On occasion, neighbouring gentry co-operated to achieve this end, though less through conscious design than as the natural outcome of their shared religious views and friendships. There is little or no evidence that puritan gentry were organizing themselves on a grand scale to buy up groups of advowsons in order to secure a puritan clergy although, occasionally, a puritan patron might purchase an advowson or a grant of next presentation in order to prefer a particular cleric. The significance of puritan patronage for our purposes lies not in the numbers of puritan clergy which it succeeded in placing in the Church (although this is important) but in some other of its characteristics. For instance, lay puritan patrons were determined to influence the character of the post-Reformation English Church in the direction of the continental Reformed churches. They wanted to see lay participation as a permanent characteristic of this Church. The medieval patronage system, unchallenged by the English Reformation changes, permitted them some degree of influence. When this was curbed by the action of the bishops and the Church courts, particularly after 1580, the puritan laity exercised their influence by by-passing the benefice system.

There can be little doubt that the puritan laity were trying to subvert the Elizabethan Church settlement by their activities. When it proved difficult to use the patronage system effectively they did not hesitate to innovate. This does not, of course, mean that groups of puritan gentry or merchants were sitting around plotting against the established Church – to some extent the activities of the puritans were organized (perhaps more so as the situation grew more desperate in their eyes in the 1620s and 1630s), but by simply interpreting their role in the Church as patrons in this way they were subversive of the spirit of Elizabeth's settlement. It is for this reason that the peculiarly close relationship between the puritan patron and his protégé is important.

Although, as we have seen, the attempts of the puritans to place worthy preachers into benefices were not at odds with the goals of at least a section of the episcopate it remains true that, after the bishops were made to bend to the will of Elizabeth in the 1580s, the puritan laity in their several guises were the chief initiators of further reformation in the English Church. It was they who gave social support to the energetic clerical puritans; it was they who helped finance innovatory measures to help this reformation along. Of course, there was also a very real tension between the aims of the puritan patrons and their clerical clients. In a sense the control which some puritan patrons sought to exercise over their protégés acted directly against the growth of professional self-determination. No doubt, most clergy saw the role of the laity in the Church in a rather different light than did the puritan patrons themselves. Within the puritan movement there does seem to be a distinction between the predominantly clerical philosophy of the *classis* organization and that of the rather loosely organized and congregationally orientated system of Independent congregations.

Lay puritans, in urban communities in particular, were grafting on to the pre-Reformation clerical structure new elements which bore some close similarity to the organization of reformed churches elsewhere. Continental Reformed churches saw the ministry not as hierarchically divided (as in England with its strictly ordered pyramid) but as horizontally divided in terms of function (the four offices of the ministry – elder, pastor, teacher, doctor). The hierarchy in England, especially the Laudian hierarchy, never accepted that all the functions of the ministry could not satisfactorily be performed by one man – the parochial incumbent. To some extent their view was governed by the reduced emphasis which they accorded to the preaching function but this was not the sole reason. However, to a substantial section of the clergy and to the puritan laity preaching was an essential mark of the new ministry – just as important as adequate pastoral care and fatherly discipline. If one man could serve a congregation in the capacity of both pastor and preacher this was all to the good; if he could not, then a separate office of preacher or lecturer must be set up to provide a *full* ministry. The hierarchy forced the puritans to innovate by failing to ensure that all recruits to benefices were able and active preachers. Nevertheless, it is to the conviction of the puritan laity and clergy that preaching is an essential mark of the ministry that the English Church owes its peculiar career structure in the seventeenth century. It appears as an odd mix of the medieval and the reformed. The establishment might oppose the institution of the lectureship, but it was unable to abolish it.

8

The use and abuse of grants of next presentation

Many lay patrons of advowsons were not puritan and there is some evidence to suggest that large numbers were not very interested in preferring clerics at all. Many patrons were passive in their role and it was the clergy who had to seek out suitable patrons rather than *vice versa*. Some patrons would leave parishes vacant for long periods through lack of interest. Yet the possession of an advowson was potentially important to members of the landowning class because it gave them power over men. Clergy put themselves in a subservient position suing for patronage. More pertinently, other laymen or clergymen were anxious to become patrons *de facto* and might be willing to pay for the right to present to a given living.

The legal ownership of an advowson implied the right to both nominate and present a cleric to an ecclesiastical benefice. The owner was known as the *de iure* patron. Those *de iure* patrons who had no personal interest in the quality of the clergy or the adequate care of the people of the parish had several options open to them. They could alienate by sale or grant the advowson itself, either separately or along with other property. They could retain the advowson but alienate the right to present to a living for a specified period or for a given number of presentations. The man who received such a grant would be known as the *pro hac vice* patron or the patron *assignatus*. He would have bought himself into the world of influence. Thirdly, the *de iure* patrons could grant away, more informally, the right to nominate a cleric but retain their own right to present him formally to the bishop. This meant that *de iure* patrons retained the right of approval and also ensured that the patronage never passed out of their hands.[1]

If patronage was readily available in this way to people without *de iure* patronage rights or with only limited opportunities for patronage, then this might have untold impact upon the composition of the clergy. Puritans might purchase grants of next presentation or advowsons and present their protégés to the livings involved. They might do this on an individual basis or in a more organized fashion. Equally, puritans might make little use of the system and allow its exploitation by men with no religious conviction.

In this chapter we shall be looking at *pro hac vice* patronage in the diocese of Worcester to see whether it was common, and who was exercising it and why. We must bear in mind that our findings will provide some indication of the attitudes of *de iure* patrons as well as the subsidiary patrons.

A total of 531 presentations to rectories, vicarages and prebendal stalls were made in the diocese of Worcester between 1559/60 and 1634. Of these 326 were made in the reign of Elizabeth and the remaining 205 in the reigns of James I and Charles I. This number does not include double presentations or, naturally, institutions for which there is no record of presentation. According to the 1603 survey ordered by Whitgift, the diocese contained 214 parishes although this number included churches with cure but without institution. The records of presentations at Worcester indicate that presentations were made to 167 of these parishes during the period (some of the others presumably falling outside the diocesan juris-diction) and that *pro hac vice* presentations were made to some 72 of them at one time or another: rather less than half the number concerned.[2]

Thus there seems to have been a pool of marketable livings in the diocese which the true patrons willingly marketed. Some of the patrons concerned were evidently little interested in the actual right to present clergy of their own choice. Ralph Sheldon of Besley granted next presentations to the following livings: Barchester (1605); Besley (1578 and 1611/12); and Stretton on Fosse (1581). He purchased a grant to Tredington in 1562/3 from William Sheldon, only to make grants of presentation to it in both 1605 and 1607. The dean and chapter of Worcester made grants of next presentation on at least 12 occasions, involving nine livings. On one occasion this was for the next two presentations to the living of Sedgeborough. These examples show a continued lack of interest on the part of some patrons. On the other hand, there were *de iure* patrons who normally exercised their own patronage right but who, for some reason, sold a grant occasionally. Grants of next presentation were not often sold by the Lucys, patrons of Charlecote, Warwickshire, but on 1 January 1621, Sir Thomas Lucy sold the grant of next presentation to Richard Hayle, gentleman of that parish. While there were certainly some *de iure* patrons who showed a consistent lack of interest in the clergy, the mere lease of a presentation in itself does not necessarily imply total lack of concern.[3]

Why then did patrons wish to sell rights to present? If a patron did not have a definite interest in presenting a particular man to his living or livings it was obviously in his financial interest to sell this right to another, rather than to allow the living to fall into lapse to either the bishop or the Crown, when no financial reward would be forthcoming. Grants of next presentation were carefully documented to protect the true patron's rights; often, also, a cleric presented under such a grant would enter a bond to move immediately if the right of patronage was found to lie with someone other than his presenter. Confusion could and did arise but, in general, careful records protected the long-term rights of the legal patron to present. Moreover, if the *de iure* patron had no definite personal preference in the choice of a cleric but was nevertheless anxious to see the parish served, he would be likely to take the advice of another in making the choice of incumbent. In this event, he might as well make his adviser pay for the privilege. The bishops and the dean and chapter obviously saw the device as a welcome source of additional revenue but they made more effort than most to retain a degree of control over the use of grants. For example, on 4 July 1577 Richard Cosin, M.A., obtained the right of next presentation to the archdeaconry of Worcester from the bishop with the proviso that it be used to present Godfrey Goldsborough, S.T.P., and that it be null and void should Goldsborough die before collation. The dean and chapter of Worcester also strove to control the use of eight of the thirteen grants which they issued. The majority of other grants were, however, unconditional.[4]

With large numbers of ecclesiastical patrons willing to make leases of the rights to present to given livings, the opportunity certainly existed for puritans within (or without) the area to mobilize their financial resources and buy the right to present substantial numbers of parochial clergy. In fact it is clear that this did not happen. On the other hand, it is probable that individual cases of energetic puritan patronage do occur via the medium of grants of next presentation in this diocese. However, an examination of the purchase of grants reveals other patterns.

Why did men want to purchase grants of next presentation? On the one side were the would-be patrons who wished to prefer a relative or friend, with or without a religious motive. When John Cookes purchased the right to present to Tardebigge from its *hac vice* patron, Laurence Childe, who was also its vicar, he did so to present a relative, Edward Cookes. At Astley in 1611 the *hac vice* patron presented a kinsman, and the same pattern had prevailed at Barton on the Heath in 1580. Other examples occur at Bellbroughton (1608); Besley (1616/17); Birtsmorton (1625); Bredicton (1578); Hanbury (1627/8); Kington (1626); Nafford (1582); Pershore (1623); Powick (1615); and Preston Bagot (1609). At Hanbury Edward Vernon, *pro hac vice* patron, presented his brother, John Vernon, M.A., on the resignation of doubtless another relative, Richard Vernon. Unfortunately it is not possible, without supporting documentation, to trace the instances where a man sought to find placement for a friend or for a relative who bore a different surname, but some grants of next presentation were evidently purchased in anticipation of an early or immediate opportunity to present and, therefore, probably with a beneficiary in mind. On 1 June 1562 Richard Tymmes, a yeoman of Abbots Morton, bought the grant of next presentation to that living from Thomas Hobbye of Bisham. He used this to present Richard Scolow on 15 July 1562. In this case, the last incumbent was already deceased when the grant was made, thus making it a grant of this presentation rather than next. On 1 November 1625, Fulk Harbach, gentleman of Astwood, bought the grant of next presentation to the parish of Feckenham from its present holder, John Culpeper, and used it on the 22nd of that month to present John Mason to the living, vacant by the death of John Trueman.

Purchase and immediate use of a grant of next presentation is a pattern especially associated with livings vacated by resignation. It is reasonable to suppose that many vacancies were engineered by the new patron and his client. For instance, in 1569/70 Robert Barker of Newcastle-under-Lyme was presented to Tamworth, and in October 1571 he was given the Crown living of Exhall. Barker eventually resigned the benefice of Tamworth in July 1573 and was granted, on 7 August 1573, a pension as retiring incumbent. Ecclesiastical officials were suspicious of such arrangements: a guaranteed pension to a retiring incumbent could be an ill-disguised bribe. It is an interesting technical question as to whether such a payment to the incumbent constituted simony or no. There is certainly some evidence of attempts by the Worcester registry to guard against the abuse of the system by simony, especially where grants of next presentation were involved. For example, on 10 February 1577/8 William Fortescue leased the right to present to Spernall to George Parsons, yeoman. On 13 February the incumbent, Thomas Philippes, resigned and the resignation was accepted by the registrar on 15 February. At the beginning of March George Parsons presented Humphrey Style to the living; on 12 April Style was made to enter a bond that he had not acquired the living by simony.

Sometimes the incumbent of a living himself urged a layman to buy the grant of next presentation to ensure the succession of the incumbent's son. The concern of the clergy to provide for their families is reflected in several grants made in Worcester diocese. Thus the grant of next presentation to St John's, Bedwardine, was made by the dean and chapter on 23 June 1570 to James Hyggyns and Robert Trawghton on behalf of the present incumbent. In September 1572 Edward Baker was presented on the death of his father, Thomas. Gilbert Backhouse of Cleeve Prior, in association with Edward Archepoll, obtained the *hac vice* presentation in order to ensure the succession of William, son of William Tomlinson. The grant was actually made out in favour of young William and, on Backhouse's death, Archepoll presented him to the vacant living. The dean and chapter allowed Humphrey Harwood, Vicar of Kempsey, to secure the presentation of his son Richard to the same when they made a grant on his behalf to Richard Wynslowe of Draycotte on 23 June 1592. The grant was to be void if Richard Harwood died before a vacancy or before admission. An arrangement of a similar nature was sanctioned at Wichenford in 1577. Here it is well to recall Cunningham's statement that it was not simony for a father to procure a place for his son; and, therefore 'his buying an advowson' with this in mind 'is not any simony'. Nevertheless, these clergymen were careful to proceed by way of a third party, avoiding any possible action against them for simony.[5]

Even in those cases where a layman or cleric purchased a grant of presentation and then used it himself to prefer a client, it is often true that the *hac vice* patron has no personal desire to be a patron. The initiative seems to stem quite often from either the man seeking a place or a doting relative. While it is true that all grants of next presentation were by no means made formally in the names of particular beneficiaries (only 13 of the total of 146 grants recorded at Worcester) a goodly proportion of them were probably informally made in this way.

However, some men bought grants of next presentation neither to pursue a religious ideal nor to satisfy the need for place of relatives or friends. They did so because of a wish to make a safe social and financial investment and, perhaps, a little profit. Some patrons sold the grant of a presentation immediately after they had placed their own choice in a living. Thus Edward Sutton, Lord Dudley, sold the next presentation to Dudley to one Abraham Trice, dyer, of London, on 18 November 1626, having recently presented William Wilson to the same on 28 October 1626. Abraham Trice can have had little hope of presenting immediately and, indeed, he sold the grant to the incumbent, William Wilson, eight years later in May 1634. So, even if the *hac vice* patron was unable to exercise his new-found patronage at a time convenient to himself, he could still regard the initial transaction as an investment. That patrons looked upon purchase of grants in this way seems very probable. On 6 November 1588, Matthew Walwyne, gent., sold the grant to Oxhill to Nicholas Clerke of Tysoe, which grant Clerke used on 4 February 1597 to present James Pallavin. Clerke applied for the next grant on 12 May 1598 and made 'a money payment'. Seven years later, he sold the grant to William Barnes of Clifford Chambers, for a sum of £50. In 1621, some 16 years later, Barnes assigned the grant to another William Barnes 'cognato meo' of Tadlington, Warwickshire. The grant was then passed to Anthony Bishop, native of Oxhill itself, on 15 June 1624, presumably for another payment. Pallavin died at long last in that year, suggesting that when Bishop bought the grant he anticipated early use in favour of his presentee, Daniel Smart, B.A. Smart was presented 26 years after the initial grant was made by Matthew Walwyne. The case of Bellbroughton was similar if less extreme: a grant was made to Robert Garvie, M.A., of Oriel College, in April 1575, which was immediately assigned to Christopher Michell of Chastleton; in October 1583 three Doctors of Law bought the grant from Michell and two of them used it to present to the living in June 1584.

From the limited evidence available in the Worcester records, it appears that a range of £30–£100 prevailed in the price of most grants. The price was probably fixed in relation to its prospect of early use – more being charged for a presentation to a living soon to be vacated by resignation or, less certainly, death. The right to present for one turn to a living was, therefore, sufficiently valuable in terms of either patronage or money to make it a worthy gift from the bishop of the diocese to one of his household for services rendered, to make it a fall-back investment for a gentleman, lawyer, merchant or yeoman, or to make it an opportunity for quick gain for the venture-some.[6]

Grants of next presentation seem to have been rather less commonly used after the reign of Elizabeth. The slight falling off in the number of grants issued at Worcester may have been due to a fall-off in demand rather than to a greater reluctance on the part of de iure patrons to alienate their rights to present. An increase in the number of lectureships or preacherships available in the English Church may have eased the placement situation considerably and thus had an effect upon demand. On the other hand, the reason may lie in a more responsible attitude on the part of ecclesiastical patrons: all the grants made by the Worcester dean and chapter, for instance, were made during Elizabeth's reign.

As already indicated, grants of next presentation were being bought by people in the gentry, merchant, professional and yeoman classes. The system, therefore, made available patronage opportunities to those who were able to pay the price. Perhaps this element of cost explains why on so many occasions two or more individuals would combine to purchase a grant. For instance, on 6 October 1560 Francis Brace, gent., made a grant to Dovedale over to James Williams, gent., and Thomas Creswell, fishmonger. In 1606 John Aperley, yeoman, joined with William Gardiner, cleric, to buy a grant to Staunton. Even more significant for a history of the profession is the fact that often the purchasers of these grants were local men. It has been said that, with the redistribution of land and advowsons at the dissolution of the monasteries, the control of ecclesiastical patronage was removed from its local base. It is possible that the system of grants of next presentation restored the balance somewhat and, moreover, permitted the local congregation (as opposed to the local lord of the manor) some say in the choice of cleric. Such a trend was bound to act in favour of local men (often from local clerical families).

Table 5

Use of patronage in the diocese of Worcester: 1559–1634

Date	De iure patron	Pro hac vice patron	Bishop	Lapse to bishop	Lapse to Crown	Crown wards	Total
1559–71	63	22	1	3			89
1571–81	57	14			3		74
1581–91	50	22	(Sede Vacante: 2)		11	1	86
1591–1601	49	9			3		61
1601–11	42	11			7		60
1611–21	48	5		1	8		62
1621–31	58	16			2		76
1631–4	15	1			1		17
Total	382	100	3	4	35	1	525

Prebendal stalls   6

Total number of institutions   531

An examination of the records of grants of next presentation issued in Worcester diocese indicates that neither the puritan movement nor any other religiously motivated movement made organized use of the opportunity before them. If puritans bought grants in order to prefer suitable clerics they did so as individuals or in small groups on an *ad hoc* basis. Those interested in transforming the parochial ministry might have made greater use of the system had it been more reliable. Sometimes it *was* possible to buy a grant and use it immediately in favour of a specific man but often a grant would be of no practical use for some years. Puritans were already impatient at the slow pace of the Reformation; they wanted some means of injecting enthusiastic Protestantism into the Church immediately. The limitations of both *de iure* and *pro hac vice* patronage were such that those intent on reform were forced to innovate.

If grants of next presentation were not used by the puritans to alter dramatically the complexion of the English clergy, they nevertheless had an impact upon the composition of that body. Local men of the lower gentry and non-landowning classes were offered, at a price, a say in the choice of local clergymen. When they took this opportunity they often exercised their rights in favour of local candidates. Local clerics were not necessarily, of course, any better than non-local incumbents but often they did encourage a greater bond and sympathy between minister and flock. The system did encourage the practice of what was but thinly disguised simony but it is by no means clear that this acted to the detriment of the Church or its clergy. It could be said that a purely business transaction was in fact preferable to the dependent relationship which often persisted between client and patron for life. Moreover, the selling of grants to present could help counter the apathy of many of the country's patrons: instead of permitting a living to remain vacant or of presenting the first suitor who presented himself, a *de iure* patron would instead sell the grant to someone who had a genuine concern to present a particular individual. Yet those bishops who did show an interest in exercising patronage at the parochial level must have regretted the fact that fewer livings were falling into lapse than might otherwise have been the case.

9

The ecclesiastical patronage of the lord keeper

So far it has been noted that the lack of patronage in the hands of the bishops was a major obstacle in the way of reformation of the parochial ministry. The bishops had little patronage initiative at this level and they had only restricted influence upon the exercise of ecclesiastical patronage by others. Lay patrons also found their lack of bloc patronage a hindrance and they were aware of the limitations of such patronage rights as they did hold. This was perhaps why they did not mobilize their resources to buy up blocs of advowsons or grants but instead preferred to bypass the traditional patronage system and endow new and more easily controllable posts in the Church. But there was one patronage holder in England and Wales who did hold large numbers of advowsons all over the country and who, in theory, could have made an enormous impact upon the religious complexion and quality of the post-Reformation clergy – this was the Crown. Did it have this impact?

The Crown was the single largest advowson holder in England and Wales: a flood of royal acquisitions at the Reformation reinforced this position. The patronage in the Crown's possession was held in two main ways. Livings valued at over £20 in the *Valor Ecclesiasticus* of 1535 were held directly by the Crown. The lord keeper customarily held in his gift all Crown livings below £20 in value. This constituted the bulk of Crown patronage. He also had the right to present to many other livings: for example, he claimed the right to present to livings under £20 in value in the gift of Crown wards, and he was entitled to present to livings which had been in lapse for 12 months or longer.[1]

Nicholas Bacon could expect in normal years to present to an average of 113 vacancies in his capacity as lord keeper – a number which was spread geographically round the kingdom. The average had dropped slightly to 108 presentations per annum during Egerton's chancellorship. This amounted to a third of the annual vacancies. It fell yet again to 98 for the period 1627–40. Perhaps many of the vacancies occurring in the early period were due to deprivations and resignations stemming from the change in régime or to deaths during the serious influenza epidemic of the mid and late 1550s.[2]

Despite the variation in presentations per annum through the period, successive lord keepers exercised great potential influence on the personnel of the clergy. Some lord keepers certainly did formulate policy and envisage themselves as adhering to certain principles in distributing favour. In a letter to Mr Maxey, Fellow of Trinity College, Cambridge, Francis Bacon declared that his purpose was 'to make choice of men rather by care and inquiry, than by their own suits and commendatory letters'. Egerton was praised by Camden for his policy of bestowing advowsons upon worthy and needy ministers – denying livings to those who already had them, rather preferring to see that 'some might have single coats, that wanted them, before others had Doublets'. He appears to have been interested in the preaching function and on two occasions in the 1590s made clergymen enter specific bonds for the provision of sermons. Thus on 9 November 1596 Richard Boyley was presented to Wigenhold rectory in Sussex and then a 'Bond entred for 12 sermons to be made yerely etc.' Bishop Parkhurst of Norwich had earlier ascribed to Nicholas Bacon attempts to ensure that simony did not enter into Crown presentations and Bacon was certainly sympathetic to the ideal of a reformed ministry embraced by the returned exiles. But despite this concern on the part of at least some of the Elizabethan and Stuart lord keepers to use their patronage wisely and in the interest of a preaching ministry, certain factors were at play which made it extremely difficult for them to follow any such policy wholeheartedly.[3]

One of the more important of these was the enormity of the task of presenting clerics to so many livings over so wide a geographical area. The lord keeper could not possibly expect to know or even to examine all candidates personally: he had to delegate this responsibility in the majority of cases and in delegation lay potential danger. Already by the reign of Elizabeth the patronage of the lord keeper was highly bureaucratized. His office had a permanent staff of registrar and two clerks in addition to one or more 'patronage secretaries'. The keeper also employed a group of chaplains whose prime duty seems to have been that of examining the suitability of candidates for Crown livings. Individual lord keepers varied considerably in the amount of personal control they exercised over the administration of their patronage by this bureaucracy. Under Nicholas Bacon it was clearly Bartholemew Kempe, the registrar of benefices and ecclesiastical promotions, who decided who would have the presentation to a particular living. Camden charged Lord Keeper Puckering not with personal corruption but with the offence of permitting his staff to sell Church livings. Yet both Egerton and Francis Bacon appear to have taken a greater personal interest in the exercise of patronage.[4]

It was, nevertheless, improbable that any lord keeper would be able to supply personally the names of candidates for the preferments in his gift. This fact alone meant that the lord keeper was open to advice from others regarding the use of his patronage. Traditionally, the lord keeper had been granted Crown patronage of livings below £20 in value to provide benefices in lieu of payment for his clerks and chaplains. Contemporaries believed that the best livings in the keeper's gift went automatically to his chaplains. Certainly Nicholas Bacon bestowed some of the better livings upon his chaplains. Arthur Sawle, in particular, profited from his position as household chaplain, acquiring a prebend worth £20 and three livings during the years 1562–6. The puritan Percival Wyborne gained rather less at the keeper's hands although he too was presented to a living wealthy in terms of the lord keeper's patronage. The household chaplains also had some influence over the lord keeper's choice of other candidates. Sawle petitioned for livings for at least 16 men between 1559 and 1575; Wyborne for another 16 between 1560 and 1575; Pedder for seven between 1559 and 1564. Under Egerton, John Williams was even more influential – on seven occasions in 1616 alone he supported the suits of petitioners. This exercise of influence by the keeper's chaplains was not necessarily harmful or corrupt. The chaplains were able men and would probably take their responsibilities seriously. Yet this gift of patronage to his chaplains did leave the lord keeper one step removed from the personal responsibility of selecting ministers for Crown livings.[5]

The lord keeper also saw his patronage as part of the wider web of patronage in society as a whole and not solely as an instrument for influence in the Church. He saw in ecclesiastical patronage a convenient way of rewarding particular groups of or individual petitioners. Sometimes he heeded such petitions because he sympathized with their religious motivation; sometimes, no doubt, he was less meticulous in his examination of the motives of the petitioner.

The bishops, for example, were regular petitioners for the lord keeper's patronage. In general they sought to extend their own influence in their dioceses. Apart from the two archbishops, only the Bishop of London regularly petitioned for benefices outside his area of immediate influence in the 1560s and 1570s. This may have been due to Grindal's personal dominance in the Church and to his concern for the ministry as well as to the fact that superior national information regarding clerical vacancies was available to London clergy. In any event, Lord Keeper Bacon showed his favour to the bishops to a marked extent, so that they had some real control over the appointment of personnel in their jurisdictions. The high point of this episcopal influence was in the mid and late 1560s. Just under half the clerics preferred in 1563 were presented upon petition and/or commendation of one of the bishops (36); a further 22 owed their success to some other eminent ecclesiastic. A similar picture emerges in 1567: 39 of the 110 presentations were made on the petition of bishops and a further 30, at least, on that of leading ecclesiastics and Church court officials. Such men as Aylmer of Lincoln, Lever of Coventry, Wattes of Middlesex, Mullins of London and the archdeacons of Huntingdon and Essex were thus playing their part in this unusual ecclesiastical control of Church patronage. These archdeacons owed their influence with Bacon not to their office but to their personal eminence within the Reformed Church. England and Wales contained over 52 archdeaconries but a mere handful of archdeacons are mentioned in the list of successful petitioners at the beginning of Elizabeth's reign. Almost all were returned exiles. (Between 1596 and 1617 there is a comparative absence from the lists of officials such as archdeacons; they have been replaced by 'certain preachers' of influence.) Similarly, Alexander Nowell, Dean of St Paul's, was accorded some influence by Nicholas Bacon.[6]

Nicholas Bacon clearly sympathized with the aims of the returned exiles but by the early 1570s the bishops and Church officials had lost their near monopoly of Crown patronage, and influence over the lord keeper's presentations became fragmented between courtiers, gentry and ecclesiastics. There is considerable evidence that men like Huntingdon, Pembroke, Leicester and Bedford sought to extend their patronage opportunities by nominating men to livings through the lord chancellor. Bedford, for example, petitioned on behalf of 20 clerics between 1558/9 and 1575. Such patrons as these were acutely aware of the importance of patronage in ensuring a reformation of the ministry. In this ultimate goal the puritan noblemen were not so far removed from the returned exiles but they did have a rather different conception of lay participation in the Reformed Church and they did remain radical longer than their ecclesiastical contemporaries. Above all, they were certainly of a different breed from the new generation of Elizabethan bishops who were achieving promotion in the 1570s.

In granting the nobles patronage, the lord keepers were assisting the advanced Protestant cause still – they were granting the laity a leading role in selecting the parochial clergy and robbing the ecclesiastical hierarchy of its earlier prominence. We have asked elsewhere whether this was a piece of conscious engineering on the part of Crown or keeper. In effect one is faced with a strange situation: the queen's choice as Archbishop of Canterbury, John Whitgift, was in the ascendant, a man who had little sympathy with the goals of the radical noblemen – and yet the Crown was granting increased exercise of ecclesiastical patronage to a group of leading Protestant noblemen who belonged to the more radical wing of the Church. It is true that, until the discovery of the Marprelate presses in the 1580s, there were attempts by the Privy Council to compromise with the puritans. Criticisms of the clergy were seen as genuine, constructive attempts to reform rather than to undermine the Elizabethan Church by men who had no objection to conformity given the establishment of a preaching, teaching, pastoral ministry. Alternatively, the situation may have been an example of those politic balancing acts of which the Elizabethan government seemed so fond – balancing puritan nobles and gentry against the conservative Whitgift and Bancroft. It could, on the other hand, be a case of inadequate Crown supervision of the lord keeper's distribution of patronage: certain of the lord keepers involved were in personal accord with the aims of the puritan nobles. Probably all of these factors contributed in some degree to the gift of Crown patronage to the puritan nobles in the 1570s and 1580s but the crux of the matter seems to lie in the fact that the group was very prominent at court. The Crown regarded ecclesiastical patronage as just another link in the chain of patronage which was much wider than the ecclesiastical world, which bound individuals to the régime, and which provided a not insignificant source of revenue. It was absolutely natural that the Crown should elect to favour the most prominent men in the kingdom in this way, especially when they were *actively* seeking patronage in the Church.[7]

It would be wrong to suggest that the lord keeper did not exercise supervision over the distribution of his patronage or ever intervene personally in particular cases. Only at the beginning of Elizabeth's reign was it possible for a cleric to petition on his own behalf for a living in the keeper's gift and stand some chance of success. It was expected afterwards that a petition would be presented formally and in writing and that it would be supported by letters testimonial. The records of the period 1596–1616/17, for example, note the very few occasions on which a petition was made orally or without letters testimonial and state the reason for this irregularity. The presentation of Edmund Gunter, M.A., to St George's, Southwark, on 16 July 1615 was 'don without any petition in writinge' because he had been commended by one of the lord keeper's chaplains. To some extent, at least, the writers of references were held responsible for their clients and we know, from other sources, that referees were often conscientious in this respect. When Bishop Parkhurst was asked for a reference for Richard Dixon, who had applied to be chaplain to Sir Henry Sidney, the bishop gave a conscientious and discriminating reference which pointed out Dixon's faults as well as his good points. Clearly suitors for benefices believed that their petitions stood a chance of success only if supported by the offices of an eminent person. In January 1592 Edward Houlden of Lincoln diocese wrote to the Archbishop of Canterbury asking for his help in obtaining a living in the lord keeper's gift, 'for the which I humbly beseech your Lordship *to stand my good Lord* into such as in the

vacancy of that offyce have the bestowing of such lyvinges'. Houlden felt confident that his suit would not fail because of delay unless
the archbishop 'by other occasions be not mayd forgetful of this my
suite unto you for the man dyed but this day and I hyred this
messenger who promysed to make more speede then my horse
because I would be sure to be the fyrst suitor'. In fact the *commender* of
a petitioner for a Crown living was not only performing a valuable
service for the client himself but also for the lord keeper. The lord
keeper respected the recommendations of men whose opinions he
valued highly – men high in the social scale, prominent at court or in
the Church.[8]

The services of the chaplains of his household were very important for this reason. The chaplains made commendations themselves.
They and other members of the household sieved the petitions of the
bishops and others regarding certain candidates and themselves
petitioned the registrar, no doubt for a gratuity. Thus on 2 October
1566 John Collyns was presented to Doddescombe rectory, Devon,
at the petition of Master Doyley, one of the lord keeper's gentlemen,
and at the commendation of the Bishop of Exeter. This system gave
the members of the household an influence which could be used for
good or ill. It was doubtless this practice which Camden found so
odious, and it certainly made it essential that the lord keeper chose his
servants with the utmost care. The chances of a client obtaining a
living at all could depend upon the services of these gentlemen and
servants of the household. They were on the spot and in an excellent
position to receive and impart information about vacancies; they
could consistently press a particular suit and check on its progress. A
cleric who petitioned unsuccessfully for one living might leave
instructions to a servant or chaplain to watch for a suitable vacancy
and press his case in his absence.[9]

The household chaplains constituted as an examining body acted
as the main check against abuse of the system. Petitioners in the
period 1627–40 (keepership of Sir Thomas Coventrey) were
examined by at least one of the chaplains for their learning and
knowledge of the Scriptures. The chaplain was required to note
down his verdict; this was usually according to a set form but there is
no reason to believe that the examination itself was perfunctory, the
phraseology used being equivalent to set grades in an examination
today. Only after this procedure had been followed and the cleric
concerned been approved, did the lord keeper's clerks go ahead with
the formal presentation of the client to a living. As an additional
check, oaths against simony were carefully administered to presentees. Unfortunately, charges of simony were difficult to prove
and, moreover, the distinction between simony and offering
'grateful thanks' was often blurred. Gratuities, not being fixed to the

same degree as fees, may have exercised some real influence upon an official's decision regarding a living or, more probably, upon his willingness to bring the petition to the lord keeper's notice initially. In October 1571 Bishop Parkhurst commented that Nicholas Bacon's practice of signing away the right of presentation or nomination to certain livings without retaining or exercising due control over the presentee allowed simony to pass unobserved. In the 1570s one William Basse, gentleman of the City of London, had obtained the nomination to West Tilbury from the lord keeper and had presented one William Gybson upon the receipt of a bribe of the tithes of the parish. The proper exercise of patronage at one or more removes was certainly difficult to monitor.[10]

It can be established that the lord keepers did delegate much of the responsibility for the selection of candidates to others and that it was difficult indeed for them to supervise personally the exercise of this responsibility. Evidently the lord keepers and the registrars of benefices did in general heed the commendations of men whom they knew and respected and such men were often themselves actively seeking the betterment of the ministry. But the quality and integrity of the members of the lord keeper's household and, in particular, of his chaplains was a crucial factor here. Only a full-scale study of the lord keeper's patronage in terms of its recipients would show whether a policy of improving the ministry was pursued by the men to whom the lord keeper delegated this task of selecting candidates for his livings. It is true that the educational qualifications of presentees to the lord keeper's livings rose dramatically during the period 1560–1642: this more than paralleled improvements in the profession as a whole and reflected the Crown's declared intention of encouraging and supporting theological studies at the universities.

It does not, however, seem that individual lord keepers used their patronage for political purposes, for example to build up a loyalist party within the Church to counterbalance the puritan. Given the organization of his patronage 'office' and the constraints inherent in his role, this would have been difficult if not impossible. In fact it appears that the lord keeper did not use his patronage very effectively to secure even a conforming clergy. In 1578 the radical puritan Humphrey Fenn was presented to the Crown living of Holy Trinity, Coventry; in June 1599 Humphrey Leach, M.A., later charged with Roman Catholic leanings and eventually a formal convert to Catholicism, was presented to St Alkmund's, Shrewsbury, with the personal support of the lord chancellor. Thomas Hodgkinson, the rebellious Vicar of Hillmorton, Warwickshire, was himself a Crown protégé. Of course, the lord keeper was also preferring many conformable and prominent diocesan clergy. In general the presentations were suggested by others and the lord keeper was evidently not overly diligent in examining the candidates for their conformity.[11]

To date only Dr Sheils has attempted a study of the use of the lord keeper's patronage within one diocese. During Nicholas Bacon's keepership 98 parish appointments in Peterborough diocese were made by the keeper, and Bishop Edmund Scambler succeeded in controlling a quarter of this patronage (23). Despite this advantageous position and his own progressive leanings, Scambler only contrived to promote three active puritans to Crown livings. Other important ecclesiastics in the diocese used their court influence to prefer 19 clergy to Crown livings during this period but none of those advanced were active puritans. As Dr Sheils points out, even Leicester, who owned land in the diocese and supported vociferously several of its clergy, does not appear to have manipulated the Crown's patronage at this time to place puritan clergy in the county. Indeed, although puritans could infiltrate into Crown livings during Bacon's tenure of office, there was no organized assault on Crown livings by puritan supporters. For instance, George Carleton did not appear as a petitioner even though Wollaston, where he lived, and Overstone, where he supported an unofficial puritan exercise, fell vacant three times during Bacon's tenure. Now it is true that Carleton and other puritan gentry may have petitioned unsuccessfully for puritan clergy but, given the climate of the times and the proclivities of the lord keeper, this seems unlikely. Certainly, therefore, the distribution of Crown patronage as between puritans and others during the entire period 1558/9–1610 does present something of a paradox. At a time 'when the movement still had a certain respectability and could reasonably expect support, not only from governmental officials but also from reforming clerics', it gained little strength from Crown appointments, yet it seems to have been more successful when the puritan movement had been discredited in official circles. Dr Sheils suggests that this phenomenon can be explained in terms of the decreasing vigilance of the bishops and the lord keeper (Bacon) would receive a list of 'the most towardly the overriding importance of the economic motive in granting patronage. However, there is a more convincing explanation: this is that the difference between the two periods is more apparent than real. Once puritanism had been, as it were, outlawed, it became more aggressive, active and distinct, and the puritan cleric himself became more easily identifiable. In the earlier period many clergy were probably presented to Crown livings who were puritan but who did not stand out from the crowd as activists. In any event, knowing what we know of Egerton's attitude towards the ministry, we would expect him to be more and not less energetic in his supervision of the exercise of patronage and to be more likely, not less, to insist upon a preaching ministry. In the early years the 'reform-minded' clergy were, presumably, less desperate. There were also fewer of them than in the later years of Elizabeth's reign.[12]

The lord keeper had sufficient patronage throughout the country to make a considerable impact upon the character of the English parochial clergy. That he seems not to have used his patronage in this way was due to a number of related factors. The task of presenting to so many livings was too great for himself and his chaplains alone. The lord keeper, even when he was committed to the support of a particular view of Church polity, still regarded his ecclesiastical patronage as a valuable means of rewarding various individuals and groups, both on his own behalf and that of the Crown. So the lord keepers actively encouraged third party patronage by rewarding members of the Church hierarchy, of the leading noblemen, of the court. The importance of the lord keeper's patronage as a channel for the influence of others is, therefore, undoubted. Moreover, on occasion the keeper would obey an instruction from the Crown as to the use of his patronage. In October 1560 the Crown announced that the lord keeper (Bacon) would receive a list of 'the most towardly divinity students' at Oxford and Cambridge and that he should in future use the prebendal stalls in his gift to support the same. Also belonging to the reign of Elizabeth is an order now in the Petyt MSS granting by letters patent to the University of Cambridge the right of presentation to half of the Crown livings which were rated between 20 and 40 marks per annum. An identical grant was made to the University of Oxford. The presentations were to be made through the lord keeper and thus still remained part of the Crown's patronage. It was hoped that the livings would be distributed geographically according to college: 'heare may be regard of laying to eache colledge the benefices of thos sheires, wheare the foundation of that colledge hath geven preferment'. The livings were again designed to support serious divinity students.[13]

In so far as the lord keeper bestowed considerable favour on particular individuals or groups and in so far as these were themselves pursuing serious policy, the patronage in his gift did have a decided impact. For example, it is true that a strikingly high number of Crown livings went to clerics with M.A.s or higher degrees. However, the records seem to suggest an increasing removal of the lord keeper's personal supervision of the distribution of livings. The keeper had the final veto on all presentations but petitions reached even the registrar of benefices via a tortuous route through bishops and courtiers to gentlemen and servants of the household to chaplains of the keeper. Only rarely did even Egerton intervene on the behalf of a personal nominee for preferment; only rarely did he exercise his veto.

An analysis of the distribution of the lord keeper's patronage, therefore, indicates that the lord keeper was not using his influence to build up a particular Crown party among the clergy. Instead he gave others the opportunity to dictate the complexion of the clergy. He may have regarded his decisions as a politic balancing act. But increasingly it seems it was others who decided which petitions the lord keeper should consider and which should be rejected at an early stage. The Crown and its servants regarded Church patronage as just one part of the patronage at its disposal – it was a political and social tool as well as a potential instrument for control of the Church. It was this conception of Crown patronage which dictated the distribution of Crown livings to a hotch potch of clerics and which forbade the granting of influence to a single 'party' among would-be patrons. Because of its essentially secular view of patronage, the Crown lost the opportunity to pursue wholeheartedly a single policy of providing a core of worthy ministers in Crown livings, preferring rather to court groups who sued for favour. Because these groups themselves sometimes desired to reform the ministry, this sacrifice on the Crown's part was not wholly disastrous for the cause of a reformed clergy but the results were far less dramatic and coherent than they might have been. There are some indications that during the 1630s the hierarchy was reasserting its control over the lord keeper's patronage but this trend had relatively little impact upon presentations, given its short duration. Yet the interest displayed by Laud in Crown patronage shows that he was well aware of the unfortunate results in terms of clerical uniformity of the Crown's willingness to distribute its favours to both Church leaders and puritan noblemen, to show interest in the would-be patrons rather than in the would-be clerics. The Crown had, through the lord keeper, furthered the cause of an educated parochial ministry and of theological studies at the two universities but it had neither produced an entirely conformable clergy nor a radically Protestant one. The result pleased neither the reforming group nor the perhaps equally radical Laudians of the reign of Charles I.[14]

In this section we have seen how the bishops in the Reformed tradition strove to reform the ministry using both old and new methods. We have seen the obstacles to improvement on a large scale caused by the survival of the medieval patronage system. Puritan laity also sought to use the patronage at their disposal to inject Protestant ministers into the Church. As we have noted, they found the patronage system limiting and unsatisfactory. Even when an instrument for extending puritan patronage was at hand – the grant of next presentation – only limited use was made of it. Instead of exploiting grants of next presentation on an organized basis, puritans preferred to go outside the traditional patronage system and innovate – creating a new position in the clerical career structure which coexisted peaceably but uneasily with that of the beneficed incumbent. The Crown, despite an interest in the support of theological studies, did not commit itself either to the ideal of reforming the ministry along puritan lines or to that of building up a Crown party among the clergy. It could not do so as long as it viewed its ecclesiastical patronage not as an instrument for change and influence within the Church but as a well of favour for politicians, courtiers and hierarchy. Possession of ecclesiastical patronage meant property, and power to those patrons who had it and those who sought it. For as long as this was the case, there would be obstacles to its use in the interests of a worthy, preaching ministry or of a particular doctrinal or ceremonial opinion.

The clerical profession which was coming into being in the late sixteenth and seventeenth centuries was not, therefore, one marked by its homogeneity. The lower clergy, at least, were not produced to the design of a single architect. The plans of many different groups and men had their effect upon the profession. In the ensuing chapters we shall be studying the extent to which the new ministry was reformed and why. We shall be examining its career structure. Above all we shall be interested in the impact of tradition, of Reformed views and organization upon the clergy's view of itself as a profession. The manner in which the clerical profession developed owed much to the theological and ceremonial controversies of these years; to social, economic and educational change, and to the drift of contemporary English affairs.

Table 6
Number of presentations granted by the lord keeper:
January 1558/9 – December 1580[1]

1559	224	1570	125
1560	144	1571	116
1561	123	1572	93
1562	123	1573	106
1563	77	1574	135
1564	98	1575	133
1565	78	1576	172
1566	97	1577	108
1567	102	1578	126
1568	102	1579	163
1569	102	1580	248

1. The modern calendar year from 1 January to 31 December has been used in the compilation of this table. The arrangement of the years into groups of high or low presentations suggests that there were complex reasons for the discrepancies between various years – epidemics; poor communications; shortage of clergy.

Table 7
Number of presentations granted by Lord Chancellor Egerton:
1596–1616/17

1596	115		1606	105
1597	165		1607	102
1598	141		1608	109
1599	99		1609	101
1600	103		1610	119
1601	107		1611	86
1602	90		1612	122
1603	84		1613	112
1604	117		1614	98
1605	119		1615	98
			1616	101

Table 8
Indications of (a) the reasons for vacancies and (b) the basis of the lord keeper's
right to present to livings appearing in the lists of presentations,
1570–80 and 1596–1616

Year	Total	Death	Depri-vation	Resig-nation	Lapse	?	De iure	Ward-ship	Sim-ony	Pro-motion
1570	125	63	2	26	7	17	10			
1571	116	68	3	25	3	1	16			
1572	93	42	5	18	2	4	22			
1573	106	43	7	29	2	12	13			
1574	135	42	5	25	12	13	37	1		
1575	133	50	3	21	25	7	24	3		
1576	172	49	1	35	25	9	53			
1577	108	31	1	23	13	9	30	1		
1578	126	32	2	33	10	9	39	1		
1579	163	33	4	37	51	3	35			
1580	248	49	1	48	23	3	124			
1596	115	27	(1)	27	25	4	25	2	1	3
1597	165	40	(5)	33	47	4	30		2	4
1598	144	43	1(4)	17	47		19	3	7	3
1599	99	27	(4)	17	21	1	20		7	2
1600	103	29	2(1)	20	31		11		7	2
1601	107	36	3(2)	20	36	2	2	1(?)	2	3
1602	90	24	(1)	17	28	9	4	2	4	1
1603	84	29		13	32	3	5			2
1604	116	25	(6)	22	44	2	12		5	
1605	119	29	7(3)	19	36	1	19		5	
1606	105	34	1(6)	19	26	1	9		6	3
1607	102	24	1(10)	18	36		9		3	1

Table 8 continued

Year	Total	Death	Depri- vation	Resig- nation	Lapse	?	De iure	Ward- ship	Sim- ony	Pro- motion
1608	109	28	(14)	14	36	1	8		7	1
1609	101	21	(8)	15	39		10		7	1
1610	119	34	2(4)	26	31	1	17		3	1
1611	86	37	(4)	11	17	1	10		2	4
1612	123	39	1(14)	24	28		12		5	
1613	112	42	(10)	15	25	1	8		11	
1614	98	43	(5)	21	16		7		4	2
1615	89	28	1(8)	13	24	3	7		5	
1616	101	32	(5)	21	16	2	11		10	4

The above years were the only ones found suitable for such an analysis.
Unfortunately the figures are not conclusive: the clerk regularly confused reason for vacancy with the lord keeper's claim to present – two
very different things. For example, the category of 'Lapse' does not
explain why the living in question had fallen vacant but why it had
fallen into the lord keeper's hands. The term 'de iure' is yet more
obscure – it probably means simply that the living concerned was
normally a Crown living valued at below £20 and therefore the keeper's
by right – as such it must include many livings vacant by death, a
suggestion supported by the figures for 1576 and 1580. Despite these
defects the figures are very useful: the number of livings falling to the
keeper for extraordinary reasons can be estimated and the rise in the
number of livings presented to during lapse, dating from the mid-
1570s, is particularly notable, The figures in brackets under the heading
'deprivation' indicate livings vacated by 'cession'.

10

The reformation of the ministry

The Reformation in England undermined the clerical position. Now that the priest was no longer necessary as a mediator between the individual soul and God, a new *raison d'être* had to be sought either consciously or unconsciously. This was to be found in the pastoral function of the Reformed ministry. Basically, this involved a change in emphasis. Catholicism had stressed the sacrificial function of the priest in offering the mass. Put simply, the emphasis was on the office and not on the man. Some even maintained that the efficacy of the sacraments was in no way dependent upon the merit of the priest in his everyday life, although this did not imply a licence for clergy to live wicked or worldly lives. The Reformed view was that the minister should offer individual and loving care and advice to each member of his congregation as well as administer a fatherly discipline. Clearly the clergy of the established Church could not successfully claim that they were fulfilling this duty as long as they were ignorant, ill-educated men. The life, training and vocational dedication of the clergyman became all important. Not all accepted that the Reformation implied a radical change in the nature of the ministry – the queen, for example, seems to have clung to something akin to the Catholic idea of priesthood, both because of her innate conservatism and because of her fear of political reprisals. For a large part of Elizabeth's reign, however, the ecclesiastical hierarchy did accept, if in a modified form, the ideal of a worthy, preaching pastoral ministry and even with the advent of Whitgift there was an espousal, for rather different reasons, of the cause of a graduate ministry.

Much has been done to document the profound transformation of the established clergy during the late sixteenth and early seventeenth centuries. There is no reason to dispute the prevailing view that the clergy of the 1630s were a far cry from the mass of ignorant, vocationally unsuitable men who formed the clerical group in the late 1550s and early 1560s. Less attention has been given to the reasons for this change. Were the efforts of the hierarchy to reform the ministry according to this new *raison d'être* wholly or partially responsible? What were the other possible influences on the nature of clerical education, recruitment and placement?

There had long been attempts to regulate entry into the ministry although there is some evidence that examination of candidates for orders was either far from rigorous, or had been allowed to lapse in the later middle ages. Restriction of entry to the suitable was difficult at the beginning of Elizabeth's reign because the rate of recruitment among such men was poor at a time when many livings were completely unserved. The reasons for this state of affairs were many but it is possible to distinguish some of the most important. The decline in the overall number of clerical recruits has been dated from the reign of Edward.[1] This may have been attributable to the apparently higher standards of admission enforced during that reign. Probably, however, it was as much due to the unsettled state of affairs and to the contempt in which the ministry seems generally to have been held. In addition there were fewer opportunities for advancement within the Church now, and the Pluralities Act of 1529 had considerably reduced a cleric's chances of raking together a comfortable living. The reign of Edward not only witnessed the dissolution of many collegiate foundations but also the removal of high civil office from the grasp of the ambitious ecclesiastic. The deprivation of married clergy during Mary's reign made many reluctant to enter the Church. Recruitment was certainly difficult during her reign also. Despite Elizabeth's own antagonism to a married clergy, this deterrent was effectively removed at her accession, but the general insecurity which had surrounded the profession for 30 years past remained.

This insecurity was largely expressed in financial terms. As late as 1585 Archbishop Whitgift was to complain that there were scarcely 600 livings (out of well over 9,000 in the country) capable of supporting a learned minister. Livings were generally poorly endowed, although the incomplete contemporary surveys which survive do suggest that in many cases income was rising and probably keeping pace with or exceeding a like rise in the cost of living. Many clergymen had additional sources of income, either from the patron or impropriator, and many employed legal or illegal means to stretch or supplement their resources: teaching, preaching, trading or practising a craft being the most common means. Moreover, the clergyman could protect his income either by legal action or adroit management. One must balance these possibilities against two considerations. Firstly, a clergyman might lose a considerable proportion of his income in tax – either tenths or payments of a clerical subsidy – and his presentation to a living involved him in heavy expense, both in securing his presentation and in paying his first fruits to the Crown: secondly, there were many rules restricting his occupational activities and, at a time when many livings offered little more than subsistence prospects in themselves, such rules proved a definite barrier to recruitment among the able.[2]

Moreover, there were excellent and sure prospects for the educated man in alternative employment. Contemporaries such as William Day, provost of Eton, bewailed the fact that it was the legal profession which was reaping the benefits of university education, and he urged that the number of places at the inns of court should be restricted to force more students to take up the Church as a career, for:

> They be taken from the universities after they have been their a whill and sent unto the lawes of the Realme wheras their is such a nomber as I understand that the houses cannot receave them. I would wishe their might be some order taken for the law as it was for the monkes, for when they so increased that the houses could not hold them and every man sought to be a monke their was a certen nomber appoynted to every house aboue the which he should not passe. And wheras god shold have the fayrest and the best appoynted for him, their is now none but the hault and lame put to ministrey which can make no better and other shifte.

Some others recommended the implementation of a quota system for the professions which would drive at least some able men into the ranks of the parochial clergy.[3]

Thus in 1558 many were aware that the ministry was not attractive to most educated men as a career and that the existence of lucrative opportunities in other fields confirmed the position of the Church as the preserve of uneducated and sometimes vocationally unsuitable men. Most of the new bishops wished to encourage recruitment of conscientious pastors and to remodel parochial and diocesan organization on Reformed lines. Their very consciousness of the importance of the pastoral role led to fresh difficulties. Between 10 and 15 per cent of livings were void at Elizabeth's accession and certain populous areas, such as the archdeaconries of Canterbury and London, had vacancies in as many as one-third of their parishes. The shortage of curates and other assistants was probably yet more acute. An unusually high death rate prevailing between about 1556 and 1560 accounted for many of these vacancies although deprivations for non-subscription and resignations for religious and political reasons also took their toll.[4]

At first the new bishops resorted to mass ordinations to fill the vacant cures, acting on the principle that an ignorant pastor was better than no pastor. For example, 167 deacons were admitted in London diocese between 28 December 1559 and 24 March 1561. Similarly, in the first eight months of his episcopate Matthew Parker, or persons commissioned by him, ordained 233 men in the diocese of Canterbury. Even at this stage there was some attempt to regulate entry but when it is appreciated, for example, that Archdeacon Mullins acted as sole examiner in London diocese and that examinations normally took place on a single day prior to ordination, it is evident that the examinations can scarcely have been searching. The 'Interpretations of the Bishops', recognizing the acute shortage of clergy, agreed that candidates without knowledge of Latin should be admitted to deacon's orders provided that they were supported by good character references. The bishops stipulated that such men should not proceed to the priesthood until they had served a 'good time of experience' as deacon, and some 'precisions' in 1563 hoped to restrict such recruits to rectories below £8 in value and to vicarages worth less than £13 6s. 8d.[5]

A note of caution must be introduced here. Few bishops were appointed or resident within their sees during the period 1559–60 and fewer still held *mass* ordinations. Ordinations held at Ely in 1560 were not noticeably large and that at Worcester in early 1561 involved only nine men. Archbishop Parker was ordaining 'men to serve in all parts of England' – a matter of expediency as the mass ordinations held in a few major centres were not large enough to flood the market.[6]

The shortage of clergy felt throughout the decade is perhaps reflected in the large number of men who were ordained both deacon and priest on the same day or on immediately consecutive days. Between 1560 and 1562, 25 men were thus ordained at Chester (out of 43 ordained priest) and a further 60 were ordained to both orders between 1562 and 1570. None of these men ordained both deacon and priest simultaneously were graduates and most were drawn from Chester diocese itself; thus there seem to have been no peculiar circumstances to take into account, the persons involved neither being particularly well-qualified nor having to travel long distances to be ordained. Of 73 priests admitted at Lincoln on 13 May 1569, 50 were ordained deacon on the same day. The practice of granting both orders simultaneously was in direct defiance of the 'Interpretations of the Bishops' which in 1561 urged that, although unlearned men might be admitted to the diaconate during this time of severe shortage, they should not be ordained priest until they had served a goodly apprenticeship. The practice of giving both orders together continued throughout Elizabeth's reign. Between 1590 and 1595 at Peterborough, 70 of the 81 men ordained deacon received priest's orders on the same day. Canon 32 of 1604 seems to have put an end to the practice but, at least in the dioceses of Oxford and Peterborough (where ordinands were often taken directly from the universities), the rules were by-passed by ordaining to both orders on consecutive rather than identical days. A distinction may be drawn between the practice of ordaining non-graduates to both orders so that they might meet the urgent situation in the 1560s and that of ordaining graduates to both orders in the later period, when there was no situation of emergency but only the individual needs of the recruit to consider.[7]

The policy of mass and almost indiscriminate ordination was intended to be temporary only. Matthew Parker was faced with a perplexing problem: in an attempt to meet the recognized pastoral needs of the nation many men totally unfitted for the pastoral role were being admitted to livings – what had been conceived as a temporary expedient would have serious long-term consequences for the standard of pastoral care in England and Wales. In August 1560 Parker felt impelled to write to Grindal, Bishop of London, and other bishops of the southern province, advising them to raise the standards of admission and to avoid ordaining those of base occupation or non-clerical background. Having met the exigencies of the moment, it was now time to curb the flow of uneducated recruits.

> Whereas, occasioned by the great want of ministers, we and you both, for tolerable supply thereof, have heretofore admitted unto the ministry sundry artificers and others, not traded and brought up in learning, and, as it happened in a multitude, some that were of base occupations . . . these shall be to desire and require you hereafter to be very circumspect in admitting any to the ministry, and only to allow such as, having good testimony of their honest conversation, have been traded and exercised in learning, or at the least have spent their time with teaching of children, excluding all others which have been brought up and sustained themselves either by occupation or other kinds of life alienated from learning.[8]

It is significant that at this very time Parker was wedded to an alternative scheme for the provision of adequate pastoral care until such time as well-trained clergy could be recruited. This scheme involved the employment of readers or lectors, usually laymen, empowered to read the prayerbook services but not to administer the sacraments. Such a band of auxiliaries was undoubtedly needed in Parker's own diocese where fewer than half the parishes had a resident incumbent in 1559. Indeed, Parker fully intended the readers to have some status, envisaging something akin to an ordination ceremony. He saw the 'order' of lectors as more than a temporary expedient: they would be used not only in parishes devoid of clergy but also as assistants to incumbents and to curates. He evolved an elaborate scheme in which the pluralist rectors or vicars would supervise and ride a circuit of parishes, each of which was to be served by a resident curate or lector. Seventy-one lectors served in Canterbury diocese alone between December 1559 and 1562: in the latter year the experiment was abandoned. After this, the appointment of lectors was left to the discretion of individual bishops and they were employed on an *ad hoc* basis, never again forming part of a coherent scheme.[9]

The advantages attached to employing lectors to serve parishes instead of permitting the ordination and consequent institution of inadequately educated clerics are obvious. The lector had no freehold right to the living which he served or its income; on admission he was required to swear 'to give place upon convenient warning . . . if any learned minister' were presented to the benefice by its rightful patron. Although a lay reader was but a poor substitute for a *good* clerical pastor, presumably having no vocation and treating the post as a supplementary source of income, at the very least he was easily removable and fully answerable to the bishop for his actions. When the number of adequate recruits to the ministry swelled, the readers could be dispensed with and, because they did not belong to the 'profession', the hierarchy was in no sense responsible for their future employment. Why then was the experiment abortive? Certainly the shortage of educated clerics was not thus short-lived. Perhaps the chief reason lay in the fact that to be well-organized the scheme depended upon the ability of a bishop to refuse legal institution to unlearned ministers, reserving their places for removable lectors. Unfortunately, the bishops were empowered to reject presentees to benefices under extreme circumstances only – the patron's rights were so well protected at common law. Had co-operation between the bishops and patrons been possible, the scheme might successfully have stretched the Church's manpower resources and could have meant that the entire income of a group of parishes (forming the circuit) could be redistributed between one learned, resident incumbent and his resident assistants, ensuring adequate support for the educated man and providing an incentive for such men to enter the Church. As things were, however, the whole scheme was unworkable because patrons were exceedingly jealous of their rights. Patronage rights in lay hands were to prove the stumbling block for this scheme as they were for plans to redistribute impropriate tithes or to pursue a policy of rigorous examination at institution or ordination. It may be also that the clergy themselves raised an outcry at the professional implications of the scheme. There was certainly feeling that deprived clergy and private chaplains, who had refused the oath of supremacy, should be employed as temporary curates in preference to laymen during this time of shortage.[10]

Parker's directive to Grindal should be viewed, therefore, as one aspect of the archbishop's plan to control recruitment and to provide incentives for university men to serve at parochial level. There are some signs that the instruction was taken seriously. Grindal's own ordinations were considerably reduced in size. At Ely the examiners were careful to inquire into the age and background of the candidates. Richard Skynner's case, for instance, was referred to the bishop because Skynner was 66. Henry Funston, earlier made lector in Norwich diocese, seems to have been rejected because of a combination of age (60) and poor knowledge of the Scriptures and Latin.

Even so, older men continued to be admitted to orders until the supply of young university trained recruits improved, and this seems to have been true in London diocese also, where the average age of priests ordained in 1560 had been 34.[11]

By the 1570s, however, Bishop Parkhurst of Norwich was making an interesting declaration of ordination policy which echoed Parker's earlier sentiments: that there was no longer any necessity for ordaining mature men who had not been specifically set apart for the ministry from youth and that the bishops should therefore abide by the canons which they themselves had approved. Parkhurst rejected at least one such candidate on these grounds. The Ely ordination lists 1560–80 suggest that where a non-graduate was concerned, the issue of clerical background was often crucial to his success.[12]

Despite all these efforts, in the 1580s and 1590s, however, both the educational qualifications and the vocational aptitude of the beneficed clergy almost everywhere were still deplorable. In 1584 only 14 per cent of the clergy in Coventry and Lichfield diocese were graduates (a number unevenly spread throughout the large area covered by this see), and by 1602/3 the percentage had only risen to 24 per cent. In part this reflects the fact that improved recruitment took time to show itself at parochial level, owing to a generally low rate of mobility and turnover, as well as to the barriers raised by the patronage system. On the other hand initial recruitment outside the university ordination centres and London showed only a gradual improvement. Between 1560 and 1570 only one of 282 ordinands at Chester was noted as a graduate; recruitment was by no means wholly graduate in this diocese in the 1590s. At small Lichfield ordinations in 1567 and 1569 no graduates were ordained. Contemporary comment and, more specifically, puritan surveys make it clear that a large number of both graduate and non-graduate clergy were unable or unwilling to fulfil their pastoral functions satisfactorily.[13]

When examining the attempts of the hierarchy to reform the ministry during the period 1558–1642 one is bound to distinguish two linked interests. Firstly, the concern that the clergy be a graduate profession: this involved an appreciation of the need for university expansion and the encouragement of theological study at the universities as well as of the need for financial and other incentives within the professional structure itself. Secondly, there was a movement to ensure the vocational suitability of ministers which ran hand in hand with a call for more congregational participation in the choice of pastor and more clerical supervision of the exercise of ecclesiastical patronage.

One or two examples must suffice to demonstrate the major characteristics of these policies. Later the question of why university recruitment accelerated to such a great extent will receive some further consideration but it is necessary to establish here that both hierarchy and Crown were concerned to foster this expansion and to direct the products of both universities into the Church. As early as 1566 John Oxenbridge had blamed the universities for not replenishing their numbers after the reign of Mary. As the Ely ordination lists indicate, those graduates who were produced right at the beginning of Elizabeth's reign were destined for immediate preferment outside the realm of parochial responsibility, becoming archdeacons, canons, bishops, chaplains, masters of colleges, fellows and masters of hospitals. There were attempts to control and correct the situation. David Marcombe has noted that the prebendaries of the cathedrals of the new foundation were required to fulfil a pastoral function. Moreover, the Crown saw the need for provision of financial incentives for the study of theology at the universities, and for an increase in the value of benefices. In 1560 Elizabeth instructed her lord keeper to make available to theology students the income from Crown prebends assessed at less than £20 per annum, thus creating in effect a sizeable number of theology scholarships. Although Elizabeth is well known as despoiler of the Church's revenues, this plan of hers for the encouragement of theological studies at a time when they were in decline at the universities was probably no less important for the redirection of graduates into the Church than was James I's ambitious but abortive project for the reclamation by the Church of tithes in the hands of the universities. Despite the claims of historians that Oxford and Cambridge were becoming increasingly secular educational institutions, there is much contrary evidence that in fact their role as seminaries was being emphasized and encouraged as never before. It is true that the universities did provide a general education for young gentlemen but to stress this aspect of their character is to effect a serious distortion. Elizabeth and her successors intervened as often as they did in university affairs because they saw the clergy as upholders of the political and religious establishment, and were duly concerned that the clergy should be educated into conformity so that they, in their turn, might ensure the political docility of the laity. The impact of a stoic humanist, non-theological education on the clergy merits more attention.[14]

Many members of the episcopate, including Whitgift, Laud, Grindal, Sandys and Morton, actively sought to encourage the education of future clerics at the universities as well as to recruit men directly from them. Bishop Morton of Coventry and Lichfield, for instance, was in the 1620s and 1630s instrumental in the establishment of scholarships for boys from Shrewsbury school to study at St John's, Cambridge. Such endowments, although important, could effect only piecemeal improvements and there are signs of a more

concerted effort to educate the clergy – an effort which aped but
lagged behind developments in the continental Reformed churches,
and which was initiated by ardent laymen in the first place. Thus
both Sidney Sussex and Emmanuel College at Cambridge were
founded with the express purpose of providing a learned and Protestant ministry. In the statutes of Emmanuel (1585) is to be found an
admonition to members of the college

> that in establishing this college we have set before us this one aim, of
> rendering as many persons as possible fit for the sacred ministry of the
> word and the sacraments; so that from this seminary the Church of
> England might have men whom it may call forth to instruct the people
> and undertake the duty of pastors

The achievement of this end was not to be left to chance: a truly
vocational training, within the terms of reference of contemporaries,
was envisaged. It is significant that by 1617 Emmanuel boasted 200
undergraduates – more than any other Cambridge college except
Trinity. The college expanded somewhat in the ensuing period and
even managed to hold its own during the civil war and the unsettled
years which followed it. Earlier endowments with a clerical complexion, such as St John's, Christ's and Gonville and Caius at Cambridge, had their seminarial function emphasized and reinforced
during the early modern period.[15]

The intention in founding and encouraging Protestant seminaries
was specifically to produce preaching ministers. There was a deep
puritan conviction that the clergy required specific training and skills
to be able to instruct the people. As already indicated, one must not
be misled by the word vocational into believing that the training
planned was practical: the course was still essentially an academic
one. There was also a deeply held belief that the office involved was a
ministerial rather than a priestly one.

Elizabethan and early Stuart England saw attempts at the diocesan
level to control the placement of ministers as well as to provide
'in-service' training for the less well-qualified. Well known are the
associations of the clergy within a region into prophesyings, exercises and classes, all of which had a specifically educational and
professional function; less well known are the continual attempts to
devise satisfactory methods of controlling the admission of men into
livings. One of these means in constant use was the ancient device of
ordination examination. As we have seen there are sufficient
examples from throughout the period to indicate that bishops often
did examine conscientiously and, when the supply position allowed,
did restrict entry into the profession when the men presenting themselves were blatantly unsuitable on grounds of education, knowledge of the Scriptures or background. Several bishops tried to

extend this means of control by granting conditional approval to certain men, who had to perform set study tasks and produce certificates of their satisfactory completion. Such methods were also employed by many bishops prior to institution and there are classic examples from both Lincoln and Norwich to illustrate that bishops would reject candidates even at this late stage. In some cases conscientious patrons would formally examine their clients. The most notable example is that of the lord keeper. It is true that his patronage was so extensive that he could not exercise stringent personal control over its distribution but it is also evident that an examination system was adhered to and that, at least under Egerton, some men were presented on condition that they provide sermons for their congregations.

These attempts to control clerical recruitment made use of long-established methods; they worked within the existing framework of the patronage system. At best the bishops could hope to control the type of man eligible for patronage and to veto the presentation of specific individuals. Used freely such powers could have achieved much, but there is evidence to suggest that bishops were only free, or only felt themselves to be free, to use these methods infrequently and then in exceptional circumstances. Various schemes were drawn up which strove to modify or even radically alter the patronage structure through which the bishops were forced to work. In the 1570s, for example, as noted, Thomas Lever, Archdeacon of Coventry, drew up some detailed 'notes for some reformacon on the mynistrye and mynisters' to be observed until the promulgation of official rules.

It is easy to establish that the Crown and the hierarchy, both 'government' and 'reformed' wings, did have a set of principles which guided their approach to the question of initial recruitment into the Church and eventual employment of ordinands, but the actions of the Church's leaders were of necessity pragmatic. They were well aware that improvement in the quality of beneficed clergy rested upon educational expansion, especially as concerted attacks upon the prevailing patronage system were clearly doomed to failure. The inability of the bishops to reject unsuitable recruits has been over-emphasized by historians but it is true to say that bishops were relatively helpless (except in extreme circumstances) before the conservative habits of patrons and their tendency to present known, and often local, men to benefices over and above well-qualified men. The answer to this predicament was that the choice of clients before patrons must be limited initially to educated ordinands – clearly this could only be accomplished when sufficient graduates to meet the Church's pastoral needs presented themselves for ordination. This dream became reality in the early seventeenth century; 109

deacons were admitted to London diocese between the beginning of 1600 and the end of 1606 and, of this number, 82 were graduate and 12 were students. Recruitment via London in the 1620s was wholly graduate. Educational standards had always been somewhat higher in London, however (for example, in 1560, 44 out of 94 incumbents had a degree level education), and more significant is the improvement in remote, previously backward dioceses: 151 candidates were ordained at Gloucester between June 1609 and May 1621: of the 87 deacons, 52 had degrees; 43 of the 60 ordained priests also had degrees. The four men who received both orders on the same day were also university men. Many of the non-graduates were students. This situation is to be compared with that of 1570 when none of the 36 ordinands had degrees. Even at Chester ordinands were better qualified, although the ratio of graduate to non-graduate ordinands fluctuated. Of 314 candidates at Lichfield between 1614 and 1632, only 62 had no obvious university connection – recruitment was, therefore, at least four-fifths graduate and student. All this is to leave out of account the staggering impression of university recruitment which can be obtained from an inspection of ordination lists at Oxford and Peterborough – huge numbers of students and graduates either leaving or remaining at university took orders here and, from an early date, recruitment was almost solely from the universities. Neither is there any reason to suppose that the story of graduate recruitment in Ely and Lincoln changed in the early seventeenth century.[16]

It is a simple matter to establish firstly that the Crown and ecclesiastical leaders had a real interest in remodelling the ministry and particularly in making it a graduate group, and secondly that new recruits into the clergy were now almost all drawn from the universities. It is less easy to establish a causal connection. Was this spectacular improvement in the educational qualifications of clerical personnel attributable to the efforts of Crown and hierarchy? Did it occur rather because patrons were showing strong preference for university men and therefore influencing the young to preface their clerical career with a university education? Was it simply the result of tremendously increased opportunity for secondary and higher education? Was it because career prospects in the Church had so improved that it now attracted graduates who would earlier have entered the law or government service?

A monocausal explanation seems both impossible and undesirable. Even hierarchical interest in raising the educational standards of the clergy was in accord with the general climate of the times. On the other hand, while provision of Protestant seminaries, the endowment of scholarships and fellowships, and bequests to schools provided the formal institutional framework necessary for expansion, they did not of themselves provide the incentive. The reasons for graduate recruitment into the Church were complicated. They deserve the attention of historians if only because the effects of this transformation upon the established Church and upon clergy-lay relations, especially during the civil war and interregnum, will never be fully understood nor their magnitude appreciated without examination of the reasons behind and the nature of this change. Just a few of the issues must concern us here. Did the arrival of a graduate clergy significantly modify the way in which patronage was exercised? Did the clergy become more geographically mobile as a result, with increased pressure on the better livings? Is this to be attributed to a widening of the channels of communication through the university experience of both patrons and clients? Did the existing non-graduate clergy find it impossible to gain preferment because of new graduate competition? Were the 'new clergy' conscious of their position as an educated group? If so, what effect did this have upon professional development and clergy-lay relations?

To answer these questions it is first necessary to come to some understanding of the manner in which patronage was distributed in the middle ages and the early modern period. The prevailing picture was one of predominantly local recruitment into livings: local connection was of paramount importance when seeking a benefice. In Durham between 1311 and 1540 40.2 per cent of institutions involved men from the diocese, and a further 37.3 per cent men from the adjacent diocese of Carlisle and York. This pattern may have been modified in certain instances, for example in the case of Crown livings but, even here, local influence was important in perhaps a majority of cases. This state of affairs can be explained in common sense terms. The rules of the Church designed to prevent over-supply and under-employment of clergy by insisting that ordinands possess a title to a benefice, thus ensuring physical maintenance, naturally militated against large-scale migration because the inexperienced tended to obtain livings where they were best known. Exeter diocese between 1598 and 1621 was served largely by men from Devonshire. Thus the very structure of society supported preferment of local men. The patronage system provided opportunities for men to present both relatives and friends – this trend being heightened by the exercise of *pro hac vice* patronage. Of course, a man did not have to be a native of an area to obtain local connection. He might have managed to obtain temporary employment as teacher, curate or servant and eventually have acquired the necessary connections in this way. Moreover, patronage was often extended through a chain of connections.[17]

Broadly speaking, it seems that locally distributed patronage had to remain the norm unless one of two situations arose. Either the horizons of patrons would have to be broadened considerably in a geographical sense, so that men from outside their immediate locality were more readily brought to their attention, or patrons, actively preferring graduate to non-graduate clerics, would have to be forced to look outside their own localities for these men.

Superficially the huge expansion in secondary and higher education would seem to have created a climate congenial to the development of either or both of these situations – a large pool of graduate clergy willing to seek preferment anywhere; and a large number of gentry and yeoman patrons who had made new connections at university or at an inn of court and who were willing to extend their patronage either to these men or to their friends and relatives. When tested against the available evidence, however, this hypothesis seems to fall far short of the truth. Basically it assumes the co-existence of two separate groups of clergy: firstly, the uneducated men who entered the ministry before university expansion and, secondly, the graduates who flooded to ordination centres in the seventeenth century and especially in the 1620s and 1630s. It envisages competition between old and new men, educated versus uneducated. This would have been the case if the Church were now recruiting men from another group – if, for example, men who might in the 1590s have entered the law were now, in the 1620s, seeking ordination. This is a tempting proposition but there is no evidence that more than a few men changed direction because of improved clerical career prospects or hierarchical persuasion. What little evidence there is of the social background of the clergy suggests no significant change other than that of the new social status conferred by education. To see the existence of two distinct groups among recruits warring for preferment is difficult if not impossible. It is surely significant that during the seventeenth century candidates for ordination were almost entirely university products. The lack of evidence of competition between the two groups at the diocesan level supports this view. There are three possible explanations: men who might have entered the Church decided not to because they foresaw insurmountable graduate competition; the new men were but the 'old' newly reformed; or a combination of the two.

Several interesting lines of approach are suggested. For some reason men seeking a clerical career were attending grammar school and university before placement. This movement was so widespread and dramatic that there was little room for competition for livings between non-graduate and graduate clergy, except where older men were looking for further preferment, and evidence presented earlier suggests that the clergy were never very mobile. It also appears that the large-scale, national improvement in educational qualifications implied little or no modification in the operation of patronage. The horizons of most patrons who attended university or inn of court remained as narrow as ever, for both colleges and inns had a marked regional complexion which cemented an existing network of connections rather than creating fresh ones.[18]

Accepting this interpretation, there is still no single explanation of why the clergy turned to the universities before seeking orders. A plausible line of argument is this. At first, the education of clerics at university stemmed from two broad movements: the declared desire of the Church's leaders and a relatively small number of patrons to see a better educated clergy; and an increased interest in education which arose from no direct professional motivation. It used to be thought that men put their money into education simply because they were no longer allowed to donate it to religious foundations such as the chantries. Now it appears that contemporaries saw, and sought to meet, a specific social need for educational expansion and that some regarded it as a vehicle for social engineering. Thus we see the foundation of Protestant colleges for the training of ministers; grammar schools providing a classical education for those destined for the professions or local government; and English schools teaching basic literacy, arithmetic and accounting to apprentices. Although the sectaries of the 1650s failed to agree, this education was seen as utilitarian. Education to a higher level was ceasing to be a luxury. To an appreciation of the value of literacy for the conduct of everyday affairs was added a conviction that the laity should be able to read the Scriptures. The religious impetus behind the cry for a mass literacy was strong. It may help the historian to realize why young men readily accepted the need for an educated ministry – that they might be able to interpret what the laymen could only read.

Both these movements had a profound effect upon the potential recruits and their parents. At a time when few clergy were graduates or even students, and when those who did have degrees were destined for early preferment, young men began to feel that the best chances of rapid promotion lay in the possession of qualifications. Perhaps more significantly, parents and particularly clerical parents saw the situation in these terms. They encouraged their sons, nephews and godsons, with both words and financial aid, to pursue a university course prior to entering the ministry. Of course, one must not be cynical in attributing a mercenary motive to these parents and sons – many shared the conviction of the Church's leaders that the standards of the pastoral ministry must be improved through education.[19] But a degree also conferred status.

The universities and their colleges must themselves take some of the credit for this revolution in thought. Colleges saw themselves as essentially orientated towards the training of professionals. The curricula of the universities, while remaining traditional, were geared subtly towards the needs of clerics within the established system. The colleges maintained efficient and extensive communications with the schools in the provinces, making certain that able boys were made aware of the desirability of a university education and of the wisdom of attending a particular college.[20]

It is true that this change of attitude as well as changes in the character of recruitment took place at varying rates throughout England. For some time, well-educated ordinands were able to move away from the remote provincial dioceses to find niches outside their native areas – there was always mobility from such areas into those of increased opportunity, which is probably why highly educated clergy without benefices were much thicker on the ground in, for example, London than Coventry and Lichfield in the period preceding the civil war. Poorer areas therefore had to provide more clergy than they truly required. The change in attitude was largely dependent upon the speed at which local educational facilities caught up with the Church's demands in that area. In fact, in almost all cases facilities expanded rapidly and their natural orientation towards professional careers, combined with hierarchical interest in directing bright boys towards the Church via the universities, benefited the profession. A slow rate of turnover through death and resignation in the parishes meant that a relatively low annual recruitment of graduates was more than acceptable.

The development of secondary education in the diocese of Lichfield illustrates this point well. During the sixteenth century rather few native scholars were being sent to Oxford and Cambridge. An examination of Clark's *Tabular View of the Counties of Matriculation, 1567–1621*, demonstrates that the four counties of the diocese – Derbyshire, Shropshire, Staffordshire and Warwickshire – sent very few students to Oxford when compared with other counties such as Devon, Gloucestershire and Yorkshire. Whereas Derbyshire was in many respects a northern rather than a midland county which had definite connections with Cambridge, the other counties might have been expected to show a regional preference for Oxford. This remains true even when school connections, such as that of Shrewsbury School with St John's, Cambridge, are taken into account. Such a situation, when we recall the limited mobility into the area and the probable level of mobility out of it into richer and more populous localities, meant that the replacement of uneducated incumbents by graduate ones was liable to be slow. Real improvement in the diocese had to wait upon the desires of patrons and even more upon the improved internal supply of graduates.[21]

Although there were schools in the diocese, some of them important, prior to 1558, it is certainly true that the reign of Elizabeth and particularly the latter years of her reign witnessed the first real expansion in the number of schools. Even the King Edward VI School, Shrewsbury, the largest school in the four counties and possibly in England, was in reality revived in the early years of Elizabeth's reign. Despite the fact that the documentation is incomplete, it can be shown that at least 200 parishes out of 388 in the diocese were at some time during the period 1584 to 1642 served by a schoolmaster and that 93 of these parishes had a continuing tradition of education and probably a proper establishment. The endowed grammar and the unendowed grammar schools (sometimes also providing more elementary instruction) grew up in the market towns and more populous areas of the diocese. Where the parish did not have its own school, the children were normally within walking distance of a school or might board during the week in a market town in the vicinity.[22]

Ecclesiastical supervision of the schools was spasmodic; however, it is significant that in the case of the larger establishments, especially Shrewsbury, hierarchical interest and control was continuous. There is every reason to believe that the pupils of such a school, or rather those who did not belong to the gentry or nobility, were directed towards the professions via the university and particularly encouraged to enter the ministry. This natural orientation of grammar school education towards the Church was further reinforced by two linked factors: firstly, many of the non–gentle pupils were the sons of clerics; secondly, the ministry had a strong dynastic element within it. Moreover, because many of the 'temporary' schools scattered throughout the diocese were run by vicars or curates, a good deal of the education outside the grammar schools proper was clerically directed.

It is easy to see that from this point onwards the re–routing of ordinands into the Church via the universities was self–generating. The chances of good preferment appeared to both insider and outsider to be slender indeed without a degree, or at least student status. Richard Baxter was almost deterred from entering the ministry because he believed that 'the want of accademicall honours and degrees was like to make me contemptible with the most, and consequently hinder the success of my endeavours'. In fact, what little evidence survives suggests that local connection might still mean more to a patron than a good education – this is particularly evident in cases of older incumbents seeking preferment. Even so, it is evident that the hierarchical emphasis upon graduate recruitment and also the general climate of opinion in favour of education as the social ladder led contemporaries to a different assessment of the situation. One probably cannot overestimate the effects of talent-spotting by many preachers and incumbents upon the attitudes of young recruits.[23]

By the late 1620s and 1630s, however, men must have realized that a degree in itself could not prove a *positive* advantage to the man seeking placement, simply because every one seeking placement had a degree or was well on the way to obtaining one. Conversely, lack of such qualification proved a serious disadvantage for some. Patrons might not be swayed by such considerations, but the more conscientious bishops examined even graduates rigorously before ordination and, faced with a more than adequate supply of well-educated candidates, felt no scruple in rejecting unsuitable applicants. It is true that the men the Bishop of Oxford rejected in the 1630s found other bishops to ordain them, but they were graduate and, moreover, can scarcely have welcomed the inconvenience.[24]

Several important points emerge. Firstly, it would be wrong to judge the actions of prospective clerics in terms of the actualities of the situation: what they believed to be true was as important as, if not more important than, the actual truth in terms of professional development. Secondly, historians have tended to assume that changes in the nature of recruitment were gradual or that educational expansion was taken at a slow pace. In fact, such developments could make themselves felt almost overnight – as is demonstrated by the ordination lists. What is true is that the effects of changed recruitment might be slow in showing themselves *in the parishes* because of low rates of turnover and mobility among the clergy already ensconced. Thirdly, the move towards a graduate profession was self-generating after a certain point, which it is almost impossible for the historian to isolate. There came a time when to have a degree was felt to be desirable, both for idealistic and professional reasons; soon the question of desirability was no longer at issue – a degree was essential for a career in the Church but it held out no promise of preferential treatment and no guarantee of the vocational training or aptitude of its owner.

This is not the place to discuss the value of a university degree to a minister nor to assess the academic worth of a university degree at this time although, obviously, these are important questions for anyone attempting to gauge the success of the reforming policy of the hierarchy. It is true to say that whereas in the earlier part of the period many of the bishops laid equal weight upon attempts to produce graduate clergy and upon experiments to improve the vocational performance of ministers, by the 1620s and 1630s there was an increasing tendency among the bishops to hide behind the success of the first policy and shirk responsibility for further improvement. There are obvious exceptions: men like Thomas Morton and the Bishop of Oxford were concerned that many graduates were unsuitable for the ministry and they acted upon their convictions. Nevertheless, the lack of evidence of attempts to reform the *type* of education offered the clergy points to the general truth of this conclusion.

It was largely because of this excessive reliance upon degree status and diminished emphasis upon pastoral performance and vocation that an unwelcome situation arose which is discussed at greater length in chapter 15 of this book.

One may conclude that the hierarchy did have a twofold policy for reformation of the ministry: an increase in formal higher education; and heightened vocational emphasis. For a combination of reasons the first of these goals was achieved with amazing ease. The second was more difficult to ensure: the patronage system proved an effective barrier to rejection of the unsuitable; it was far more difficult to examine men for pastoral suitability than for possessing a paper qualification. In the event, decreasing emphasis was placed upon pastoral suitability by members of the episcopal bench. The effects of this situation were far-reaching and occurred where they might least have been expected.

11

The clerical élite

This book is concerned in the main with the lower clergy of the Church of England. In fact Protestant thought envisaged an entirely new clerical organization, which negated the old priestly function and stressed the overriding importance of the pastoral aspect of clergy. This new thought encompassed both the upper clergy and the parochial clergy. A new emphasis was placed upon the pastoral function of the bishops and other dignitaries (who were pastors of the clergy); there was a concerted effort to draw the lower clergy into this new 'ministry' by educating, training and supervising them. The development of the ministry as a profession depended essentially upon the quality of leadership which it received from the hierarchy, which itself depended in part upon the extent to which the hierarchy formed an integrated part of the profession. The clergy, high and low, had to be unified by vocation and function and also by career structure.

Unfortunately the present was caught in the trammels of the past. The reluctance, or the inability, of either Crown or hierarchy to inaugurate a new method of paying Church dignitaries and officials meant that there could be no clean break away from the medieval practice of supporting officials in both Church and university from the proceeds of prebendal stalls and benefices with which they had little true connection. The irregular availability of such positions in itself meant that there could be no natural career structure in the same diocese from parochial ministry to prebend and hence to greater responsibilities of a pastoral nature. Similarly, the Crown's attitude to the function of prebendal incomes (that they should be used to finance the students of theology at the universities or to supplement the incomes of prominent preachers and dignitaries) directly contradicted attempts by some bishops to stress the diocesan, pastoral responsibilities of its clerical élite. If the leadership of the Church clearly fell to those without pastoral experience then there was a danger that the more ambitious clergy with a bent for organization or theology would circumvent pastoral work as far as possible and, more seriously yet, that the emphasis in religious writing and preaching would be removed from the pastoral function. In theory the key to promotion to the upper echelons of the clerical ladder in a Reformed church would be successful pastoral service and evidence of preaching ability and enthusiasm. These were certainly ingredients in many clerical success stories but whether they were the most telling is doubtful.[1]

Some light can be shed upon the question by examining the lower clergy in particular areas at a number of dates, and seeing how many of the men concerned ever achieved promotion (to prebendal stalls, cathedral offices, diocesan offices) within the same diocese. For example, of the 91 incumbents in Coventry archdeaconry in 1584 only four were promoted to such positions, three to prebends and one to an archdeaconry. Eight out of 95 incumbents in the archdeaconry of Derby in 1584 achieved promotion. One was an archdeacon, one was the vicar general of the diocese and another was the treasurer of the cathedral. Similarly, a return for 1620 of clergy in the four archdeaconries of Lichfield diocese revealed that six out of 64 incumbents in Stafford archdeaconry entered the upper echelons; in Derby the figure was only two out of 86; in Warwick five out of 98 and in Salop two out of 61.[2]

One might conclude that this was a fairly good showing on the part of the parish clergy but, in fact, the statistical information is misleading. In few cases was it a simple matter of promotion from pastoral to non-pastoral functions, from the parishes to the upper reaches of the hierarchy. Several men were given cures of souls to help support them financially in their diocesan work. Zachary Babington, for instance, was Chancellor of the diocese before presentation to a living of any kind. When he was given the prebendal stall of Curborough in 1583 and the rectory of Sudbury, Derbyshire in the same year it was to support his official work and not to introduce him to pastoral functions. Babington accordingly leased out the prebendal estates for three lives at a low reserved rent, and drew £900 in entry fines.[3] This was clearly not a case of local man makes good: Babington was a lawyer and administrator and not a pastor. Christopher Gill's is also a case in point. Although he held a living in 1584 this was undoubtedly to help remunerate him for his services as Chancellor of the cathedral and as treasurer. William Hinton, Archdeacon of Coventry from 1584 until 1631, was given the living of St Michael's, Coventry, to supplement his income as archdeacon. Hinton supplied the place with a curate. John Fulnetby's heart also was in cathedral affairs and diocesan administration. He entered the diocese as a prebendary in 1605 and not as a parish priest. He was precentor of the cathedral from 1608–36 and Archdeacon of Stafford from 1614–36. Although he held two livings (Handsworth from 1608–36 and Aldridge from 1622–36), they acted as a supplement to his livelihood and both were served by curates. Now this is not to say that Hinton and Fulnetby did not take their pastoral duties seriously, but they were the responsibilities of clerical supervision incumbent upon an archdeacon and not those of the parish. In neither case had parochial experience furthered promotion.

For some others, however, the situation is not so clearly defined. Sampson Hawkshurst came from a clerical family in Shropshire. He proceeded B.A. from Balliol College, Oxford, in 1593 and in 1599 was presented to Dunchurch vicarage in Warwick archdeaconry. But it seems that Hawkshurst was not content with his lot and, motivated by a mixture of ambition and love of learning, he studied for both his M.A. and his B.D. at the university. By this time the rules allowed him to complete his studies largely *in absentia* from the university and it is not necessary to assume that he was non-resident during this period. It is clear, however, that Hawkshurst thought that a higher degree brought with it strong chances of promotion. In 1607 he proceeded B.D.; in 1608 he was collated to the prebend of High Offley. This prebend carried with it the patronage of the vicarage. Hawkshurst leased out the prebendal estates for three lives and took an unspecified amount in entry fines. Hawkshurst retained both Dunchurch and High Offley until 1627, when he became Vicar of Nuneaton. It is hard to know how to treat a case like this. It is not the case of one who was already prominent in diocesan or cathedral administration or in university circles, but it is still difficult to ascertain what part his parochial experience played in securing him a place in the cathedral élite of his home diocese. At least it meant that he was known by the bishop (who collated to the prebend in question). Hawkshurst may have been a diligent parish priest and this may have been what commended him to his superiors. Yet Hawkshurst seems all along to have been one of Bishop Overton's protégés – Dunchurch was in the bishop's gift – and he was probably one of the bishop's chaplains. Academic achievement seems to have swayed the bishop to a greater extent than parochial service, and it suggests that Hawkshurst had been singled out on graduation for eventual promotion on the basis of his academic promise.

The career of the puritan John Walton, Archdeacon of Derby from 1590 until his death in 1603, was apparently also furthered by academic prowess. During his career Walton held at least three livings, two of them in Lichfield diocese, but his entry to the cathedral circle preceded his parochial experience. Walton took his Cambridge M.A. in 1575, was collated to Wellington prebend in 1576 and was presented to Breadsall rectory, Derby, in 1577. Breadsall was served by a curate and Walton's parochial involvement was probably minimal. Walton used his preferment to support his academic studies and he added two further livings to his portfolio before becoming archdeacon in 1590. He continued to hold all five preferments to his death.

In fact, this brief examination of groups of clergy at two dates –

1584 and 1620 – suggests not that some parochial clergy did become members of the clerical élite but that some members of the cathedral/diocesan hierarchy were given, for one reason or another, cures of souls within the diocese. Moreover, education was clearly a mark which most members of the hierarchy bore. In only one of the 27 cases mentioned above was the man involved not certainly a graduate, and he was a student of both Oxford University and the inns of court. Of the graduates not one was less than a Master of Arts and many possessed a higher theology degree. Although it was possible to fulfil the requirements for an M. A. outside the university, it still at this date represented a set period and programme of study.

It is worthwhile here to examine the use of patronage to these higher positions in the diocese by one of the bishops. We possess a good deal of information concerning the episcopate of Thomas Morton, Bishop of Coventry and Lichfield from 1618–32. Morton was concerned in the early years of his episcopate to draw up a survey of all the resources of the see – rentals, fees, and rights of patronage. Morton was anxious to muster sufficient resources to remunerate his officials and his chaplains, and he knew that he had to do this by collating them to available prebendal stalls and cures of souls. Unfortunately, there was no regular availability of such places and, even when places were available, no reliable source of income. As Richard Baddiley, the bishop's secretary who compiled the survey, commented wistfully in 1631, 'My Lord hath given 27 collation of prebends and yet 11 of them not void.'[4]

Of course, the archdeaconries had a set value, ranging in Coventry and Lichfield from £20–£60 per annum. Three prebends were allocated to the cathedral offices of chancellor, treasurer and precentor. There were two other canons residentiary. The residentiary canons of the cathedral were provided with houses in the Cathedral Close. There were other houses at the bishop's disposal, which he presumably allocated as he thought fit. Certainly in 1623 two archdeacons were said to have the right to a house, but only by virtue of holding a specific prebend: Dr Hinton was a canon residentiary as well as Archdeacon of Coventry, and Dr Masters was prebendary of Pipe Parva as well as Archdeacon of Salop. Two of the houses were presumably let out by their occupants, the non-resident prebendaries of Eccleshall and Colwich. A house was a valuable supplement to income: most incumbents of cures of souls had them as of right but few prebendaries gained a house at the centre of diocesan administration. Perhaps the lack of housing in Lichfield did much to encourage the collation of prebendaries to benefices which provided housing. Certainly the bishop of this diocese could only guarantee residence in the city of eight members of the élite at a maximum.[5]

In theory the bishop had at his command the patronage of 27

prebendal stalls, 14 cures of souls and four archdeaconries. As noted above, the manner in which he used this patronage was to some extent predetermined, as some officials had fixed sources of income. As the income for the archdeaconries was scarcely adequate in terms of 1623 prices, and as it stemmed from procurations and other dues which it was not possible to increase, it was also probable that the bishop would choose to give his archdeacons preferments to help them to meet their expenses. A bishop would also wish to remunerate his vicar general and his domestic chaplains. He might also be asked by the Crown or some powerful figure to bestow preferment upon one or more of their protégés.

However, prebendal stalls did not become vacant *en masse* at the start of a new episcopate and, as there was almost always some attendant change of diocesan personnel and certainly of domestic chaplains, this posed a problem. A prominent official might have to take an inadequate preferment simply because nothing else was available, or the man in question might have to seek preferment outside his diocese to achieve solvency. Even a technically adequate prebendal estate might be next to useless as remuneration because it was encumbered by leases which were unlikely to fall through quickly. The implications of the complexity (and unreliability) of this method of paying diocesan and cathedral officials for achieving a professional structure which approached the Protestant ideal were enormous.

None of the Lichfield prebendal stalls was precisely wealthy although several had a respectable valuation in the King's Book. One, Sallow, was valued at £56 13s. 4d., and five were valued at £20 or above. But several had nominal values even in 1534. Nine were valued at £2 10s. or less, and of these three were valued at £1 or less. Receipt of one of these prebends, in normal circumstances, neither greatly increased a cleric's income nor made him one of the élite: it could only confirm his membership and give him a say in cathedral administration. The value of some of the prebends had risen sharply in the period between 1534 and 1623, as Baddiley noted. This was presumably due to a combination of the effects of inflation on land values and of improvement of the estates (usually by lessees). Where a prebend did not show a significant increase in value this was probably due to the nature of its endowment. When a prebend had little or no workable land to start with, it was nigh on impossible to increase its revenues. This was the case with Dernford which had income only from its mill, which yielded 10s. in 1534 and 13s. 4d. in 1623.[6]

Even this information does not really tell us what income potential the prebendal patronage yielded either for the Bishop, in his search to finance his chief advisers and officials, or the recipients. The estates of the prebends were heavily leased and several prebendaries serving under Morton suffered because of leases arranged by their predecessors. The general practice was for a prebendary to lease out the estates and tithes at a reserved rent (which probably represented its taxable value under the *Valor* or that amount plus an increment allowing for rising costs) and an entry fine, which was as high as the land value and the market would permit. Such a practice could benefit the prebendary considerably. The entry fine probably yielded a welcome capital sum such as would not often be within the grasp of the ordinary parochial cleric (and which could be invested in a personal estate or used to supplement income and cover extraordinary expenses), in addition to a reserved income upon which only minimal tax was payable. Moreover, the prebendary benefited however short his stay in the prebend in question. He could relinquish the preferment without qualms on the day after collecting his entry fine if he so wished. For his successor in the prebend the benefits of the system were less certain. The lease might fall through within his own occupancy and leave him free to make a similar arrangement with all its attendant immediate advantages. However, leases were made for long periods of time even after the act of 1571 which restricted leases to periods of 21 years or three lives (except in the case of leases to the Crown). A successor might, therefore, never have the benefit of a heavy entry fine and be stuck with a rental which was constantly being undermined by inflation. What one made out of even a wealthy prebend was, therefore, a hit-and-miss matter. If it were unencumbered with leases one stood to gain considerably from such a collection, but if it were leased and the lease had a good while to run one stood to benefit little.[8]

Baddiley mentions the case of Stockett Lutwich who held the prebendal stall of Flixton, valued at £7 in 1534. The prebend had doubled in face value by the 1560s and was thought to bring in £16 per annum by 1623 under the terms of a lease made by the present incumbent. Lutwich, a non-graduate but an ex-student of both Oxford and the inns of court, took £400 in entry fines. Lutwich's rental probably affected only himself as he occupied the prebend until the early 1640s. But Edmund Merrick, LL.D., prebendary of Bobbenhull, Warwickshire, in the period 1563–1606, leased out his prebendal estates to his own children on a long lease which was still in effect in 1623. It is improbable that he required of his own kith and kin heavy entry fines or even reasonable reserved rental. Yet the prebend, valued at only £1 in 1534, was thought to be worth £50 in potential income in 1623.[9]

It is small wonder that in the 1630s Archbishop Laud and his 'party' were intent upon preventing excessive leasing of prebendal estates: it was undermining the very necessary method of subsidiz-

Table 9

Table of values: prebendal stalls in Coventry and Lichfield, 1535, 1560s/70s, 1623[7]

Prebend	King's Book	Bishop Bentham	Richard Baddiley	Comment
Alrewas	£26 13s. 4d.		£27 13s. 4d. rr	
Berkswich & Whittington & Baswich	£13 6s. 8d.	£18	£16 0s. 0d. rr	estimated worth £100 in 1623
Bishopshull	£2 0s. 0d.	£2 5s. 6d.	£2 5s. 6d. rr	estimated worth £29 2s. 9d. in 1623
Bobenhull	£1 0s. 0d.	£3 3s. 0d.	?	worth £50 in 1623
Brewood	£2 0s. 0d.		£44 0s. 0d. rr	worth £300 in 1623
Colwich	£13 6s. 8d.	£26 6s. 0d.	£22 0s. 0d. rr	worth £66 5s. 6d. in 1623
Curborough	£6 13s. 4d.	£8 0s. 0d.	£6 13s. 4d. rr	worth £90 in 1623
Dassett	3s. 4d.	4s. 0d.	3s. 4d. rr	
Dernford	10s. 0d.	13s. 4d.	13s. 4d. rr	from the mill in 1623
Eccleshall	£20 0s. 0d.		£20 0s. 0d.	
Flixton	£7 0s. 0d.	£16 0s. 0d.	£16 0s. 0d. rr	£400 in entry fines to Stockett Lutwich
Freford	£14 0s. 0d.	£33 3s. 0d.	£20, £9 rr	in 1623 money drawn from two separate leases
Gaia Major	£5 0s. 0d.	£7 0s. 0d.	?rr	worth £26 6s. in 1623
Gaia Minor	£2 0s. 0d.	£4 0s. 0d.	?rr	worth £13 2s. 9d. in 1623
Hansacre	£20 0s. 0d.	£14 0s. 0d.	£20 0s. 0d. rr	William Hinton has much improved the estate
Itchington Episcopi	£26 13s. 4d.		£26 0s. 8d. rr	worth £100 in 1623
Longden	£8 0s. 0d.	£16 0s. 0d.	£16 13s. 4d. rr	worth £100 at least in 1623
Offley	£16 0s. 0d.	£18 0s. 0d.	£22 0s. 0d. rr	

Table 9—*continued*

Prebend	King's Book	Bishop Bentham	Richard Baddiley	Comment
Oloughton				
First Half	£2 3s. 4d.			worth £26 6s. in 1623
Second Half	£2 3s. 4d.			worth £26 6s. in 1623
Pipe Parva	£1 6s. 8d.	£3 3s. 0d.	£1 6s. 8d. rr	plus a house in the close of 1623
Prees	£19 0s. 0d.	£26 6s. 0d.	£20 0s. 0d. £6 13s. 4d. £5 0s. 9d. rr	rent on 3 parcels in 1623; worth at least £100 in 1623
Rinton	£11 6s. 8d.	£10 0s. 0d.	?rr	worth £50 in 1623
Sallow	£56 13s. 4d.	£66 6s. 0d.	?rr	worth £300 in 1623
Sandiacre	£10 11s. 5½d.	£10 0s. 0d.	£7 6s. 8d. rr	overcharged in King's Books
Stotfold	£5 0s. 0d.	£7 0s. 0d.	?rr	tithes worth £100 in 1623; increase in rr by Lord Chancellor's order
Tachbrook	£10 0s. 0d.	£16 0s. 0d.	?rr	worth £50 or £60 in 1623
Tarvin	£26 13s. 4d.	£38 0s. 0d.	£36 0s. 0d. rr	worth £200 in 1623; reported £300 entry fines in 1603 on current lease.
Weeford	£14 0s. 0d.	£20 0s. 0d.	£14 0s. 0d. rr	
Wellington	£10 0s. 0d.	£13 2s. 9d.	£10 0s. 0d. rr	worth £66 6s. 0d. in 1623
Wolvey	£2 3s. 4d.	£6 0s. 0d.	?rr	

rr = reserved rent.

?rr = query as to amount of reserved rent in survey; estimated worth in 1623 is Baddiley's assessment of *per annum* value of land.

It is probable but not certain that the figures in the King's Book and in Bentham's Survey represent the annual reserved rental; this would make them directly comparable with those for 1623. As we are not sure whether an economic rent was being received even in 1535, however, it would be dangerous to assume that the land had risen in value between 1535 and 1623 by the difference between the two figures of 1535 rr and estimated worth in 1623.

ing the income of important Church officials. Although at least one cathedral chapter (that of Ely) had in 1588 imposed upon itself a rule that no lease should in future be made for a period of lives but only for a maximum of 21 years, and although something was done through the acts of 1571 and 1576 to prevent the worst abuses of the system, the rentals obtained from prebendal and other estates were in no way equivalent to the true value of the lands concerned. In 1633 Laud finally persuaded Charles I to forbid leases for lives of such estates altogether. In 1634 the instructions were extended to include not only deaneries but also individual prebendal estates. Surveys were ordered to see that the instructions were being punctiliously observed. Yet although the leasing of prebendal estates for long periods was undoubtedly a grave abuse and did undermine the system of financing Church dignitaries and officials, the irregular availability of preferments had even more serious consequences for the profession and its roots in pastoral service. When one sees the Archdeacon of Sarum being given the treasurership of Lichfield Cathedral with its appendant prebend, the most valuable in the diocese, one begins to realize the implications. It was necessary to give Church dignitaries and officials places when and where they became available, *irrespective* of their principal responsibilities in terms of geography or interest. The placement of the clerical élite was divorced from the diocesan and parochial structure.[10]

How did Bishop Morton use the patronage which came into his hands? During the 13 years or so of his episcopate, opportunities arose to present 28 times to 17 different places (15 prebends and two archdeaconries). In no case did Morton collate a non-graduate to one of the preferments in his gift. Moreover, in all but one case the men appointed had at least an M.A. degree and, in several cases, a higher degree, usually in theology but in one case in medicine. The man who possessed only a B.A. on preferment in 1630 had obtained his B.D. by 1632. In several cases Morton used his patronage quite evidently to provide for his personal chaplains – men whom he had selected for their promise and potential as leaders in the Church. William Jeffray obtained a living (Sheriffhales vicarage) in the diocese in 1622 at the hands of Sir Walter Aston, whether or not with the bishop's connivance, but he had certainly been noticed by Morton by 1625 when he was collated to Gaia Major prebend as Morton's domestic chaplain. In 1627 Jeffray was collated to Offley prebend and in 1628 to the archdeaconry of Salop. A puritan patron presented Jeffray to Hampstall Ridware in 1631, following his appointment as Chancellor of the cathedral in 1630. Jeffray was an active deputy in the consistory court during the 1630s. His prominence no doubt owed something to his close kinship (nephew) with the chancellor of the diocese, Charles Twysden.

Another puritan minister, Alexander Howe, pluralist Rector of Draycott in the Moors and Caverswall, Staffordshire, was collated to a prebend (Ulveton) in 1626 as the bishop's domestic chaplain. He, too, was active in the diocesan courts, and he appears to have acted as the equivalent of a rural dean when the consistory court met in his church of Caverswall. James Povey, M.A., Rector of Willey since 1601, was another diocesan cleric whom Morton made his domestic chaplain and protégé. Povey was active in the Church courts and sufficiently prominent for Morton's successor, Bishop Robert Wright, also to make him his chaplain and collate him to a prebend. There can be little doubt that Nathaniel Williams, B.A., later B.D., was a particular protégé of Morton. The bishop groomed him for a successful career. Williams, who graduated in early 1620, was presented to no fewer than four livings during Morton's episcopate. Two were livings in the bishop's gift – Dunchurch and Tachbrook in Warwickshire. The career of Williams seems to have dovetailed very closely with that of another episcopal protégé, William Jeffray. Probably Bentham persuaded Sir Thomas and Lady Katherine Leigh to present first Williams and then Jeffray to their rectory of Hampstall Ridware; when Williams resigned Hampstall Ridware in Jeffray's favour he was collated to the prebend of Offley which Jeffray had just vacated; Jeffray was now Archdeacon of Salop and Chancellor of the cathedral and so Morton's manoeuvre secured a place in the diocesan élite for both chaplains.[11]

By a judicious use of the preferments at his disposal and of goodwill of some lay patrons, the bishop was able to further the careers of the most able men in his entourage. Morton's use of patronage at parochial level echoes that of the prebendal stalls – he clearly demonstrated great and practical interest in the careers of particular individuals. The men whom he preferred at all levels appear to have been of moderate puritan persuasion and to have been enthusiastic preachers: this was no less true of George Canner, blind curate of Clifton Campville, than it was of John Burges, M.D., the Rector of Sutton Coldfield (1617–35), preferred to Wellington prebend in 1625. Morton was concerned to ensure that the diocesan administration, itself a prime pastoral function, was conducted by able and conscientious clerics, and to this extent the Protestant view of the clerical élite can be seen at work in his exercise of patronage. He did appoint as his chaplains some learned clerics who were already based in the diocese as ministers and, once he had promoted their careers, he involved them fully in the rather different pastoral functions of lay and clerical discipline. Even so, Morton imported key figures such as Jeffray and Williams. Moreover, he was evidently much guided in his selection of chaplains by the level of education attained by a client: university record and preaching activity, rather than pastoral experience, singled out his chaplains from the mass of the parochial clergy. (Perhaps this was natural enough at a time when a high proportion of new recruits to the Church possessed a first degree.) This fact meant that, while Morton's choice of prebendaries was to a great degree dictated by a Reformed vision of what the cathedral élite should look like, his appointees were not entirely drawn from the ranks of the diocese's parish clergy.

Morton used some of his patronage to give place to men with little personal connection with himself. In this he was caught up in the traditional web of patronage: he bestowed favours on suitors, expressed his own gratitude to his personal benefactors, or bowed to the superior wisdom or power of others. Stephen Haxby, for example, seems to have been recommended to Morton by St John's College, Cambridge, Morton's old college. Haxby was collated to Wolvey prebend in 1619 and in 1620 was presented by the Crown to Ashover rectory, Derbyshire. Haxby left Ashover for Coppenhall, Cheshire, in the following year. There were, of course, a considerable number of able men seeking places in the Church at this time, and Morton collated several other men whose academic record served as their principal recommendation for promotion in the diocese and whose subsequent connection with diocesan life seems to have been slight. George Murray was a Bachelor of Divinity and a Fellow of Queen's, Cambridge, when collated in 1623 to Bishopshull. He was perhaps one of those men who left university life for reasons of marriage: he appears not to have achieved great heights within the Church. William Sherbourne, B.D. (later D.D.), had connections with the dioceses of Hereford and Llandaff and a distinguished career at Oxford. William Bridges, B.D., presumably needed an additional income to help support his activities as Archdeacon of Oxford and Fellow of Winchester College. George Gippes, M.A., perhaps gained promotion to Freford prebend because of his connection with St John's College, Cambridge. He left university teaching in 1619 and certainly had no known previous connection with Coventry and Lichfield diocese. None of these men seem to have developed any real connection with the diocese after receiving their collations.

In one similar case, however, Morton may be said to have recruited the services of an able theologian for the diocese by establishing an early link. Ralph Brownrigg, collated to the prebend of Tachbrook in 1629, was a man already marked for position in the Church and with whom Morton shared strong theological sympathies. At the time of the collation Brownrigg had a distinguished academic record, a prebendal stall in Ely cathedral and four benefices (none in Coventry and Lichfield diocese). In 1631 Brownrigg became Archdeacon of Coventry, a position which he held until

1642 when he was elevated to the see of Exeter. Of course, from 1635 onwards Brownrigg was at least equally involved with the academic life of the University of Cambridge: from 1635–45 he was Master of St Catherine's and he was Vice-Chancellor of the university from 1637–9 and from 1643–5. Nevertheless, it could be said fairly that Morton gave his patronage to this distinguished man and enlisted his services for a diocese with which he had no prior connection. Whether Brownrigg ever demonstrated great personal interest or activity in his capacity as Archdeacon of Coventry, or whether the interests of the Church in the diocese at this delicate juncture were well served by a theologian is, of course, a debatable point.[12]

Bishops such as Morton were vigorous in their pursuit of the Protestant ideal when promoting men to positions in the diocesan hierarchy but even they were unable to live up to this new ideal entirely, or to avoid the graver implications of the need to finance officials throughout the country from the proceeds of prebendal estates. Constant lobbying for place by the theological students of the universities, the criteria by which the Crown selected its own clients for advancement in the Church's hierarchy, and the various tugs upon the loyalties of the bishops themselves, made it impossible for the bishops or other patrons of prebendal stalls to allocate them in an entirely idealistic manner.

If one examines the occupants of Lichfield prebends over the period circa 1558–1680 one is struck by the patterns which emerge. First of all, turnover of place was much more rapid in some stalls than in others. This frequency of turnover seems to have owed something, but not everything, to the monetary value of the prebend concerned. Predictably enough, it seems to have been related to the promise and prominence of the occupants – men destined for further promotion in the Church held on to particular preferments for a shorter time, in general, than did men who had reached, with a prebend, the pinnacle of their clerical careers. A few such men had entered via an academic teaching career; a few were parochial clergymen promoted within their own diocese. The prebend of Flixton, for example, was occupied by only eight men between 1553 and 1719. For all except one of these men there was no further promotion. Stockett Lutwich held this prebend for nearly 40 years. Dernford prebend (where the occupant was resident) saw only eight occupants in a similar period and only one of these climbed higher on the ladder of preferment. Dassett Parva had nine prebendaries between 1557 and 1697. Some of the other stalls had more prominent incumbents: Colwich was in the hands of 14 different men between 1531 and 1684. Seven members of this group achieved further promotion as deans, archdeacons, bishops, chancellors, or treasurers. This pattern is repeated in a number of other prebends. It suggests a certain continuity in cathedral administration which was achieved in the main by the collation of a few of the better educated diocesan clergy to prebendal stalls (or by the appointment of the bishop's chaplains during a long episcopate). It also supports the suggestion that there were other, more common routes to promotion within the Church than that via parish and prebend.

Many of the men collated to prebends in Lichfield owed their promotion to their academic careers. Of the 11 graduates who held Colwich, all had an M.A., six had a higher theological degree, and four held college Fellowships. Although several (nine) held cures of souls during their careers, these were often to support them in their academic roles: for example, the Master of Balliol held livings during his term as Master. It was even more common for a university teacher, particularly one qualified in theology, to obtain a prebendal stall either to support him in his studies (as the Crown would have had all prebends below a certain value used) or to provide him with an income on his resignation from university teaching. At Eccleshall, for instance, seven of the 15 prebendaries serving between 1554 and 1689 had held Fellowships at the universities. Freford provided four ex-Fellows with a living and Gaia Major three, while Gaia Minor supported four ex-Fellows and Hansacre five. Thus, while prebends were certainly not meted out exclusively to ex-Fellows of colleges, they equally certainly represented an important source of preferment for ex-university teachers. University teaching had its attractions for young men but its financial remunerations were, no doubt, limited and, moreover, a Fellow was not permitted to marry. On marriage, or on feeling that the financial rewards and promotion prospects were not good enough, a Fellow would search for an equivalent or better position in the Church. Since many Fellows had high academic qualifications and since their colleges had connections with prominent patrons, ex-Fellows were regarded as natural candidates for the richer livings in the country and for a say in cathedral and diocesan administration. They were not, however, as a body destined for yet further promotion. This was in the nature of things: there were far fewer higher positions in the Church than able men to fill them and, moreover, the qualifications and interests of ex-Fellows generally limited them to seek promotion to deaneries and sees rather than to legal/administrative positions.

Another common route to a prebend in this diocese was that through official position in another diocese or a continuing position at the university. A man would acquire preferments in various places to support his principal activities in another location. Thomas Dod, M.A., had an academic career until 1603 when he acquired the patronage of James I: he was collated to a prebend at Chester in 1607 and to one in Lichfield in 1619 (via Morton's connivance – he had previously been Bishop of Chester), to support his positions as Archdeacon of Richmond (1607–47) and chaplain to the king. Dod was later promoted Dean of Ripon. In this way the services of one diocese (Chester, and later Ripon) were being subsidized by the resources of another. Similarly, Clement Colmore's position as Chancellor of the diocese of Durham in the early seventeenth century was financed from the proceeds of Durham and Lichfield prebends as well as from those of various cures of souls. Edmund Diggle's functions as Archdeacon of York (1663–88) were in part supported by the treasurership of Lichfield cathedral and a Ripon prebendal stall. It is hard to believe that Thomas Laurence, B.D., was more than an occasional visitor to Lichfield, where he was treasurer and holder of the richest stall in the cathedral, when he was simultaneously Master of Balliol, Professor of Divinity, and a royal and noble chaplain.

Clearly the patronage of monarchs or great men also provided a path to preferment. John Bridgman, one of James I's chaplains, acquired Eccleshall prebend in 1616 as the third of such places given him on the strength of his favour at court, before his elevation to the episcopate in 1619. Thomas Laurence also received considerable preferment from the king. Samuel Brook, Master of Trinity College, Cambridge, had royal patronage. In 1625 the Archbishop of Canterbury intervened to collate Richard Pilkington, D.D., to the treasurership of the cathedral.

What we are really concerned about here are the implications of such paths to promotion for the 'élite structure' within a particular diocese. Past service in pastoral care in the diocese provided one route to élite membership as did pastoral service in other dioceses, but preferment came more readily via other paths. The immediate protégés of a diocesan bishop, recruited from among able undergraduates and scholars and with sympathetic religious views, were employed in the work of the diocese and groomed for leadership; ex-Fellows of the colleges sought extra-university employment with the help of their university patrons; Church and university officials and dignitaries found preferment through their network of connection; clients of Crown, nobility, university or cathedral hierarchy were able to achieve rapid promotion. There is certainly no evidence at Lichfield of nepotism or outright corruption playing a part in the administration of patronage at this level. The nature of the documentation (generally restricted to a few dates and biographical particulars) and the probability of overlap makes a statistical breakdown of the men following differing paths to preferment inadvisable. Nevertheless, it seems apparent that the Protestant ideal of a preaching, caring ministry in close contact with its flock stood little chance of full realization (even under a sympathetic bishop) as long as the current system of financing Church government and of distributing preferments persisted. To a great extent the criteria by which the Crown selected candidates for the episcopate and deaneries determined the criteria for promotion to prebendal stalls and archdeaconries.[13]

Was it, in fact, those men with a long experience of pastoral service and non-courtly preaching who were promoted to the highest positions in the hierarchy? The answer is a resounding *no*. The reformation of the upper echelons of the ministry, at least, still had far to go before it achieved the ideal. There was no single career ladder in the English Church, reaching from assistant curate to bishop, which was accessible to all recruits to the profession.

12

The community of the clergy

Considerable problems of definition arise in studying the consolidation of the clerical profession during the early modern period. In the course of the past chapters it has been established that now (by about 1620), in contrast to the medieval period, the majority of new recruits to the clergy were graduates or had spent some time studying at a university. Most of these men were resident upon their benefices or their cures. A new situation had arisen: now the *resident* cleric, however humble, was much better educated than his medieval counterpart and it was not only the higher clergy and dignitaries or absentee rectors who had received a university degree. The significance of this change both for the clerical profession and for its relations with the laity was enormous, even when it is remembered that there were still members of the clergy ensconced in benefices who had done no more than attend the local school.

In his discussion of the professions in sixteenth-century England, Professor Kenneth Charlton includes as one of the chief criteria for distinguishing a profession a period of organized professional training – normally of a theoretical nature – on an institutionalized basis. The seminarial function of the universities; the foundation of puritan colleges to produce fit ministers; the energy devoted to 'in-service' training, all help the clergy to fit this description. The term 'learned profession' implies that the members of a professional group are not involved in manual labour. The canons of the Church and the statutes of the realm all worked to restrict the cleric's participation in non-clerical or intellectual pursuits. They did so in order to ensure that the clergy devoted their time and energy to pastoral care but such measures had the side effect of divorcing the clergy occupationally and socially from the working community of the parish. Of course, the training which the clergy received was not vocational in the modern sense, being theoretical and general, with an extra-curricular emphasis on knowledge of the Scriptures.

The entire body of the clergy, therefore, upper and lower clergy alike, fits neatly into Professor Charlton's model of a profession. It was a distinct group with its own accepted internal hierarchy, its own rules and regulations, its own 'training programme' (which was becoming accepted as the norm for new recruits) and its own emphasis on non-manual work. Increasingly, the hierarchy was trying to educate the lower clergy and bring them within the professional network. There are, however, other aspects of Professor Charlton's definition which need further consideration. Was the clerical group not only a vocational group but a social one?

The clergy may not have been vocationally trained but most of the younger clergy had a degree and had been separated from the rest of the community since childhood in preparation for a clerical career. This development had been actively encouraged by the hierarchy. The clergy had shared a common education with entrants to other professions (law, medicine, teaching) and with some members of the gentry and noble classes, but they were isolated by education from the majority of the working population whom they would have to serve. Theirs was not a wealthy profession – although there is reason to believe that it was not as impoverished as has generally been maintained – but its position in society was important and the clergy as a group appear to have been anxious to assert their superiority and indispensability. Certain of the hierarchy were anxious to accentuate the dignity of the clergy – men like Thomas Morton, Bishop of Chester, Lichfield and Durham consecutively, no less than Arminians such as Richard Neile and William Laud. The Calvinist bishops chose to do so on grounds of the clergy's unique ability to interpret the Scriptures for the layman as a consequence of calling and training; the Arminians concentrated more on the nature of the priestly office.

It has already been observed that whereas during the reign of Elizabeth many of the bishops laid equal weight upon attempts to produce a graduate ministry and upon experiments to improve the pastoral work of ministers, by the 1620s and 1630s there was a tendency to shirk responsibility for the vocational training of ministers. There was an excessive reliance upon degree status and a seriously diminished emphasis upon pastoral performance and vocation. As will be shown, this led to an unwelcome situation in the 1640s; certainly the clergy set great store upon their own educational background.

Research has demonstrated that there was a 'community of the clergy' in early modern England. It is, of course, true that there were opportunities for the medieval clergy to feel kinship with their fellows – for example on the occasion of the ruridecanal general chapter meeting which dealt with local business and problems. Developments in the post-Reformation period saw a strengthening of these bonds – professional consolidation. One basic cause of this professional consolidation was undoubtedly the possession of a higher degree of education than the majority of the lay community. Clerical gatherings – now made more important by the hierarchical drive to see a better educated clergy and also by the impulse of the puritan lower clergy towards fast days, prophesyings and exercises – extended this process. Clerical marriage – leading in its turn to direct clerical dynasties and to marriages between clerical families – produced many important reverberations. Shared clerical experiences, problems and interests bound the community even tighter together. Where the clergy did have relationships outside their professional group, they tended to mix with other professionals or with the educated gentry. The historian finds evidence on occasion of close relationships between 'puritan' patrons and their clerical protégés.

The beneficed clergy were quick to seize the opportunity to increase the status of their calling through education – their wills indicate that they promoted their sons to university careers. Edward Peers, Rector of Sudbury, Derbyshire, willed his two sons the use of £50 apiece to keep them at university for four years. On occasion a godson benefited from such generosity: John Hill, Rector of Elford, Staffordshire, had, before his death in 1621/2, given to John Dowley '£10 alredy payd toward maintayninge him at Oxfourd And I give him more £3 6s. 8d.' Richard Browne, Rector of Norbury, Derbyshire, determined that both of his sons should have a clerical career or at least follow an academic calling. Enthusiasm for a university education was shown even when financial rewards were not forthcoming. Jonathan Jephcott entered Oxford in the 1590s, supporting himself from the proceeds of a short-term teaching appointment. He stretched the money as far as it would go and then returned to similar employment to finance further periods of study. Even when he found employment in the Church he still found it necessary to travel two miles a day away from his parish to supplement his income by teaching. Jonathan Jephcott the younger, probably his son, entered New Inn Hall, Oxford, in April 1627 and appears to have financed his stay there by serving as curate of Shilton, Warwickshire, for a period. The bishop (Thomas Morton of Lichfield) even appears to have ordained him deacon under the canonical minimum age so that he could serve the cure. This enthusiasm for a university education can probably be explained in terms of family tradition, puritan conviction and episcopal encouragement. A university education lent status to an impoverished professional. Moreover, contemporaries did believe that without a university degree preferment to a benefice was difficult to obtain and further promotion out of reach.[1]

It is difficult to establish just what percentage of the clergy belonged to clerical families. In her study of Exeter, Irene Cassidy estimated that between 20 and 25 per cent of clergy actually succeeded their fathers over the entire period of Bishop Cotton's episcopate. Dr Owen recorded that the dynastic element was strong among the London clergy in Elizabeth's reign. Figures for Stafford archdeaconry suggest that Miss Cassidy's figures may be a little high, but the web of clerical connection was extremely complex and were we to trace the more distant relationships – those of cousin, uncle, son-in-law, brother-in-law and grandson – the proportion of clergy belonging to long-standing clerical dynasties would exceed 25 per cent. The family of Bourne, for example, had as its representatives in the diocese of Lichfield at one point in the 1620s three brothers – Immanuel, Elisha and Nathaniel. Immanuel, the eldest, sent two of his sons into the ministry and provided for the education of his grandsons to that end. The Bourne brothers themselves were the sons of a Northamptonshire puritan cleric, who survived until 1649, and none of them succeeded their father. The connections were not always so obvious as between father and son or brother and brother. William Leigh, Rector of Edgmond, Salop, owned William Deacon, Rector of Hodnet, as his son-in-law, as well as William Leigh, clerk, as his son. Humphrey Steel, Vicar of Cheswardine (variously Staffordshire and Shropshire) was both cousin and patron to Nathaniel Pudyfatt, who was a member of an extra-diocesan clerical dynasty. Roger Daker's nephew was Thomas Colley, incumbent of both Drayton in Hales (at his uncle's demise) and Ightfield, Salop. The Taylors, father and son, held the livings of Moreton Corbet. This phenomenon was not confined to the later years of our period. In his will of 1585 Richard Stonnynaught spoke of his relationship with Mr Pennyfeather, parson of Draycott in the Moors, apparently his uncle. The Leonard Harresons, father and son, were serving in the archdeaconry of Coventry simultaneously in the 1590s.

Relationships such as these could and did cross diocesan boundaries, making it doubly difficult to estimate how many of the clergy of Elizabethan and Stuart England belonged to families with a strong clerical tradition. Whereas there was an element of dynasticism in the medieval Church (particularly at the higher echelons) the dramatic growth of clerical dynasties is a post-Reformation development, post-dating the acceptance of clerical marriage. By 1576, 61 of 146 clergy in Leicester archdeaconry were married men and two were widowers. Thus just over half of the clergy were married, a proportion which presumably increased as the diehard celibates or merely elderly clerics disappeared. Twenty-eight of the 38 men aged over 55 were unmarried; a mere nine of the middle age group of 32 men (aged between 35 and 55) were unmarried; 19 of the 28 men for whom there is relevant information in the under 35 age group were still single (this group contained 47 men but information is poorer than for the other groups as many were curates who made no return). These figures suggest that it was normal for the clergy to marry and that economic considerations prevented early marriage.[2]

This tendency towards dynasticism was important in the consolidation of the clerical profession but no less so was the sense of community engendered by common interests.

The contents of clerical wills at Lichfield, for example, provide some interesting information about clerical friendships which often seem to have had their roots in a common educational background and in shared 'scholarly', 'professional' and religious interests. Such friendships had often developed perfectly naturally between clergy of neighbouring parishes or between incumbent and assistant curate. Although not unusual or new, the cementing of personal relationships was important in the process of professional consolidation: the minister of an adjacent parish was possibly the only other man of equivalent education nearby, apart perhaps from the local gentry family which may or may not have welcomed the incumbent into their midst on terms of parity. Ministers themselves had much in common, not least being problems with their respective parishioners. Henry Clarke, vicar of Willoughby, Warwickshire, became fast friends with George Beale, Vicar of the next parish, Grandborough. Beale was but two years Clarke's senior and their careers at the university of Oxford had overlapped, both proceeding B.A. in 1612. Clarke was probably the son of Henry Clarke, minister of Leamington Priors in the same archdeaconry. He remained at Oxford until 1621, whereas Beale took up the Warwickshire living after receiving the degree of M.A. in 1615. When the time came for Clarke to find a benefice (perhaps on marriage) he returned to the neighbourhood of his boyhood, presented to the living by the president of his college, Magdalen. Occupied for the first time in pastoral work, he was doubtless grateful for Beale's advice and help, and both were pleased to preserve their scholarship and discuss common experiences. Clarke, and probably Beale, were puritan in sympathy. For the last few years of his life Clarke was in very poor health and receiving treatment in London. Nevertheless, despite long absences, he bequeathed to George Beale all his 'Lattin bookes standinge in the sayd Press [cupboard] in my studdye' (which were worth £10 at his appraisors' estimate) and forgave the same George a bonded debt of £30.

Similarly, Thomas Walker, Rector of Grendon, Warwickshire, shared his interest in books with Richard Latimer, vicar of neighbouring Polesworth. When Walker died in 1607 his bequest to Latimer was of 'one booke and my part of a booke which are both in his hands', suggesting that the two men exchanged books and had on at least one occasion co-operated to purchase a copy of a book which would normally have been beyond the means of either man acting alone. James Hall, Rector of Thorpe, Derbyshire, recorded in his will that he had lent the Rector of Kingsley 'a booke called calvyne upon Paules epistles' which had never been returned, in addition to a sum of five shillings. In 1625 the puritan Vicar of Sedgley decided to give 'unto Mr. Taylor the rector of Burwarton the bookes I have lent him'. It is possible that John Thomas of Flintshire had access to the library of William Overton in 1607 when he observed in his will that,

> There remayneth in my custodie fowre books which I borowed of my Lord bushop . . . Perapast upon the gospells Johis baptista uppon the psalmes the third booke reasoninge whether the Church or scripture are of greatest authoritie and John (?) booke of Churchgay Item remayninge allso in my custodie a booke of Humfrey Winsor a booke intreeatinge of the Sacraments.[3]

Simon Presse of Egginton, Derbyshire, made the chancellor of the diocese, Dr Zachary Babington, the overseer of his will and gave 'to the said Mr. Doctor Babington my best lawe booke'.

Many of the clergy participated in the late Elizabethan and early Stuart fashion for funeral sermons and often bequests to neighbouring clergy were in compensation for such services. In 1634 William Tomlinson, Rector of Thorpe, Derbyshire, wrote: 'I give unto Mr. Griffin Parson of Bentley five shillings to make a sermon in remembrance of me.' However, the clergymen whom they appointed to give these sermons were usually friends of long standing, with whose religious views they were in agreement. Brian Heppenstall left Roger Newham, parson of Staley 'in my good friend xs in gould & my best tannye cassock hopeing he will preach at my buriall'. George Higgs desired his 'good friend Mr. Orgell if hee bee alive and in health then to preach at my funerall and in remembraunce of my love I give him an angell'. Similarly with the men they chose to be executors and overseers. When Edward Peers, Rector of Sudbury, Derbyshire, drew up his will he stipulated that his son Edward should inherit his estate when he attained the age of 21 'if in the judgement of my good freind Mr. George Glen, Vicar of Doveridge, he shall then be thought fitt to manage the same'.[4]

The clergy who lived and worked close to one another often lent one another a helping hand financially. Thomas Walker of Grendon forgave Richard Latimer his neighbour 'all other reconinges which are betwixt him & mee saving the xxs aforesaid'. In 1597 the Vicar of Wednesbury, Staffordshire, died owing the Vicar of Walsall the sum of five pounds. Other gifts were made purely as free will offerings. In a will of 1 August 1623 William Hull, Curate of Ashbourne, Derbyshire, called his employer, Thomas Peacock, 'my loving freind' and bequeathed to him his 'best gowne save one, his old study bible in quarto and a piece of gold of 5s. 6d.' and made further bequests to local ministers. Arthur Hildersham received 11s. in gold and Messrs Rowlandson, Tailor and Brinsley were given 5s. apiece. In 1591 Thomas Warde of Monks Kirby, Warwickshire, gave to 'William

Hobson preyste' his 'cloke wyth sleeves & mi common places in Inglysshe wythe all my other Inglysse Bookes'. John Sprott bestowed a complete outfit of clothing upon the Vicar of Baddesley in 1597.[5]

This tightness of the clerical community, underlined by professional and educational ties, was further strengthened by bonds of kinship. Philip Ward was the brother-in-law of two Derbyshire clergymen, Arthur Rickards and John Porter. He was himself schoolmaster at Repton for a few years and served the cure there for a very brief period. His will of 29 May 1640 shows his connection both with the puritan ministers in Derbyshire and with Repton school:

> I give unto my father and mother to eich of them a booke either of them chuse And Mr. Arthur Rickeards my brother in lawe one Booke to chuse the next, and I give unto Mr. Roger Jackeson one Booke to chuse after the have chosen before and Mr. Ullocke one Booke to chuse the next.

His father Francis was named as executor but Arthur Rickards became overseer to the will and his consent was required before the estate could be sold in favour of Ward's younger children. John Porter, wealthy Rector of Aston on Trent, was also Ward's brother-in-law and in his own will bequeathed 30*s*. apiece to Arthur Rickards, Philip Ward and another brother-in-law, John Somerfield, clerk and curate of West Felton, Salop. A cousin, John Browne, Rector of Loughborough, became overseer to the will, acting in conjunction with Philip Ward of Repton. Porter's curate, Mr Wheildon, completed the clerical circle, receiving at his employer's hands 'five pounds to buy him a booke'. Gervase Wheildon had received his board and lodging in the parsonage as part of his salary.[6]

A network of clerical families emerges from these two wills alone. The marital relationships were in a sense both the cause and the effect of the closeness of the clerical community. The daughters and sisters of the clergy met and married persons of equivalent social and educational standing, often clergy. The daughter of the Vicar of Chebsey, Staffordshire, was expected to marry her father's successor but, in the event of her not doing so, she was to be accorded an annuity of £60 out of the estate. There were, of course, exceptions to the pattern of relationships enjoyed by the daughters and sisters of the clergy – it was common for such girls to be sent away into service in the homes of neighbouring gentry, merchants, tradesmen or yeoman farmers as well as of clergy, or even to the metropolis, and there they might meet and marry men with no clerical connections or ambitions. Whatever the deviations from the pattern described, the professional community of the clergy was strengthened by familial relationships at every level and account should be taken of the marriages of female siblings and offspring as well as of male.[7]

Both my own researches and those of Professor Patrick Collinson suggest that this entire web of clerical connection through friendship and kinship should be set within the context of organized clerical gatherings which in part fulfilled the functions of modern professional associations. Professor Collinson has drawn attention to the phenomenon of the 'combination lecture' which stood firmly in the tradition of 'exercises', 'prophesyings' and 'fast days' in the England of Elizabeth and the early Stuarts. A panel of ministers (varying in number), drawn from the natural catchment area of the preaching centre (normally a market town) or the same deanery provided sermons by rotation. Others of the 'combination' would also be present and the sermon would sometimes be followed by a conference among the ministers and a dinner paid for by the town magistrates or by the preachers. Professor Collinson sees these combination lectures as characteristic of the Anglicanism of this epoch and containing little that was inherently unorthodox – although schismatic views might be preached by individual members of a 'combination' there was little feeling that the entire enterprise was schismatic or subversive of the Church. The device was not simply one of providing sermons for the populace; it had another function 'as imparting some element of collegiality to its members' and as such it became an important element in the cohesion and common life of the Church. The lectures by combination strengthened the emergent sense of professionalism among the clergy, as did any clerical gathering – their importance was increased by the regularity and frequency of the gatherings which might be monthly or weekly.[8]

When arguments were put forward in the diocese of Norwich in the reign of James I in favour of combination lectures, the following points were made:

1. First, the propagation of the Ghospell and edefieng of the church.
2. Incouraging of the meaner sorte of preachers.
3. Exciting of sluggards to the studie of divinitie by meanes whereof their owne parishes also shallbe the better served.
4. Increase of love and acquaintance amongst preachers.
5. Increase of religion and learning, by meetinges and conference.
6. Varietie will more delighte the people's attention.
7. Advauncement to the clergie man, when their guiftes shalbe knowne.
8. People wanting preachers shall or maye be there taught.
9. Benefit also to the inhabitauntes for their markett by concurse of people.

This interesting conglomeration of religious, professional and commercial arguments and considerations demonstrates the awareness of the clergy of the need for professional cohesion, best brought about by frequent and regular meetings, the desirability of improved preaching standards and scriptural knowledge among the parish clergy, and the promotional advantages inherent in public preaching. As Professor Collinson points out, this was a Church consolidated by local loyalties, not characterized by ardent conformity, and emphasizing non-parochial patterns of religious life, but there can be little doubt that the long-term effects of such a programme would be improved pastoral performance, more and better preaching, and a preferment situation where patrons could sample the preaching of clients before taking the almost irrevocable step of presentation to a benefice.[9]

As Professor Collinson also points out, clerical gatherings at episcopal visitation and synod as well as prophesyings, exercises and fast days provided similar opportunities for the cementing of relationships among the clergy, for a sharing of common experiences and for general discussion. Technically a prophesying consisted of several sermons preached consecutively on the same text (taken from Scripture or a commonplace) and summed up by the moderator to the assembled company of clergy. Afterwards discipline was administered by the clergy to the clergy in a private conference. The renowned prophesying at Southam, which had a long tradition and which occasioned the suppression of all prophesyings in 1577, was conducted on this model. Other prophesyings grew out of the orders made for the further education of the unlearned, non-graduate clergy in Elizabeth's reign. The archdeacons set tasks or 'exercises' for the clergy to perform; the clergy gathered together to invigilate and correct the work. In some places (London and Durham, for example) the gathering was institutionalized into a 'regular quasi-synodal meeting, lasting two or three days'. The St Albans prophesying grew out of this system, and in both Essex and Kent the supervision of the written work was provided for within the context of a prophesying. The suppression of the prophesyings gave rise to two divergent traditions: clandestine conferences on the *classis* model and occasional prophesyings known as fast days or fasts.[10]

One of the best known examples of an organized clerical gathering is that of the Dedham *classis* of the 1580s. A set of rules was drawn up on 22 October 1582 by 20 ministers, to govern the behaviour of the *classis*. The first meeting was held on 3 December 1582 and the eightieth and last on 2 June 1589. A three-hourly meeting was held on the first Monday of each month. The frequency and regularity of the meetings is in itself a point of some significance. The *classis* discussed and reached decisions on points of doctrine, ceremonial and clerical behaviour. For instance, it advised Mr Dore to accept the church of Stratford, discussed the issue of the baptism of the children of the unmarried, and argued over whether one of its members should be permitted to publish a catechism. The issue of catechizing became an important one: at the thirteenth meeting, in December 1883, the meeting agreed 'that some certayne forme of catechisinge might be followed by the mynisters in the churche, especially for the use of the younger sorte, as a preparatyrie to the publike and ordenary exercises of the worde and prayer'. The *classis* organized collections to help colleagues who had fallen on hard times. It imposed conditions on Mr Morse when advising him to accept a chaplaincy in Sir Drew Drury's house. It took upon itself the responsibility of providing sermons for parishes deprived of their incumbents in 1584. In July of that year 'it was thought good that enquiry should be made of the number of mynisters nere unto us which are both insufficient in leringe and notoriously offensive in liffe' and the *classis* set out to procure men of good life to fill the cures. On 7 September the clergymen consulted together as to whether to subscribe to the articles. The *classis* did not hesitate to discipline its members. On 1 February 1585, for example, Mr Andrews was rebuked for being absent from his cure, and an extraordinary meeting was called to discuss his wish to leave the cure for another. The *classis* organized a rigorous examination of the Book of Common Prayer, studied parts of the Scriptures, and reserved a part of its proceedings for preaching.

From our point of view the *classis* is most interesting because it was a wholly clerical gathering which exercised considerable authority over its membership and which organized clerical responses to diocesan and central directives within the parishes. It is true that several members of the *classis* were unbeneficed and that the membership ignored diocesan boundaries: it is also true that it overwhelmingly represented the puritan connection on the Norfolk/Suffolk boundary. Its importance is not reduced by these facts. The puritan connection was of great importance in underlining and strengthening professional bonds and professional consciousness. The words 'group identity' may be heavily overworked in works of contemporary social anthropology but they do express the essence of this situation. The Dedham conference, like so many others, was both an expression of and creator of clerical group identity. As Patrick Collinson has commented, 18 of the members of the *classis* were university men, 17 of them graduates, and almost all from Cambridge. The university connection, then, was part of the strength of this puritan clerical gathering.[11]

Fasts were the occasions not of wholly clerical meetings but of gatherings of both clergy and laity. They occurred in centres of radical puritanism, such as Southam, Warwickshire. A group of clergy in a locality would call a meeting, which resembled a prophesying in that several different sermons were preached for the edification of the fellowship of ministers and the assembled laity. The laity did not otherwise participate. The occasion for such a fast day was often a visitation of plague or a bad harvest in the area. The market towns as usual were the focal points of this activity. In 1596 five ministers from Warwickshire joined to proclaim a fast day. The authorities were particularly interested in the participation of John Oxenbridge, erstwhile moderator of the Coventry and Southam prophesyings. The other participants were Henry Bradshaw, Vicar of Bulkington; Ralph Fox, Vicar of Coleshill; Mr Barbon; and Mr Dod of Hanwell. One of Oxenbridge's errors, in the episcopal view, had been that he advertised the gathering a fortnight beforehand, naming the preachers involved. The meeting was, moreover, held at Southam, late a centre of intense and radical puritan activity, and the administration feared the re-establishment of a permanent exercise there.

In 1639 Ithiel Smart, Vicar of Wombourne, Staffordshire, was cited for proclaiming a fast in direct contravention of the king's recent proclamation. Also in 1639 Immanuel Bourne organized a fast day at Ashover, Derbyshire and was brought before the Court of High Commission as a result. Large-scale clerical/lay meetings were evidently part of the normal religious life of the Peak District around Chesterfield. During the interregnum a meeting was called by leading Derbyshire ministers (including Bourne) to refute the teachings of the Quaker Richard Farnsworth and a further meeting was held in 1654 to confront the notorious itinerant Quaker preacher, James Nayler. As will later be indicated, this set-piece provided the perfect vehicle for professional defensiveness against those who sought to attack the very idea of a clerical *profession*.[12]

Is it merely coincidence that many of the references to clerical friendships and connections discovered in the Lichfield wills occur in areas of the diocese where clerical gatherings of one kind or another were prevalent? Beale and Clarke were within the direct catchment area of Southam and Clarke was certainly an ardent puritan. Ward, Rickards and Porter were all participants in the famous Repton lecture by combination and Porter refused to subscribe to the three articles in 1621. William Hull, curate to the puritan Thomas Peacock, was himself settled in a centre of puritan preaching to which were drawn such as Arthur Hildersham, John Rowlandson of Bakewell in the High Peak and Joseph Tailor, who was appointed public lecturer at Ashbourne in the year 1624. It would be precipitate to conclude that clerical associations only emerged within the context of such gatherings or within the puritan connection, but it is evident that in these gatherings a sense of professional cohesion and awareness was fostered and that tremendous enthusiasm for improved preaching and scriptural learning through communal effort was engendered.

M. Vogler, when discussing the post-Reformation Rhenish clergy, concludes that one of the most important features distinguishing the Protestant clergy from post-tridentine Catholic clergy was not the emphasis upon pastoral work, which had its place in the new Catholic thought, but the clerical right to marry. When the clergy married they drew themselves closer to their parishioners both physically and psychologically. They also established clerical dynasties. In examining the network of friendships and kinship among the parochial clergy of the period, it is not the simple existence of such connections which appears novel (medieval clergy must have had clerical friends) but rather the fact that such connections were invited and encouraged to take place within the context of professional life and gatherings. In the reign of Elizabeth there was a concerted effort to improve the educational standards of both graduate and non-graduate ministers, as well as an attempt to increase the amount and standard of preaching. This programme had far-reaching professional implications. More and more of the clergy (and certainly not only those whom we would call radical puritans) were agreeing that there should be a high standard of entry into the ministry and that the clergy should be offering a minimum level of pastoral care to their congregations far in excess of that which was normal in the 1580s. A man such as Richard Latimer of Polesworth, who had been denounced as a 'dumbe-dog' in 1586 by the puritans and as of poor scriptural learning, was nevertheless drawn into the local clerical network and was participating in some book-buying by the end of the reign. The situation changed slightly in the Stuart period, in the sense that a majority of the new recruits into the clergy were graduate – a common educational background was already in existence to link the members of the local 'exercise by combination' but, in other respects and in underlining this shared characteristic, the clerical gatherings were equally potent as instruments of professional consolidation. The work of these gatherings was cemented in the area of family relationships.[13]

The sort of evidence cited above seems to suggest that through professional activities performed in common the clergy were also emerging as a distinct social group and were becoming aware of this fact. It is interesting to note that M. Vogler has come to a similar conclusion regarding the development of the Rhenish clergy, who possessed 'la solidarité engendrée par le ministere, le genre de vie, la culture et surtout les liens familiaux', which gave them a consciousness of being a social group, and counteracted the effects of declerification and the doctrine of the priesthood of all believers.[14]

Before we can assume that the clergy formed a separate group, it is necessary to assess the closeness of the average incumbent or curate to the community which he served. The following chapter attempts such an assessment.

13

Clerical standards of living and life-style

No conclusions about the standard of living and social place of the parochial clergy can be drawn without some consideration of the actual value of clerical livings. It is impossible to explore this complex subject fully here, but an outline can be drawn without too much over-simplification. In studying the value of livings during the period 1535–1660 the historian has at his disposal a variety of surveys, constructed for a variety of purposes and according to a variety of criteria.

The *Valor Ecclesiasticus* of 1535 is by far the best known of these surveys. It was compiled to provide a new taxation assessment for the entire body of the beneficed clergy and the religious in England. There has been some controversy about the basis for the assessment of income. In general it seems clear that where the living was leased out it was the rental value which appeared in the *Valor Ecclesiasticus*. Generally this rental value was an underestimate of the actual value. In some cases, however, the assessment was based upon the value of tithe or upon the actual income of the living (gross or net) over a number of years, in an average year, or in the year of the valuation. This changing base for the valuation makes the *Valor* exceedingly difficult to use but, even if one is not able to pin down the actual value of the property or its potential within the context of contemporary market conditions, at least one is able to estimate roughly the sort of income which the incumbent involved could expect, assuming average harvest, payment of tithes and rents and so forth. The Crown exempted incumbents of vicarages worth below £10 and of rectories worth less than £6 13s. 4d. from the payment of first fruits and tenths. Taxation assessment was based upon the income of the living concerned after the deduction of synodals and procurations. There were continuing complaints that no allowance was made for the necessary payments made to assistant curates. Moreover, after the reign of Mary many clergy, and perhaps most incumbents, had wives and families to support from their income. Furthermore, the income stated for each living was by no means a guaranteed income.[1]

The number of ecclesiastical benefices in England and Wales has been estimated variously at between 8,803 and 9,244 parishes. Jeremy Collier analysed the contents of the *Valor Ecclesiasticus* relating to 8,803 livings. Of these, 4,503 rectories and vicarages were assessed as worth less than £10. Among these, 2,978 were rated below £5 and of these, 1,000 at below £2. Of the 1,445 rectories and vicarages were given an annual value of between £10 and 20 marks; 1,624 were assessed at between 20 marks and £20; 790 were assessed at between £20 and £30; and a mere 392 at over £30. Of the benefices of England almost 90 per cent were assessed at less than £26 yearly income and 75 per cent were worth less than £20 per annum. There were certain regional discrepancies in the distribution of clerical income. According to R. G. Usher, most of the livings worth £25 or over were situated south of the Wash. Dr Barratt illustrated the discrepancy between various dioceses in her examination of figures for Worcester, Oxford and Gloucester, but the percentage distribution appears to be roughly equivalent for all three midland dioceses and compares with the national percentages. Dr Barratt was able to show how the more favourably endowed livings had heavier concealed expenses than the so-called poorer livings. Thus of 20 benefices valued at £20 plus in Worcester diocese, nine had chapels of ease attached; of 33 such benefices in Gloucester, another nine had chapelries; and of 13 such benefices in Oxford, four had attached chapels.[2]

The majority of beneficed clergymen in the post-Reformation period were dependent upon glebe and tithe for their incomes. Long leases did occur but, in general, when the glebe or the tithe was leased, it was for a short period and at favourable terms for the incumbent. Because most benefices were endowed in kind, it could be expected that most would rise in money value over the period up to 1660 unless land was rented or tithe payments commuted. Even assuming this situation, however, the rise in the money value of livings was likely to be uneven. It has been demonstrated that the price inflation of the sixteenth century affected different commodities at varying rates. By about 1580 the price of wool, lambs and sheep had trebled since 1535 and the price of hay and corn doubled, but after this date grain and hay were rising much more rapidly in price than livestock. So far as the clergy went, this meant that the value of small tithes, upon which the vicars depended for their income, was rising much more slowly than that of the great tithes of corn, which formed a large part of the average rector's income. Thus by the civil war the price of wheat was perhaps six times as high as it had been during the period of the *Valor* and hay as much as eight times dearer, whereas the price of lambs was only five times higher and that of calves only four times higher. Moreover the value of the land was increasing more rapidly than that of any commodities and therefore more than that of tithe, great or small. A living with an extensive glebe therefore stood to profit more dramatically than one which was dependent for most of its income upon tithe produce.

Those livings which had increased by seven or eight times in value by 1650 seem to have been those with large glebelands.[3]

The type of endowment possessed by a living determined to a great extent the proportionate rise in income over the period 1535–1660, but all rectories did not prosper equally nor all vicarages lag behind equally. It was, for example, common to commute tithe hay payments in many areas. Hay was a difficult tithe to collect and because of this it became the only agricultural product of much importance to be commuted frequently and on a regular basis; because of this rectors were losing out considerably on the steep rise in hay prices over the period. Yet it was rare that there was general commutation of tithe products in any parish, although almost every incumbent accepted some commuted payments, either for particular products (such as milk, eggs and cheese, or livestock under a certain number) by *modus*, or from particular persons or pieces of land by composition. At a time of rising prices the *modus* (prescriptive or customary) was in the long run to the incumbent's detriment. On occasion this disadvantage was compensated for by the convenience of the method.[4]

Other factors affected the incumbent's income pattern. Enclosure might help the recipient of sheep and wool tithes, but it hit the owner of the great corn tithes quite severely. Similarly, some clergymen were dependent for a proportion of their tithe income from the tithe on wages, or the personal tithe. Personal tithes did not die out completely during the period but they were normally changed into fixed and trivial money payment, which may easily be confused with the Easter offering. The Act for the True Payment of Tithes of 1548 had made the recovery of personal tithes extremely difficult. Day labourers were specifically exempted from making such payments. Other persons refusing to pay personal tithe were to be brought before the ordinary for questioning 'by all lawfull and reasonable meanes, other than by the parties owne corporall oathe'. This meant, in effect, that no tradesman was compelled to declare his profits on oath in a Church court. The clergy were discouraged from suing such cases in the courts as a consequence. There were continual complaints by the Church against the general refusal to pay personal tithes. The puritans wished to establish a *modus* for their payment and in 1610 Bancroft asked for the return of the oath. The matter was of more crucial importance to incumbents of urban livings. In a few Worcestershire parishes Dr Barratt discovered that personal tithes were still being paid by servants in the reigns of Elizabeth and James I. Certain allowances were made for clothing and other expenses before the wage was assessed for personal tithe at Alcester (1616) and Bretforton (1617). In 1647, Sir Henry Spelman wrote that this was the practice in various parts of the country but one suspects that personal tithes were more often than not left unpaid. There is evidence for the existence of *modi* for personal tithe: in the late seventeenth century servants in Berkswell, Packington and Curdworth parishes (Warwickshire) were paying a flat rate of 6*d*. a head, maid servants 4*d*. and communicants 2*d*. The 2*d*. paid by each householder and communicant represented the ½*d*. traditionally paid at the four chief festivals to the cleric in medieval times and now collected all together at Easter. The higher rates for servants (presumably those hired by the year and not by the day) included the assessment for wages as well as the Easter offering. In the 1692 terrier of Coleshill the Easter Dues claimed included 4*d*. from every tradesman and 4*d*. from every craftsman.[5]

While it is true that by the Restoration all traces of offerings made at other times than Easter had disappeared from terriers in the midland counties at least, Usher's statement that the abolition of mortuaries, oblations, fees, dues and payments at the Reformation dealt the finances of the parochial clergy a crushing blow must be suspect. No offerings were statutorily abolished at the Reformation. Naturally fees for masses and other Catholic ceremonies were no longer paid. Fees were still claimed for marriages, burials and churchings. Mortuaries and other offerings were still paid where the incumbent could collect them. In parishes in Worcester diocese the proportion of income received in the form of offerings appears to have been around 6 per cent at the time of the *Valor Ecclesiasticus*. The real value of such offerings declined during the period, but they were still claimed.[6]

Were the majority of livings showing increases in value commensurate with the rise in prices? Various studies have shown that on average livings had increased three times in value by the middle of Elizabeth's reign, four times by the beginning of James's reign and five times by 1650, when compared with the assessment in the *Valor*. This would indicate that most clergymen were keeping their heads above water. As has already been suggested, however, the incomes of rectors and vicars were affected differently on many levels. Livings with extensive glebeland and uncommuted great tithes intact stood to gain much more than those with little glebe and with an income drawn mainly from small tithes and commuted payments.

The period saw increased inequality in the value of livings. A study of the value of Derbyshire livings in 1535 and 1650 shows this quite well. In 1535, 59 out of 82 assessed livings were worth less than £10 per annum. Even if we allow that this was probably an underestimate, this means that about three-quarters of the livings were incapable of supporting a learned minister according to Archbishop Cranmer's contemporary opinion. No living in the archdeaconry was worth more than £50. By 1649/50 the picture had altered; 102 livings were assessed: 44 were valued at over £50 in value – well over one-third as against one-quarter in 1535 were capable of supporting a minister if we calculate that a rise of five times the 1535 figure was sufficient, but a large number of livings were really plumbing the depths of poverty. Four were worth less than £10, 17 worth less than £20, 15 worth less than £30 and 11 worth less than £40.

When one recalls that the majority of these incumbents in the later period were graduate and married with families then one can appreciate the new, unprecedented demands on income and the expectations of a comfortable, professional life-style which were never realized. It is this overall picture which is all-important to the historian, not the fact that on average livings had risen five times in value. The vicarage of Ashbourne, for instance, had been worth £5 5s. in 1535 and was valued at £31 6s. 8d. in 1650 yet it was still below the poverty line when related to mid-century price levels, and was made to support a learned preacher and four chapelries. Almost without exception it was the reasonably comfortable rectories of Henry VIII's reign which increased in value over and above the rise in prices. Barlborough, worth £10 1s. 5d. in 1535, was worth £80 in 1650; Brailsford, £9 19s. 1d. in 1535, was worth £100 in 1650; most dramatically of all, Seckington, one of the richest livings in 1535 at £40 13s. 4d., had increased by eight times in 1650 to £320. The poorer livings would have had to increase by far more than five or eight times to do more than maintain their initial level of poverty: thus Lullington vicarage increased by eight times during the period but was still worth only £36 13s. 4d. in 1650. Significantly enough the urban livings were tremendously hard hit: often they were entirely dependent upon the town corporation for endowment, which was meagre, and upon other payment for sermons which were irregular and never princely. The Vicar of St Michael's, Derby, received only £8 in 1650 as against £4 14s. 11d. in 1535 and the Vicar of St Werbergh received £18 compared with £5 12s. 8d. Bakewell's vicar, surely one of the most hard-worked ministers in the county, was expected to live and pay an assistant curate out of an income of £53.[7]

One is thus led to the conclusion that, whereas a large number of rectors were keeping their heads above water economically and even prospering as a result of rising prices, a great number of the country's 3,800 vicars were remaining impoverished and in real terms being more stretched than ever, as families and changing life-styles made their relentless demands.

While it is true that the very poorest rectories and vicarages were exempt from the payment of first fruits and tenths to the Crown, taxation did prove a burden to many of the clergy in the mid-sixteenth century. In Holinshed's *Chronicle* we are told that of a benefice of twenty pounds by the year, the incumbent thinketh himself well acquitted if all ordinary payments to the Queen being discharged, he may reserve thirteen pounds six shillings eight pence towards his own sustentsion or maintenance of his family.

In particular the year of entry to a benefice could be a very expensive one, when an entire year's profits were surrendered by the Crown. Of course, the fact that the *Valor* seems to have underestimated the income of most livings proved an advantage to the incumbent involved but this can scarcely have completely outweighed the burden of taxation. As the years passed and the value of livings rose, the *Valor* assessment in the King's Book remained the basis of ecclesiastical taxation. A living worth £14 in 1535 and £70 in 1640 was still taxed as if it were worth £14. As time progressed, therefore, for some incumbents Crown taxation proved a mere pinprick – the responsibility of looking after a family in a time of rising prices proved the main new drain on resources. For some, however, the burden of taxation was still significant: those livings which remained impoverished according to 1640 price levels and which still paid tax at the old rate did not receive as much effective 'tax relief' as did their wealthier brothers. All the evidence points to the conclusion that there was a strong, indeed overwhelming, case for a new tax assessment in the mid-seventeenth century both from the Crown's and the poorer clergy's point of view. As it stood the system was scarcely equitable.[8]

The wages of curates, be they curates of chapels of ease or assistant curates, were increasing very slowly during the period under discussion. This situation usually benefited the incumbents who employed them – most of the larger livings were rising in value much more rapidly than were curates' wages. One can only speculate as to how far the incumbents were forced to compensate the curates for meagre salary by providing bed and board, and as to whether curates were in the seventeenth century even more than previously compelled by poverty to engage in by-occupations such as school-teaching.

In a situation where there was increasing inequality in the value of livings, most incumbents shared one benefit: they were provided with a house and (in country areas) with farm buildings and some land. In itself this was an enormous advantage, although it left the incumbent then, as today, with the problem of providing a roof for his widow and an inheritance for his children on his death, or a house for his own retirement. The type and quality of house provided varied tremendously.

Most rectories and vicarages in the diocese of Lichfield boasted some sort of house for the incumbent although there were exceptions. In 1584 the vicarage at Shilton, near Coventry, was said to be 'decayed and Kepte from the minister' and in 1626 the 'parsonage howse' of Stapleton, Shropshire, was 'decayed by reason of fire 2 yeares since'. At Stapleton the situation had still not been rectified by 1635 when a visitation return reported that 'it was burned downe before the now Incumbent', who was instituted in 1625. In the case of a rectory, the rector was responsible for repair of the parsonage house and chancel; in the case of a vicarage this responsibility lay with the lay rector (impropriator). At Stapleton the court ordered that the clerical rector build a new and convenient mansion within the next two years and certify this to the court on the next court day after completion. If the rector responsible (whether lay or clerical) refused to comply with such an order the court concerned would sequester the fruits of the parsonage until the work had been completed by specially appointed sequestrators. On 15 August 1621 Thomas Somerfield, Rector of West Felton, was charged with responsibility for the ruin and decay of both chancel and rectory; the fruits of the living were sequestered to three named persons made responsible for the repair. On 3 July 1623 a similar case was brought against Edward Langley, curate and farmer of Ladbrook rectory, Warwickshire. One might consider such rectors negligent, yet the financial burden of rebuilding a house (at a time when fire was a very common hazard) could be considerable. A public collection was made in Shrewsbury to ease the cost of building anew the parsonage house of Smethcott.[9]

Recent studies have shown that both vicarages and rectories reflect the regions to which they belong, in both materials and disposition of rooms. Moreover, because the parochial clergy varied greatly in wealth, 'their dwellings invite comparison with the houses of men of all sorts, from lesser gentry at one extreme to poorer husbandmen, if not labourers, at the other'. It has been suggested that because the clergy were involved to some extent at least in agricultural pursuits, their housing and living standards reflect the vicissitudes of the entire rural community. Yet it has also been suggested that many of the houses occupied by the clergy offered a higher standard of comfort than could have been supported from most of the livings involved. This fact has been attributed to the prevalence of pluralism, at least in the mid-sixteenth century, which often led to the endowment of a particularly handsome and commodious house in one or other of the parishes held. A cautionary note must be struck here, however: if Mr Barley is deriving the value of such livings from the *Valor Ecclesiasticus*, this was probably already an underestimate when compiled and was certainly seriously out of date by the end of the sixteenth century. Mr Barley has posited that the clergy as a group displayed less interest in improving their farms and farm buildings than did others of similar economic status. This could, if true, have been because they had at most a life interest in their holding (although one must remember the importance of dynasties in the same parish) but it is probable that the clergy diverted their funds into other channels – in the purchase of private property or in pursuit of professional interests.[10] And vicars had no obligation to build a house.

Information garnered from Lichfield terriers of 1612 (mainly for Shropshire and Staffordshire parishes) indicates that the average rectory or vicarage consisted of four bays of building. This seems to have been true elsewhere also, for example in Lincolnshire. A bay was technically the stretch of building between two main timbers in the structure of a house. The length of a bay was not consistent even within an area and, by the seventeenth century, the term was used in such a general way as to make estimates of the exact size or type of building impracticable. For instance, the rectory at Moreton Corbet was described as being of 'three small bayes' whereas that at Draycott contained four large bays of building in 1633. Normally a house containing 12 bays, as that at Kemberton, would be of superior size and accommodation to one of six bays, but it is hard to believe that many parsonages were more commodious than that at Caverswall in 1635, having three bays, each in length 20 feet, 18 feet and 14 feet.[11]

Descriptions of houses contained in terriers are normally brief but are occasionally useful. Several houses were thatched, as at Cheswardine, but the use of tiling and slate shingles for roofing was also common. The terrier of High Ercall, Shropshire, recorded the possession of 'one fair antient dwelling house of timber covered with slate shingles and tyle' in 1612. The rectory at Drayton Bassett showed the transition between the two styles: in 1613 its four bays were part tiled and part thatched.[12]

Houses varied enormously in their plan. At West Hallam, Derbyshire, the parsonage house consisted merely of 'a parlor and chamber ioyning to the church'. In some cases the dwelling house and the kitchen were contained in two separate buildings. At Kinnersley the parsonage was described as containing 'two bayes of buildinge beinge thatched with straw and havinge two fier places' – by all accounts a small house – but the kitchen here was housed in a separate structure of two bays. Stirchley Rectory, Shropshire, had only two bays but again there was a separate 'backhouse' of 'one lettell bay' where the cooking was done. Yet Staundon parsonage was a very small dwelling 'contayninge a hall parlor and hall parlor and kitchin' (sic). Harley rectory in 1612 had a 'dwelling howse and kitchin under on Roofe', and that at Yoxall had merely 'one chamber and parlor called the Curats chamber'. Many parsonages were on one floor only but some incumbents were improving their property and providing extra sleeping and studying accommodation by lofting them over. Arthur Hildersham, Rector of West Felton, Shropshire, made his house more commodious and luxurious by repairing its six bays and providing lofts and glass windows in the early 1630s.[13]

As indicated, the general groundplan of the houses varied considerably. Some were still moated: the parsonage house or hall at Stoke-on-Trent possessed a court yard and two gardens and was 'motted about' in the style of the fifteenth century. The 'dwelling house' at Whitchurch was 'scituate within the moate conteigning seaven bayes' and still possessed its own gatehouse of three bays, with accomodation for servants, plus a considerable mass of outhouses and cottages within and without the moat enclosure. The terrier of Longford, Salop, recorded a gatehouse leading up to the rectory in 1635. In 1631 the rectory at Drayton Hales was described as having 'an Inner courte and an outward courte' and in 1616 Church Eaton parsonage had gardens within its moat. Houses are occasionally shown to have had an upper storey. In 1635 that at Bolas, Shropshire, had '2 baies floored over head as alsoe 2 baies more of Crosse-buildinge floored over & 2 shores'.[14]

In general one is presented with a picture of timber-built, thatched or tiled houses of the hall-type. Much of what was in use was old property. The terriers yield information about additions to existing buildings and improvements but rarely mention the erection of an entirely new mansion. Cheswardine in 1636 had a new 'kitchinge' of one and a quarter bays. Additions to the outbuildings of clerical dwellings were more frequently noted than improvements to the houses themselves. It is possible, despite Mr Barley's conclusions, that the clergy as farmers were more concerned with their farms than with building more roomy and comfortable accommodation for their families. In 1611 when two bays of the barn at Aldridge, Staffordshire, fell down, the parson – John Scott – hired a carpenter immediately to knock down one further bay and built three completely new bays. Richard Taylor, Rector of Moreton Corbet, was also active in building anew, as was Abdias Birch of Shifnal, who added seven bays to the existing house and outhouses.[15]

Certainly the terriers do indicate that the most noteworthy part of the rural clerical establishment was not the house but the barn and barnyard, the pastures and the arable strips. In almost every case the parsonage was first and foremost a farm house and the buildings were clearly situated about a farmyard. Thus the rectory at Whitchurch stood within the line of the moat alongside a barn, a dovehouse, a 'sheepcoate' and a 'kill' and malting house, whilst a gatehouse commanded entry to the dwelling, and a large barn (of a size roughly equivalent to the house) stood outside the moat. It was not unusual for the great barn to be almost as large or even larger than the parsonage itself. Caverswall boasted two barns, neither quite as large as the vicarage but certainly roomy: one was 15 ft by 47 ft and the other 10 ft by 43 ft. The great barn at Yoxall (which was called the 'Tithe barne') far outstripped with its seven bays the meagre vicarage, and a tithe barn of five bays stood next to Rolleston's rectory of six bays.[16]

The type of farming practised by the incumbent is often reflected in the nature of the outbuildings. A great barn, probably normally the tithe barn, was a constant feature. Most farms had an additional smaller barn, sometimes called 'the hayhouse'. Stables and cowhouses appear in dairy farming areas particularly, whereas on some farms sheeprearing was obviously more important. So we find that at Alcester, Warwickshire, there were barns, stables and cowhouses amounting to 13 bays plus 'foldyards' near the house but that at Whitchurch there was no accommodation for cattle but a sheepcote of three bays. At Stirchley the rector concentrated upon sheeprearing but kept a few cattle.[17]

Mr Barley's contention appears to be that throughout England the parochial clergy demonstrated an unwillingness to employ new building styles and techniques thus fixing their 'social position as a member of the village community rather than as a poor member of the gentry class'. This may have been true as regards house and farm buildings but one should not allow this to colour one's estimate of the cleric's overall social position *vis à vis* his parishioners: the benefits of any improvements would be felt, after all, not necessarily by his kin but by his successor. Clergy would farm their glebe to the best effect, maintaining farm buildings but resisting investing money in the land and house – they were far more likely to invest any profit in the purchase of property which could be handed down to their children. One can scarcely conclude from evidence concerning the condition of Church property that the clergy were in the same social or economic class as husbandmen or yeomen farmers. At the same time it is difficult to deny that the situation was detrimental for Church property – there was a tendency to continue to occupy old housing and farm buildings, with occasional refurbishment and additions, rather than to build anew, until disaster struck and decaying property was replaced. The clergy were farmers, often relatively impoverished ones, who had fewer incentives than most to plough back their profits into better buildings, techniques and equipment.[18]

What type of farming activities did the parochial clergy pursue and on what scale? Clerical inventories yield some information of value but these sources are difficult to use: for instance, if the inventory was drawn up in winter many of the cleric's livestock would have been killed off and only store cattle would remain; inventories, naturally enough, do not give particulars of the amount of land under the plough although they may on occasion give an estimate of the acreage of a particular crop if it is yet to be harvested. Terriers often provide a specific statement of the amount of land belonging to the glebe, but care has to be exercised here also as the terms of land measurement varied in their usage according to region and according to the farming system (open field or enclosed) which was in use. The 1693 terrier for Keele, Staffordshire, speaks in terms of 'days work': 'One parcell of land conteining seven day works called by the name of the Parsons Croft'. A day's work appears to have meant three roods of land in some counties (Yorkshire, Lancashire and Lincolnshire) and one can only assume, perhaps wrongly, that it did so in the midland counties also. One is on more certain ground when interpreting 'day-math' (used in the same terrier) as twice a statute acre or the equivalent of one day's mowing for one man. Variations in the terminology employed, in the units of measurement used and their exact meanings, combined with a tendency in some terriers to describe the glebe very loosely in terms of 'meadows' or 'butts' or 'parcels', makes any attempt to give the average size of a clerical farm impossible. It is sufficient probably to say that the glebe of parish churches varied enormously in size.

Although the general assumption that the wealthier livings possessed the largest glebelands is probably broadly correct it is nevertheless true that some small, insignificant livings possessed quite extensive glebe. Where the glebe was small the incumbent had several choices before him: he could rent or purchase land to farm; he could rely on his tithe receipts for subsistence; or he could take by-employments. The glebe land, however large or small, seems to have been arranged according to a specific pattern. The house was surrounded by a close, a paddock or two, orchards, outhouses, stables, coach-houses, a backside, and the church yard. The remaining glebe land might be widely scattered through the village. Drayton Bassett in 1613 had besides the dwelling house a corn barn, a hay barn, a bakehouse and kitchen, a garden, an orchard, a croft enclosure, and over four acres of meadow divided into five plots (the largest being two acres in area), and several strips scattered over four common fields. At the same time, Loppington in Derbyshire had a house surrounded by outbuildings (the stable being attached to the house itself), a garden, a 'little orchard', a yard and six enclosures. The area around the dwelling was often described as the 'backside' and this was the part of the glebe used for market gardening and tended by the women folk. Norton in Hales in 1635 had a backside 'intended for a garden' of half an acre, a parsonage croft of three acres, one and a half acres of meadow pasture and eight and a half acres of enclosed arable land. Some of the glebe nearest the house was used for livestock, especially for sheep during bad weather, at shearing time and in the lambing season. The 'fould yard' at Rolleston was about half an acre in size.[19]

Although the clerical farmer might have a glebe of several acres, the majority of such farms appear to have been well under 30 acres in size. The terriers give occasional glimpses of the enclosing activities of clergymen. At Rolleston four acres of the glebe were 'latly included by the said incumbent', and Edward Rolleston had also straightened the boundaries of a five-acre field by judicious exchange with neighbouring land owners. As this was a family living, Rolleston may have had more incentive to be enterprising than other clerics. In 1635 the terrier of Moreton Corbet noted that Lewis Taylor, last incumbent, had exchanged three acres of land with the bailiff of Sir Richard Corbett for an enclosed pasture. The terriers reveal the progress of enclosure, usually in accord with local patterns, but indicate that the ownership of arable strips was still very widespread and that these were often held in many different common fields throughout the parish.[20]

A parson sought to meet all the material needs of his family from his establishment, whether as a direct result of farming his glebe or as a result of tithing receipts. Therefore, whereas he might concentrate upon dairy farming in dairy country, he would also practise mixed farming – grow cereal crops, keep chickens, rear a few sheep and perhaps some pigs, and tend his orchard and garden plot. There are interesting variations in this pattern: for example, a rector or vicar who drew heavy tithes from wool and sheep in a sheep-rearing area might well decide not to produce sheep himself and to concentrate on providing grain or dairy produce for his family. The Rector of Leigh, Staffordshire, seems to have kept no sheep himself in the mid-seventeenth century – after all, he garnered the produce of an average sheep flock from his parishioners as it was – but his curate who received no such tithes kept 32 cattle and 26 sheep. Because of this it may be that while the agricultural preoccupations of a given area are reflected in the farming activities of the clergy there, the correspondence is not necessarily an exact or startling one.

Clerical inventories give the impression that mixed farming on the following pattern was very common with slight regional variations. Most clergy farms kept cattle, slightly fewer also reared sheep, and many kept a few pigs and poultry, with most possessing horses or oxen to work the farm. Crops such as corn and hay were common and in some regions hemp, flax and peas were grown. In the seventeenth century there is some evidence of dairy production (cheese and butter) for the market in dairying areas such as Staffordshire. In Staffordshire the emphasis seems to have been on livestock – of 55 farms examined 33 had flocks of sheep and 47 had herds of cows – particularly in the moorland areas. Few of the flocks and herds were large. Only seven farms had flocks of more than 70 sheep and only one more than 200 – almost half had fewer than 20 animals. Only five cattle farmers had more than 20 head of cattle. A general view of clerical farms in the west midland counties of Staffordshire, Shropshire, Warwickshire and Derbyshire suggests that few clergymen had either the acreage of good enclosed arable land or the acreage to support a large herd of sheep which Mr Bowden suggests would have brought a peasant cultivator or sheep farmer a profit of around £14 9s. 3d. a year. The type of farming practised by a reasonably wealthy cleric in the Peak District of Derbyshire seems to have been as typical of this sheep-rearing district as it was of lowland Staffordshire – Immanuel Bourne set 11 acres of his land under wheat, kept pigs, a small number of cattle and a flock of 39 sheep, as well as mowing clover grass and hay for feed, and producing a supply of peas, rye and barley. The existence of regional variations in emphasis seems to reveal itself in the by-products of a clerical establishment rather than in the types of farming (arable or pasture, sheep or cattle) practised.[21]

As already indicated, the clergy were dependent not only upon their own farming activities for subsistence but also upon the tithe which they received on the produce of all the farms within their parishes. The incumbent drew much of his livelihood from tithe rather than from the glebe which he worked himself. In terms of the *Valor Ecclesiasticus* there was normally a huge discrepancy between the two sources of income in favour of tithe. There is some evidence that it was the livings with extensive glebe which increased most rapidly in value in the following period but the issue is complicated by the fact that most of these livings also had valuable tithe income. Nevertheless it may well be true that the onus for increased prosperity was placed more and more upon the cleric's efficient exploitation of his glebe in the period after the Reformation. To the more hostile of parishioners it appeared that the cleric was in fact receiving unearned income from tithe, although it in fact represented a rendering to God that which belonged to God and a payment for the services which the minister rendered.

The clergy were farmers, but they were farmers with a difference because in addition to the income from their own farming endeavours they had a source of considerable additional income in tithe, be it collected in kind or in the form of money payments. To say that the clergy rarely possessed as large a farm as the small peasant cultivator with his 30 acres is relatively meaningless, therefore. The total produce of farm and tithe might give the cleric a considerably larger income than a cultivator on this scale.

Other factors set the clergy apart from their parishioners. Clerical housing may have been very similar to that of the neighbouring farmers but the parson's life-style was necessarily very different. Very few lay wills or inventories contained references to books during the period, particularly to books other than the Bible. Clerical wills and inventories, on the other hand, were full of such references. Books were to the clergy the tools of their trade – as the last was to the cobbler or the wheel to the spinner. Immanuel Bourne, Rector of Ashover in Derbyshire, had complained that his library was destroyed during the civil war, yet when he died in 1673 he left 'Bookes of severall sorts in the studdy' including '15 folio's 45 quarto's 40 octavo's & twelves & 20 stitched bookes'. Nathaniel Puddyfatt left an unremarkable library of 119 volumes when he died in 1642. Robert Revell, the allegedly scandalous minister of Dronfield, Derbyshire, possessed a small but quite valuable library at his death in 1648. The presence of such collections points to the fact the parson was instructed by his superiors to set aside a part of every day for study: for the reading of Scripture and commentaries; for the annotation of what had been read; and for meditation. The contents of the libraries seem to represent acquisitions made as an undergraduate as well as books acquired during later life. Laymen felt so ill-equipped to value these works when appraising the deceaseds' goods that they often called in clerical evaluators to deal separately with the study contents – thus Robert Revell's library was dealt with, and that of Nathaniel Puddyfatt. The 'praysers of the bookes' of Henry Bellingham of Stoneleigh in 1632 were four neighbouring clergy, including Edward Maunsill, his successor in the living; yet of the general appraisors none seem to have been clergy. Of course one would hestitate to argue that no husbandman, yeoman farmer, tradesman or craftsman shared such scholarly interests, especially where the Scriptures were concerned – this would be patently untrue – but the fact remains that such interests were incumbent upon the clergy as a profession even when the individual inclination was lacking (particularly in an age when there was increased emphasis upon academic training for the clergy and upon the clerics' role as interpreter of the Scriptures for laymen) whereas they were not upon farmers, tradesmen or craftsmen. When Henry Smith, Rector of Matlock, gave his curate, Mr Haslam, 'xs and my little blacke sermon booke', he was motivated both by the friendship which he felt for his assistant and the knowledge that the sermon book would be useful to him in his work. For the same reason that he bestowed his 'Ministers cloke with sleeves' Roger Daker gave his nephew Thomas Colley 'all my Bookes Printed and Manuscripte whatsoever, wishinge my lybrarye were better for his sake, and besechinge the Lorde to give a specyall blessinge to his studyes and labours in that Cure'.[22]

If the clergy felt that intellectual work was in some degree at least a part of their work, they also acknowledged their need for a place in which to study. Many of the wills examined in Lichfield diocese indicate that rooms were allocated as studies within their houses, generally on the upper floor. Occasionally it is clear that the 'study' was no more than a large cupboard or that it was used as much as a storage place for beds and bedding as it was for studying. At Henry Alsop's death, as late as 1675, his study held not books but a bedstead, a table, wool and other small things worth just over a pound. Yet a man such as Richard Orgell, who died in 1647, dedicated his study to work: it contained a table, a desk, a trunk for papers and documents, shelves, a stool and a large library of books, in itself worth £30. The study chamber in the home of puritan Humphrey Fenn was remarkable in that it contained not only a library of books, a folding table, a close stool and 'one boxe which the Evidences are in and 2 smale boxes' but also '4 pictures in cullers', '80 little pictures', '36 mappes' and 'other paper pictures'. The Rector of Ansley, member of a long-established clerical dynasty, bequeathed to his son and namesake, Francis Bacon, in 1682 all his 'mathematical instruments' from his study. Such casual references as these suggest that some at least of the parochial clergy had active academic interests which were not related to their clerical vocation but which stemmed from their intellectual background and training.[23]

The parson's duties required him to spend considerable hours in the preparation of sermons if he were licensed to preach. The manner in which professional life was apportioned depended to a great extent upon whether the parson were a graduate and, if so, whether he was also a preacher. It must have taken an Immanuel Bourne or a Simon Presse long hours to produce such lengthy and extensively annotated sermons, whereas one can scarcely imagine a Henry Trickett devoting time voluntarily to study. Indeed it was said of this pluralist Vicar of Marston and Doveridge in 1599 that he was 'never knowne or supposed to be a favorer of the Gospell: In regarde he never endevowred him selfe to Reade, Studie or geve care to his preachinge of the same'. Perhaps significantly it was Trickett who was simultaneously accused of 'as a layman' purchasing land, buying leases, lending money at interest, 'huntinge fysshinge and Breedinge Beastes. . . and sellinge them your owne selfe at fayres and marketts wherein you dalie exercise your selfe still nothinge regardinge your charge & callinge'. There is the unmistakable implication that too great an interest and initiative displayed in farming was contrary to the professional interests of the clergy. Whereas no doubt there were graduate clergy who farmed for profit and concentrated their energies outside their pastoral duties, it is probable that as the graduate numbers within the profession increased, so did the emphasis in the life-style of the clergy shift. Without a very different sort of documentation than is available, this is impossible to prove, but a glance at the attitudes and life patterns of a few of these clergy supports the position.[24]

James Whitehall was born at Sharpcliffe, Staffordshire, on 13 October 1579, the son of Robert Whitehall. In 1591 he was sent away to Loughborough School, where he remained for six years. In February 1597 'I came to oxford beinge then abote 17 years old' and was admitted to Broadgates Hall which was popular among those from the midland counties. It was two years before he was admitted to Christ Church, where he apparently remained for the next 21 years in varying capacities. In 1602 he 'determined in the scholes' and in 1604 'proceeded Master of Artes'. His commonplace book, a small volume $4\frac{1}{2}$ in. by 3 in. and written in minute and scarcely legible characters, covers the years 1608 onwards, concentrating in the main upon his Oxford career. It provides some insight into his way of life which apply also to his career as Rector of Checkley, Staffordshire. Whitehall was interested both in his own *curriculum vitae* and in his ancestors': on page 65 of the book he inserted a list of the chief dates in his own life, from his birth and his having smallpox to his coming to Christ Church. In 1607 he noted 'I am almost 28 yeares old' and in 1611 on his birthday recorded that he was now 32. On the following page he gave the dates of death of various members of his family, including information evidently drawn either from the family Bible or from parish registers. References to land purchases and leases reaching back as far as the reign of Edward III (1365) found a place in this section. His interest in his ancestry was further manifested in a rough sketch of the family coat of arms, uncoloured but with the colours indicated, and a written description of the crest in heraldic terms. This concluded with a statement that the arms were granted either at the end of Henry VI's reign or at the beginning of that of Edward IV.

Whitehall had inherited some property from both his grandfather and his father. The book is in part concerned with his management of this land and the rents which he collected. He seems also to have had the custody of his brother, Robert, who was some years his junior and still an undergraduate at Christ Church when James was already a Master of Arts. Whitehall was an ambitious man and the book reveals some of his intrigues to achieve college office. He seems to have held some office in the buttery as the book contains his accounts for meals for both fellows (students) and undergraduates and estimates of income and requirements. He also described some of his tutorial and supervisory responsibilities. Like many diarists of the period, he reveals his life as carefully planned. He kept a close eye on his diet and its effects upon his work; he wrote down the maxims by which he tried to live. His day began early, at six in the morning and he was regular in his habits. The first hour of the day and the last

(from 9 until 10) were spent 'warmeinge myselfe in winter, walke-
inge etc. meditating how the day hath been spent'. The day for
him held 15 hours but the danger was that he would sit too long in
the hall after meals, so he restricted himself to one hour after lunch
and one after supper. The hour from 9 a.m. until 10 a.m. was devoted
to personal business. This was followed by separate periods dedicated to the study of law; the humanities; sermons; theological
exercises; disputations arising out of divinity lectures; teaching his
'readinge pupilles' and seeing their studies; supervising the finances
of these students and writing to their guardians; and attending to
business for friends. Sunday was rather differently arranged with
more time allocated for reading, prayer and listening to sermons.
The foundation of this approach to work was 'Let not cogitations
bee fixed longe upon any thinge though never so necessary . . . longe
restinge on one thinge causeth dulness and forgetfulness'. His diet
and health were matters of great concern for him because 'The belly
was the first bayte the devill used to deceive mankind (Eve saw that
the tree was good for meate, pleasant to the eyes, & to get knowledge)' and it had no less power over Whitehall! In August 1608 he
reported 'reume, winde and feare of stone & slowe digestion upon a
great supper of cold meate & tong and chese'. On 24 September, not
surprisingly, he recorded 'slow digestion after eating of a rawe leg of
mutton' and on 26 September he had 'dimnes of eyesight for halfe an
houre walking after dinner', as on the next day 'after dinner, in the
university library'.

At length Whitehall married Elizabeth, the daughter of John Hollins of Christchurch, who seems to have been a relative of Whitehall.
By his marriage he renounced his Fellowship and position in college
and Hollins obtained a benefice for him, that of Checkley in his
native Staffordshire. Whitehall was instituted to the living on 16 June
1620 but was not ordained priest until the following September. His
entry into the pastoral ministry was not forced upon him but his
vocation can scarcely have been in this direction in view of his past
career. It is doubtful whether his way of life changed significantly
although he may have been as conscientious a minister as he was a
tutor.[25]

Whitehall was a member of the minor gentry and an academic. It
would be foolish to claim that all the clergy of the early seventeenth
century planned their lives according to the demands of academic
work, strove to be accepted as members of the gentry, or had private
sources of income. Equally it would be unwise to claim that all
clergymen were so introspective as a Ralph Josselin. Nevertheless, it
seems fair to say that many of the clergy who attended the universities – particularly but not only those who remained as Fellows –
acquired while there habits and values which they took with them

into their parochial work, and which associated them in life style with members of the professional classes and the educated gentry rather than with peasant farmers or artisans and tradesmen.

In the seventeenth century there is some evidence that the clergy were, at least in the larger and wealthier parishes, beginning to share the more opulent life-style of the lesser gentry. The great chamber of John Porter's house at Aston in Derbyshire made some pretence to magnificence with its 'one great chaire' and 'sixe lesser chaires, wrought with Irish stitche, two needle worke chaires, one of them silke, a redd velvett chaire and a Cushion of Irish work' alongside the 'hambrough chests' the two feather beds with their 'Tapestrie Coverings and 'East Indie Quilt' and the walls lined with 'greene cloth'. Moreover the chief parlour boasted a set of leather chairs with brass buttons and matching stools and also a set of embroidered stools. Here the walls were not decorated only with hangings but with nine maps and 17 framed pictures. The hall was decorated with armour, which spilled over also into the study. This room was well furnished with a desk, a table, a writing desk, a trunk, and a large library. Evidently a high proportion of Porter's income was spent upon embellishments to the parsonage and provisions for his comfort and his pursuit of study. Poorer clergymen such as John Sherrard of Arley, Warwickshire, and John Dicher, Vicar of Shawbury, Salop, made little pretence of stylish or even comfortable living and spent most of their money and energies upon their farms and their studies. As Mr Barley has commented it was the existence of the study and the activities which went on therein which distinguished the clergyman from the peasant farmer, the small tradesman and the craftsman, rather than the opulence of his dwelling. It is this fact that one must carry forward into one's thinking of the clergy as a separate, distinct social and professional grouping. Sections of the clergy belonged economically to the peasant cultivator class, others to the minor gentry, but all were drawn together by professional interests and duties to make them one social group. Of course, it is true that some of the clergy (whether because of birth or better education or wealth) would have mixed more easily with the gentry than did the others, although it is probable that the raising of educational standards in the seventeenth century rather smoothed out this distinction also.[26]

14

Lay attitudes to the clergy before the civil war

1

During the period the clergy became increasingly separated from the laity because of their education, their awareness of a separate, special and important vocation, and the hereditary nature of the profession. Relatively few of the clergy were arrogant about this separation from the laity before the civil war, just as very few laymen thought that an educated ministry was totally unnecessary. The interregnum period in England, however, saw the polarization of thought concerning the nature of the ministry and its relevance to salvation. Groups of laymen were questioning the very *raison d'être* of a ministry. The activity of the sects during the era put the Anglican clergy *en masse* on the defensive and provoked from them a much more uncompromising response than had been needful prior to the revolution. All this has long been accepted by historians, yet many have neglected an important fact: whereas the division and hostility between some sections of the laity and the clergy was not made explicit before the civil war, the seeds of radical anticlericalism were nourished by pre-civil war developments.

The extreme anticlericalism apparent in some circles during the war and after had multifarious roots. The clergy were appearing as a separate caste because of professional training, interests and habits. The clergy were attacked for all those attributes which set them apart. Special clerical dress came under attack because it suggested superiority or at least difference in kind from laymen. In the sixteenth and seventeenth centuries style of dress was deemed not only a reflection of social reality but also a determinant of it. The Elizabethan Vestiarian controversy, the objections to Laudian wearing of vestments and, above all, the opposition of sects such as the Quakers to the wearing of any distinct clerical uniform should not be passed over as irrelevant to the issue of anticlericalism.[1] An increasingly literate laity was beginning to question the clergy's monopoly of interpretation of the Scriptures as well as of preaching. The clergy were also in a delicate position – that of authority. A godly pastor might be the friend, ally and consoler of his flock but in his disciplinary and teaching role (even when righteously exercised) he inspired rebellion, dislike, even hatred among some members of his congregation. Some questioned the authority of the minister just as they challenged the authority of the Church courts. The division between 'puritan' and 'Laudian' wings of the Church must have exacerbated this tendency. Anticlericalism also had its roots in the scandalous lives of a small section of the profession. Anticlerical members of the laity tended to produce a caricature of the clergyman which resembled no individual minister but incorporated the worst features of many. Dislike of the clergy was also inspired by their personal economic litigation and by their evident position as watchdogs of the establishment.

It has already been noted that the rural clergy were very much part of the village community in that they were farmers but that they were alienated from that community in another very real sense: they were not wholly dependent upon the fruits of their own labour for their livelihood. Most farms were reasonable in size but certainly not large, and the parish priest drew much of his income from tithe rather than from the glebe which he worked himself. There was normally a discrepancy between the two sources of income in favour of tithe. To the more hostile of parishioners it appeared that the cleric was receiving unearned income, particularly if these parishioners did not regard the services rendered by the cleric as strictly essential. Of course, as has been pointed out, large numbers of laymen neither raised nor saw any objection to the clergy or to their means of subsistence. Many objected violently to the lay ownership of tithes but saw some justification for clerical tithe ownership. More still complained about the jurisdiction of the Church courts over tithe litigation. The vocal opposition to the clergy throughout the century was nevertheless strong and at the end of the period it was gaining the ascendancy.

In recent years much valuable work has been accomplished on the nature of tithe and upon the methods of payment adopted. Attention has been drawn to the political controversy surrounding tithe payment in the civil war period, but very little has been said about the contribution of clerical tithe litigation at the local level to the general unpopularity of the clergy. The immediate impression gained from the court books of Coventry and Lichfield diocese is that tithe litigation almost monopolized the instance side of consistory and that a large number of cases were initiated by clergymen, suggesting a real foundation for lay grievance. Information gleaned from court books, papers and terriers can be examined in the light of biographical and other data, however, to produce a more refined view of the extent and pattern of clerical economic litigation and to point to some of the probable consequences of their activities.[2]

During the period 1600–40/1, 2,235 separate tithe cases were brought into the consistory court at Lichfield by clergymen. The huge majority were beneficed clergymen within the diocese. Clerical tithe cases appear to have represented just under one-third of the total number of tithe cases brought in the court over the 40-year period. That the parish clergy were all equally litigious is, however, patently untrue. A total of 441 clerics brought new tithe cases into court but only 61 men brought 10 or more tithe cases apiece, accounting for 1,037 of the total. The extent of antagonism aroused by individual incumbents was therefore likely to vary: clergy such as the archlitigant (and pluralist) John Weston, who brought 54 cases, or Henry Stevenson, who brought 41 cases into court against the parishioners of Wolstanton, could expect hostility but many parish clergy brought only one or two cases in the course of a long ministry.[3]

Many clergy also brought cases for defamation of character against parishioners. In one case a parishioner retaliated in a case suing tithe payment. Valentine Overton was Rector of Bedworth and Archdeacon of Derby. He held Bedworth rectory, Warwickshire, for at least 39 years (1600–39) and during that time brought 13 tithe cases, scarcely a phenomenal number considering the length of his ministry there. On 23 September 1600 he brought a case against Michael Saunders of Bedworth, 12 days after his institution. Saunders resisted and in September 1607 Overton brought a further suit against him for arrears. On the same day he sued Margaret Saunders, Michael's wife, for defamation. Her offence had been that she:

> bid the said Valentine Overton leave his fleecinge and follow the kings iniunctions and doe what as he shold do And further said unto the said Valentine Overton Sir Domine Preist plucke they lippes & hide they tieth for one of they cote ought not to fleece

either in reality or metaphorically! Margaret Saunders was objecting to Overton's preoccupation with tithe because her own family had fallen victim to this concern. The laity were probably only acutely aware of an economic grievance against the clergy when they were individually affected. But before one falls into the trap of accepting that what we are looking at is a very restricted, personal feeling against one clergyman rather than even a localized anticlericalism, one should remember that all parishioners were in potential danger of pressure from the cleric about tithe payments. Obviously any grievance was intensified if an expensive, long drawn out court case was the consequence, yet it would be futile to estimate the extent of lay objection to tithe by measuring the amount of litigation. The court books show us only the tip of the iceberg.[4]

It is instructive, however, to analyse this peak. It is only too easy to see the more litigious among the clergy as careless of the welfare of their parishioners. This was doubtless sometimes the case. The reluctance of some farmers to acknowledge the parson's right to gather tithe in the manner which he thought fit, and the average cleric's extreme dependence upon the income from tithe, should always be borne in mind, however. The number of cases brought in any one year fluctuated. A deficient or terrible harvest could bring a flood of clerical and lay suits against impoverished farmers. Thus the bad harvest of 1608 produced 272 cases at Lichfield, a full 88 cases above the average. A comparatively good harvest in 1635/6 (preceding the near disastrous one of 1637) brought only 103 new cases, whereas the deficient harvest of 1611 brought 189. It must indeed have been more difficult to collect tithe in a year of poor or even average harvest and, of course, the clergy dependent upon the land for their own livelihood and for the money to pay tenths and subsidies to the Crown found it imperative to press their claims in those years more urgently than in others, when they themselves had had a prosperous harvest. It would be interesting to see whether lay tithe litigation rose to a greater extent in such years than did clerical.[5]

A combination of reasons induced the clergy to take their parishioners to court. On occasion the incumbent would bring a case or cases immediately upon entering a living or after his first harvest therein. Possibly the living had been vacant for some time and the parson found it necessary to show who was boss immediately, before it became impossible to collect arrears of tithe and before enterprising parishioners had the opportunity to assert and consolidate new 'customs'. This was the more necessary if the year was a hard one.

In 1628, shortly after entering the living of Castleton, Derbyshire, Isaac Ambrose introduced 12 cases into consistory. In the ensuing years of his ministry he brought no new cases. Just over one-tenth of the clergy appearing as litigants prosecuted parishioners in the Church courts for subtraction of tithe or mortuaries shortly after institution, although some of this number also brought subsequent cases. Eleven of the cases brought by John Weston in his capacity as Rector of Stoke-on-Trent (a total of 36 cases) were brought within 12 months of his institution; six of those which he prosecuted as Rector of Checkley came before the court in a similar period. Here the incidence of the cases did not coincide with that of bad harvests. For example, the years 1604 and 1605 apparently produced good harvests, yet Weston sued 11 cases within that timespan. 1619 brought another good harvest but Weston saw fit to cite eight parishioners for refusal to pay tithe. The year 1613, which Professor Hoskins noted as a year of deficient harvest, brought only one new case from Weston. Even if one allows for a time lapse, he brought only five in the following year after another harvest had passed. Of course, one meets with several methodological problems here: there must, for example, have been regional, even local, variations in the abundance and quality of a harvest. Moreover, in the absence of cause papers at Lichfield it is impossible to say what proportion of tithe cases normally involved arrears of tithe covering a period of years, which would not permit any direct comparison between the year of incidence and the type of harvest involved.[6]

In general, the evidence suggests that whereas the overall number of tithe cases might fluctuate somewhat in accordance with harvest yields, the truly litigious among the clergy, or those who arrived in a parish where tithe payments were seriously in arrears, were scarcely affected by such consideration. The picture becomes blurred, therefore, and one cannot reasonably expect to see a close correlation between the number of cases brought in any one year and the state of the harvest. Rather it was that many clergy never prosecuted parishioners at all unless circumstances were truly adverse.

Yet the cases brought by the 61 'litigious' clergy may not have been motivated by avarice: the figures are deceptive. To take up the case of John Weston once more: firstly, he was a pluralist and so his 54 cases were not directed against members of the same parish; secondly, as Rector of Stoke he was responsible not only for the parish church but also for a considerable number of outlying chapels of ease: Bucknall, Bagnall, Burslem, Newcastle-under-Lyme, Norton in the Moors and Whitmore. The rector also owned tithes in other parishes, including Barlaston and Trentham. Parishioners from Horton, Trentham, Barlaston, Seabridge (Newcastle), Whitmore and Audley are concerned in the tithe cases within Stoke and more, listed as of the parish, probably lived in the outlying chapelry districts. That the clergy found difficulty in controlling remote parts of their parishes is documented elsewhere. That tithes were difficult to collect in both Stoke and Checkley seems to be underlined by the absence of cases arising in the parish of Clifton Campville. However, Weston was there for a brief time only and may have been so preoccupied with the affairs of Stoke and Checkley that he had little time or money to pursue causes elsewhere. His successor at Clifton at three removes was certainly litigious enough.[7]

Henry Gilbert's problem, however, seems to have been that he aroused considerable personal hostility within Clifton. He brought 15 tithe cases altogether: four in 1633, a year after his institution; seven in 1636; two in 1637; and two in 1638. It is probable that he found the collection of tithe nigh on impossible because of the non-activity of the past 20 years when Clifton was held *in commendam* by successive bishops of Lichfield. In any event, his activities agitated his congregation. In 1638 one James Woolferton, gent., 'did assault and strike the said Henry Gilbert his rector' for lying and Gilbert returned the compliment. Gilbert's litigation had twice been directed against Woolferton and this may have been the root cause of the latter's anger. Gilbert, however, seems to have been a quarrelsome and opinionated man. The son of Thomas Gilbert, gentleman of Alrewas, he appears to have attended the inns of court (Middle Temple) and to have proceeded B.A. from Oriel College, Oxford, in 1629. On his admission to Clifton in 1632 he was a bachelor of civil law and appears to have stood very much on his dignity. When he met with contempt from John Webster in 1640 he replied by suing him for defamation. Significantly, Webster had asserted that Gilbert had no claims to higher status than his parishioners because he, Webster, was 'as well bredd and borne' and as 'good a man . . . excepting by cloath'. Undoubtedly Gilbert also met with antagonism because of his political and religious views: he was a devoted royalist and later claimed to have lost £10,000 through the civil war and subsequent imprisonments. The cumulative effect of all these characteristics – economic litigation and harassment, arrogance, and extreme royalism – seems to have been the alienation of a section of his congregation. This must not lead the historian into the trap of believing that Gilbert's tithe litigation was therefore unwarranted and the result of avarice: we have noted the peculiar circumstances of his incumbency (falling immediately after a succession of non-resident incumbencies) and some of the actions and attitudes of members of his 'flock' appear to have been provocative in the extreme.[8]

One should not, of course, equate the litigious clergy or the unpopular ministers with the conformists or the politically royalist. It was incumbent upon the clergy to protect their tithing rights: most of the ministers who supported the parliamentary cause in the civil war maintained the right of the clergy to a tenth no less ardently than did their royalist brethren – even emphasizing the divine right of tithe. Moreover, it appears that the amount of tithe litigation actually reaching the courts represented only the tip of the iceberg. It is most difficult to fathom the depth of the resentment engendered by clerical economic husbandry or harassment *outside* the courts. Those who brought no cases into court, or very few, still badgered their parishioners to surrender the dues, maintained carefully kept ledgers, and strove to protect their rights and those of their successors by judiciously worded agreements. The tithe cases brought before the courts did not represent accurately the number of tithe defaulters but were brought in defence of particular principles or to recoup serious arrears. The non-litigious clergy may have been among the most efficient businessmen and their very efficiency may have caused their unpopularity.

In the terrier of Ercall Magna, Salop, we are told that the rector, George Wood, had fought in the consistory court on behalf of his right to collect tithe in kind from his parishioners, particularly from those living in outlying chapelries and hamlets. He also found it difficult to collect tithes from John Taylor, which had been settled by a composition made before Wood's incumbency. 'We present that the vicar or Ercall aforesaid hath received by composicons beyond the memory of man three strike of eels every year for the tyths eels of the half ware of Mr John Taylor of Long alias Longdon' which had lately been withheld.[9]

The clergy were becoming increasingly aware that compositions often had the effect of complicating the collection of tithe and blurring the rights of the clergy to draw tithe according to custom. The tithe book of the rectors of Leigh provides excellent illustrations of the ways in which ministers attempted to safeguard these rights without necessarily resorting to litigation. Leigh was a parsonage in mid-Staffordshire in the deanery of Leek. The Rector's income, according to the *Valor*, was drawn largely from tithe worth £14 11s. 8d. a year rather than from glebe worth £1 13s. 4d. and other land valued at £1 16s. 8d. At this date it was not wealthy. By 1604 it was thought to be worth £100 and a terrier of 1612 suggests a glebe of large stretches of pasture land. The parish itself was largely a sheep-farming community. The rectors of the parish were not litigious. Richard Aston (1583–1601) brought few if any cases; John Palmer (1601–39) pluralist Rector of Stafford St Mary's and Leigh, brought six cases as Rector of Leigh; Richard Chapman (1639–46) brought no charges. But this does not mean that the successive rectors were careless of their rights or any the less anxious to protect them: on the contrary. The tithe book presents the rectors' accounts of tithes and dues from 1639 onwards. The first accounts are for customary payments – the rector (probably Chapman) carefully noted down

> A true and perfect declaration of certaine customes used time out of minde within the parish of Leigh in the county of Stafford touching the payment of certaine dutyes yearly at the feast of Easter unto the parson of the parish of Leigh aforesayd or to his farmer or deputy as hereafter in presents is specified.[10]

Following this summary of tithing customs within the parish are accounts running from 1639–86. These are kept in decent order until 1648: tithe payments being recorded in separate columns under clear headings. From 1648 the entries steadily deteriorate: amounts are entered in little boxes which often bear no certain relation to the headings. The accounts provide numerous instances of composition and a few examples of long-term composition for emparked land. The existence of such an agreement, however, did not always imply commutation to a money payment. The latter part of the book presents an entirely different type of material, less indicative of the parson's concern to keep his accounts in order and more of his awareness of the legal value of carefully worded and recorded tithe agreements and compositions, which could be produced as evidence in court of law if necessary. We are constantly reminded of the importance of literacy in an increasingly litigious age. Often this type of information was also inserted in terriers. Even when not needed in court, such documents acted as proof of the regularity of the parson's claims, making clear the customs of the parish, and perhaps making litigation unnecessary.

The rectors of Leigh were wary of signing away their rights for extended periods, preferring short-term arrangements which could be revised in their own interests should conditions change. For instance, on 4 April 1657 Deliverance Fennyhouse let to William Belcher and George Parker of Middleton Green the 'whole tythes of the house and landes which they have now in tillage, being in quantity 6 dayes workes with Easter booke, wool and lamb and all other their tythes' for three years until Easter 1660 for 14s. per annum. Sometimes the rectors allowed men to compound for tithes on one part of their land while demanding ordinary payment for their other property.

In the past, whereas long-term compositions benefited the parties who initiated them, succeeding parsons often suffered from their terms as conditions altered. The clergy of Leigh were aware of this, perhaps as the result of bitter personal experience. They tended, when drawing up agreements for an unspecified number of years, to safeguard the rights of their successors. In 1653 the tithe of William Keen was commuted at the rate of 18s. per annum for three years 'yf that the said Deliverance Fennyhouse of Leigh doe hold and enjoy the same otherwise the bargayne is voyde'. Occasionally the clergy demonstrated concern for the tithe payer, making allowances for harvest fluctuation or for the amount of land actually under cultivation.

The example of Leigh underlines several points. The cases brought before the court for non-payment of tithe are evidently not a reliable index of the amount of concern which the clergy displayed in this matter. Whether they are a reliable indicator of non-payment of tithe is a separate issue. The parsons of Leigh took great care to protect their rights, kept careful accounts, and insisted that persons in arrears paid up. They may have been just as resented for their efficient methods of tithe collection as were men like John Weston who were reduced to taking their parishioners to court. At Leigh the value of the tithes which the clergyman drew must have courted unpopularity in some circles. In the 1640s the rector was claiming on average 51 fleeces; £1 0s. 5d. for sheep and lambs; 33 geese; tithes on crops, cattle and dairy produce; as well as personal oblations and the products of *modi* – representing the produce of a modest farm. As has been noted, Deliverance Fennyhouse needed to keep livestock of his own and no sheep, whereas his curate owned 32 cattle and 26 sheep, being so much more dependent upon his own farming activities. There also seems to be some suggestion that the clergy did take into account the peculiar circumstances of their parishioners. Where a *modus* was involved, of course, such consideration may have been the condition for the parishioners' agreement. Nevertheless, the historian must constantly remind himself that he is dealing with human beings who had to live together; a good pastor did not purposely alienate his flock or seek to cause their economic downfall. At this point it seems pertinent to ask whether the non-resident parson would be more likely to ride rough-shod over his parishioners than his resident counterpart, whether he would have less control of the actual collection of tithe, and whether he would have more need, as a consequence, to resort to court litigation?[11]

This brief examination of clerical tithe litigation at Lichfield during the early seventeenth century calls into question any prior assumption that the number of clergy involved in such causes and the amount of litigation itself were sufficient to explain lay anticlericalism and, more specifically, lay opposition to tithe payment during the civil war and interregnum. Relatively few clergy brought such cases: fewer still brought much economic litigation. On the whole, the clergy seem to have regarded legal process as a last resort – when they succeeded a lax administration, faced extreme geographical difficulties in collection, or met with resistance on matters of principle. Probably only the reasonably well-off clergy could afford to prosecute in the courts. It appears that the clerical attitude to tithe both inside and outside the Church courts contributed to their unpopularity. The noise and commotion connected with the court proceedings was, moreover, completely out of proportion to the actual number of cases or the number of laymen sued. The personal grievances of parishioners against individual clergy were used in the interregnum period by men who wished to see the abolition of tithe and the payment of the clergy by other means – they were subsumed into a more general onslaught on the economic rights of the clergy. In stressing lay hostility to tithe in the pre-civil war period one is not, therefore, claiming that this constituted the root cause of lay anticlericalism before or after the civil war nor that the traditional explanation for the campaign to abolish tithe is inaccurate. Above all the activists wanted to pay the clergy directly because they wanted direct control of the pulpit. What one is saying is that clerical tithe collection and litigation following upon it was one of the contributory causes of clerical unpopularity in many circles.

2

The clergy aroused some hostility among the laity through personal litigation. Perhaps even more interesting is the reaction to the clergy in their disciplinary role – when the parish clergy appeared to be in alliance with authority. This was, of course, something which was inherent in the pastor's position: he had to discipline his flock as well as to instruct them. Whereas the more extreme puritans would have made the parish priest a pope in his own parish, dispensing justice among those he knew intimately, the Church of England made the minister at parochial level just one link in the traditional chain of justice and administration. The minister was very much involved in ecclesiastical discipline – it was he who presented (along with the churchwardens) offenders at the triennial episcopal and archidiaconal visitations – out of which presentments most correction cases in the diocesan consistory court arose. The clergy read out citations issued by the court and delivered by apparitors. When the time of sentence arrived, the clergy saw to it that the convicted performed penance and obeyed the court's other instructions. It was they who enforced excommunication. Unfortunately, in all these processes the minister stood as the immediate representative of a hated, remote, diocesan court and, as such, it was against him that animosity towards the entire judicial system was directed. Ironically enough, it was often the puritan ministers, who took their disciplinary role most seriously, who provoked the greatest measure of resentment among parishioners both before and after 1642.

Occasionally one finds clear-cut evidence of the annoyance which the situation engendered. When Ralph Leadbeater attempted to prevent Isaac Ambrose's institution and induction to Castleton a long conflict ensued. Leadbeater objected to Ambrose's attempts to read orders to the churchwardens of the parish to render accounts to the bishop's consistory court of the profits of the vicarage during the vacancy. He likened Ambrose to an apparitor of the court and become so violent that the congregation did 'move up towardes the chauncell both men and women in a greate thronge as though they woulde have thrust the said Mr Ambrose forth of the chauncell'. And there are further instances of this feeling that the clergy were acting in alliance with the unpopular church courts against the interests of the laity.[12]

Some of the parish clergy actually held office in the courts, either at the level of the consistory or at that of the visitation. Arthur Cresset, Vicar of Shenstone, near Lichfield, acted as surrogate from January 1618/19 to at least 1632. The excommunication books of the diocese are interesting in that they show him actively excommunicating people throughout these years. There was, of course, strong feeling that excommunication and absolution should be administered by a cleric rather than by a lay chancellor. Cresset acted as deputy for the Official Principal more regularly than did any other during the years 1622–5. During that period the consistory court (correction side) sat 189 times: Robert Master, Official Principal, presided on 113 occasions; Cresset on 42. Cresset was possessed of no particular legal qualifications, had no degree and apparently never attended a university or an inn of court. He was probably drawn into court work by the prospect of supplementary income and because he lived but a few miles from the court and had connections in the city. He was by no means the only cleric to act as surrogate of the court. Nine others appear in the court records of 1622–5; there was parallel participation during earlier and later years by different clergymen. During the 1630s, for example, Cresset's place as chief deputy was assumed by William Jeffray, an archdeacon, and by James Povey.[13]

This clerical participation was often brought home to the local population by the fact that surrogates other than the deputy tended to preside when the court was sitting outside Lichfield. For instance, on the three occasions when Thomas Peacock acted as president of the consistory court, it was sitting in his own parish church of Ashbourne, chief church of the deanery. The cases heard were those arising from an earlier visitation in the area and it was Peacock's duty, perhaps unpleasant for himself also, to pronounce sentences of excommunication upon local offenders. Alexander Howe sat when the court met in the church of Caverswall, his second parish. Is it significant that so many of the clergy who were thus actively involved in the disciplinary work of the Church at court level were known to be of puritan persuasion? Was it that these men, believing that the duty of the Reformed pastor lay in administering a fatherly discipline, participated eagerly in this work even though they would have preferred to have seen the system overhauled along Reformed lines? Whatever the reason there seems to be every reason to believe that the laity, urge though they would the administration of discipline and correction by clergy, and the restriction of excommunicatory powers to a cleric, reacted with hostility to clerically dispensed justice. In Peterborough diocese in 1605 Robert Williamson, Rector of Tichmarsh, surrogate, a known puritan, was used by the bishop to mediate with the bishop's puritan opponents and to attempt to reconcile the non-subscribing clergy to the settlement. He seems to have had little success. Indeed, Dr Sheils notes that 'the authority of the courts was bound to be diminished when one incumbent sat in judgement upon another' and that there were considerable dangers inherent in the delegation of responsibility for order in the diocese to surrogates drawn from the ranks of the parish clergy. Yet the puritan clergy were often heard to demand a discipline administered in a situation of parity – the cleric admonishing and correcting his brethren. Most bishops appear to have been aware of the unreality of this proposal and to have made sure that they themselves heard correction cases brought against the clergy.[14]

Certainly the court records and excommunication books of Coventry and Lichfield diocese impress upon the historian the manner in which the Church utilized its manpower for the administration of justice: binding the clergy, even or especially the puritan, to official policy and, in consequence, drawing upon the ministers themselves some of the public odium inspired by the courts Christian. The enlistment of clergy to serve on commissions further identified them with the work of the courts. Irene Cassidy has noted that this was a prominent feature of Bishop Cotton's administration at Exeter; we see it also at Lichfield. For instance, on 16, 17 and 18 May 1622 a commission appointed to hear a marriage case brought by Ellena Fletcher against Vincent Bradshaw of Duffield comprised Richard Sale, Rector of Weston on Trent; Robert Smith, Rector of Langford; William Fowler, Rector of Kedlaston; John Porter, Rector of Aston on Trent; and William Bennett, Rector of Morley. The commission sat in the church of All Saints, Derby.[15]

In view of the number of clergy who were involved in the work of the courts in some way and who regarded this as an important and accepted part of their ministry, it is not surprising that there was an identification with the unpopular Church courts in the minds of laymen. As John Corney wrote to registrar Walker of Lincoln in 1627, 'Jove made that thunder & every pigmy must cast it' when referring to excommunication. If the offender were put to inconvenience and expense by the Church courts, the clergyman found that some of the culprit's hard feeling was directed against his person. This was the case when Francis Colley, Vicar of Bushbury, Staffordshire, announced to Richard Langworthe

> being present there in the church that he had received a letter or notice from the official of Wolverhampton (a peculiar jurisdiction) that he the sayd Langworthe was excommunicated for not cominge to his parishe churche of Hampton and therefore told him he would not receive him to the church as his parishioner

despite the fact that Langworthe had paid 1*s.* per annum for his tithes to Colley and had paid his church lewnes (rates). Colley was doing his duty: it was an offence to seduce men from the congregation of another church; it was also an offence to admit strangers to the communion. The result of Colley's action, however, was a costly law suit for this and a conglomeration of other offences, including neglect, sowing discord among the parishioners, including himself in playing bowls, and drinking with 'low' company. A charge of preaching 'that he that will goe to god must never thinke good thought nor doe good deede' was also cast against him.[16]

This feeling against the Church courts was apparently becoming more vocal in the 1620s and 1630s. Perhaps under the Laudian régime clergy were simply more willing to bring such cases of defamation before the courts. The administration itself was increasingly conscious of the need to protect the clergy as a body from the attacks of sections of the laity. Bishops such as Richard Neile wanted to improve the status of the clergy. It is also possible that during these years the clergy, encouraged by the hierarchy to stand on their dignity, proved more odious to the laity. Whereas instances of spoken contempt of the court do occur in the act books of earlier years, there were three distinct cases before the Lichfield consistory court in 1639, one of which was directed specifically against a clergyman as instrument of the court. William Simcox of Stoneleigh was cited, 'for sayinge that my Lord Grace and all the beggerley Bishopps would never be quiett until the King had turned them out of their services and sent them a begginge with the chancellors their hangers on'. Henry Motteram of Uttoxeter did not mince words in saying that 'this court was the basest court in the world and the basest officers belonged to it'. Sutton of Aldridge was served with a citation in the same year for 'prophaning the saboth' and, with his eyes upon the minister, Mr Barton, said 'that the apparitors man (meaneinge the sayd Mr Barton) did weare a blacke coat'. And this takes no cognisance of the many instances of active contempt of both the Church and the court revealed at visitation and at court appearances.[17]

Whereas it would be wrong to maintain that such cases provided the bulk, or even a large part, of the business of the consistory court during Charles I's reign, it does seem that the resentment which some laymen felt against the disciplining activity of the clergy was to some extent being shaped and finding expression in the courts.

3

The cleric's way of life, as determined by his calling, set him apart from his parishioners, but it did not necessarily lead to unpopularity. As has been indicated, however, the cleric's position of authority sometimes did. As a teacher, the clergyman might be loved and respected but he was certainly a man set apart – a man separated from the community which he served. Depending upon the individual, this position could be abused and the cleric appear to assert a superiority which his flock refused to acknowledge. The following chapter examines the case study of Immanuel Bourne, a Derbyshire clergyman, who took his pastoral responsibilities extremely seriously and who held a high Calvinist doctrine of the ministry. In some men the admixture of concern for congregational interests and for self was not so happy and friction between pastor and flock resulted. Even in the case of Bourne, his beliefs sometimes made him seem arrogant in the face of lay attacks during the interregnum.

It is dangerous to rely too heavily on the evidence of court depositions which are naturally extreme in tone. However, some of the cases brought against clergy in the Lichfield court do suggest a lay reaction to this 'arrogance' in the ministry, especially when it is present in the morally corrupt. Christopher Capron, curate of Trentham, Staffordshire, was accused in 1607 of abusing his parishioners from the pulpit. It was said that he,

> about ii or iii monethes sythens A dead mans scull being digged forth of the earth the sayd Capron took yt and placed yt uppon the toppe of the cover of the font and afterwards being in the pulpitt he tooke occasion to preache agaynst his parishioners saying they were envyous malitiouse covetous etc. And poynting his finger toward the scull sayd and soe was the owner of that head but what is he the better for yt now?

In the case of Capron his independence of the wishes of the parishioners enabled him to be arrogant. As long as he retained the support of his patron, Sir John Leveson, he could not be ousted:

> Mr Coxe you maye well be called an Attorney because you turne more often then some weather cocks do, but excepte the weather cocke doe crowe louder then all the cocks in Trentham you shall never turne me out of my livinge . . . your friend Christopher Capron curatt of Trentham, and wilbe by gods permission and the favour of the right worshipfull Sir John Leveson till death resignaction or deprivacion and this you knowe to be lawe without dissimulacon which you use too often.[18]

If Capron could be removed at his patron's displeasure, most beneficed clergymen were protected from such fickleness by their freehold, having to fear only due process of court. The sixteenth and seventeenth centuries saw a succession of attempts to make the parochial clergy answerable to their congregations and more easily removable but, due to the barriers erected by property rights and hierarchical opposition, as has been shown, they met with little success. The laity, however, remained resentful that the 'unsuitable' clergyman could still abuse them, collect tithes and so forth and retreat behind the parson's freehold. The radical anticlericalism of the war years and interregnum could be seen as in part the result of this failure of the congregations to control ecclesiastical patronage at parochial level.

In the Church courts this resentment against clergy who set themselves up in judgment over their erring parishioners was further fuelled by the fact that many of the same clergy were living unworthy lives or even scandalously. An adverse reaction to the clergy as a whole was nurtured by this discrepancy between the requirements of the office and the frailties of the men themselves. Clement Austen of Sudbury, Derbyshire, for example, was charged with keeping fish in the font and draping his fish nets and tackle over the pews of his church. Drunkenness seems to have been a real problem amongst the clergy at this time, as was also incontinency. Recently Dr Stephen Lander has suggested that 15 per cent of the clergy in Chichester diocese prior to the Reformation were accused of fornication: it would be interesting to know whether the percentage decreased once the clergy were allowed to marry. In Lichfield diocese, many clergy were charged with having been incontinent before marriage. It is impossible to arrive at satisfactory statistics for either drunkenness or fornication among the seventeenth-century clergy at Lichfield. The court books are not consistent in stating the nature of a cleric's offence; although cause papers do stipulate the type of case involved, they survive in such small numbers that it would be foolish to hazard an opinion as to the proportion of clerics committing such moral offences. Moreover, most of the charges brought against the clergy were composite: to bring a strong case the prosecution found it necessary to rake up almost every crime on which it might be possible to convict the clergyman. Henry Trickett, Vicar of Doveridge, Derbyshire, for example, was immoral, inebriate, recusant, quarrelsome and simoniacal to boot! Capron got drunk regularly in the ale-house so that he could not stand and could not make his own way home; he was also immoral and quarrelsome; he was illegally possessed of his cure; and he was intent upon sowing seeds of discord in the parish. The case against a clergyman had to be stacked to secure his deprivation and, more often than not, this was what the court was seeking. The relative weight which the historian should attach to individual charges in a case is, therefore, doubtful. In the case against Capron it is his possession of the cure which is disputed: all other charges were designed to improve the case against him by showing that he was a thoroughly bad lot. The case against Trickett was fundamentally one of simony – in such cases, even were the case proven, the courts found it difficult to deprive without treading on lay toes, so they sought another peg to hang their case on – Trickett's nonconformity and immorality.[19]

When religious differences entered the picture it is true that the issues hardened still further. Christopher Capron had consorted with recusants and had made no attempt to convert them to the true religion. He was 'much fallen from his vocacon and callinge and is great shame to the ministrie'. Henry Trickett thought so little of his calling that he employed one Creswell to be his curate 'not for anie sufficiencie in the man beinge neither minister nor preacher nor other wise learned but for the lykinge and desyre' he had taken for Creswell's wife. Trickett also was said to be a papist, presumably because he had recusant friends and preached a doctrine of good works.

If what one is seeing is the Church courts seeking to correct and deprive clergy for nonconformity or moral offences, one must not be blinded to the important effects of the exposure of these moral failings. Psychologically the effect could be devastating – the laity (or a large number of them) obviously did believe that the clergy as a group were scandalous even though all knew of individual exceptions – their own minister, for example! It was court exposure of the criminous clerk which provided the necessary material for the caricature portrait of the clergy which emerged in the mid-century. (The Chancellor of Lichfield in the 1680s showed himself aware of the detrimental effect of correction cases against the clergy when he demanded that before a case against a specific cleric was brought, it be carefully scrutinized, for he 'would not have the clergy needlessly exposed'.) Moreover, a small section of the community was actually *invited* by the Church authorities to bear witness against members of the clergy; they were being trained in vituperation.[20]

The clergy had certainly alienated a section of the laity by the time of the civil war and some of the reasons for this situation have been discussed above. The publicity impact of the activities of the church courts has been emphasized. By bringing tithe cases into the courts, the clergy were inadvertently drawing attention to their activities. Because it was widely believed that the courts treated their tithe cases prejudicially, yet more resentment was whipped up. General antagonism towards the clergy as agents of authority was reinforced by any exhibition of arrogance or taint of moral or religious corruption in the clergy. The Church courts provided a display case for scandalous ministers – normally ones of which the hierarchy wished to purge itself – and a practice ground for attacks by the laity.

Puritan and non-puritan clergy alike were working with the Church courts. The puritans believed in discipline and, traditionally, claimed that the clergy should correct their own congregations. Although they could not ignore the Church courts which stood in their way, many chose to work through them. Certainly the puritan minister was ecclesiastically as authoritarian as his Arminian counterpart. Yet the puritan ministers always stressed their contempt for the strictly conforming clergy, encouraging disobedience to certain ecclesiastical orders. As a result their congregations became preoccupied with the problem of freedom – from clerical control; from ecclesiastical dictation about what to believe and what not to believe. Soon many laymen were objecting to puritan as well as to conforming discipline.

J. F. Maclear may have been correct in saying that it was the threat of Presbyterian dominion in England (with the meteoric rise of

Scottish influence, the conclusion of the Solemn League and Covenant, and the convening of the Westminster Assembly) and consequent suppression of the sects, which made general anticlericalism a necessity if the sects were to survive, but it remains true that the seeds of this anticlericalism had already been sown during the post-Reformation period and the ground well prepared. If they cannot demonstrate the whole picture, the records of the Church courts can certainly underline some of the tensions between Church and society before the war. Men had already had the opportunity to flex their muscles, build up an arsenal and train with future weapons before the advent of war itself.[21]

15

Clergy on the defensive

The interregnum period in England saw the polarization of thought concerning the nature of the ministry and its relevance to salvation. Twenty years ago, James Fulton Maclear classified the anticlericalism which matured during these years in three ways: anticlericalism based on mounting class consciousness and bitter resentment against the pretensions of the clergy; anticlericalism rooted in political antagonism (the determined stand which some clergymen had made for the king tended to brand the whole body of the clergy as royalists in the minds of many laymen); and the anticlericalism to be discerned in the thought of men such as William Walwyn, which was moralistic, anti-theological and indifferent to ecclesiastical problems. Most historians have discussed the issue of a settled ministry with reference to the writings of the leading controversialists – Milton, Walwyn, Lilburne, Winstanley, Fox and Jubbes – leaving the reaction of the clergy themselves well alone. But this is precisely what interests us here: how did the established clergy react to attacks upon their position in the period 1640–60?[1] The question seems especially pertinent when we realize that large numbers of the pre-civil war clergy were still in their benefices in the late 1640s and early 1650s.

The years of the civil war and interregnum provided their own setpiece contests between ministers and sectaries which the historian may use to advantage to illustrate the major issues. Such public disputations between the two groups were apparently a regular feature during the late 1640s and the 1650s and, on occasion, the parties involved published a record of the proceedings in order to demonstrate their case and reach a wider audience. A well-known report of such a gathering is Thomas Hall's *The Pulpit Guarded* which was 'occasioned by a dispute at Henley-in-Arden in Warwickshire' on 20 August 1650, involving Hall and four mechanic preachers. But whereas we are familiar with the history of the mechanics' objections to a settled ministry through various recent studies, we remain rather ignorant of the origins of the position adopted by so many of the ministers themselves.[2]

In a sense this whole study has been dedicated to illuminating this issue but, to get to grips with the matter, one needs to examine the careers of some of the clergy involved and look at the crisis of the 1650s through their eyes. Although no one man can or should be regarded as 'typical', either of his age or of a small professional group, it seems that two case studies will help us to pinpoint the ways in which some, and perhaps many, established clergy reacted to the attacks upon the ministry in the light of their own past experiences, training and thought. To this end I have selected the careers of two very different representatives of the established Church, Immanuel Bourne, a beneficed clergyman from the east Midlands, and Ralph Josselin, Vicar of Earls Colne, Essex. The two men were separated by almost a generation in age and by a great deal in attitude to Church government but they were both nevertheless very much attached to the need for a settled ministry.

In January 1654 a confrontation took place in the town of Chester-field, Derbyshire, between ministers of the neighbourhood and the Quaker, James Nayler. The leading speaker among the Chesterfield ministers was Immanuel Bourne, rector of the large and wealthy Peak District parish of Ashover. By this time Bourne was a man in late middle age, old by the standards of his day. He was born in Northamptonshire on 27 December 1590. His opponent, James Nayler, was of a different generation, being some 26 years younger. More than age separated the two men, however. Bourne's father, Henry, was the minister of East Haddon, Northamptonshire, from 1595 until his death in 1649. Immanuel had attended Oxford, taking his B.A. in 1612 and his M.A. in 1616. In 1617 the Dean of Christ-church used his influence to acquire for Bourne the position of preacher at his own rectory of St Christopher-le-Stocks in the City of London. Here Bourne became closely associated with the family of Sir Samuel Tryon, baronet, wealthy scion of a Flemish Protestant exile. Bourne lived with the family and was given a study in their household: two of the sermons which he wrote during this period were preached at Paul's Cross and eventually published, with dedica-tions to his patrons. Immanuel was firmly in the tradition of puritan ministers who obtained strong gentry support for their preaching activities and in return acted as private chaplains. In 1621 Tryon purchased the grant of next presentation to Ashover and presented Bourne to the rectory. Two years later Immanuel married Jemima Beckingham, cousin and companion of Lady Elizabeth Tryon, and an heiress in her own right. As a dowry Tryon bought the advowson of Ashover and gave it to Bourne. Little is heard of Bourne from then until the outbreak of war. He preached an assize sermon at Derby in 1623; sat on the Commission of the Peace; took a few parishioners to court over tithe; and in the 1630s was hauled before the High Commission for proclaiming a public fast day in time of plague contrary to royal orders.[3]

The life of James Nayler before the outbreak of the civil war is for the most part shrouded in shadow. He was born at Ardislaw, near Wakefield, in 1616 of yeoman stock, although he maintained that he was by occupation a husbandman. After his marriage he moved to Wakefield. During the civil war Nayler served in the parliamentary army for about nine years: he was a quarter-master in Lambert's regiment and in 1656 Lambert was to dub him 'a man of unblameable life and conversation'. At Appleby in 1652, when charged with blasphemy, Nayler denied that he had ever been a Leveller and, indeed, there is little reason to believe that he was ever linked with so secular an organization. Even while he was in the army and long before he met with George Fox he was preaching and converting. The effect of the New Model Army on his life is manifest: here he received his spiritual training and here he developed his deep-felt belief in religious equality. On his return home he appears to have attempted to settle down once more to life behind the plough. His account of his personal conversion sheds some interesting light on the way in which the civil war unsettled men's lives and is also of paramount importance to any understanding of the clash between the ordained ministers of the Church before the war and the sectaries.

> I was at the plow [he wrote] meditating on the things of God, and suddanily I heard a voice, saying unto me, 'Get thee out from thy kindred and from they Father's house'. And I had a promise given with it. Whereupon I did exceedingly rejoyce, that I had heard the voice of that God which I had professed from a child but had never known him.

Soon afterwards, he left his wife and child without even taking his leave of them. Thus began his career as an itinerant preacher: like Fox, he reached a belief in the 'Inner Light' by an independent and personal process.[4]

The difference between the paths which these two men followed to their ministry of the word is immediately apparent. Bourne came from an established clerical dynasty and from the start he was both set apart and trained for the ministry of the Established Church. Although his inclinations and talents probably made this course congenial to him, he can scarcely have experienced an inner call at the early age when he was marked for this career. Nayler, although far from illiterate, was brought up a farmer and, but for the incidence of the civil war, would probably have continued as such in his native Yorkshire: when called to preach the Gospel, the call was both intensely personal and immediate, requiring no preparation. In their printed works both men made virtues of their own experiences, thus in their persons summing up the issues at stake in the 1650s.

The reformers of the sixteenth century all held by the doctrine of the priesthood of all believers, but maintained no less strongly that there was a need for a special ministerial order in the Church. The Second Helvetic Confession of 1566 demonstrated the distinction between a priesthood and a ministry:

> The Apostles of Christ indeed call all believers in Christ priests, but not by any reason of a ministerial office, but because through Christ all who are the faithful, having been made kings and priests, are able to offer spiritual sacrifices to God. Accordingly, there are great differences between a priesthood and a ministry. For the former is common to all Christians, as we have just now said, but the same is not so with the latter.

Within England itself, Elizabeth was not amenable to a Church organization of the Reformed type and no doctrine of the ministerial order was clearly defined: within the Church of England, however, many ideas were advanced both by men of Reformed views and others. The priesthood of all believers may have been the underlying assumption behind the pronouncements of the Church's hierarchy but, naturally, the emphasis was upon the nature of the ministry and the qualifications necessary for admittance. The preface to the ordinal reads:

> It is evident unto all men diligently reading Holy Scripture and ancient authors, that from the Apostles' time there hath been these Orders of Ministers in Christ's Church: Bishops, Priests and Deacons. Which offices were evermore had in such reverend estimation, that no man, by his own private authority might presume to execute any one of them, except he was first called, tried, examined and known to have such qualities as were requisite for the same; and also by Public Prayer with Imposition of hands, approved and admitted thereunto. And therefore to the intent these Orders shall be continued and reverently used and esteemed in the Church of England, it is requisite that no man (not being at this present Bishop, Priest or Deacon) shall execute any of them, except he be called, tried, examined, and admitted thereunto, according to the Form hereafter following.

Whereas there was considerable argument between men of Reformed views and others concerning the internal structure of the ministry, both sides were in favour of a carefully ordered ministry with controlled entry. For guidance on such points the Reformed ministers appealed to Scripture, whereas when Hooker and Whitgift tried to establish the foundations of church polity they held firmly to the belief that no particular form was exclusively prescribed in the Scriptures and that local conditions and needs had to be considered when formulating practice.[5]

The Elizabethan and Stuart Church hierarchies were obsessed with the problem of recruiting a well-qualified clergy. Whatever the possible vocational deficiencies of the clergy, by the 1620s they formed a largely graduate group. It can be argued that this development had a profound effect upon the clergy's view of themselves as a profession. Certainly, as a group they appeared even more caste-like and self-perpetuating, with a strong element of dynasticism and a conviction that in university education lay the key to professional advancement. Natural common interests stemming from this educated background and from professional duties bound the clergy together yet more firmly. The remoteness of which the clergy were accused stemmed less from their physical than from their psychological distance from the community.

It was in part to this professional consolidation, rooted in education, that the sectaries objected. In 1647 Thomas Collier drew a parallel between the settled ministry of the day and Simon Magus. He maintained that the clergy paid for a university education in order to ensure greater future profits: 'it was the great end for which they were by their parents dedicated and set apart of purpose to get a living, even as they binde their children Apprentices, etc.' When admitted to the Church they search for

> the greatest and fattest livings, where there are most calves, lambs & tythe-pigs, corn, hay and glebe-land, there usually is their call; witness their often removing from a lesser living to a greater . . . witness their first quaere, what it is worth per annum . . . witness their indenting for thus much by the year, in case there be no tythes'.

Most important of all, he compared preparation of boys for the ministry directly with apprenticeship for a trade. Walwyn's earlier criticism of the clergy along similar lines introduced the additional point that the clergy argued that they were made ministers by divine right simply to deter laymen from questioning their pronouncements.[6]

The ordination controversy which came to the fore in the 1650s was, in fact, one aspect of this reaction. Basically it was a quarrel between those who urged the spontaneity of a ministry, called directly by God without the mediation of either man or Scripture, and those who were convinced that 'Besides the internall call of God, and due qualification through the Spirit, an externall mediate calling by men . . . is necessary to put a man into the office of a minister, and to enable him for the work' for 'the Scripture puts a difference between gifting, and sending men for the work of the ministry'.[7]

Immanuel Bourne was one of those who were convinced of the necessity of a ministerial order. His writings suggest that from his youth onwards he had held a very high doctrine of the ministry, setting great store on the necessity for a ministerial order although always within a traditional Calvinist framework. A careful training was necessary to equip a man to serve as a pastor to a congregation. The theology which Bourne expressed in his work was of an orthodox Calvinist nature. In his earlier sermons he devoted a great deal of space to a lucid exposition of the doctrine of Justification by Faith and not by the process of reason. For Bourne the Scriptures were the ultimate source of knowledge: he appealed both to Scripture and to the practice of the primitive Church – the Church of England had to measure the extent of her reformation by these two yardsticks.[8]

He felt that the Scriptures should be open to the laity and denounced the Pope for keeping the word of God from the people for so long 'contrarie to the command of Christ who bids, Search the Scriptures: John,5,39' and to the practice of the apostles. Ironically enough, he charged the Romish priests with the identical fault for which Walwyn chastised the Presbyterian ministers:

> These hereticall priests shut up the gates of truth, for they know that if the truth be one laid open, their church shall be forsaken, and they from their pontificall dignitie shall be humbled and brought downe to the common and bare estate of the people.

Yet it was not sufficient in his view that the people should be allowed to read the Scriptures: the laity should be well instructed in the word of God and the clergy were to ground their congregations in the faith. As a minister Bourne had a vested interest in the national Church and in the system of government which set the clergy apart from the laity but he, for other and purer reasons, did not want the faith to become a matter of personal interpretation. The Scriptures and not the individual man, or the Inner Light, were his milestone. The minister was necessary, as one set apart and specially educated for the task, to guide the people along the right paths; he should teach the principles of the faith by systematic instruction. As a product of a university education, Bourne held these institutions in veneration and believed that the ministry should consist of learned men, but this did not mean that he was blind to the deficiencies of the system. The universities did not concentrate upon preparing a man to execute the office of a pastor: in a modern phrase, they were not vocationally orientated.

> And heere [he wrote] you may soon espie the cause, why so manie students in the universities, and lawyers at inns of court, come so unfurnished, the one to the pulpit, the other to the barre; the one to feed the soules of their flockes, the other skilfully and honestly to plead the rightfull cause of their poore clyents.

It was small wonder that there was such a ready market in prepared or printed sermons and catechisms. Bourne placed the blame for the evident ignorance of many of the laity upon this neglect of vocational training. A teacher had to possess three attributes: knowledge, vocation and aptness of method.[9]

Fully aware that ministers required some guidance beyond academic training, he urged the use of catechisms. From internal evidence it seems clear that he had early evolved a catechism for use within his own parish and in 1645 he published one version of it. In this Bourne stands as part of a strong tradition within the Church of England: a tradition in which his own father had stood. A catechism was as much a teaching manual for the preacher as a book of guidance for the catechumen. These catechisms of the late sixteenth and early seventeenth centuries were the forerunners of Richard Baxter's *The Reformed Pastor*, which constituted a detailed appreciation of the need for vocational training and awareness. The methods used were the traditional ones of question and answer. Learning was by rote. Even in non-official catechisms, the answers were presented in a set and unchangeable form.[10]

Bourne's view of the teaching ministry fits into his general conception of the office. Ministers are 'ordained by Christ, in a speciall calling above others, to be instruments or outward means of converting men and women unto Christ'. Question 19 of his catechism asked whether there was a common ministry of all believers and whether all had the right to preach and teach publicly the word of God. Bourne's reply was that all Christians must bear witness to their faith privately, within the family, 'yet the great offices of the publike ministration belongeth to none but such as are specially called and appointed thereunto by their lord and king Christ Jesu' for God has 'inwardly furnished them with grace and experimental knowledge of Christ's power and grace in their souls'. The minister was not a priest in the Roman sense of the word, but was there to unfold Christ's message to the people. Bourne's treatment of the absolution of sins in an early pamphlet further illustrates this aspect of his thought. If a man is unable to reassure himself of God's infinite mercy in the forgiveness of sin then he 'must flye to the minister of God, whom he hath appointed for theyr help herein'. To him the sinner should make confession, as far as he is able, so that the minister 'may apply the promises of mercy, the refreshing oyle of the Gospel unto thy soule' and that 'the minister of God may pronounce the sentence of absolution (of the free remission and reconciliation with God in Christ)'. He was convinced that the minister alone had this power to reassure:

> And this power though it be not absolute, but ministerial (Christ absolving by his ministers) yet . . . the same words of absolution being pronounced by any other, cannot have that power to work on the conscience, or to perswade to peace, as when they were pronounced by him, that hath this ministeriall office; because the promise only is given to God's ministers, who are sent forth to this end. Ioh. 20.12.13.[11]

Thus the minister should serve his flock: teaching and reassuring them in the faith. The pastor was empowered to do this in two ways. Certainly Bourne introduces a *jure divino* – the minister is given grace and knowledge when called directly by Christ. The minister must also receive approval and training from Man. Moreover the task incumbent upon the minister is so important and so time-consuming that financially he must be in a position to devote his whole attention to its fulfilment. Significantly enough, these views on the nature of the ministry were set forth by Bourne before the settled, established ministry was being threatened seriously by the sects during the interregnum. They were not called into being simply because his livelihood was being threatened. Moreover, there is nothing original about Bourne's doctrine or about his views of the importance of the ministry. What is interesting is this simple fact – these views are expressed in the sermons which congregations all over England and Wales were hearing; these were the arguments for a trained ministry most frequently presented to the laity in the early seventeenth century. The style of these sermons suggests that they were directed chiefly to the better educated members of the congregation: they are learned sermons, based on a careful reading both of the Scriptures and the Fathers, and when they concern themselves with social ills they do so from the vantage point of one untouched by such problems, although nevertheless outraged by social injustice. This was not a deliberate stance, rather it was the natural product of the cleric's training and his professional and social position within the parish. Nevertheless, the type of argument which Bourne used and the way in which he presented it probably had little appeal for the husbandman or labourer with little education and even less money. It was among these people that the message of the sects made its chief impact.

During his ministry, Bourne exhibited many of the concerns voiced by his fellow puritans, both lay and clerical. For example, he attacked the social ills peculiar to Jacobean England: enclosure, engrossing and depopulation. He saw the evil of depopulation as arising from the oppression of the poor by the rich. Yet, in this respect, Bourne, even when commenting upon a social question, displayed a religious/ecclesiastical interest which related very much to the functions and interests of his own order. Enclosure had caused a shortage of corn and because of this patrons were anxious to sell livings to the men most willing to offer a handsome price. Simony had, in consequence, become prevalent in the Church. Bourne would have agreed with the bishop who in 1597 said 'one of the best ways to further the ministers to become learned is to revise the statutes for tillage'. Although, in the short run, some clergy profited from the increased tithe on sheep resulting from enclosing and engrossing, the decline in great tithes from corn and in small or vicarial tithes was ominous. It is significant that the seventeenth century saw a majority of tithe struggles over these small tithes.[12]

At the same time Bourne was ranging himself with those puritans who urged the introduction of a godly rather than a secular discipline into the Church. He attacked the Church courts, where offenders commonly were permitted to commute their penances for money. He claimed that officers of the courts were often corrupt. Although Bourne was willing to use the courts for civil suits, he believed that the business of correction belonged in the parish. The use of excommunication for petty offences and for non-appearance in court, and the arbitrary use of fines, met with his utmost disapproval. Once again Bourne demonstrated that he was a puritan clericalist who wanted to see the parochial clergy administering fatherly discipline to their congregations. Already Bourne stood in that tradition of the Reformation which was highly censorious of the Church and of the clergy, but from a standpoint of high clericalism. Because his standards were high, Bourne was critical of the clergy: ultimately he saw the only hope of general reform in a reformed clergy.[13]

Bourne later claimed that at the onset of war he adopted a neutral position, intending 'to attend to my own parishes and leave them to fighte it out'. He thought that Parliament had gone too far and that the king's actions could not be justified. This decision to stand aside from the fray did not ensure his safety: commanders on both sides demanded sums of money and, when Sir John Gell left Derbyshire to the Earl of Newcastle's men, the Cavaliers 'like demons, destroyed all they came neare and left the poore to starve'. As a result Bourne and many others began to side with Parliament. Bourne, in 1646, listed his attempts to comply with Parliament's wishes: after Laud's death he obeyed the ordinances; ceased to pray for the king in public; left marriages to the J.P.s; and 'when the kyng's cause became hopeless' accepted an appointment on the commission of sequestration 'thinking thereby to soften some of the hard measures dealt out to the kyng's friends'. Instead, however, it made him enemies among former friends and still the parliamentarians thought him a malignant in disguise. At some point he became assistant lecturer at St Sepulchre's, London, living as a banished man because Derbyshire was neither 'safe nor comfortable abiding'. After 1645, Bourne and others hoped that the war had left Derbyshire, but in June 1646 Parliament decided to destroy castles and halls there to prevent their falling into the malignants' hands. Bourne, presumably recently returned to Ashover, used every available cart to move his possessions from his large home, Eastwood Hall. Although he surrendered his house to the company of dragooners, they blew the hall up and 'they then sung a psalm and afterwards marched to the church'. Bourne followed them there and:

> to my great surprise did find scout master Smedley in the pulpit where
> he did preache a sermon two houres long about popery, priestcraft, and
> kyngecraft; but, Lord, what stuff and nonsense he did talke, and if hee
> could have murdered the kyng as easily as hee murdered the kyng's
> English, the war would long since have been over.

The dragooners proceeded to ransack the church for remains of the
old order and made a fire of surplice, prayer books and so on.[14]

Although Bourne, on his own private admission to a relative, had
had no real faith in the cause of either side and was swept into the
parliamentary ranks by circumstance, he publicly sought to align
himself with the parliament in London and to persuade it to inaugurate the much needed reform of the clergy. Part of his concern was
personal and materialistic: he asked compensation from the
authorities for his plundering at the hands of the Duke of Newcastle's royalist army.

> I was plundred, not only of my goods and study of books above twenty
> years in gathering, and my house barbarously torn in pieces and spoiled
> . . . but which was worse my manuscripts, near thirty years studies and
> pains night and day rent in pieces and taken away.

The royalists had treated him in this manner because they thought he
was a malignant from their cause. However, his greater concern was
to see the ministers of the Church better provided for financially so
that they could perform their duties to better advantage. A preaching
and teaching ministry simply could not be secured for between £10
and £30 a year, when ministers had to keep common ale-houses in
order to make ends meet. Parliament, in his view, had been accorded
victory in order to 'confirm the settled maintenance of the ministers
of the gospel by tithes' and to increase their livelihoods by redis-
tributing impropriate tithes among the clergy. If there had been
sufficient right preaching in England so many 'poor blind souls'
would not have 'run to the king's standard set up in Nottingham'.[15]

Bourne's defence of the tithe system was essentially a historical
one – the system goes back into antiquity and is condoned in Genesis;
tithes are to be exacted as of divine right. Theft of tithes had in the
past been severely punished: both William the Conqueror and Henry
VIII met with unpleasant retribution. Bourne also declared that it
was far preferable for the clergy to be maintained by tithes, already
God's property, than to be dependent upon men for their maintenance. Pure teaching of the Gospel would not be corrupted or cur-
tailed. Bourne was speaking from bitter personal experience with
regard to tithe. During the year 1657 he was forced to sue lead miners
from Ashover for tithe on lead: parishioners had apparently taken
advantage of his frequent absences from the parish during the interregnum to break the 'custom' of tithe payment. Bourne was hard

pressed financially by the system of composition for tithe. It was imperative that he prove that he had always had a claim to tithe in kind and that the agreements he had made for commutations in individual cases were not, in fact, a renunciation of this right. Yet Bourne's living was worth between £136 and £141 per annum in the period 1650–7, a comfortable living by contemporary standards. He had also been able to go some way towards recouping the losses of the 1640s and the repair of his house. Yet his point remains valid – that ministers of God should not be forced to worry over financial problems at the expense of their pastoral work.[16]

Bourne's contact with the separatist sects, and particularly with the Quakers, brought his high clericalism into stark relief. The independent sects which sprang up in England represented to Bourne two of the ills which he had always denounced: schism and the claim that every man could interpret the Scriptures and the Faith for himself. The fundamental anticlericalism of the Reformation itself had contained a potential threat that the need for a ministry would one day be denied. Contact with the Quakers, who did not believe in an established and regularly maintained clergy and who thought that man had no need of aid in interpreting the light of God which was within each and every man, drew from Bourne a spirited and entirely characteristic defence of the settled ministry as it then stood.

In common with all Quakers, James Nayler had a firm belief in the immediacy of his call from God: one of his main criticisms of the settled ministry was that they denied this fact. To him it seemed that both the civil and ecclesiastical authorities had their values all wrong. He hoped to convince the authorities that they were serving selfish interests and not God when they persecuted fellow Christians. For Nayler, the function of the ministry was essentially that fulfilled by prophets such as Amos and Hosea – warning and chastising the people of God and showing them the right road. On receiving the call from God, however, a man had no further need of the minister. He became conscious of the 'inner light' within him and began to live in accordance with that light. He was able to see the discrepancy between the world as God would have it and the world as men have made it. At this point every man would be moved to denounce the sinfulness of Man's world and persuade others into the right frame of mind to receive God's word. Nayler's main concern was to reform men spiritually: he saw the social grievances around him as the outcome of spiritual disease which could only be cured by a spiritual remedy. Thus the Quakers approached the problem from an entirely different angle from that of secular groups such as the Levellers. Nayler, for instance, went to great lengths to prove that present disillusionment concerning the civil war was due to a fundamental misapprehension shared by ruler and ruled: they had believed that they could, by their own efforts, remove a tyrant from his seat and replace him with a godly government. The new government was still ruling in the interests of one section of the community and without God. In his desire for the establishment of a new theocracy, Nayler saw the clergy and the lawyers as oppressors of the people and upholders of the *status quo*. He agreed with the view that the clergy were mainly concerned to preserve their professional interests and because of this were maintaining that all ministers must be well educated. For Nayler, if man had God's spirit within him he had no need of earthly learning to interpret God's word. Ministers were necessary to make men aware of the presence of the inner light. There was a need to prepare the ground, but God had planted the seed and would nourish the plant. Truly Nayler must be classed with those who wished not to reform the settled ministry but to destroy it.[17]

The Quakers had been active in the midland counties since the mid-1640s and in Derbyshire since 1647. The leaders had been engaged in a missionary campaign in the north Midlands since that time. In the year 1653 Richard Farnsworth concentrated his ministry in the county of Derby; significantly he entered into disputation with the preachers of the town of Chesterfield and its hinterland. These men were so incensed by the Quaker challenge that they threw down the gauntlet to yet another leader in early 1654, James Nayler. Some time before the meeting was held, the issues to be discussed were sent to Nayler so that he could prepare replies. The central issue of the meeting was whether there was a need for a formally ordained, educated and settled ministry. Other questions were whether the Scriptures or the inner light were the final authority in matters of faith, and whether it was permissible to address any man on earth as mother or father. On 3 January Nayler and the ministers met in the church of Chesterfield in front of a large congregation. The questions were read aloud by John Billingsley, preacher of Chesterfield, and then Nayler 'began to read his answer in writing' which was then subjected to intense criticism.[18]

The Chesterfield disputation was essentially a clerical meeting. Although several 'understanding' laymen did take part, the leading speakers were all clergymen – John Billingsley, Immanuel Bourne, Mr Gardiner, minister of Eckington, Mr Maudstey, minister of Dronfield, and Mr Moor, minister of Brampton. There can be little doubt that these men felt their very livelihoods to be threatened. If man needed to consult the Scriptures to ascertain God's will then the foundation of traditional puritanism went unscathed: the position of the minister as pastor and teacher of his flock was unassailable. The *type* of training for the ministry might still be open to criticism and suggestion, and the validity of the academic syllabus at Oxford and Cambridge in this context might be disputed, but the need for some vocational training was acknowledged. Should however, the Quaker's point be conceded that it was not the written word in the Scriptures but the spirit within each man which provided all the guidance necessary for individual salvation, the foundation of the ministry was undermined. Similarly, if it were not allowable to honour any man or own his authority, this would be tantamount to saying that the clergy were not in a position of honour or authority – that they had no greater qualification to teach than did any private individual and no special grace bestowed upon them by God, over and above that accorded to each layman, in order to shepherd and teach God's people.

Although there was some attempt at argument, the meeting did bear a distinct resemblance to the 'bull-bayting' which James Nayler saw in it. As he said, the ministers chose their own ground: 'The things they would dispute upon were what they themselves had chosen, so that there was no place for any other thing, that I would have had them to have proved as their own practice.' The contempt which a man such as Bourne felt for an uneducated and simple wandering preacher completely coloured his own account of the meeting. This was clearly partisan, designed, in his own words, to convince Cromwell that, although his measures against the Ranters had had a beneficial effect, the Quakers presented a yet more fearful threat to the 'quietness in our exercises of religion', lives and property. The document provides interesting insight into the view of the uneducated sectaries taken by the settled ministry. Nayler is portrayed as quite unable to argue on traditional lines. Time after time Bourne notes that Nayler evaded the questions put to him. Bourne refused to let him escape with such tactics and insisted on pressing home his points. Nayler obviously felt himself to be cornered by the verbal quibbling in which Bourne and the rest engaged. For example, when Bourne maintained that Christ himself had referred to the Scriptures as chief judge in points of controversy, Nayler could summon up no real answer but yelled out: 'Liar, liar, hold thy peace, the Spirit is the judge, not the written word.' When Bourne rejoined with the logical argument that the word of God was the chief judge and, as the Scriptures equal the word of God, *ergo* the Scriptures are the chief judge, Nayler did not reply by disagreeing with the premiss but fell back upon yet another emotional outburst. Immanuel Bourne, accustomed to men who argued according to the traditional rules of the schools, told Nayler he was the most 'brazen fac'd, foule mouth'd fellow he had heard, when his own mouth was stopped, then he could not answer an argument, he still cried out, liar, liar, stop thy mouth'.[19]

Nayler was getting progressively out of his depth and the assembly sought to trip him up in argument. One John Bunting, 'an honest yeoman (of more true spirituall understanding than many Quakers)' sitting by Nayler at this disputation, writing in shorthand what Nayler said, was charged by Nayler with writing down lies: Bunting's quick reply was that, as he was merely writing down Nayler's own words, he was indubitably writing down lies. The disputation ended abruptly with Nayler and his followers leaving the church. In conclusion Bourne described the meeting as more of 'a wrangling by that man, who had not artificiallie, scarce naturall order of reasoning, but like a boisterous, railing fellow, who by loud cries, little or nothing to the purpose, sought to deceive the people', than a disputation. One among the congregation commented that his name should rather be James Rayler.[20]

The two sides were arguing at cross purposes throughout and little progress was possible. Bourne and the ministers concluded that, whereas each man could generally discern good from evil by reference to his conscience, in the last resort the Scriptures were the chief judge. Nayler disagreed with this point – he did not equate the inner light with Man's conscience, it was truly God in Man. The ministers thought that the Quakers were heretically claiming a oneness with God, whereas Nayler was really claiming that God was working directly within Man. The Quaker position was somewhat confused by their inheritance of the traditional puritan dependence upon Scripture – Nayler's works were as littered with Scriptural references as were Bourne's own. Nayler stressed that truths arrived at through direct communication with God were always in accord with the written word of God, but he emphasized that the inner light expressed the living word of God, whereas the Scriptures, unless read through this light, were a dead letter. The settled ministers were, however, able to demonstrate that the Quakers were misapplying passages of Scripture.[21]

In 1659 Bourne returned to the fray in defence of human learning. The sectaries denied that the ministers possessed any greater portion of God's grace than did the laity and asserted that the only distinction between the two groups was one created by the clerical profession: 'Take away that which you had at Cambridge and Oxford, and then you have no ministers but laymen might preach as well as you.' Bourne countered that the self-called preachers of the sects themselves made use of human learning. He thought that they were merely envious of the clergy and of their opportunities for education. Yet the gulf between Bourne and Nayler, for instance, was more fundamental. To Bourne's mind a separate ministerial order of men specially trained for the pastoral ministry and educated in human learning was not merely an adjunct of the Church's apparatus but a necessary part of it. The Church on earth could not function without the ministry. To Nayler it was Anti-Christ which denied that the call to the ministry was immediate and maintained that it was mediate, 'by which all are called by commission from men'.[22]

Whereas it is true that Bourne formulated his thoughts concerning the nature and necessity of a separate ministerial order much more quickly during the 1640s and 1650s, an examination of his career shows that he had always been a high clericalist by conviction and that the war years merely served to emphasize this part of his credo. In claiming that the sectaries threatened the vested interests of the settled clergy, one is not being unduly cynical and suggesting that the clergy defended their own worth for material reasons alone – Bourne, for example, was convinced of the truth of his own defence – but such considerations did play their part in determining the reaction of these ministers to the wandering sectarian preachers. It was small wonder that the ordination controversy of the 1650s produced such strong feeling.

We are fortunate to be able to complement this dicussion of attitudes to the settled ministry with an examination of Ralph Josselin's ministry at Earls Colne, Essex, during the mid-seventeenth century. The appearance of a complete edition of Josselin's diary has provided us with a much fuller description of the day-to-day life of a clergyman of the established Church than we can ever glean from Church records and published pamphlets. Once again, we have to be careful not to rely too heavily on this individual case study. Indeed, the case of Josselin is especially interesting simply because it *is* so different from that of Immanuel Bourne. Clearly the clergy of the established Church itself came from very divergent backgrounds and, because of the variations in their experiences, shared very different views on many topics. Yet, despite such differences, they joined together in opposition to the sectaries and to the idea of a non-maintained ministry. Bourne was a product of the Elizabethan and Jacobean ecclesiastical age. He was a learned Calvinist minister, who set great store on the pastoral and teaching functions of the clergy and thought that learning and reasonableness were necessary attributes in a minister. A puritan of the old school, if you like, he had no spark of 'enthusiasm' in his religious make-up. In addition, Bourne came from an ecclesiastical family background and accepted the fundamental structure of the English Church.

Josselin, on the other hand, like Nayler, grew up in the age of Laud and was subjected to different influences at a susceptible age. His diary shows him to have been a Millenarian, for example. In this way his religious thought had more in common with that of Nayler than that of Bourne. Josselin grew up in the household of an educated yeoman: the vested interest which Bourne's family had always had in the Elizabethan *status quo* was never present in Josselin's family conversation. Perhaps as a result of this, Josselin's diary reveals him as more critical of the method of recruiting, training and approving clergy than Bourne. He still believed in the necessity of a settled, maintained ministry but he was less concerned that the procedure of episcopal approval of presentations to livings be perpetuated, for instance. Nevertheless, when one has read the diary, one can scarcely be left in any doubt that the attack on the settled ministry was a matter of immediate, personal concern to Josselin. He was prepared to live with an 'Independent' Church organization but his personal involvement dictated that he could never countenance the abolition of a settled, maintained ministry.[23]

We are not arguing that this was a purely *generational* difference. Age in itself did not dictate that Bourne be a 'conservative' and Josselin an innovationist. The difference in their past experience (a result, if one likes, of age) did shape their reactions to the situation.

Accepting these reservations about the typicality of the Josselin case study, nevertheless, the diary does enable us to say exactly what a seventeenth-century clergyman did with his time – something which it was impossible to be certain about previously. It also enables us to define the professional relationships of one clergyman – both with his fellow-ministers and also with members of his own and neighbouring congregations, and it permits us to assess the strains and stresses placed on those relationships during the period of turmoil in the 1640s and 1650s. We are able to see what impression issues such as that of the settled ministry made upon Josselin's parochial ministry. What place did such major issues take in Josselin's daily life? Was he absorbed by them or not?

Ralph Josselin was the son of a yeoman. He was born in January 1616. It is interesting to note his words: 'I confesse my childhood was taken with ministers and I heard with delight and admiracion and desire to imitate them from my youth, and would be acting in corners.' Josselin underlines the fact that, although he had this natural inclination for a career in the Church and a love of learning, he was also motivated in his desire to be a scholar by insecurity (his mother was dead and he feared that a stepmother might bring financial and emotional ruin to him) and the feeling that a good education would bring him financial independence. (It was not likely that such a man would ever willingly agree to a withdrawal of payment from ministers.) Josselin persuaded his father to prepare him for the ministry. First he attended Bishop's Stortford School. Then he was sent to Cambridge and was admitted pensioner at Jesus College in March 1632/3 at the age of 16. Josselin's time at Cambridge was much interrupted by financial exigencies.

I was forced to come from Cambridge many times for want [of] meanes and loose my time in the contry yett would I endeavor to gett it up and I thank God notwithstanding all hindrances I was not behind many of my time and standing.[24]

Even at this time Josselin was troubled by ceremonial aspects of the services of the Church of England. Josselin's father died before he took his degree and, as he left Ralph only £20, Josselin was undecided as to his future occupation. He contemplated farming, the law and so on. The minister of Steeple Bumpstead persuaded Ralph to return to Cambridge and take his degree and another minister seems to have sought employment for him. Eventually Ralph obtained the post of usher (under master) with a Mr Neale's school at Deane in Bedfordshire. He occupied the place for two years and used the time for study. He became friends with Mr Dillingham and used his library; he gained access to Lord Mandeville's library through acquaintance with Mandeville's chaplain. Josselin appears to have concentrated on the writings of members of the Reformed Church on the Continent: he mentions studying and abridging the works of Daniel Chamier. In October 1639, over two years after taking his B.A., Josselin moved to a curate's position at Olney, Buckinghamshire, at the request of Mr Gifford, the Vicar. Gifford had presumably heard Josselin preach at Wormington, Northamptonshire, on 1 September – yet another indication of the importance of the pulpit in furthering the careers of prospective clerics.[25]

Josselin was not in orders and he spent the first quarter of his term at Olney as schoolmaster (and perhaps reader). In the December he was ordained deacon by the Bishop of Peterborough, a supporter of Laud. On his return to Olney Josselin took up preaching duties and the reading of prayers – by February he was preaching once a fortnight and receiving 10s. a quarter more for this. In February Josselin received priest's orders at Peterborough and expressed his disapproval of the ceremonial adopted. 'I was ordayned minister at Peterburg by the Bishop and six ministers: I would not bowe towards the Altar as others did and some followed my example.' Then Josselin proceeded to take up his M.A. at Cambridge – a further drain upon his financial resources as the ordination ceremonies and the degree ceremony together cost him £25 9s. 7d. (the equivalent of almost twice his annual money income).[26]

Josselin had by now decided to marry but 'could not see any convenience how to live'. This spurred him on to search for a place which paid more than the £14 plus diet offered by Mr Gifford. (The sum of £14 includes the £2 additional payment for preaching and reading prayers.) Josselin preached two sermons at Cranham, Essex (in part, a publicity campaign); he turned down a chaplaincy in Lord

Mandeville's household (for moral or spiritual reasons); and sought a place, unsuccessfully, at Kimbolton. Eventually he was offered and accepted a post, presumably as curate but perhaps as lecturer, at Cranham, for which he was to receive £24 per annum from the minister; diet or £10 from his uncle; and £10 from the town. Josselin felt that this arragement made it possible for him to marry and he did so in October 1640, when he was aged 24. The Josselins moved to Cranham immediately but the post seemed less satisfactory in fact than it had in prospect. Josselin served as schoolmaster of Upminster, which took up much time but yielded little financial reward. He and his wife had no home of their own.[27]

Ralph was again open to offers of other positions.

> The Inhabitants of Horenechurch layd in for mee and made mee [good offers] of 80li. per annum viis et modis certayne without any trouble on my part: [only] to preach twice on the Lords day, without medling with other dutyes.

Then, through the mediation of the Vicar of Felsted, the people of Earls Colne became interested in his services. Significantly enough, Josselin first met and talked with the patron, Mr Richard Harlakenden. He then preached a sermon and 'upon their approbacion they desired mee I would come and live with them as their Minister'. Josselin agreed on condition that they matched the financial offer made by Hornchurch. For a brief period the Josselins rented accommodation for £24 a year but were able to move into their own, apparently newly built, house in October 1641 and to employ a maid servant. Josselin was disappointed by the financial returns of the living – that he felt that he had been misled by the initial promises and that he sensed that some of the congregation were hostile to his ministry finds clear expression in the diary.

This first section of the diary account is most interesting because it sets in a more personal perspective several important points which have already emerged in this study. Firstly, the setting apart and separate training of a child for the ministry; secondly, the diverse motives for entering the Church; thirdly, the extreme insecurity of the period preceding the acquisition of a benefice and the natural place of schoolteaching within this 'apprenticeship' period; fourthly, the importance of preaching and patronage in obtaining a place; fifthly, the role of neighbouring clergy and of the congregation in searching out a suitable minister and approving him; sixthly, the number of practical considerations which had to be weighed before accepting a place – all appear as relevant to Josselin's own case. But most importantly, the account sketches in Josselin's underlying assumptions about these matters. In some ways his views already seem to diverge from those which we know were held by Immanuel

Bourne. The contents of the diary reveal Josselin as a puritan who was rather further to the 'left' than was Bourne. For example, he seems to have always assumed the correctness of congregational participation in Church appointments and to have been enthusiastic about conferences with parishioners on delicate issues. During the Commonwealth his leanings were definitely towards independent rather than Presbyterian church forms, although he was willing to live with Presbyterianism.

Although Josselin collected his tithes and believed that adequate fixed maintenance for the clergy was a necessity, one gets the impression that his attitude to the divine right to tithe was rather more flexible than Bourne's. Bourne would not have accepted that maintenance by tithe could be replaced successfully by other means, and he would not have countenanced gladly such extensive congregational participation. This divergence of views between men who were both believers in a separate, educated and maintained ministry is an intriguing one. Is it attributable to Bourne's clerical background and inherited assumptions? Is it, as already suggested, a product of the generation gap? Josselin was the same age as James Nayler. Is it simply attributable to a difference in personality, Josselin being more flexible and questioning than Bourne? Weight should be given to all these explanations: together they may provide the answer. But the fact that Josselin was only first generation clergy seems very significant. He was one of the people in a sense that Bourne was not: Josselin was simply the well-educated son of a prosperous yeoman; Bourne had an entirely different sort of background – separated in his upbringing as well as his profession.

The diary gives so full an account of Josselin's daily life that it would be idle to pretend to be able to cover all the important passages here. Blocks of entries, however, should indicate the range of Josselin's activities as pastor and preacher and his reactions to contemporary issues. It has proved impracticable to present the entries unabridged: the entries quoted here relate specifically to clerical duties although some references to financial preoccupations have been included. The reader is advised to consult Alan Macfarlane's edition of *The Diary of Ralph Josselin* to set such entries in the context of Josselin's daily life.

In August 1644 Josselin bought a share in a ship for £14 10s., an investment designed to supplement his income from the living. On 11 August he used the Sunday sermon as an occasion to remind his congregation that if they did not pay him he would be forced to find other employment. On Thursday 15 Josselin preached at neighbouring Coggeshall and returned to bury two parishioners. A feast was provided and Josselin conversed with members of the congregation. The entry for Tuesday 20 August shows him hard at work building his new hall but on the following day he kept a day of humiliation at a parishioner's house (the Parliament's Wednesday Fast), at which he extemporized on a text from the Book of Ruth. Josselin dealt with a drunkard on Tuesday 27 August. A further day of humiliation was held on Wednesday 28 August: Josselin obviously found these occasions a strain. On Sundays Josselin apparently spent the whole day either taking public services or preparing for them: when on 1 September the Bentons visited he commented, 'Mr Benton and his wife with us which shortned my time for studdy, yett god inabled mee in some measure for the Sabbath'. He was called to the bedside of a sick parishioner on the following Tuesday (3rd) for spiritual comfort. Josselin 'urged him to a Covenant with god to bee a new man if he recovered'. On Friday 6 September Josselin rode to the sermon at Halstead and conversed with a gentry patron of his, Sir Thomas Honeywood, who entertained him to a meal. Josselin was reading and reflecting on Prynne's Breviate of the Life of Archbishop Laud on Monday 9 September and on the Wednesday following held a burial service in the parish. On Monday 14 September he rode to Colchester to appear before the Committee for the Sequestration of Scandalous Ministers in Essex: while in the city Josselin conferred with one Mr Ellis on the issue of separation from the established State Church. During the week beginning 22 September Josselin attended both a day of humiliation (the Parliamentarian Wednesday Fast) and also the lecture at Clare. On Tuesday 1 October the vicar rode to Wethersfield to keep company with friends and purchased some books. On Wednesday 9 and Monday 14 October Josselin was away from his parish conferring about the choice of a minister for Stisted.

> I rid to Stisted to assist in the choyse of their minister, both parts stiffe; divided, a most sad towne, no care almost of any thing, I spoke to them but could not drawe it to a conclusion though I hope to a good forwardness; Mr Alstone made a serious offer to mee of 10li. out of his owne purse, and great likelyhood to carry it if I would yeeld to them but I would not, I was ingaged in the busynes and therefore would not endeavour any such thing to myselfe: the place hath: 140 acres of glebe and the tith are worth about 100li. per annum.

At this time Josselin's pastoral and preaching activities were well spaced out throughout the whole week. Josselin was a farmer but he did not confine his clerical duties to Sundays and evenings by any means. Study and preparation for preaching were but one aspect of his clerical function. In some weeks Josselin was attending both an extra-parochial sermon and a fast day in addition to Sunday services. He was involved in pastoral activities such as sick visiting and holding burial services. Yet it is evident that preaching provided the highlight of his week's work. No doubt, quite apart from its reli-

gious significance, Josselin liked the variety which trips to neighbouring communities brought to his life. They also brought an
element of risk: as the diary shows, Josselin was always sharply
aware of the grave dangers involved in so much travel even over
relatively short distances. The roads were abominable and horse
accidents frequent, but for the most part the activities mentioned are
unremarkable. The only really new departure from the norm of
Josselin's life was the conversation regarding separation at Colchester: a foretaste of the discussions about the ministry, Church
government and the visible and invisible Church which were such a
feature of later years. But in the main, in 1644 the Vicar of Earls
Colne was the unchallenged religious leader in the community,
whose advice was sought on spiritual matters, and whose claim to
maintenance by the parish did not yet need to be voiced.

By 1647 the situation appears to have altered. The issue of the
settled ministry was sufficiently important by the spring that the
Essex clergy were discussing it. On 1 April Josselin wrote: 'This day
[Tuesday] rid to Mr Downings [Rector of Layer Marney], six of us
mett, we agreed to conferre about the lawfulnes of our ministry, to
meete next month at Mr Westlyes.' A sense of insecurity seems to
have underlined the bonds which already held together the clerical
community. Such meetings became far more frequent from this time
onwards. During April and May 1647 there were three clerical
gatherings. Such activity was in part a response to national political
events and to the fears aroused by opinions voiced by the soldiers of
the army. These fears were intensified in the summer of 1647.

> This weeke there is a sad turne and change on the face of the kingdome,
> what god will doe wee knowe not, the counsell of Jehovah shall stand,
> the poore ministers are in straites on all hands, but the name of the lord
> is a tower unto his . . . (6 June 1647).
> The times were sad the reproaches on the ministry, and threats against
> them very great, and many gaping for evill to come upon us, yett god is
> our helpe and refuge . . . (27 June 1647).

When, in early April 1647, 60 of Desborough's troops had quartered
in Earls Colne and cast abuse against ministers, the current feeling
against the ministry, which was running high in the army ranks, was
brought home to the Essex clergy. No matter what the spiritual
comfort provided by colleagues such as Daniel Rogers, Ralph Josselin was subject to ominous feelings: 'this weeke seemed blacke and
darke in providences as if mutinies and troubles were yett neare at
hand, the lord in mercy prevent them, and fitt us for whatsoever he
will bring upon us'.[28] Josselin's practical reaction was to try to
prevent the rot spreading to his own parish but congregations were
small and Josselin was able to speak only to the minority of the
parish. On 20 June Josselin held a parish meeting, at which a petition

was drawn up requesting a reformation of Church discipline. A subcommittee worked on the petition at Josselin's house on 21 June and the petition was presented to Parliament in early July. On 5 July Josselin held a conference with his parishioners about Church discipline: he was obviously finding it more and more difficult to curb the 'particular fancies' of certain parts of his flock. So much so that on 12 July Josselin held another conference. Fear of renewed civil war gave rise to more clerical gatherings to pray for peace and a solution to the Church's and the nation's problems. By August the issue of infant baptism was exercising the minds of some of the laity and on 26 July Josselin rode to talk the matter over with the Rector of Lexden. Both agreed with the position of the Church of England that it was not essential for the parent of the child to be a believing Christian. With all this talk of Church discipline, the ministerial order and the Church's position on infant baptism one might have expected some expression of discontent with the settled ministry of the parish, yet the following comment suggests that this was not the case: 'went about to gather tith, but I have not yett at twice received one penny: mony is dead, people are bare'.[29] The war, rather than discontent with the ministry, was having its impact upon tithe revenue.

The religious life of the parish in the 1650s was transformed. For some time Josselin had been preoccupied with his studies – with a careful reading of Deuteronomy, with research into the history of the Protestant Reformation in Europe – as well as with reflections on the state of the nation. By late 1650 he was expressing interest in apocalyptic literature and his interest blossomed during the 1650s. In February 1653 his uncle was urging him to carry on with his apocalyptic studies. During the years following, he had several apocalyptic dreams. As Alan Macfarlane points out in the introduction to the *Diary*, Josselin was at first a convinced Millenarian although he became sceptical in the mid-1650s.[30] If Josselin's dreams were obsessed with the second coming they also reflected some of the day-to-day worries of the settled ministry. On 7 August 1653 he thought an Anabaptist was throwing stones at him; on 8 June 1656 he heard a sermon preached in the lane by Mr Sams and had to prompt the preacher who forgot his text; later in March 1656 he himself preached without collar or surplice and without knowledge of the psalms or scriptural passages. All this seems to suggest a horror of the preachers of the sects. Certainly, in his waking life he also expressed fear that the ministry would be put down.

It is during the 1650s that Josselin's accounts of parish meetings are most informative. That of 23 February 1651 is very noteworthy. According to Josselin, for the first time in nine years the communion was celebrated in both kinds. The service was suggested by Josselin's patron, Mr Harlakenden and, although there was some obstruction, the group resolved to go ahead with the service. Public notice was given 'to prevent offence' and a resolve was made to admit none to the supper but those who were 'disciples'. During January this suggestion gave rise to considerable discussion as to who should be admitted to communion: Josselin spoke to the effect that any who professed the faith should be admitted, against a suggestion that only those who could prove that they were called should be admitted to fellowship, but persons wishing to participate in the fellowship had to present their names for scrutiny. 'I admonisht divers, admitted others with consent, divers Christians hung backe'. The precisians' ideal of pastoral excommunication was being realized. Clearly the restoration of the sacrament of the Lord's Supper after such an absence made a profound impression upon the 'fellowship'. But Josselin was absorbed with the relevance of the apocalyptic prophecies to the political situation in England. His obsession seems to have communicated itself even to his youngest children and certainly to his congregation through sermons preached at services and days of humiliation.[31] In this context, perhaps his rather casual attitude to tithes and the issue of maintenance and a settled ministry is rather more explicable.

> 19 September 1651. A great Rabbi's saying. If the Messiahs coming bee not before 1656. of the Christians account then expect no other Messiah but the Christians Messiah.
> I am perswaded the present dispensacon is the breaking in peices the kingdomes of the earth which god is entring on, and some time when this worke is advanced, will the Jewes appeare; and then comes in the happy season of the flocke.

Although he regarded the Quakers in his parish as deluded, his reaction was not as impassioned as that of Bourne in the mid-1650s. Bourne was fighting the Quakers with reason, Josselin with a millennial hope akin to that of the Quakers themselves. He was undoubtedly alert to the Quaker threat and *worried* but he seems to have contented himself with private discourse with the offenders in his parish and confident assurances in the pulpit.[32]

It would be possible to continue describing Josselin's daily life during the 1650s but the main point has already emerged. Josselin was increasingly concerned by attacks on the ministry and the Church but he found refuge in Millenarian belief until the later 1650s. Sceptical comments begin to creep in in 1656. His absorption with the parousia lends a slightly surrealistic air to his accounts of parish life. It is as though the realities of the political situation were so unbearable a shock to his sensibilities that he was forced to rely even more on his belief in divine providence and a solution to the country's problems completely outside man's control. This is a far cry from his reasoned discussion with the Anabaptist Oates about the necessity for a settled ministry in 1646.

One should not read too much into two individual case studies, although the instances of Bourne and Josselin indicate how varied the responses of two educated clergymen of the established Church could be in the crisis of Church order in the period 1640–60. Age, experience, background and personality all played their parts in determining such reactions. We are warned not to accept that all clergymen adopted such a defensive position as Immanuel Bourne or reconciled themselves to the new régime easily. Ralph Josselin, despairing of help from Cromwell in the 1650s, was falling back upon Millenarian dreams for comfort in his distress; Immanuel Bourne, equally sceptical of state assistance, was nevertheless already fighting for his cause in the same period.

16

Comparisons

To argue that the English clergy emerged as a professional group in the late sixteenth and early seventeenth centuries is to say that there was no clerical profession in the middle ages. This assumption is itself worth examination. Of course, it is neither possible nor desirable here to describe in detail the medieval clergy or their organization but it is useful to draw some comparisons between the medieval and the post-Reformation clergy in the parishes.

Studies of the clergy in the fourteenth, fifteenth and early sixteenth centuries support the view that the word *clergy* meant something very different in pre-Reformation days. First of all, it encompassed large numbers of people, mainly boys, who merely intended to enter holy orders and therefore took the first tonsure and who later, when in minor orders, undertook rather menial functions in connection with the Church's liturgy. Such boys had no pastoral responsibilities whatsoever and lived a partly lay life. The word also took in those men who had finally committed themselves to a clerical life and taken the major or holy orders of subdeacon, deacon and priest. These young men possessed a patrimony or title on ordination but most had to serve as unbeneficed parish auxiliaries for some time in order to supplement this source of income. For some, such work was casual and temporary, for others more permanent as they became hired priests of the parish, chantry priests, chaplains or parish priests.[1] Dr David Robinson has estimated that before the Black Death in the archdeaconries of Cleveland and the East Riding there were approximately four unbeneficed to every one beneficed clergyman.[2] As late as 1525 there were twice as many parish chaplains as incumbents in the East Riding (and this excludes consideration of less permanently employed clerics).[3] The word clergy also included, of course, those more comfortably settled: the beneficed rectors and vicars, the members of deans and chapters, the archdeacons, the bishops and the archbishops. A statistically significant proportion of the beneficed parish clergy were given benefices as a reward for their services to Crown, noble household, episcopal administration or monastic house. Many were non-resident and continued to hold benefices as sinecures while pursuing administrative, legal or scholarly careers elsewhere.[4]

Before the Reformation the word clergy implied being set apart from the laity: ordained eventually to mediate between man and God. The priesthood involved only partly a pastoral charge. Men were ordained into it who had no immediate prospects of presentation to a benefice or charge of a parish, and those who did obtain benefices either before or immediately after ordination as priest often promptly delegated the pastoral responsibilities associated with a benefice to an auxiliary or deputy. The large number of men belonging to the clergy made it perhaps inevitable that the more junior would bear the brunt of pastoral work, particularly when a substantial proportion of the beneficed confessed to no vocation. The rector (where resident) or vicar devoted himself largely to the liturgical duties of the office and delegated duties of instruction, baptismal, churching and funeral services, the hearing of confession and sick visiting to hired priests. Many of the men who on ordination technically possessed no cure of souls certainly exercised one in reality, but the fact remains that the ultimate ambition was to be able to relinquish that responsibility. Although a good many of the parish priests had no hope of ever obtaining a benefice, the majority of beneficed clergy, excluding graduate rectors and vicars, did serve an apprenticeship as parish assistants. They often served as auxiliaries or deputies for long periods before acquiring benefices. One contrasts this with the situation in Reformation Kent or in late sixteenth-century Coventry and Lichfield where such curacies normally provided a dead end for the occupant and where the beneficed normally secured their places soon after ordination even in the 1620s. Had the medieval clergy continued to exercise a largely pastoral function once beneficed, such an apprenticeship might have been invaluable. As it was served in circumstances of financial insecurity or hardship and with little or no specific training, it is doubtful whether it was of great service to the parishes concerned.[5]

After the Reformation, it was normal to see the priesthood not as an office but as a pastoral vocation. Although the degree of emphasis on the nature of the separation between laity and clergy might vary, the ideal remained that a priest should have a parish. The function of the archdeacon, the dean and the bishop was also seen in pastoral terms. In point of fact, we know that the English Protestants were fighting a continuing battle against the old concept of the benefice as a piece of property, dispensed by patrons for a variety of non-religious reasons and eagerly sought after by the penurious cleric. We know that attempts to reform the upper echelons of the diocesan clergy were foiled by the traditional method of rewarding servants of state and church with cathedral prebends and wealthy benefices.[6] Despite the fact that the traditional structure of the medieval Church remained, there was, however, a continuing and articulate attempt to reform the attitude of the clergy to their role. Ironically enough, this may have been helped by the comparative shortage of clerical recruits in the immediately post-Reformation years. With so few qualified parish priests outside benefices, there was far more onus upon the beneficed to assume full pastoral responsibility. Laws against non-residence and pluralism undoubtedly helped, as did the emergence of a non-ecclesiastical route through the universities to royal and noble service.

Probably the most obvious difference between the pre- and post-Reformation Churches lay in the attitude towards training for the ministry. This does not mean that the medieval clergy were ignorant illiterates and their late sixteenth-century counterparts well-educated. In fact, the number of graduates among the clergy was on the increase in the fifteenth and early sixteenth centuries. About a fifth of the beneficed in Canterbury and Durham were graduate in the 1520s and 1530s, about a sixth in Norwich between 1503 and 1528, and about one-third of those beneficed or vacating benefices in London between 1522 and 1530. There were some dramatic regional variations: Stafford archdeaconry in 1531 contained no graduate clergy, for example. Nevertheless, a statistically significant proportion of England's parochial clergy had been to university and of the rest most were literate in a real sense. According to Mr Peter Heath's researches, quite a high proportion of the clergy owned books: approximately one-fifth of a largely non-graduate population examined. Moreover, it can be shown that in some instances the level of education of the parish clergy actually fell during the years immediately following the Henrician Reformation. In Surrey 34.1 per cent of identified incumbents between 1520 and 1530 possessed degrees; the percentage fell to 14.3 per cent under Edward VI, rising to 22.62 per cent in 1562 and eventually to 29.5 per cent in 1581.[7]

However, Peter Heath identifies the real distinction between the medieval and the Reformation clergy. The former were literate, even graduate, but their education was conservative and little touched by new ideas of humanism and, moreover, it was in no sense systematic or planned. To quote Peter Heath,

> There was plenty of private educational enterprise by bishops but no concerted plan and no blueprint even of how a priest should be trained – or even that a priest should be trained at all *as a priest*. The post-Reformation Church in England was constantly hindered by tradition yet, however far attempts to train the clergy for their pastoral function fell short of the Protestant ideal, there can be no doubt that the ideal existed and was actively sought after.[8]

The reformers in England and Wales reacted against the medieval concept of clergy. They were aware that the pastoral function of the priesthood had also fallen into disrepute – because it was disowned by the established and executed by the ill-prepared and poor clerics of low status. There must have been many unbeneficed priests who did serve their parishes faithfully and impeccably but the leadership was lacking which would have made this pastoral service the ideal. The Protestants attempted to restore the pastoral function, not only to see that it was fulfilled but to see that it was exalted. The battle was not won overnight – indeed, in some cases it was not won at all – but falling recruitment until the Protestant ideal had taken hold, and improved training of recruits and of some of the beneficed helped the Protestant bishops (and those who remained outside the hierarchy) to win some of the major battles of the war.

It was because this leadership was lacking that the late medieval clergy never formed a true professional group. Too many of the clergy were priests in name only and too many of the natural leaders – the graduates – were included within this group for the clergy to develop a true sense of group identity. Although there was some movement from curacies to benefices in the late medieval Church, there was no career structure of the type that was emerging in the early and mid-seventeenth-century Church. One might conclude that the medieval Church consisted of several distinct clerical groupings with no common cause to bind them together into a profession. Because the episcopate offered no real leadership in this respect the clergy were unlikely to develop any common cause or identity. On the other hand, in the post-Reformation English Church the removal from benefices of well-educated men pursuing a non-ecclesiastical career seems to have removed the chief obstacle to cohesion among the parish clergy. Moreover, as the minor orders were abolished and there were far fewer unbeneficed clergy in major orders, the clergy now possessed a more regular career structure. Above all the clergy through their training were made aware of the their role in the Church. Even if some men lacked vocation, even if training for the ministry was still somewhat traditionalist and inadequate, the clergy recognized that the goal of the Church was fatherly care of the people through well-prepared pastors. The acceptance of the pastoral ideal as a noble one and the need to train men to fulfil it provide the key to the professionalization of the English clergy. Indeed, I believe that this becomes even more apparent when we compare the situation in England after the Reformation with that in Germany and France. But the English clergy already possessed some of the essentials for professionalization before the Reformation: a hierarchical structure; the machinery for association; control over its recruitment and its discipline; and some measure of control over patronage. If the pastoral ideal were to be fulfilled within the English Church then it had to take account of the existence of these factors also.

The tradition of English Protestantism after 1558 has for long been treated in isolation from the European Protestant tradition. This insular approach to late sixteenth and early seventeenth-century developments has been dictated, in part, by the circumstances of the official Reformation in England and Wales; in part, by the attitude of the Crown to continental Protestantism after 1558; and, in part, by the distinct Anglican tradition which emerged after the Restoration, which was foreshadowed during the period 1620–42, and from which it is difficult to disengage our minds in viewing an earlier stage of development. But any study of the clergy as a group in the period would be short-sighted indeed if it did not take cognizance of continental developments in both the Catholic and the Protestant communions.

There are at least three respects in which the development of the clerical profession in England and Wales seems to stand in the mainstream of continental events. The first concerns that process of laicization in the Churches of Protestant Europe (including England and Wales) which produced a reaction against a privileged and distinct clerical caste. The second relates to the movement in both Catholic and Protestant countries for the reform of the Church as an institution and for the purification of religious life. The third is connected with a phenomenon to which I have already drawn attention: the fact that recruitment into the ministry increased during the late sixteenth and early seventeenth centuries in several countries or, at least, that the career offered by the Church became sufficiently attractive that men were willing to obtain the more rigorous requirements for entry in order to take orders. These three phenomena were closely interconnected, as I have tried to demonstrate in this book, in the case of England, but I think that it is well worth the effort to try to disentangle the strands to some extent.

In his study, *The Reformation in the Cities*, Steven Ozment has written:

> Protestants broke down the medieval distinction between clergy and laity not only by permitting the clergy to enter the estate of marriage, but also by having them assume many of the duties of citizenship. The Protestant 'priesthood of all believers' which enhanced the importance of secular life and vocations, also had a reverse effect. If it 'sanctified' the laity, it also worked to 'secularise' the clergy. If lay Christians were now to be a 'priesthood' clerics were expected to enter certain estates of the laity.[9]

As we have seen, in England there were lay attacks on the concept of a privileged and in some way superior clerical caste: attacks which were levelled both at the Catholic priesthood of the late middle ages and also at the Protestant clergy of the late sixteenth and early seventeenth centuries. These last were themselves men who rejected the idea of a superior mediating priesthood but who clung to the idea of a separating vocation for which they were especially fitted, and which many laymen found equally abominable. Once we appreciate this fact we are acknowledging perhaps that the anticlericalism of the pre-Reformation period was not an attack on clerical abuse but on clergy itself. Scandalous clergy merely underlined the more fundamental belief that the clergy did not form a superior religious caste, able to mediate on the layman's behalf with God, and so it is interesting to see that the laymen of Europe (including England) often found the *raison d'être* of the new ministry as difficult to accept as that of the old priesthood, even when its exponents were upright, honest Christians. Increasingly articulate definition of clerical professionalism was, as we have seen, liable to spark off increasingly articulate counter-attack. In this context it is pertinent to note Christopher Hill's comments on the opposition to professionalism in general in the mid-seventeenth century. Dr Hill associates anti-professionalism closely with fears of social oppression, and certainly the fervent expression of anti-professional views in the mid-seventeenth century by radicals and sectaries in England reinforces this view. The uneducated took exception to the socially exclusive learned professions of Church, medicine and law because the members of these professions claimed that their training gave them a prescriptive right to rule and to dominate certain areas of thought.[10]

Steven Ozment comments in his book that the popularity of Protestantism in Europe was largely attributable to the fact that 'the Protestant movement was an unprecedented flattering of secular life'.[11] If this last assessment of the appeal of Protestantism to the laity is even partially correct, does it not follow that any tendency to the contrary would meet with determined opposition? So we have here two complementary views of lay reactions to clerical domination which undoubtedly contain a good deal of the truth but not all: the one sees laymen objecting to clerical claims to a special position in the Church for social reasons; the other sees men accepting Protestantism with enthusiasm because it suggests that the active Christian citizen is as important in the Church's life as the minister, and spends much time lauding the secular virtues. It is tempting to see these two views as presenting a well-rounded picture of the layman's reasons for espousing the Protestant cause and for objecting to the new justifications for clerical dominance which the clergy were producing during the seventeenth century. Indeed, I share to some extent this behaviouralist approach to the problem but I think it is dangerous to accept an entirely materialist interpretation of religious behaviour and thought. It can be misleading to underline too heavily the very definite links between social aspiration and religious opinion. Ozment's comment in itself places the whole issue in the context of developments in humanism during the sixteenth century. Men were now more openly extolling secular virtues. They were perhaps more unwilling to curtail their own freedom of thought: when pushed they were less able than their forebears to accept that someone else's opinion held undoubted sway over their own. In England, it may be that the intellectual or spiritual roots of this objection to clergy were exposed only because its exponents were thrust to the forefront by political and social accident. England was in political and social flux in the mid-seventeenth century, and as a result the opinions of the sectaries mattered; there was a public forum for views which had long been suppressed; the peculiarities of the political situation meant that pressure groups could influence the outcome of events and the formation of new institutions; the issue of whether or not there should be a state Church and a maintained ministry seemed actually to be being *debated*. The intellectual freedom of the layman in England may have been secured by political and social occurrences and it may have had its roots in the structure of early modern society, but this is not to say that its motivation is materialistic in a derogatory sense.

While not wishing to examine in any detail the reasons for the ready acceptance of the Protestant message in Europe in the sixteenth century, it seems that Steven Ozment has something further to contribute to this debate about fundamental anticlericalism. While he rightly stresses that no head count of the first Protestant groups according to vocation and economic self-interest can tell the whole story of the attraction of Protestantism, he goes on to point out that the initiators of reform in the cities of Germany and Switzerland tended not to be members of the fixed political élite (i.e. the magistrates or higher clergy) but men from among the ideologically and socially mobile, 'either by reason of social grievance (as with clergy and workers), ambition (as among certain guilds and the new rich), or ideals (as witnessed by university students and various humanistically educated patricians)'. Preachers, who sought escape from control of the bishops over their cure of souls and who thought it wise to place the Church under the joint control of magistracy and clergy, provided the initial stimulus for change. Support came from the lower and middle strata of the citizenry (burghers and not below). The magistracy, conservative and slow to take action, finally consolidated and moderated the reformation, giving it an institutional framework. The reformation in these cities was not the result of popular revolution but of an attack on the inner ring of government by ambitious burghers. The magistracy implemented reform when they saw that it had to come; when they saw that radical religious and not radical social changes were envisaged; and when they appreciated that without magisterial support, popular revolt might be the

next step. Into this general pattern of change consequent upon the
Reformation, we must fit the attitude to the clergy. All the supporters of reform recognized the need for magisterial implementation
(i.e. lay government) of reform. This was a practical necessity if the
Reformation were to survive but it also marked a revolt against
episcopal bureaucratic control of the choice and conduct of the
ministry. The preachers initiated the movement for civic reformation and necessarily advocated a distinct ministry – but this ministry
was conceived within a citizen context. This both clergy and laymen
accepted.

> Protestant ministers accordingly renounced traditional clerical
> privileges and immunities and assumed many of the normal respon-
> sibilities of citizenship. . . . Although the clergy were never to become
> citizens as other citizens were citizens – they were, for example,
> excluded from holding public office – they did pledge allegiance to their
> cities, pay certain taxes, and become completely subject to the civic law
> code.[12]

Steven Ozment shows us the clergy in Strasbourg praising civic life
and virtues and advocating clerical subjection thereto. In August
1524 the government moved to take over appointment of parish
clergy and subjected all to a civic oath of obedience. Citizenship was
required of all resident clerics after 1525.[13] Dr R. W. Scribner, while
seeking to explain why the Reformation made no headway in Cologne, points out that in that city the pulpits were controlled by the
university which was itself in the grip of the ultra-conservative
theological faculty. The clergy, therefore, gave no lead to the
Reformation in Cologne as in other German cities – rather they gave
their support to opponents of Luther. The government of the city,
while it shared the anticlerical preoccupations of its counterparts to
some degree, was prepared to support this stance when social unrest
seemed to be the alternative. Dr Scribner, of course, sets this argument in the context of Cologne's geo-political situation, but he does,
nevertheless, make it clear that there was no ministerial support for
the Reformation within the university or the parishes and that the
proposals for a 'reformed ministry' put forward by the leaders of a
disturbance in 1525 stood no chance of success without clerical
support because to the council, the Reformation was linked with
social upheaval.[14]

It is interesting to note the extent to which doctrines of the
ministerial order evolved within this context of civil allegiance and
active citizenship during the century and beyond. Sixteenth-century
reformers in England would have liked this situation to prevail in
England and Wales also: few at this stage contested that there should
be a ministry but the idea of a separate clerical allegiance was

anathema, as this in itself spelled privilege. The views of the Crown
and of the ecclesiastical hierarchy towards the question of episcopal
control and episcopal reform and towards a separate disciplinary
procedure for the clergy within the Church, should all be examined
in this context. The position of the Crown, in particular, was an
ambivalent one. The Crown, as instanced especially by the suspension of Archbishop Grindal in 1577, was unwilling that the bishops
and clergy should claim allegiance to any higher authority than itself
as justification for independent action. Yet it was *as* unwilling to
abolish the old clerical hierarchy and countenance a congregational
polity within the Church. The bishops, in the main, implemented
royal policies and enforced conformity to the State Church. This was
a powerful argument in favour of their retention even had the
Crown not been bound to them by bonds of tradition and scriptural
justification. Indeed it was only when the bishops themselves
seemed to be seeking the introduction of a further reformation that
Elizabeth I opposed Grindal's stance. Why the Crown did nothing to
strengthen the hands of the bishops in the cause of the established
order is another question. Nevertheless, neither Elizabeth nor her
successors did anything to remove the apparatus of the ecclesiastical
courts or to suggest that the clergy should be tried in civil courts. The
steady erosion of the benefit of clergy cannot be instanced to the
contrary because in reality it did not relate to true clergy.

Interestingly enough, Charles I, who seemed to share a view that
the episcopate should control doctrinal matters, actually tried to
strengthen the ecclesiastical court system. The courts were certainly
concentrating upon punishing contempt of ecclesiastical forms and
discipline, and clergymen were themselves being disciplined constantly. It has been suggested that Charles' support for the Laudian
attitude to clergy tipped the balance which had been maintained by
the ambivalent attitude of both Elizabeth and James and provoked
the laity into action.

The views of the reformers in England were more clear cut and, in
a very real sense, less conducive to further professionalization of the
clergy. This is true even when we acknowledge the definite contribution of the puritan clergy to professional consolidation. In the
1570s, for example, Thomas Cartwright was advocating congregationally appointed and answerable ministers even though he envisaged them as working within a system of distinct, provincial and
national assemblies or synods. The discipline within this presbyterian church would have applied to clergy and laity but a real
separation would still have been effected between laity and clergy.
The advocates of more congregationalist forms normally made the
individual congregations much more independent and responsible
for discipline, choice of pastor and forms of worship. This tended to

emphasize the relationship between the minister and his congregation at the expense of the relationship between the minister and other clergy and thus to act against the development of a clerical profession. The extent to which there was a hierarchical structure within such a system; the extent to which there was central control from national government and/or Church; and the extent to which there was institutionalized provision for association between ministers would all affect the degree to which the clergy might professionalize. In practice, in England the strivings of some Protestants to accomplish such a congregational church had to take place amid the apparatus of the existing national Church: one might look to the Church during the commonwealth or to the Church in colonial New England for some indications of the anti-professional tendency of congregational forms of church organization. In England one is faced with a confused picture of some Protestants trying to impose forms of Church government hatched in the very different political, religious and social circumstances of the continent onto the English Church, forced as it was to retain so many of the forms of the pre-Reformation Church. The feeling of supporters of congregationalism against a separate clerical 'profession' (with all its implications of separateness, exclusiveness and worldly ambition) was, therefore, swamped by the tendencies of the English Church and of the Presbyterian reformers in its favour.

As we have noted, there was a common preoccupation in both Catholic and Protestant countries with the need to purify religious observance and reform the institutions of the Church. Dr Wright has recently suggested that these efforts to reform and purify had a common root – the need to eradicate the hold of the 'old religion' (which fed on witchcraft and superstition) in Europe as a whole – and he draws attention to the similarity between the reform programmes of 'Anglican' bishops and those of Catholic episcopal reformers. Enforcement of ecclesiastical discipline; provision of a resident clergy; education of the laity in right doctrine; attitudes to censorship; suppression of superstition and witchcraft through the Church court machinery and attempts to enforce social control through the same – all were marks of these programmes.[16] It is not the expression of these concerns which most interests us in the present context of the history of the clerical profession so much as the firm conviction that the programme should be led and controlled by the episcopate. This was a clerical battle against the 'old religion' and its manifestations, and the clergy were to be specifically trained and armed to fight it. Moreover, it was the clergy who could be relied upon to fight obediently for the cause as delineated by their superiors. One would hesitate to say, of course, that the laity were denied a role. Even the most ardent supporters of episcopal reform of the Church in England were willing that the laity should participate on given terms. Hitherto the emphasis upon conformity has been upon its political implications – the Crown wanted the unquestioning allegiance of the clergy because of the threat of sedition – but it is surely important to emphasize that the bishops saw conformity as ensuring that the clergy were unified in their fight against the forces of superstition. In a situation where a congregation was permitted to formulate its own rules about worship and where discipline was administered in the congregational setting, no such assurance existed. Whereas most congregations might insist on pure religion, the old religion might flourish in pockets when central control was to all intents and purposes removed. From our point of view, the implications of such a decentralized system are interesting – it could have lessened the bonds between cleric and cleric even as the bonds between laity and minister within the congregation were strengthened. Whether in fact such a thing happened to the clergy in, for example, Cromwellian England is a moot point. Lay participation by the few in Josselin's Essex was great but the opportunities for clerical meetings were not reduced: instead, they multiplied as the number of sermons proliferated. However, one could speculate that the particular nature of the professional bond was diluted during this period until there was a marked attack on clergy itself which reunited the clergy as a profession. This is something upon which further research may throw light. However, there can be no doubt that the episcopal framework of reform and the emphasis upon the clergy as its necessary agents were important for the emergence and consolidation of the clerical profession in the early seventeenth century. I hope that during the course of the book I have made it clear that the bishops played an important part in promoting the growth of a clerical profession which embraced both the clerical élite and the parochial clergy.

I have drawn attention, specifically in chapter 9, to the numbers entering the Church at various times, to the changing standards of admission to orders, and to changing qualifications possessed by ordinands. It seems that we must set this discussion within a more general European context. Marc Venard, who has worked on clerical recruitment in the Province of Avignon, suggests that the prospect of priests' orders was not attractive to young men in sixteenth-century France until after the meeting of the Council of Trent. Before this, entry into religious houses was much more popular. Having received the tonsure only, a man was entitled to possess a benefice without any commitment. Entry into orders, on the other hand, implied vocation and the pursuit of a given career. In response to the Council of Trent's rulings, however, there was a movement of sacerdotalism – mainly in association with the emphasis upon the

Mass – and the late sixteenth and seventeenth centuries saw a rising number of priestly candidates for benefices. At a time when bishops were much more strict in their interpretation of the rules regarding ordination, more candidates were coming forward and proving willing to obtain the necessary qualifications. The profession was becoming more attractive to young men just as the requirements for entry were effectively being raised. Perhaps the increased status accorded the parochial clergy by the Council of Trent had this effect. Marc Venard, however, does point out that the career of cleric did not attract local men from the prosperous Avignon region but rather increasing numbers of 'imports' from the backward, mountainous areas of Vivarais and the Dauphiné and, late in the century, Provence. He also suggests that the proportion of outside clerics amongst the resident perpetual vicars of Avignon province meant that, just as parochial duties were being stressed, most parishes in the area were in the care of outsiders.[17]

Of course, it would be precipitate to conclude that the whole of Catholic Europe fitted this southern French model, but there are several points of interest which it would be worth exploring further. The role of the central policy makers and the bishops in emphasizing the importance of the parochial clergy and in demanding higher entrance qualifications for ordinands; the interesting fact that resident bishops appear to have been more rigorous in enforcing such regulations; the rising numbers of recruits with improved qualifications in the early seventeenth century – all have their parallels in the English situation. Was the situation similar in the rest of Catholic Europe – in counter-Reformation Italy or Spain, for example? In his study of the universities of Castile Richard Kagan seems to imply that, in the adverse social and economic conditions of the late sixteenth and early seventeenth centuries, the Jesuit emphasis on clerical training had a distinct appeal for lay students, entering Jesuit colleges and swelling the ranks of the regular clergy. This would suggest that, in the case of Spain, Tridentine reform alone did not make clerical careers more attractive to lay youth. Yet, coupled with the frustrated ambitions of products of the universities who could not obtain legal or administrative posts of sufficient status, the new emphasis upon the priestly vocation did have its impact. In the absence of a detailed study of the Spanish clergy, one has to rest content with this analysis.[18]

Episcopal reform programmes emphasized the status of the clergy but, in saying this, are we denying that the status of the clergy could be enhanced in a church without episcopacy? The Calvinist Geneva Academy and the Lutheran University of Marburg, seminaries in theory and in practice, were every bit as insistent upon the need to train and equip the clergy as their counterparts in Catholic countries or in England. Late sixteenth-century and early seventeenth-century Europe in general seems to have been obsessed with the ideal of a resident, worthy parochial clergy. This obsession was not peculiar to either Catholic or reformed countries. Of course, the manifestations of the obsession differed – one might emphasize the need for a preaching ministry, another a learned, catechizing clergy; one might stress the sacramental role of the cleric, another his role as pastor and teacher. But the importance attached to the parochial ministry was always present and the status of the ministry thereby increased. Far from saying that episcopacy was a requisite precondition for enhancement of the clerical profession, one should say that all forms of Church discipline in the period, in their different ways, tended to increase the status of clergy. One of the interesting things about the emergence of the clerical profession in England in the period 1550–1642 is that it occurred in a context which included both episcopalian and non-episcopalian elements. In their differing ways both the puritan and the Laudian groups were emphasizing the importance of the clergy as a separate group. They would not, of course, have agreed about the *nature* of this importance or the nature of the distinction between clergyman and layman. Yet, when pressed, the Presbyterians and Independents in religion would not countenance an end to a separate, educated and maintained ministry any more than would the Laudians.

This book, it is hoped, has indicated some of the major influences which shaped the clerical profession in the course of the period between the death of Henry VIII and the interregnum, and which led to its consolidation as a profession. Not all of these influences were new or peculiar to England – there is a sense in which the clerical élite had always had an awareness of group identity and an accepted career structure and there are, as indicated above, noticeable continental parallels to be drawn. But it was during this period that the lower clergy became conscious of and insistent upon their status. It was also during this period that the clergy came to see their role in terms of pastoral service within the parish rather than in the state. 'I am no parson. No, I am no vicar. I abhor these names as Anti-Christian. I am pastor of the congregation there', a Shropshire puritan told his bishop in the early 1580s. Many would not have expressed themselves so radically yet would have shared the basic sentiment.[19] The old situation persisted among the cathedral clergy but even here increasing effort was spent in pastoral duties and there were attempts to make the cathedral clergy resident.

Both theory and practice were important in shaping the clerical profession in England. The views of the *raison d'être* of the clergy articulated by supporters of the Reformed continental Churches and also by their opponents played an important part in forming the attitudes of both patrons and clergy to the role of minister. But practical considerations also played a part – because the clergy shared similar interests and similar responsibilities, they developed a group identity which was heightened by opportunities for contact. Although the life of a minister is in some ways a solitary, independent one, this fact in itself probably predisposed the cleric to seek out his fellows and identify closely with them. Not only the group identity of the clergy was heightened during the period but also their status. This stemmed equally from a variety of contributory causes – the role of the clergy in episcopally inspired programmes of reform and control; the stress on the pastoral role in those most influenced by the Reformed disciplines; and the interest shown by patrons in securing a learned ministry. There seems to be overwhelming evidence for the view that it was increased status and not increased prosperity which made the Church an attractive profession in the early seventeenth century. There is rather less support for any view that the Church attracted recruits away from other more lucrative professions such as the law or the burgeoning government service. Equally there is some doubt as to whether the seventeenth-century Church was attracting more recruits than it could absorb into rewarding service – at least before the late 1630s. More convincing is the argument which sees the bishops rigorously enforcing ordination rules along with some lay patrons and laying emphasis upon the status of clergy, and thus causing candidates for orders to undertake the required education before presenting themselves for ordination. Such an explanation allows that there was some increase in recruitment but makes it clear that what we are talking about is a profession with increased status and higher standards of admission rather than a Church attracting the vocationless candidates who had failed to make a career in the law or government service.

For our study of the Church as an emerging profession, it is particularly interesting that in this situation patronage, normally considered to be a factor acting against the professionalization of a group, was actually essential to the consolidation of the clerical profession. A system in which laymen elected their own ministers would have acted in the opposite direction. Moreover the pressures of society favouring a revolution in university education, and making posts in the Church dependent upon the recruit possessing a university degree, allowed the Church to counteract those tendencies in the patronage system which were detrimental to professionalization – that is, that the patronage system is not easily controlled and does not acknowledge a set of given criteria in distributing places. The fact that some patrons were sincerely affected by puritan ideology when presenting men to livings also had some effect upon standards but this aspect should not be exaggerated. No doubt the process of professionalization would have been more efficiently accomplished had the bishops held all the Church patronage. Nevertheless, the episcopate was better equipped to work to achieve an educated clergy within the patronage system than within any projected congregational church, meeting centrally imposed standards.

This book has been concerned not only with the shaping of the clerical profession but also with the effect of this developing situation upon the laity. Heightened emphasis upon the separate nature and status of the various professions seems to have been a feature of the early modern period in Western Europe. Its relationship to class consciousness and its roots in the educational revolution have not yet been examined in detail. There is a strong connection between the new professionalism and the shift from the contemplative to the active life in both the Renaissance and the Reformation, which found expression in the education of both gentry and clergy. It is an interesting phenomenon and there can be no doubt that the anti-professionalism which emerged in England during the interregnum combined some of the features of a class struggle and of a reaction against education and specialization as a force for good in society.

Notes

Note Places of publication are given only for those books published outside the United Kingdom

Chapter 1
The career structure of the clergy

1. C. Hill, *Change and Continuity in Seventeenth Century England* (1975), 162–3 *et passim*.
2. K. Charlton, 'The professions in sixteenth-century England' in *U.B.H.J. 12* (1969).
3. P. Orpen, 'Schoolmastering as a profession in the seventeenth century: the career patterns of the grammar schoolmaster' in *History of Education 6* (1977), 193; B. Levack, *The Civil Lawyers in England, 1603–25* (1973); G. Clark, *A History of the Royal College of Physicians*, I (1964); W. Prest, *The Inns of Court* (1972); Hill, *Change and Continuity*; Charlton, *op. cit.*
4. P. Collinson, *The Elizabethan Puritan Movement* (1967); see P. Collinson, 'Lectures by combination: structures and characteristics of Church life in seventeenth-century England' in *B.I.H.R. 48* (1975), *passim*, which shows heightened awareness of the situation and of the importance of puritanism in this context; see also W. J. Sheils, 'The Puritans in Church and politics in the diocese of Peterborough, 1570–1610' (unpublished Ph.D. thesis, University of London, 1974); P. Tyler, 'The status of the Elizabethan parochial clergy' in *Studies in Church History 4* (1967).
5. M. Curtis, 'The alienated intellectuals of early Stuart England' in T. Aston (ed.), *Crisis in Europe* (1965), 295–316; P. Seaver, *The Puritan Lectureships* (Stanford, 1972); M. L. Zell, 'The personnel of the clergy in Kent in the Reformation period', in *E.H.R.* (1974), 513–33; this confirms the point already made by Dr Barratt concerning the Lincoln clergy in D. M. Barratt, 'Conditions of the parish clergy from the Reformation to 1660 in the dioceses of Oxford, Worcester and Gloucester' (unpublished D.Phil. thesis, Oxford University, 1950), 54–5.
6. See pp. 136–43, also I. Cassidy, 'The episcopate of William Cotton, Bishop of Exeter, 1598–1621' (unpublished B. Litt. thesis, Oxford University, 1963), 50; M. Steig, 'The parochial clergy in the diocese of Bath and Wells' (unpublished Ph.D. thesis, University of California at Berkeley, 1970), 90 *et passim*. R. Donaldson, 'Patronage and the Church' (unpublished Ph.D. thesis, University of Edinburgh, 1955), 315–17, 332–5, points out that the tendency to present local men became more and not less pronounced in the early sixteenth century.
7. G.L.MS. 9535/2; C.C.R.O., EDA 1/3; L.R.O., B/R 27a, fos. 57r–62r; C.U.L., E.D.R. 5/1, fos. 75r–80v; 55r–60r.

8.   C.U.L., E.D.R. A.5/1.
9.   D. Marcombe, 'The Durham dean and chapter: old abbey writ large' in R. O'Day and F. Heal (eds.), *Continuity and Change* (1976), 125–44, esp. 144.
10. See pp. 138–43.
11. L.J.R.O. B/A/1/16; B/A/1/18.
12. Seaver, *op. cit.*, 174; see pp. 105–12.
13. L.J.R.O., B/A/1/16; B/A/4A/18; P.R.O., E331, Manuscript Index of Institutions and Bishops' Certificates.
14. See p. 113; Dr Richard Christophers has discovered the same trend amongst the Surrey clergy; 1557: 10 of 13 vacancies caused by death; 1558: 14 of 17; 1559: 6 of 10; 1560: 10 of 16; the number of vacancies there was in sharp contrast to the norm of *circa* 4–8 per annum.
15. Coke MSS., Melbourne Hall, Derbyshire.
16. This section is based upon material from a variety of sources. L.J.R.O. B/A/2ii/1 contains a list of institutions in Coventry archdeaconry for 1537–1603; L.J.R.O., Black Book of the diocese of Lichfield, I, contains a list of presentations to livings and dates when fees were received for 1604–9; L.J.R.O. B/A/1/16, Register of Bishop Thomas Morton, 1618–32, lists institutions for these years. Relevant material was also garnered from the P.R.O., E331 Bishops' Certificates; Borthwick Institute of Historical Research, York (hereafter Borthwick I.H.R.), Subscription Book RIV Be, Coventry and Lichfield subscriptions for 1610–14; L.J.R.O., B/A/4A/17 and 18, Lichfield subscriptions, 1614–18, 1618–32 and 1635–45. Class B/V/1 of the L.J.R.O. (visitation records), Lichfield Wills and Inventories and other classes of material in the Diocesan registry were also consulted. Further biographical material was drawn from J. and J. A. Venn, *Alumni Cantabrigienses* (1922–7); A. Foster, *Alumni Oxoniensis* (1891–2); and from the ordination lists of other dioceses. Information for the group of 1584 was based upon L.J.R.O. B/V/1/15, 16, 17, 19. Supplementary information was drawn from visitation *comperta*; consistory court act books; institution records mentioned above, L.P.L., C.M. XIII; Lichfield Dean and Chapter Muniments, A.A.I.I.
17. L.J.R.O. B/V/1/37, *Liber Cleri* for 1620; supplemented by Lichfield Dean and Chapter Muniments, Jurisdiction XVIII.
18. N.R.O., Ordination Books of the Diocese of Peterborough, 1570–1642; Bodleian Library, Oxford Diocesan Papers, C.264, II; e.9; e.13.
19. Curtis, *op. cit.*, *passim*, esp. 304; G.L.MS., 9535/2, fos. 97v–214v.
20. L.J.R.O., B/A/4A/1; B/A/4A/18.
21. This finding is based on Lichfield ordinands, 1614–32, L.J.R.O., B/A/4A/17 and 18. H. G. Owen suggests that the average age of London ordinations in the early 1560s was 32 and that it had dropped to around 27 by the late 1570s (H. G. Owen, 'The London parish clergy in the reign of Elizabeth I' (unpublished Ph.D. thesis, University of London, 1957, 70). His figures were based on very small groups: fuller information exists for London from 1598 onwards. The average age on ordination as deacon was: 1598–1607:

28.21 years (standard deviation 5.82); 1607–11: 26.26 (s.d. 4.75); 1611–17: 26.06 (s.d. 5.05); 1617–21: 24.97 (s.d. 3.11); 1621–8: 25.02 (s.d. 2.50). These figures are based on groups of 150 ordinands. The drop in standard deviation from the mean suggests that a lower age at ordination was much more generally accepted in the 1620s than it had been in the 1590s.

22. L.J.R.O., B/A/4A/17 and 18; Seaver, *op. cit.*, 195, 171–200.
23. Bacon Collection, Folger Shakespeare Library, Washington, D.C., L.d. 305.

Chapter 2
The context

1. P. Heath, *English Parish Clergy on the Eve of the Reformation* (1969), esp. 187; C. Haigh, *Reformation and Resistance in Tudor Lancashire* (1975), *passim*.
2. Heath, *op. cit.*, 189; in fact, most of these revolutions can be said to have occurred during the century after the official Reformation in England.
3. See S. Lander, 'Church courts and the Reformation in the diocese of Chichester, 1500–58' in R. O'Day and F. Heal (eds.), *Continuity and Change* (1976), 237 *et passim*.
4. A. G. Dickens, *Lollards and Protestants in the Diocese of York* (1966 edn), 184 *et passim*; M. L. Zell, 'Church and gentry in Reformation Kent, 1533–53' (unpublished Ph.D. thesis, University of California at Los Angeles, 1974), 188–9; Haigh, *Reformation and Resistance*, 30, 40–1, 44–5, *passim*.
5. D. Palliser, 'Popular reactions to the Reformation', in F. Heal and R. O'Day (eds.), *Church and Society in England from Henry VIII to James I* (1977), 42; C. Cross, *Church and People, 1450–1660* (1976), 81–100, presents a good general account of progress during Edward's reign.
6. R. W. Henderson, *The Teaching Office* (1962), 233.
7. F. D. Price, 'Gloucester diocese under Bishop Hooper' in *T.B.G.A.S.* (1939), 51–151.
8. Henderson, *op. cit.*, 233–4.
9. H. E. P. Grieve, 'The deprived married clergy in Essex, 1553–61' in *T.R.H.S.* (1940), 142–5; N.L.W. MS.4919D, fos. 57–8; C.U.L. E.e.2.34, doc.36.
10. See P. Tyler, 'The status of the Elizabethan parochial clergy' in *Studies in Church History* (1967), 93 *et passim* for the argument that the status of the Elizabethan clergy was low and that of the Jacobean clergy still lower.
11. D. M. Barratt, 'Conditions of the parish clergy from the Reformation to 1660 in the dioceses of Oxford, Worcester and Gloucester' (unpublished D.Phil. thesis, Oxford University, 1950), 7. *C.S.P.D Elizabeth, 1547–78*, vol. lxxvi. Register of dispensations for pluralism, 1560–5.
12. P. Collinson, *The Elizabethan Puritan Movement* (1967), 59, 64.

See M. Bowker, 'The Henrician Reformation and the parish clergy' in *B.I.H.R.* (May 1977), for evidence concerning the lag of recruitment after 1536. Barratt, *op. cit.*, *passim*, is also interesting on the number of Edwardian ordinands.

Chapter 3
The Reformed episcopate and its problems: a case study

1. P. Collinson, *The Elizabethan Puritan Movement* (1967), 46. More recently he has suggested that the conflict concerned England's foreign policy.
2. *D.N.B.,* iv, 284.
3. D.W.L., Morrice MSS., 'L' xi, no. 2, fos. 3–4.
4. B.L. Harleian MS. 594.
5. N.L.W. MS. 4919D, The Letter Book of Bishop Thomas Bentham of Coventry and Lichfield, f. 95, 8 May 1561, Bentham to the Queen.
6. Letter Book, fos. 61, 62, 71.
7. Letter Book, fos. 54, 56, 64, 65.
8. Letter Book, fos. 33–8, 43, 44, 59, 60, 62, 63, 66–9, 77, 78.
9. See R. O'Day, 'Cumulative debt: the Bishops of Coventry and Lichfield and their economic problems, c. 1540–1640' in *Midland History* (Autumn 1975), 77–93.
10. L.J.R.O. Dean and Chapter Act Book, IV, fos. 32v–35r.
11. L.J.R.O. C.C. 12410, f. 8.
12. Letter Book, fos. 88, 93, 99.
13. Letter Book, f. 39.
14. L.J.R.O. C.C. 12410, fos. 28–30.
15. See O'Day, 'Cumulative Debt', 82–4, and R. O'Day, 'Thomas Bentham: a case study in the problems of the early Elizabethan episcopate', in *J.E.H.* (April 1972), 140–3 *et passim*.
16. Letter Book, f. 90.
17. Letter Book, fos. 71, 77.
18. Letter Book, f. 54.
19. Cf. L.J.R.O. B/V/1/2; B/V/1/4; B/V/1/15 *passim*.
20. W. N. Landor, 'Staffordshire incumbents and parochial records, 1530–1680', *Staffordshire Historical Collections* (1915), xli.
21. *Ibid.*, xxxiii–xxxiv, 361–6.
22. *Ibid.*
23. Letters and Papers, Henry VIII, xii(I), 335; L.J.R.O., B/V/1/2.
24. Letter Book, fos. 57, 58. Bentham's personal experience of the situation is referred to on f. 58.
25. Letter Book, f. 58.
26. L.J.R.O. W.P. 3 September 1571.
27. L.P.L. MS. C.M. xiii/58.
28. Letter Book, fos. 85–6.
29. For an illustration of this point see S. Lander, 'Church courts and the Reformation in the diocese of Chichester, 1500–1558' in R. O'Day and F. Heal (eds.), *Continuity and Change*, 215–38. Also the introduction to the same volume, p. 24.
30. P. Collinson, 'Episcopacy and Reform in England in the later sixteenth century' in *Studies in Church History 3* (1966), 99 ff.
31. *Ibid.*
32. B.L. Add. MS. 29,546 f. 52r.

250

33. Collinson, *Elizabethan Puritan Movement*, 172.
34. M. Bateson (ed.), 'A collection of original letters from the bishops to the Privy Council, 1564 . . .', *Camden Society Miscellany*, IX, 1895, 39–41.
35. A. Hamilton Thompson, 'Diocesan administration in the middle ages: archdeacons and rural deans', *Proceedings of the British Academy* (1943), 15.
36. P. Collinson, 'The Puritan classical movement in the reign of Elizabeth I' (Ph.D. thesis, University of London, 1957), 293, n.2, refers to Lever 'ruling in the southern half of the diocese'.
37. Letter Book, f. 76.
38. Letter Book, f. 94.
39. See below, p. 66.
40. J. Strype, *Ecclesiastical Memorials*, III pt i (1822), 169; C. H. Garrett, *The Marian Exiles* (1938), 74; L.J.R.O., B/A/1/15; Bateson, *op. cit.*, 39–41. With Aston's help, Bentham seems to have surveyed and valued his estates. L.J.R.O.. C.C. 12400.
41. Letter Book, f. 98; B.L. Add. MS. 29,546, f. 52r.
42. Letter Book, fos. 90, 91, 94, 95 and 97 for examples.
43. Bateson, *op. cit.*, 39–41; see also Collinson, *Elizabethan Puritan Movement*, 182 for comment on office and function of rural dean.
44. Collinson, *Elizabethan Puritan Movement*, 183; R. A. Marchant, *The Church Under the Law* (1969), 14–15, 111, 161; W.R.O., 716.02. BA2056 no. 3; G.C.L., K4/1(I).
45. L.P.L. MS. C.M. XIII; L.J.R.O. B/C/3/3, 21 April 1596.
46. L.J.R.O. B/A/1/15.
47. *D.N.B.*, xvi, 8.
48. Lever, Ashton, Aston, Nowell, Morweyn and Sale (as well as the difficult Bolt) were all in benefices at this time.
49. L.J.R.O., B/A/1/15; Letter Book, f. 91.
50. Letter Book, fos. 47, 48; L.J.R.O. B/A/1/15 f. 37v; Letter Book, f. 55; L.J.R.O. B/A/1/15 f. 35v.
51. L.J.R.O. B/A/1/15; B. L. Lansdowne MSS. 443, 444.
52. Letter Book, f. 94.
53. Letter Book, f. 64.
54. Letter Book, fos. 62, 87, 88.
55. Letter Book, fos. 85, 86; W. H. Frere (ed.), *Visitation Articles and Injunctions of the Period of the Reformation*, Alcuin Club Collections, XVI, 1910, iii (1559–75), 166.
56. D.W.L. Morrice MS. 'W' Life of Thomas Bentham by Roger Morrice, no. 9, 41; Letter Book, fos. 46, 49, 55, 64, 73; B.L. Add. MS. 29,546 f. 52r.

Chapter 4
Recruitment

1. R. Houlbrooke, 'The Protestant episcopate, 1547–1603: the pastoral contribution', in F. Heal and R. O'Day (eds.), *Church and Society in England from Henry VIII to James I* (1977), is a valuable survey of the pastoral efforts of the Elizabethan bishops.
2. H. S. Bennett, 'Medieval ordination lists in English episcopal registers', in J. Conway Davies (ed.), *Studies Presented to Sir Hilary*

Jenkinson (1957), 23–34; *Lyndwood's Provinciale*, Lib. 1. tit. 5 v.
Canonice Examinatus; R. J. Phillimore, *Ecclesiastical Law* I (1873),
100; P. Heath, *English Parish Clergy on the Eve of the Reformation*
(1969), 16; Letter Book, fos. 49, 65, 81; C.U.L., E.D.R. A5/1, fos.
75–80, f. 2, f. 15r.

3. C.U.L. E.D.R. A5/1, f. 25v; *ibid.* f. 74r for articles of 1561; *ibid.* f.
    86r for interrogatories of 1569; E. Cardwell, *Synodalia* I, (1842), 113
    for Canons of 1571; *ibid.* 132ff. for regulations concerning entry
    into deacon's orders, 1575; E. Cardwell. *Documentary Annals*, I, 44,
    141ff. for Whitgift's regulations of 1585; Cardwell, *Synodalia*, I,
    140ff., 148ff., 266, give articles for Canterbury Province, 1585 and
    1597 and Canons of 1604.
4. C.U.L., E.D.R. A5/1, f. 2r.
5. C.U.L., E.D.R. A5/1, the ordination book contains a record of
    examinations, subscriptions to the articles, and a record of the
    actual ordinations. It covers 82 folios with two enclosures. *Ibid.*,
    fos. 75–80, 21 March 1561; *ibid.*, fos. 60v–63v, December 1568;
    ibid., fos. 55r–60r, April 1568; *ibid.*, fos. 25v–32r, April 1580.
6. *Ibid.*, f. 29r (Anthony Iveston); *ibid.*, f. 71v (John Dawsbury); *ibid.*,
    f. 70v (John Clarcke).
7. *Ibid.*, f. 73v (William Ashton, 7 June 1561).
8. *ibid.*, fos. 73r–74r; see fos. 52r–v, 67r–69v for July 1560. See below
    p. 130 for Parker's Directive.
9. See below for comment, p. 131.
10. C.U.L., E.D.R. A5/1, fos. 75–80 (March 1561); f. 30r (Thomas
    Michell, 14, 15 April 1580); f. 58v (William Reynolds, 15 April
    1568).
11. *Ibid.*, fos. 3r, 7r (John Dun); fos. 6r, 13r (Lancellott Ellys); fos. 7r,
    11r, 14v (Thomas Everard).
12. W.R.O., 732.2 (I), no. I; see also, G.L.MS. 9535/1, dated 1550.
13. For example, that on 18 December 1568 was held in the chapel of
    Jesus College, Cambridge, C.U.L., E.D.R. a5/1, f. 60v.
14. H. G. Owen, 'The London parish clergy in the reign of Elizabeth I,
    (unpublished Ph.D. thesis, University of London, 1957), 111;
    compare for example E.D.R. A5/1 fos. 55r–60r with f. 85r.
15. For reluctance of clergy to alienate gentry see Owen, *op. cit.*,
    115–16; R. B. Manning. *Religion and Society in Elizabethan Sussex*
    (1969), 186; J. E. Neale, *Elizabeth I and Her Parliaments*, I (1957), 79.
    For the grave shortage of ministers see C.C.R.O. EDA 1/3 and pp.
    126–32 below.
16. See below pp. 126–42.
17. Cardwell, *Synodalia*, I, 267; L.J.R.O. 17th Century Precedent Book,
    unpaginated; Richard Baddiley, *LIfe of Thomas Morton*, (1669), 96.
18. *Ibid.*, 95–6.
19. J. E. B. Mayor, 'Materials for the life of Thomas Morton, Bishop
    of Durham', in *Cambridge Antiquarian Society 3*, 13.
20. E. Calamy, *Account of the Ministers Ejected and Silenced*, I: 112.
21. L.J.R.O., B/A/4A/18 (Peter French, B.A.; Richard Winterburne,
    divinity student; Richard Cotes; Timothy Mountford; Josiah
    Lightfoote).
22. Samuel Clarke, 'Life and death of Mr Richard Mather' in *Lives of
    Sundry Eminent Persons* (1683), 128; Calamy, *op. cit.*, I: 112, but in

fact Shaw's name appears in the list of those who subscribed in L.J.R.O. B/A/4A/18.
23. W. Scott and J. Bliss (eds.), *Works of William Laud V*, 363; see also C.U.L. Baker MSS. Mm.L.35, f. 80, for Bishop of Norwich's comments to the Vice-Chancellor of Cambridge, 1 November 1598; *Works of Laud V*, 330 for Goodman of Gloucester; G.C.L., G.D.R. vol. 27A.

Chapter 5
Experiment

1. I.T.L., Petyt MS. 538/38, fos. 71–4 *passim*.
2. J. L. Ainslie, *The Doctrines of Ministerial Order* (1940), 140–6, 149.
3. W. P. M. Kennedy, *Elizabethan Episcopal Administration*, Alcuin Club Collections, XXVII (1924), 161–74.
4. For Becon's part in the plan see P. Collinson, *The Elizabethan Puritan Movement* (1967), 183–4; D.W.L., Morrice MS. vol. A. N.L.P. f. 180 for Axton's attack on Overton.
5. P.R.O. S.P. 12/138 no. 67, 7 April 1586.
6. *H.M.C. Rep*. ii, 26ff. Marquis of Bath's MSS.
7. R. G. Usher, *Reconstruction of the English Church* (1910); see also D.W.L. Morrice MSS., vols. A, B, and C.
8. B.L. Egerton MS. 1693, f. 118. Ironically, the *Advertisements* of 1584 represent a detailed response to a directive from the Privy Council itself via Whitgift to the diocesans. Articles were sent to Whitgift in late 1583 and were then distributed to the bishops: for this see J. Strype, *Whitgift*, I (1822), 238–9; for attacks on the bishops by the Privy Council, see *H.M.C. Rep*, ii, 26ff. and Morrice MS. I.V. f. 13.
9. H. G. Owen, 'The London parish clergy in the reign of Elizabeth I' (unpublished Ph.D. thesis, University of London, 1957), 122–37, gives a detailed examination of these attempts to educate the clergy. See also H.R.O., Acta Books of the Archidiaconal Court of St Albans, ASA, 8, f. 282v; H. R. Wilton Hall (ed.), *A Calendar of Papers . . . of the Old Archdeaconry of St Albans*, St Albans and Herts A.A.S. (1908), 21; L.P.L. MS. 2003, f. 23.
10. L.C.C.R.O. Lib. Corr. 1583–6 offers evidence of punishment meted out to those who ignored the exercises. G.L.MS. 9537/6 fos. 108r, 115r and 122r give the names of the examiners and their responsibilities; L.C.C.R.O. DL/C/334, fos. 131–2 is an interesting letter to one of the examiners, Richard Vaughan which suggests that unlearned ministers were evading the exercised by obtaining preaching licences – this suggestion finds support in the records of preaching licences granted; J. E. Neale, *Elizabeth I and Her Parliaments*, II, 217; W. P. M. Kennedy, *Elizabethan Episcopal Administration*, III, *passim*; *Calendar of St Albans Papers . . .*, 68.
11. Collinson, *Elizabethan Puritan Movement*, 171.
12. *Ibid.*, 173.
13. *Ibid.*, 191–200.
14. *Ibid.*, 201 for changes on the episcopal bench.

Chapter 6
Jus patronatus

1. This account is based upon R. J. Phillimore, *The Ecclesiastical Law* (1873) and W. Prynne, *Jus Patronatus* (1654).
2. *S.R.*, 13 Henry VIII, c. 14; 14 Henry VIII, c. 2; L.J.R.O. B/A/1/15, f. 13; *S.R.*, 14 Car. II, c. 4; *S.R.*, 13 Elizabeth I, c. 12; reinforced by Constitutions of 1575: E. Cardwell, *Synodalia*, I (1842), 135–6; C.U.L., Ee.2.34, Correspondence of Bishop Parkhurst, doc. 117.
3. Phillimore, *op. cit.*, 412; *S.R.*, 13 Elizabeth I, c. 12; P.R.O. E101/521/8.
4. Cardwell, *op. cit.*, II, 503; I, 128, 145, 150, 271–3; The historian is fortunate in possessing a register of dispensations granted for pluralism in the years 1560–5, which permits analysis of the problem on a diocesan basis: *C.S.P.D. Elizabeth, 1547–78*, vol. lxxvi, 1570, Register Book of Grants of Dispensation for Plurality of Benefices, 1559–70; see D. M. Barratt, 'Condition of the parish clergy from the Reformation to 1660 in the dioceses of Oxford, Worcester and Gloucester' (unpublished D.Phil. thesis, Oxford University, 1950), 148; e.g. P.R.O., E101/523/8, William Savage, clerk, paid £4 10s. to hold two livings in 1571; at a time when he was already expected to surrender first fruits to the Crown this was an added burden.
5. *S.R.*, 5 Elizabeth I, c. 28; see also Phillimore, *op. cit.*, 435; Cardwell, *op. cit.*, I, 132ff.; C.U.L., Ee.2.34, doc. 111.
6. Phillimore, *op. cit.*, 437.
7. I owe this point to Professor Patrick Collinson who criticized an early draft of the article upon which this chapter is based.
8. H. G. Owen, 'The London parish clergy in the reign of Elizabeth' (unpublished Ph.D. thesis, University of London, 1957), 252.
9. C.U.L., Ee.2.34, doc. 37.
10. See below, chapter 9, for the Crown's exercise of patronage.
11. C. W. Foster (ed.), *Lincoln Episcopal Records in the Time of Thomas Cooper*, Lincoln Record Society Publications, II, (1912), 138.
12. L.R.O., COR/R/2.6.6, 30 November 1601; R. Baxter, *Reliquiae Baxterianae* (1696), 176.
13. C.U.L., Ee.2.34, doc. 36.
14. W. H. Frere (ed.), *Registrum Matthei Parker*, Canterbury and York Society, III, 1,117–1,123.
15. L.J.R.O., B/V/1/13, unpaginated.
16. *Ibid.*
17. G.L.MS. 9531/13, Sandys, fos. 181r–183v.
18. C.U.L., Ee.2.34, doc. 88.
19. Phillimore, *op. cit.*, 456–7; as the living in question would by this time presumably have been in lapse, the patron's continued right to present was debatable, even if the living were still vacant.

Chapter 7
The puritans and patronage

1. M. C. Cross, 'Noble patronage in the Elizabethan Church', *H.J.* 1 (1960).

2. D. M. Barratt, 'Conditions of the parish clergy from the Reformation to 1660 in the dioceses of Oxford, Worcester and Gloucester' (unpublished D. Phil. thesis, Oxford University, 1950), 358 ff.; R. G. Usher, *Reconstruction of the English Church*, 2 vols., (New York, 1910), *passim*, L.J.R.O., B/V/1/2, Visitation of Salop Archdeaconry, 1558; B/A/1/16, Register of Bishop Thomas Morton, 1618–32.

3. Cross, *op. cit.*, *passim*; p. 116 below; P. Collinson, *The Elizabethan Puritan Movement* (1967), 63–4.

4. Cross, *op. cit.*, 5–15; Collinson, *op. cit.*, 107, 147; R. C. Richardson, *Puritanism in North-West England* (1972), 116–17.

5. *Ibid.*, 117–18, 121.

6. *Ibid.*, 128–33.

7. W. J. Sheils, 'Some problems of government in a new diocese: the bishop and the Puritans in the diocese of Peterborough, 1560–1630' in R.O'Day and F. Heal (eds.), *Continuity and Change* (1976), 176, 183, 185.

8. R. B. Manning, *Religion and Society in Elizabethan Sussex* (1969), 185.

9. I. Calder, *The activities of the Puritan faction of the Church of England, 1625–33: a seventeenth-century attempt to purify the Anglican Church'*, *A.H.R.* (1948), p. 238; C. Hill, *Economic Problems of the Church* (1956), 245–74.

10. W. J. Sheils, *op. cit.*, 50–69.

11. Melbourne Hall, Coke MSS., Bundle 43, letters dated 5 December 1639, 26 January 1639/40.

12. *Ibid.*, 2 January 1639/40; L.J.R.O., B/C/3/15, 16 March 1635/6.

13. *Ibid.*, 2 January 1639/40.

14. *Ibid.*, 8 August 1640.

15. *Ibid.*, Bundle 44, John Jemmat to Sir John Coke, 19 September 1640.

16. P. S. Seaver, *The Puritan Lectureships* (Stanford, 1970), 66–7.

17. L.J.R.O., B/A/1/76, Register of Bishop Thomas Morton.

18. Hill, *Economic Problems*, 57.

19. Seaver, *Puritan Lectureships*, 22–6.

20. P. Collinson, 'Lectures by combination: structures and characteristics of Church life in seventeenth-century England', in *B.I.H.R. 48* (1975).

21. Seaver, *Puritan Lectureships*, 125–9, 133–42, 143.

22. *Ibid.*, 91 ff.

23. L.J.R.O., B/C/3/14, 26 May 1631; T. S. Willan, *Studies in Elizabethan Foreign Trade* (1959), 195–6; H.M.C. *9th Report*, Appendix 2, 394 (H. Chandos-Pole-Gell MSS. Bundle of Papers including an information by Attorney-General Noy); Coventry Record Office, A100 Mercers' Accounts, fos. 51r, 52r, 53r, 57r, 59r, 60r, 62r, 67r, 72r, 73r, 76v, 79r, 81r, 86r, 91r, 92r, 95r, 99v, 101r, 105v.

Chapter 8*
The use and abuse of grants of next presentation

1. The fullest treatment of the sale of advowsons and of the grants of next presentation appears to be in D. M. Barratt, 'Condition of the clergy from the Reformation to 1660 in the dioceses of Oxford,

Worcester and Gloucester' dioceses (unpublished D. Phil. thesis, Oxford University, 1950), 362–70, which draws mainly upon material for Gloucester diocese.

2. W.R.O., 778.7324, doc. ref. BA2337 (Calendar to Presentation Deeds, BA 2442 vols. 1 and 2.)

3. W.R.O., 778.7324, vol. 1, nos. 552, 479, 598A, 701, 755A, 590, 1060, 605, 775A, 1108, 1059 (no. 552 concerns Sedgeborough).

4. *Ibid.*, vol. 1, no. 751; *ibid.*, vol. 1, nos. 750, 755A and 627, etc.

5. Thomas Cunningham, *The Law of Simony* (1784), 28.

6. *Ibid.*, vol. 1, nos. 1181–2; vol. 2, nos. 101.271, 286, 428, for examples of amounts paid for grants; vol. 2, no. 386 for gift of grant to a bishop's servant.

* Where dates are fully given in the text, I refer the reader to the relevant calendar for further details.

Chapter 9
The ecclesiastical patronage of the lord keeper

For a detailed survey of the ecclesiastical patronage of the lord keepers see R. O'Day's 'The ecclesiastical patronage of the Lord Keeper, 1558–1642' in *T.R.H.S.* (1973), 89–109.

1. The patron of a living had six months in which to fill a vacancy; if he failed to do so, the right to present fell to the bishop of that diocese for a further six months; at the end of that time the living fell in lapse to the archbishop for six months and then to the Crown.

2. B.L. Lansdowne MS. 443, 1560–80; Bodleian Library, Tanner MS. 179; B.R.L., Croome Court Collection; F. J. Fisher, 'Influenza and inflation in Tudor England' in *Economic History Review* (1965), 120–9; W. G. Hoskins, 'Harvest fluctuations and English economic history, 1480–1619' in W. E. Minchinton (ed.), *Essays in Agrarian History* I (1968), 105; L.J.R.O., B/A/2ii/I, 29 out of 33 vacancies in Coventry archdeaconry, 1557–9, were caused by death.

3. William Camden, *The History of the Most Renowned and Victorious Princess Elizabeth* (1688), 528; B.L. Harleian MS. 6997 (Puckering Papers) sheds little light on the problem; J. Hacket, *Scrinia Reserata: A Memorial . . . of John Williams, D.D. . . .*, part i (1693), 29; J. Spedding, *The Letters and Life of Francis Bacon*, VI, 172; Bodleian Library, Tanner MS. 179; C.U.L., Ee.2.34., letter 57; H. G. Owen, 'The London parish clergy in the reign of Elizabeth I', (unpublished Ph.D. thesis, University of London, 1957), 89, for difficulties which the lord keeper encountered in filling poor livings in London.

4. J. Ayre (ed.), *The Works of John Whitgift*, iii, Parker Society (1853), 246; L.C.R.O., DL/C/212, f. 125r.

5. Bodleian Library, Tanner MS. 179; B.L. Harleian MS. 385, f. 112; C.U.L., E.2.34., letter 81; P. Collinson (ed.), *Letters of Thomas Wood, Puritan, 1566–1577*, B.I.H.R. Special Supplement 5 (1960), 21.

6. B.L. Lansdowne MS. 443.

7. See M. C. Cross, 'Noble patronage in the Elizabethan Church', in

H.J. I (1960), 1–16; B.L. Lansdowne MS. 443, Huntingdon petitioned successfully for nine livings in the period 1558/9–79; in the same period Bedford petitioned for 20 clerics; see also R. O'Day, 'Ecclesiastical patronage: who controlled the Church?', 142–5, in F. Heal and R. O'Day (eds.), *Church and Society in England, Henry VIII–James I* (1977).

8. Bodleian Library, Tanner MS. 179; C.U.L., Ee.2.34, letter 107; W.R.O., 732.2 (1) nos. 1–40; G.L.MS. 9535/2, f. 155r; B.L. Harleian MS. 385, fos. 74–5; L.P.L., MS. 705, f. 45.
9. B.L. Lansdowne MS. 443; Bodleian Library, Tanner MS. 179.
10. Bodleian Library, Tanner MS. 50; W. J. Jones, *The Elizabethan Court of Chancery* (1967), 165; numerous examples of letters of presentation are to be found in C.H.R.O. Benefice Papers (unsorted) and W.R.O., 778.7324 BA2442, index vols. 1 and 2.; L.C.C.R.O., Lib. Examin. 1591–4, 24 November 1592; Lib. Act. 1589–93, f. 292v; B.L., Lansdowne MS. 445; this case is described in Owen, *op cit.*, 290; C.U.L. Ee.2.34., letter 57.
11. W. J. Sheils, 'The Puritans in Church and politics in the diocese of Peterborough' (unpublished Ph.D. thesis, University of London, 1974), 58, 60, 61, 62; Bodleian Library, Tanner MS. 179.; O'Day, 'Ecclesiastical patronage', 144–5.
12. Sheils, *op. cit.*, 58–62.
13. *C.S.P.D. Addenda, Elizabeth I, 1547–1565*, 505–6; I.T.L., Petyt MS. 538/38 f. 137 (no date but by location in collection reign of Elizabeth and possibly early 1570s).
14. There are some other problems in assessing the impact of *policy* upon the lord keeper's exercise of patronage. These include the question: how much competition was there for such livings? In fact, the keepers found difficulty in filling the poorer livings in their gift (see 3 above) and in the records there is very little evidence of competition for individual livings (see Bodleian Library, Tanner MS. 179; and B.R.L. Croome Court Collection, vol. 901, nos. 452–54, August 1633, for examples). In addition, we need to know how keen the Crown was upon using its own patronage and exercising its rights in cases of lapse, simony, wardship and deprivation. Dr Sheils, for example, has suggested (*op. cit.*, 54) that the Crown was aggressive in its approach to lapse, on occasion even infringing the diocesan's rights, but this claim does not seem to be borne out by a study of the lord keeper's exercise of patronage overall.

Chapter 10
The reformation of the ministry

1. D. M. Barratt, 'Conditions of the parish clergy from the Reformation to 1660 in the dioceses of Oxford, Worcester and Gloucester' (unpublished D.Phil. thesis, University of Oxford, 1950), 54–5.
2. J. Strype, *The Life and Acts of John Whitgift*, I (1822), 536; e.g. L.J.R.O., B/V/1/63, Curdworth, Astley, Lee Marston vicarages; D.W.L., Morrice MS. B. pt. i, fos. 122–9; R. O'Day, 'The role of the registrar in diocesan administration' in R. O'Day and F. Heal

(eds.), *Continuity and Change* (1976), 88; *S.R.*, 21 Henry VIII, c. 13; E. Cardwell, *Synodalia*, I (1842), 290.

3. Bodleian Library, Tanner MS., 50, f. 53; L. Stone, 'Communication: the alienated intellectuals', *P. and P. 24* (1962).

4. Barratt, *op. cit.*, 7; F. J. Fisher, 'Influenza and inflation in Tudor England' in *Economic History Review*, 2nd ser. *18* (1965), 120–9; see p. 8.

5. G.L.MS. 9535/1; J. I. Daeley, 'The episcopal administration of Matthew Parker, Archbishop of Canterbury, 1559–75' (unpublished Ph.D. thesis, University of London, 1967), 178; W. P. Haugaard, *Elizabeth and the English Reformation* (1968), 164.

6. Daeley, *op. cit.*, 183: only 30 of the 233 men whom Parker caused to be ordained served in Canterbury diocese; Bath and Wells was vacant from October 1559 to March 1560; Chester from June 1559 to May 1561; Gloucester from 1559 to April 1562; Lichfield from June 1559 to March 1560.

7. C.C.R.O., E.D.A.1/3; L.R.O. Bishop's Register XXViiia, fos. 59ff; Haugaard, *op. cit.*, 164; N.R.O. Ordination Books, 1, 1570–95 fos. 25ff; Cardwell, *op. cit.*, I, 265; Bodleian Library, Oxford Diocesan Papers, C 264, vol. II; e9, e12, e13.

8. J. Bruce (ed.), *Correspondence of Matthew Parker*, Parker Society (1853), 120–1.

9. Daeley, *op. cit.*, 185–9.

10. Haugaard, *op. cit.*, 165.

11. C.U.L., E.D.R.A.5/1, fos. 67, 70–4, 75–80.

12. C.U.L., Ee.2.34, letter 146, f. 123r.

13. L.J.R.O., B/V/1/15; L.P.L. CM XIII; Lichfield Dean and Chapter Muniments MS. A.A.11; C.C.R.O., EDA 1/3; P.R.O. S.P.D. Eliz. vol. 36, no. 41 and vol. 118, no. 17 and enclosure 17i.

14. Bodleian Library, Tanner MS. 50. f. 35r; *C.S.P.D. Addenda, 1547–65*, 505; H. Kearney, *Scholars and Gentlemen* (1970), *passim*.

15. J.E.B. Mayor, 'Materials for the life of Thomas Morton, Bishop of Durham' in *Cambridge Antiquarian Society Journal 3* (1865), 29; G. W. Fisher, *Annals of Shrewsbury School* (1898), 38; H. C. Porter (ed.), *Puritanism in Tudor England* (1970), 186; S. E. Morison, *The Founding of Harvard College* (Cambridge, Mass. 1935), 96; but see J. Simon, 'The social origins of Cambridge students', in *P. and P. 26* (1963), 64.

16. G.L.MS. 9535/2; G.C.L., G.D.R. Bishops' Act Books; L.J.R.O., B/A/4A/17 and 18; Bodleian Library, Oxford Diocesan Papers, C 264 vol. II; e9, e12, e.13; N.R.O. Ordination Books of the Diocese of Peterborough, 1570–1642.

17. D. B. Robinson, *Beneficed Clergy in Cleveland and the East Riding, 1306–40*, Borthwick Papers, 37 (1969), 20–1; R. Donaldson, 'Patronage and the Church: a study in the social structure of the secular clergy in the diocese of Durham, 1311–1540' (unpublished Ph.D. thesis, University of Edinburgh, 1955), 315–35; I. Cassidy, 'The episcopate of William Cotton, Bishop of Exeter, 1598–1621 . . .' (unpublished B. Litt. thesis, University of Oxford, 1963), 50; see p. 224 for the interesting example of Ralph Josselin's search for a living.

258

18. For example, see pp. 6–7.
19. E.g. L.J.R.O. W.P. 1646: Edward Peers, Rector of Sudbury, Derbys., willed the use of fifty pounds apiece to support his two sons at the university as 'poore schollers or servitors . . . for the space of fower yeares'; W.P. 1613: Richard Browne, Rector of Norbury, Derbys., divided the rents from two-thirds of his lands in a ratio of 2:1 between his two sons. Two parts were to support his son Richard at university until he acquired either a college fellowship or a benefice worth £30 a year; the other was to support his younger son John in the same way. See R. O'Day, 'Clerical patronage and recruitment in England during the Elizabethan and early Stuart periods' (unpublished Ph.D. thesis, University of London, 1972), 269, for further examples.
20. See, for example, R. Tyler, 'The children of disobedience: the social composition of Emmanuel College, Cambridge, 1596–1645' (Ph.D. thesis, University of California, Berkeley, 1976). Dr Tyler shows that of the 1,090 freshmen entering St John's, Emmanuel, Jesus and King's during the period for which particulars of school survive, no fewer than 800 (73.4 per cent) had attended a school with an intimate relationship to Cambridge through patronage or the master's education or a closed scholarship and thus had sources of information about the university and its houses. 606 (55.6 per cent) had ties with the colleges of admission (still 42.4 per cent even without King's and its heavy reliance on boys from Eton). Of 617 boys entering St John's between 1631 and 1645, the indication is that 62.2 per cent had received education in a school with strong Cambridge ties and 41.6 per cent in schools associated closely with St John's. After including the information conveyed by relatives, friends and local clergy, Dr Tyler estimates that three out of four freshmen had advance information about Cambridge and its colleges (91–2).
21. Andrew Clark, *Register of the University of Oxford, vol. 2, 1571–1622, Matriculations and Tables*, Oxford Historical Society, 2 vols. in 5 (1885–9).
22. O'Day, thesis cit., 275; *idem*, 'Church records and the history of education in early modern England, 1558–1642: a problem in methodology', in *History of Education 2* (1973), *passim*.
23. Richard Baxter, *Reliquiae Baxterianae* (1696), 12.
24. See p. 56.

Chapter 11
The clerical élite

1. J. H. Pruett, 'Career patterns among the clergy of Lincoln Cathedral, 1660–1750' in *Church History* (1975), 204–16, presents an alternative approach to a study of the clerical élite. My decision to approach entry to the cathedral chapter from the vantage point of the parish clergy and from the perspective of various influences and pressures upon the growth of a reformed profession was dictated by interest in the clergy as a whole, a conviction that a statistical approach is not entirely satisfactory, and a belief that rather

different questions need to be asked about the paths to preferment at this level of clerical employment.

2. L.J.R.O., B/V/1/15; B/V/1/19; Jurisdiction XVII, list of parochial clergy, 1620.

3. The dates of collation to prebendal stalls, cathedral offices and archdeaconries are based on those given in J. Le Neve, *Fasti Ecclesiae Anglicanae*, ed. T. D. Hardy (1854) (3 vols.) corrected in the light of Lichfield diocesan records, especially B/A/1/16. Biographical information was garnered from J. A. Venn, *Alumni Cantabrigienses* (1922–7) and J. Foster, *Alumni Oxoniensis* (1924).

4. L.J.R.O., C.C. 124100.

5. *Ibid.*, fos. 33, 34.

6. *Ibid.*, fos. 18–36.

7. *Ibid.*, fos. 18–21 and 22–36.

8. *S.R.* 13 Elizabeth I, c. 10.

9. L.J.R.O., 124100, fos. 28, 30.

10. C. Hill, *Economic Problems of the Church* (1956), 310–11.

11. L.J.R.O., B/a/1/16; Will of William Jeffray, 1642; B/C/3/10–16.

12. L.J.R.O., B/A/1/16.

13. For the criteria for Crown promotions see the following, J. A. Berlatsky, 'The Social Structure of the Elizabethan episcopacy' (*sic*), (unpublished Ph.D. thesis, Northwestern University, 1970); R. Houlbrooke, 'The Protestant episcopate, 1547–1603, the pastoral contribution' and R. O'Day, 'Ecclesiastical patronage: who controlled the Church?' in F. Heal and R. O'Day (eds.), *Church and Society in England, Henry VIII to James I* (1977); H. R. Trevor Roper, 'King James and his bishops' in *History Today* (1955); A. P. Kautz, 'The selection of Jacobean bishops' in H. S. Reinmuth (ed.), *Early Stuart Studies: Essays in Honour of D. H. Wilson* (Minneapolis, 1970). That there was an emphasis upon the pastoral work of both bishops and cathedral chapters is, however, certain: see J. B. Gavin, 'An Elizabethan Bishop of Durham: Tobias Matthew 1595–1606' (unpublished Ph.D. thesis, McGill University, 1972), and D. Marcombe, 'The Durham dean and chapter: old abbey writ large?' in R. O'Day and F. Heal (eds.), *Continuity and Change* (1976), for some pertinent comments on this changed situation.

Chapter 12
The community of the clergy

1. L.J.R.O., W.P. 1646, Edward Peers, Rector of Sudbury, Derbys.; L.J.R.O., W.P. 1621/2, John Hill, Rector of Elford, Staffs.; L.J.R.O., W.P. 1613, Richard Browne, Rector of Norbury, Derbys.; information on the Jephcotts from J. Foster, *Alumni Oxoniensis* (1891–2); L.J.R.O., B/A/4A/18; E. Calamy, *The Nonconformists' Memorial*, ed. S. Palmer, 2 vols., 1775; see p. 141:

2. I. Cassidy, *The Episcopate of William Cotton, Bishop of Exeter, 1598–1621*, 53–5; information on the Bournes in H. Longden, *Northamptonshire and Rutlandshire Clergy*, vol. 2, s.n.; and L.J.R.O., B/A/1/16, B/A/4A/18.; L.J.R.O. William Leigh, Rector of Edgmond, Salop, W.P. 1598; Humphrey Steele, Vicar of

260

Cheswardine, Salop, W.P. 1617; for Pudyfatt see under John Pudyfatt, Vicar of Cold Ashby, Northants, in Longden, *op. cit.*; Roger Daker, Vicar of Drayton Hales, W.P. 1618; Lewis Taylor, Rector of Moreton Corbet, Salop, W.P. 1623; Leonard Harreson, Vicar of Hardwick Priors, 1569–1602/3 c, L.J.R.O., B/V/1/15; Leonard Harreson, his son, curate of Marston Priors and Lower Shuckborough, L.J.R.O., B/V/1/15 and B/V/1/23; Richard Stonnynaught, Vicar of Wirksworth W.P. 1586; figures for marriage in Lincoln drawn from L.P.L., CM XII/4, printed in C. Foster (ed.), *The State of the Church in Lincoln Diocese*, vol. I, Lincoln Record Society, 23 (1926).

3. J. A. Venn, *Alumni Cantabrigienses* (1922–7); Foster *op. cit.*; L.J.R.O., B/A/1/16, George Beale instituted to Grandborough vicarage, 19 September 1615; 14 May 1621, Henry Clerke M.A. instituted to Willoughby vicarage; Henry Clerke, W.P. 1635/6; Thomas Walker, W.P. 1607; James Hall, W.P. 1591; Richard Browne, W.P. 1625; John Thomas, W.P. 1607.

4. L.J.R.O., William Tomlinson, W.P. 1634; Simon Presse, W.P. 1612; Brian Heppenstall, W.P. 1639; George Higgs, W.P. 1617; Edward Peers, W.P. 1646.

5. L.J.R.O., Thomas Walker, W.P. 1607; Thomas Parkes, W.P. 1597; William Hull, W.P. 1623; Thomas Warde, W.P. 1591; John Sprott, W.P. 1597.

6. L.J.R.O., Philip Ward, W.P. 1640; Venn, s.n.; John Porter, W.P. 1637.

7. L.J.R.O., Humphrey Whitmore, W.P. 1617; see Alan Macfarlane, *The Family Life of Ralph Josselin* (1970), *passim*.

8. P. Collinson, 'Lectures by combination: structures and characteristics of Church life in seventeenth-century England' in *B.I.H.R.* 48 (1975), 183–4, 187, 208, 213.

9. *Ibid.*, 212, 213.

10. *Ibid.*, *passim*.

11. John Rylands Library, Manchester, Eng. MS. 874: Minute Book of meetings held by Puritan ministers at various places in Essex, and papers relating to them; P. Collinson, *The Elizabethan Puritan Movement* (1967), 225.

12. L.J.R.O., B/C/3/3, 21 April 1596; B/C/3/16, 18 April 1639; Immanuel Bourne, *A Light From Christ Leading unto Christ*, 2nd edn (1646), 11; Immanuel Bourne, *A Defence of the Scriptures* (1656).

13. Bernard Vogler, *Le Clergé Protestant Rhenan Au Siècle De La Réforme (1555–1619)* (Strasbourg, 1976), 366–8.

14. *Ibid.*, 368.

Chapter 13
Clerical standards of living and life-style

1. J. and J. H. Caley (eds.), *Valor Ecclesiasticus*, 6 vols. (1810–34); *S.R.* 26 Henry VIII, c. III; *S.R.* 27 Henry VIII, viii, modifies earlier statute.

2. J. Collier, *An Ecclesiastical History of Great Britain*, IX (1852), 362–3; R. G. Usher, *The Reconstruction of the English Church*, 2 vols, 222; D. M. Barratt, 'Conditions of the parish clergy from the

Reformation to 1660 in the dioceses of Oxford, Worcester and Gloucester' (unpublished D.Phil. thesis, Oxford University, 1950), 192.
3. Barratt, *op. cit.*, esp. 196–7; 201; 205.
4. Barratt, *op. cit.*, esp. 210, 250–1, 271.
5. Barratt, *op. cit.*, esp. v, 297–308 *et passim*; see also *S.R.* 2 and 3 Edward VI, c. 13 for Act For True Payment of Tithes.
6. Barratt, *op. cit.*, 287.
7. *V.E.*; B.L., Lansdowne MS. 459.
8. Reprinted in Usher, *op. cit.*, vol. 1, 224. The reader who is specifically interested in the taxation of the clergy would be well advised to read two recent articles by F. Heal: 'Clerical tax collection under the Tudors', in R. O'Day and F. Heal (eds.), *Continuity and Change* (1976), and 'Economic problems of the clergy', in Heal and O'Day (eds.), *Church and Society from Henry VIII to James I* (1977).
9. L.J.R.O., B/V/1/17: Shilton; B/V/1/48, B/V/1/55, under Stapleton L.J.R.O., B/C/3/11, 1621, Thomas Somerfield, Rector of West Felton; L.J.R.O.., B/C/3/12, 1623, Edward Langley, curate and farmer of Ladbrook rectory; *H.M.C.Rep.*, 15, X, Shrewsbury Corporation Papers, 59.
10. M. Barley, 'Rural housing in England' in J. Thirsk (ed.), *The Agrarian History of England and Wales, IV, 1500–1640* (1967), 724–5, 734
11. L.J.R.O., B/V/6: M.16, Moreton Corbet, Salop. 1612, D.9, Draycott in the Moors, Staffs. 1633; K.2, Kemberton, Salop, 1612; C.5, Caverswall, Staffs., 1635.
12. L.J.R.O., B/V/6: C.8, Cheswardine, Salop, 1636; H.11, High Ercall, Salop, 1612; D.7, Drayton Bassett, Staffs., 1613.
13. L.J.R.O., B/V/6: H.1, West Hallam, Derbys., 1612; K.5, Kinnersley, Salop, 1612; S.25, Stirchley, Salop, 1612; S.22, Staundon, Staffs., 1612; H.20, Harley, Salop, 1612; Y.1, Yoxall, Staffs., 1613; W.13, West Felton, Salop, 1633.
14. L.J.R.O., B/V/6: S.26, Stoke-on-Trent, Staffs., 1635; W.20, Whitchurch, Salop, 1612; L.12, Longford, Salop, 1635; D.8, Drayton in Hales, Salop, 1631; C.13, Church Eaton, Staffs., 1616; B.19, Bolas, Salop, 1635.
15. L.J.R.O., B/V/6: C.8, Cheswardine, 1636; A.7, Aldridge, Staffs., 1612; M.16, Moreton Corbet, 1612; S12, Shifnal, Salop, 1612.
16. L.J.R.O., B/V/6: W.20, Whitchurch; C.5, Caverswall; Y.1, Yoxall; R.4, Rolleston, Staffs., 1612.
17. L.J.R.O., B/V/6: A.23, Alcester, Warwicks., 1635; W.20; S.25.
18. Barley, *op. cit.*, 726.
19. L.J.R.O., B/V/6: K.1, Keele, Staffs., 1693; Keele Churchwardens' Accounts c. 1693; D.7, Drayton Bassett; L. 15, Loppington, 1613; N.11, Norton in Hales, Salop, 1635; R.4, Rolleston, Staffs., 1612.
20. L.J.R.O., B/V/6: R.4; M.16.
21. Analysis of clerical inventories in the L.J.R.O., L.C.R.O., Will and Inventory of Immanuel Bourne, 1673.
22. L.C.R.O., Will and Inventory of Immanuel Bourne, 1672/3; L.J.R.O., Nathaniel Puddyfatt, W.P. 1642; Robert Revell, W.P. 1648; also Robert Porter, Rector of Aston on Trent, Derbys., W.P.

1617; William Orton, Rector of Sheldon, Warwicks., W.P. 1628; William Hull, Curate of Ashbourne, Derbys., W.P. 1623/4; Simon Presse, Rector of Egginton, Derbys., W.P. 1612; Henry Bellingham, W.P. 1632; Henry Smith, W.P. 1640; Roger Daker, W.P. 1618. For Ralph Josselin's views on the need for books see Alan Macfarlane (ed.) *The Diary of Ralph Josselin* (1976), 53–4 *et passim*.

23. L.J.R.O., Henry Alsop, W.P. 1675; Richard Orgell, W.P. 1646/7; Humphrey Fenn, W.P. 1634; Francis Bacon, W.P. 1682; Peter Clark, 'The ownership of books in England, 1560–1640: the example of some Kentish townsfolk', in Lawrence Stone (ed.), *Schooling and Society* (1976), 95–114, has some interesting comments on the use of 'studies' and on professional book-buying in general.

24. Preaching was seen as the expression of this studious attitude among the clergy: see for example the bishops' discussions after the Hampton Court Conference, B.L., Add. MSS. 28571, fos. 187–92, when rejection of non-preachers at ordination was suggested as a means to prevent the infiltration of ignorant clergy.

25. W.S.L., HM.308/40, Commonplace Book of James Whitehall, Rector of Checkley, Staffs.

26. L.J.R.O., John Porter, W.P. 1637; John Sherrard, W.P. 1635; John Dicher, W.P. 1620/1.

Chapter 14
Lay attitudes to the clergy before the civil war

1. I owe this point to Mr Keith Thomas.
2. Especially D. M. Barratt, 'Conditions of the parish clergy from the Reformation to 1660 in the dioceses of Oxford, Worcester and Gloucester' (unpublished D. Phil. thesis, University of Oxford, 1950); M. James, 'The political importance of the tithes controversy in the English revolution' in *History*, (1941); L.J.R.O., Class B/C/1/.
3. Clerical tithe cases seem to represent under a third of the tithe cases brought between 1600 and 1640/1: 2,235 cases out of an estimated total of 7,480.
4. L.J.R.O., B/C/5/1607: instance case brought by Valentine Overton, Rector of Bedworth v. Margaret Saunders of Bedworth for slander.
5. L.J.R.O., B/C/2/45; B/C/2/70; B/C/2/50.
6. L.J.R.O., index of instance cases brought by clergy, 1600–1640/1, compiled by R. O'Day, arranged alphabetically under cleric's name.
7. *Ibid.*; W.S.L., HM 308/40, Commonplace Book of James Whitehall, f. 100r: according to Whitehall, Weston's successor at Checkley, Weston had to pay Bishop Overton £300 'because of the 80li per annum which he had presented to his kinesman dureinge his liffe' from Stoke-on-Trent Rectory. Even on a rich rectory this would be quite a large initial sum to recoup. It may have spurred Weston to abnormal litigation.
8. L.J.R.O., alphabetical index of tithe cases; W.S.L., Q.S.R./Michaelmas/1638/20, Clifton Campville; Q.S.R./Michaelmas/1640/30, Clifton Campville; J. Foster, *Alumni Oxoniensis*, s.n.; W. N. Landor, *Staffordshire Incumbents and Parochial Records, 1530–1680; Collections for a History of Staffordshire* (1915),70;

J. Walker, *Clergy Sequestered . . . in the Great Rebellion* (1714); B.L., Add. MS. 15670, fos. 341, 444.

9. L.J.R.O., B/V/6/H.11; see also N. Adams, 'The judicial conflict over tithes' in *E.H.R* (1937).

10. Staffordshire Record Office, Tithe Book of the Rectors of Leigh, Staffordshire; see also alphabetical index of clergy bringing tithe cases.

11. L.J.R.O., Deliverance Fennyhouse, W.P. 1672; Francis Swineshead, W.P. 1647.

12. L.J.R.O., B/C/5/1628: Office Case v. Ralph Leadbeater, clerk of Castleton, Derbys.

13. L.J.R.O., B/V/2: Excommunication Books; B/C/3/10, 11, 13, 14 and 15; B/C/3/12–13 cover 1622–5; according to Landor, *op. cit.* 231, Cresset was vicar from 1598–1631 resigned; B/C/3/16: 1632/3, William Jeffray, Archdeacon of Salop; B/C/3/13: 1627, James Povey, Rector of Willey and chaplain to Bishop Morton.

14. L.J.R.O., B/C/3/12; W. J. Sheils, 'Some problems of government in a new diocese . . .', in R. O'Day and F. Heal (eds.), *Continuity and Change* (1976), 182.

15. L.J.R.O., B/C/2/60. Enclosure 5.

16. L.R.O., COR/L/2, 15.25, 20 July 1627; L.J.R.O., B/C/5/1600.

17. L.J.R.O., B/C/3/16, 6 September 1639, 2 November 1639, 6 August 1639.

18. L.J.R.O., B/C/5/1607.

19. L.J.R.O., B/C/5/1601; B/C/5/1598/9.

20. L.J.R.O., B/A/19/1: Correspondence of Richard Raines, Chancellor of Coventry and Lichfield Diocese, letter 77, 11 June 1687.

21. J. F. Maclear, 'Popular anticlericalism in the Puritan revolution', *J.H.I.* 17 (1956).

Chapter 15
Clergy on the defensive

1. J. F. Maclear, 'Popular anticlericalism in the Puritan revolution', *J.H.I.* 17 (1956), *passim*; examples include C. Hill, *Change and Continuity in Seventeenth Century England* (1974), 127–48; R. L. Greaves, *The Puritan Revolution and Educational Thought* (Rutgers, 1969), *passim*; R. L. Greaves, 'The ordination controversy and the spirit of reform in Puritan England', *J.E.H.* (1970).

2. T. Hall, *The Pulpit Guarded with XVII Arguments* (1650).

3. I. Bourne, *A Defence of the Scriptures* (1656); J. Foster, *Alumni Oxoniensis*, I (1891–2), 156; H. I. Longden, *Northamptonshire and Rutland Clergy from 1500'* II (1939–52), 177; I. Bourne, *The True Way of a Christian to the New Jerusalem* (1622), dedication; *The Godly Man's Guide* (1620), dedication; L.C.R.O., Will of Immanuel Bourne, W.P. 6 February 1672/3; L.J.R.O., B/A/1/16, Immanuel Bourne instituted to Ashover rectory, 11 July 1621; I. Bourne, *The Anatomie of Conscience* (1623); I. Bourne, *A Light from Christ leading unto Christ* (1646 edn), 11 (introduction); P.R.O. Exchequer Depositions, 1657: Michaelmas, Derby, no. 33.

4. George Whitehead (ed.), *A Collection of Sundry Books, Epistles and Papers written by James Nayler . . .* (1716); see *An Examination of*

James Nayler upon an indictment of Blasphemy at the Sessions at Appleby, January 1652 and *The Power and Glory of the Lord . . .* 42–3.

5. Helvetic Confession cited in J. L. Ainslie, *The Doctrines of the Ministerial Order in the Reformed Churches of the Sixteenth and Seventeenth Centuries* (1940), 8; English Ordinal, *The Second Prayer Book of Edward VI*, in the Ancient and Modern Library of Theological Literature (1552) facsimile.

6. T. Collier, *A Brief Discovery of the Corruption of the Ministry of the Church of England* (1647), 17–18, 23–4; W. Walwyn, *The Compassionate Samaritane Unbinding (1644), 22–7*.

7. J. Ferriby, *The Lawfull Preacher* (1652), 15.

8. I. Bourne, *The Rainebow* (1619), 4–5 *et passim*.

9. I. Bourne, *The True Way of a Christian*, 16, 18, 24, 28.

10. I. Bourne, *A Light from Christ*; R. Baxter, *The Reformed Pastor*, (1841).

11. I. Bourne, *A Light from Christ*, 129, 104–5.

12. I. Bourne, *The Rainebow*, *passim*; D. M. Barratt, 'Conditions of the parish clergy from the Reformation to 1660 in the dioceses of Oxford, Worcester and Gloucester', (unpublished D.Phil. thesis, Oxford University, 1950), *passim*; C. Hill, *Economic Problems of the Church* (1956), 100.

13. Bourne, *The Anatomie of Conscience*, 40.

14. Derby City Library, Ashover Collection, letter from Immanuel Bourne, dated 28 August 1646, to William Bourne of Manchester, printed in *The Derbyshire Times*, 28 May 1910, original now missing.

15. I. Bourne, *A Defence and Justification of Ministers' Maintenance by Tithes And of Infant Baptism, Humane Learning and the Sword of the Magistrate* (1659), dedication.

16. *Ibid.*, 2, 19, 87, 89; P.R.O., Exchequer Depositions, 1657, Michaelmas, Derby, no. 33.

17. Whitehead, *A Collection of Sundry Books, passim*.

18. W. C. Braithwaite, *The Beginnings of Quakerism*, (2nd edn, 1970), 127; for accounts of the disputation see Bourne, *A Defence* and J. Nayler, *A Dispute Between James Nayler and the Parish Teachers of Chesterfield, by a Challenge against him . . . occasioned by a Bull bayting* (1655).

19. Nayler, *A Dispute*, 1; Bourne, *A Defence*, dedication, 954.

20. *Ibid.*, 976, 991.

21. *Ibid.*, 983–4.

22. Bourne, *A Defence*, 9, 10; J. Nayler, *The Power and Glory of the Lord . . .*, 42–3 and *Antichrist Discovered*, in *Works*, 204.

23. References in this chapter are to Alan Macfarlane's edition, *The Diary of Ralph Josselin, 1616–1683* (1976). As a general policy, relevant dates are given in the text of the chapter for ease of reference. When the work is referred to in a footnote it is as *Diary*; A. Macfarlane, *The Family Life of Ralph Josselin* (1970), 189–90; *Diary* during the early 1650s is even more preoccupied with Millenarianism than Macfarlane suggests; *Diary*, 1–5, gives information on Josselin's family background.

24. *Ibid.*, 1, 3.

25. *Ibid.*, 5–8.

26. *Ibid.*, 7–8.
27. *Ibid.*, 8–10.
28. *Ibid.*, 91.
29. *Ibid.*, 103.
30. *Ibid.*, evidence of Josselin's common-sense scepticism c. 1656–7 about parousia on 360, 365, 412.
31. *Ibid.*, 237, 339.
32. *Ibid.*, 348, 349, 350, 362, 366–7, 384 etc.

Chapter 16
Comparisons

1. P. Heath, *English Parish Clergy On the Eve of the Reformation* (1969), 13–15, 19–22.
2. D. Robinson, *Beneficed Clergy in Cleveland and the East Riding*, Borthwick Papers, no. 37 (1969), 8.
3. Heath, *op. cit.*, 21.
4. On this aspect, Heath, *op. cit.*, 27–36 and M. Bowker, *The Secular Clergy in the Diocese of Lincoln, 1495–1520*, (1968), 64–109 are particularly helpful.
5. See pp. 1–21.
6. See p. 157.
7. Heath, *op. cit.*, 81–2; R. Christophers, 'Social and educational background of the Surrey clergy, 1520–1620' (unpublished Ph.D. thesis, University of London, 1975), 50.
8. Heath, *op. cit.*, 91.
9. S. E. Ozment, *The Reformation in the Cities* (Yale, 1975), 84.
10. C. Hill, *Change and Continuity in Seventeenth-Century England* (1974), 176–8, 157–63.
11. Ozment, *op. cit.*, 89.
12. *Ibid.*, 85.
13. *Ibid.*, 86, 124.
14. R. W. Scribner, 'Why was there no Reformation in Cologne?' in *B.I.H.R* (1976), *passim*.
15. See P. Collinson, *The Elizabethan Puritan Movement* (1967), 112.
16. A. D. Wright, 'The people of Catholic Europe and the people of Anglican England' in *H.J.* 18 (1975), 452.
17. M. Venard, 'Récherche sur le récrutement sacerdotal dans la province d'Avignon', in *Annales* (1968).
18. R. Kagan, 'Universities in Castile, 1500–1700' in *P. and P. 49* (1970), *passim*.
19. A. Peel (ed.), *The Seconde Parte of a Register* I (1915), 71.

Index